# THE MELTING POT

To Tom, Richard, Diana and Sophia-Mary, with love

# THE MELTING POT

## BALKAN FOOD AND COOKERY

BY

## MARIA KANEVA-JOHNSON

*with a foreword by*
ALAN DAVIDSON

PROSPECT BOOKS
1999

Published in paperback by Prospect Books in 1999,
at Allaleigh House, Blackawton, Totnes, Devon TQ9 7DL.
First published by Prospect Books in 1995.

© 1995, 1999, text and illustrations, Maria Kaneva-Johnson.
Map by Philippa Stockley.
Cover design for paperback by Maria Kaneva-Johnson.

The author, Maria Kaneva-Johnson, asserts her right as the author in accordance with the Copyright, Designs & Patents Act 1988.

All rights reserved. No part of this publication may be reproduced, stored in a retrieval system, or transmitted in any form or by any means, electronic, mechanical, photocopying, recording or otherwise, without the prior permission of the publisher.

Text designed and set by Tom Jaine.

British Library Cataloguing in Publication Data:
A CIP record for this book is available from the British Library.

ISBN 0 907325 96 3

Printed by The Cromwell Press, Trowbridge, Wiltshire.

# Contents

| | |
|---|---|
| Weights and Measures | viii |
| Foreword by Alan Davidson | ix |
| Acknowledgements | x |
| Pronunciation and Transliteration | xi |
| A Lesson in History and Geography | 1 |
| A Cook's Tour | 10 |
| Pots and Pans | 31 |
| Unfamiliar Ingredients | 43 |
| Meze and Zakouski | 59 |
| Soups | 74 |
| The Garden Crop | 88 |
| Cheese and Eggs | 113 |
| Milk, Yoghurt, Cream and Butter | 120 |
| Fish and Shellfish | 124 |
| Meat | 145 |
| Poultry and Offal | 187 |
| Game | 201 |
| Grains, Seeds, and Porridges | 208 |
| Pasta, Tarhana and Dumplings | 223 |
| Breads, Pancakes and Fritters | 230 |
| Leaf Pastry | 259 |
| Biscuits, Cakes and Pastries | 271 |
| Fruit Desserts, Creams and Ice-creams | 285 |
| Syruped Sweets and Sweetmeats | 304 |
| Preserves | 317 |
| Non-alcoholic Drinks | 333 |
| Sauces and Standard Preparations | 340 |
| Bibliography | 355 |
| Indexes | 361 |

# WEIGHTS, MEASURES AND TEMPERATURES

The measures used in this book are entirely metric. Since the end of 1995, imperial measures were effectively outlawed in Britain's shops and markets, save for a tiny number of instances such as pints of draught beer and pints of milk in glass bottles. It seemed simpler to reflect this fact by saving the need to translate one set of measures to another as we trek between home and shop and back again.

The spoon measures that I have used are also metric. These are very close to American spoons, but smaller than the imperial set you may still guard in your equipment drawer. A metric tablespoon is 15 millilitres (ml); a dessertspoon is 10 ml; a teaspoon is 5 ml. Spoon measurements are for a level spoon, unless I state otherwise.

For the sake of consistency I have also given only metric dimensions of cooking pans and baking dishes. I realise that kitchen equipment has a longer life-cycle than greengrocers' stock, therefore your pots and pans may still be imperial. Remember, therefore, that 1 inch is 2.5 centimetres (cm).

I have given oven and other temperatures in Celsius (C) and Fahrenheit (F), as well as Gas regulos. The recommended times and temperatures in this book are for conventional ovens. If you use a fan (circotherm) oven, you may wish to reduce the cooking time by approximately 10 minutes and lower the temperature by 20–25°C/68–75°F, or at least consult the manufacturer's recommendations.

# Foreword

The qualities which have enabled Maria Kaneva-Johnson to present this book to the world are not commonly found in combination. A certain intrepidity has been necessary, dealing with what is, in culinary as well as ethnic and political terms, one of the most intricately convoluted patches of territory on the face of our planet. A fundamental bank of knowledge, gained directly in the course of a lifetime, was patently required; but so was a diligence bordering on fanaticism in pursuing over mountain ranges and through the numerous language frontiers every last little fact and nuance. Equally essential for the sifting and arranging of these, were faculties of discrimination, analysis and collation such as are normally found only in the brains of higher grade encyclopaedists. Yet everything had to be firmly anchored to the kitchen and to cooking skills.

Yes, a 'job description' would have sounded impossible. Yes, it was unsurprising that no one had hitherto tried to assume a role so daunting, and that the food and cooking of the Balkans had persistently been 'gap in the literature'.

Yet it does not surprise me to see the gap now magnificently filled by this book. I have, after all, been watching its progress from concept to finished product for nearly twenty years. It was in the '70s that I solicited Maria's aid over the Black Sea aspect of my book on Mediterranean Seafood and I still recall vividly the simple but wonderfully good array of Bulgarian fish dishes which she then prepared especially for me. Ah, that *Tikvitchki s Anshoa*, and the *Riben Kebap v Giuvetcheta*! It was at that time that I learned of her own grand project and began to be aware of the extraordinary tenacity with which she would pursue it to this triumphant conclusion.

I am deeply content to think that Prospect Books, whose book publications were such a big part of my life until my wife and I handed over to Tom Jaine in 1993, is the publisher. My affectionate blessings on the author; and may her book have the long and successful life which it eminently deserves.

*Alan Davidson*

# Acknowledgements

It remains for me to thank those who have helped me with this book: Tom Jaine, my publisher and editor, without whom this book would not have been possible; Alan Davidson, my mentor and friend of many years, for whose journal *Petits Propos Culinaires* I wrote my very first cookery essay; Caroline Davidson, my literary agent, for her calm and wise guidance in the presentation of this book; my Balkan friends, relatives and chance acquaintances who gave me their most valued home recipes; and especially my sister Mrs Lyudmilla Staneva from the town of Russe in Bulgaria, who provided me with a few forgotten recipes that belonged to our mother and grandmother.

I would like to acknowledge my indebtedness for permission to quote from the following books: Patrick Leigh Fermor, *Between the Woods and the Water* (1986), by permission of John Murray (Publishers) Ltd, London; Leslie Gardiner, *Curtain Calls, Travels in Albania, Romania and Bulgaria* (David and Charles, 1977), by kind permission of the publishers; M.E. Durham, *Through the Lands of the Serb* (1904), and *High Albania* (1909), published by Edward Arnold (Publishers) Ltd; D.J. Hall, *Romanian Furrow* (1933), by permission of Peters, Fraser & Dunlop Group Ltd; Robert Halsband (editor), *The Complete Letters of Lady Mary Wortley Montagu* (1965), by permission of Oxford University Press; Maud M. Holbach, *Dalmatia* (1908), by permission of The Bodley Head; Skeat, Walter W. (editor), *Chaucer, Complete Works*, 'The Book of the Duchess' (1973), by permission of Oxford University Press. My thanks to the History Museum, Stara Zagora, Bulgaria, (Mincho Dimitrov and Peter Kalchev), for permission to redraw two photographs; Marshall Cavendish Ltd, London, for permission to use recipes which I contributed and which first appeared in their publication *Robert Carrier's Kitchen*, 1980, 1981, 1983; and the Editors of Time-Life Books, for 'Quail grilled over charcoal', reproduced from page 132 of *Outdoor Cooking*, a volume in the *Time-Life Good Cook Series*, by kind permission of the publishers. My special thanks to Nevin Halıcı for her permission to quote from *Nevin Halıcı's Turkish Cookbook*, a Jill Norman Book, Dorling Kindersley, London 1989, and her *Türk Mutfagı*, Güven Matbassi, Ankara 1985. I am also particularly grateful to Michael Bateman, Caroline Conran and Oliver Gillie for permission to use my recipes which first appeared in their book *The Sunday Times Guide to the World's Best Food*, Hutchinson, London 1981, and to Michael Bateman and Heather Maisner who have permitted the use of my recipe for 'Dee-Dee Cake', which first appeared in their book *The Sunday Times Book of Real Bread*, Rodale Press Ltd, Aylesbury 1982.

Lastly, but by no means least, I wish to thank my husband, Tom Johnson, for his endless, stalwart support, constructive criticism and valued advice; and our daughter Dr Diana Bonella, the biochemist, who was my scientific advisor in the preparation of this work.

# PRONUNCIATION AND TRANSLITERATION

Three alphabets are used in the Balkans: Latin, Cyrillic and Greek. The Albanian, Croatian, Romanian, Slovenian and Turkish languages are written with Latin script, while Bulgarian, Macedonian and Serbian with Cyrillic. Modern Greek has its own distinctive alphabet. In this book, I have transliterated Greek and Cyrillic words into the Latin alphabet to enable you to recognise common elements in the various languages. There is hardly a standard system of transliterating modern Greek. Even in Greece itself, road signs show a good deal of inconsistency. However, in this book I have used the acute accent to mark emphasis where the Greeks used to use either the acute, the grave or the circumflex.

Pronunciation of Balkan languages is simple because each letter has the same phonetic value, and any exceptions follow fixed rules. The tables below are an abbreviated guide for those readers who feel the need of it.

ALBANIAN
| | |
|---|---|
| a | a in bar |
| c | ts in bits |
| ç | ch in Cheddar |
| dh | th in they |
| ë | u in curd |
| gj | g in ambiguous |
| j | y in yoghurt |
| nj | ni in onions |
| q | ky in stockyard |
| rr | rr in burr but highly trilled |
| x | ds in seeds |
| xh | dg in porridge |
| y | yu in yule or eu in the French fleur |
| zh | s in measure |

BULGARIAN
| | |
|---|---|
| a | a in bar |
| j | y in royal |
| u | u in curd |

GREEK
| | |
|---|---|
| ai | e in egg |
| ay,ey,iy | av, ev, iv, but af, ef, if before f,h,k,ks,p, ps,s,t,th |
| d | th in this |
| ei,oi,yi | i in machine |
| g | g in grill but soft and more guttural, save before a vowel when y in yeast |
| gg | ng in finger |
| gh | ngh in bung-hole |
| gk | g in grill at the beginning of a word, but as ng in finger when in the middle of a word |
| gks | nks in links |
| mp | b in bake at the beginning of a word, but as mb in crumble in the middle |
| nt | d in dish at the beginning of a word, but nd in blend in the middle |
| s | s in sausages, but z as in zest before d,g,l,m,n,r,v |
| tz | ds in seeds |
| x | ks in box |
| y | y in syrup |

## MACEDONIAN

| | |
|---|---|
| dž | dg in porridge |
| ǵ | g in ambiguous |
| j | y in royal |
| ḱ | cky in dockyard |
| u | ou in soup |
| ž | s in measure |
| - | not marked by any symbol, but pronounced as u in curd before the so-called vocalic r, when the r is preceded and followed by a consonant |

## ROMANIAN

| | |
|---|---|
| ă | a in farther |
| â | u in burn |
| c | k in kitchen, but as ch in Cheddar when followed by e or i |
| cc | kch in pork chops |
| ch | cky in dockyard |
| e | e in egg, but at the beginning of a word or syllable, or when combined with a vowel, as ye in yet |
| g | g in grill, but as dg in porridge when followed by e or i |
| gh | g in get, but palatized (softened) |
| i | i in machine, but at the beginning of a word or at the end of a word and combined with a vowel, as y in yeast |
| î | u in burn |
| j | s in measure |
| ș | sh in fish |
| ț | ts in bits |
| u | ou in soup |
| q | kv in milk-van (only occurring in foreign words and names) |

## SERBO-CROAT

| | |
|---|---|
| c | ts in bits |
| č | ch in Cheddar |
| ć | cky in dockyard |
| dj | dy in 'How d'ye do?' |
| dž | dg in porridge |
| j | y in royal |
| nj | ni in union |

## SLOVENIAN

| | |
|---|---|
| c | ts in bits |
| č | ch in Cheddar |
| j | y in royal |
| l | l in lard, but if at the end of a word, as w in cow |
| š | sh in fish |
| v | v in vinegar, unless it is at the end of a word or before a consonant when it is pronounced as w in cow; or in between consonants when pronounced as ou in soup |
| ž | s in measure |
| - | not marked by any symbol, but if r is preceded and followed by a consonant, it is pronounced as u in curd |

## TURKISH

| | |
|---|---|
| a | u in bun |
| â | a in far, but after k, g, and l as a in apple |
| c | j in jam |
| ç | ch in Cheddar |
| ğ | g in grill but hardly perceptible and guttural, and sometimes just lengthening the preceding vowel, except with soft vowels when it is pronounced y as in paying |
| ı | i in cousin |
| j | s in pleasure |
| ö | eu in French peu, or as ö in the German König |
| ş | sh in fish |
| ü | yu in yule |
| û | u in cute |

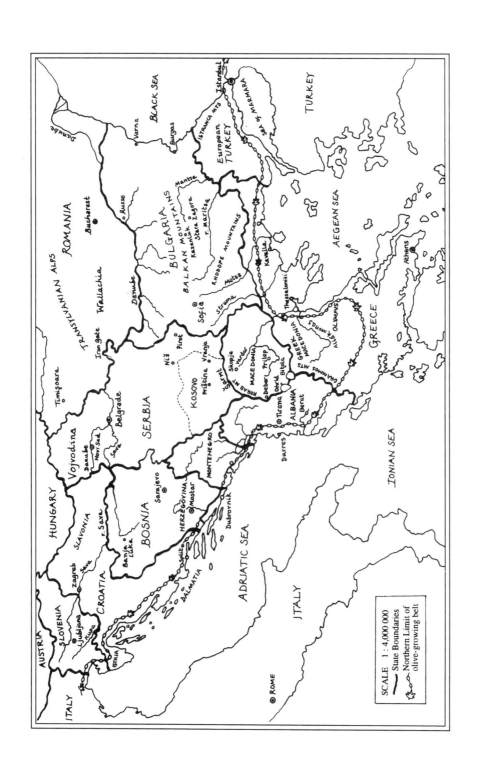

CHAPTER I

# A Lesson in History and Geography

Centuries of integrated life under Turkish rule have created a common Balkan culture, a sameness in demeanor, outlook, eating attitudes and habits. The region's cookery is an amalgam of centuries of practice enriched by Greek, Turkish and Central European adoptions. It spans between the Middle East and Western Europe. *Ćevapčići*, moussaka, *köfte*, baklava, sour soup—sound a roll-call of dishes that are part of an older shared heritage, despite variations of climate, belief, nationality and economic circumstance. This needs a tithe of history to explain.

Even near neighbours view the Balkans as a cohesive entity, regardless of its centripetal politics (which in a sense define it still further). Step north of the Sava and the Danube, and 'Balkan' is unanimously thought not even remotely related to local lifestyle or food; in reality, however, the cooking remains essentially Balkan in character in northern regions such as Vojvodina in Yugoslavia or the Wallachian plain of southern Romania. But such is the strength of geography and history they virtually refuse to recognise it. Even further north, in Transylvania, Romanian and Hungarian shepherds still produce the two most common Balkan cheeses—the white, brine cheese similar to feta, and the hard, yellow *kashkaval*.

The Balkan peninsula projects into the Mediterranean south of the rivers Sava and Danube. It takes its name from the mountain range which stretches across the entire length of Bulgaria and just enters the eastern part of Serbia. The term itself did not occur before the Turkish occupation. It is a literal translation of the Bulgarian *Stara Planina*, Old Mountain, into Turkish, *Koca Balkan*.

There are three climatic regions: temperate in the north and centre; more extreme Central European conditions in the high mountains; Mediterranean in the south and on the Adriatic. This last area is defined by the growth of the olive tree: its northern limits form a great U shape, starting from the Black Sea in the east and running up to the north-western tip of Slovenia.

While ten countries lie entirely or partially within the Balkans, for our purposes

2 *A Lesson in History and Geography*

*1 & 2. Four-legged dish and jar from the settlement mound (tell) at Karanovo, near Nova Zagora. Late Stone Age, c. 5,400 BC, in the National Archaeological Museum, Sofia.*
*3. Illyrian earthenware pot, from Maliqi, Korça district, Albania. Middle Bronze Age, c. 1,800 BC, in the Archaeological and Ethnographic Museum, Tirana,*

*4. Earthenware water carrier and cooler, from Sarvaš, Croatia, Middle Bronze Age, between 2,300 and 1,800 BC.*
*5. Marble figurine from the settlement mound at Soulitsa, near Stara Zagora, c. 3,500 BC, in the District History Museum, Stara Zagora. Similar bone and clay figurines of the same period have copper earrings from hammered copper nuggets.*

Greece and European Turkey have been largely excluded, since Greece belongs climatically and culturally to the Mediterranean and European Turkey looks more today to the national homeland of Anatolia than to its small European region of eastern Thrace.

## THE BEGINNINGS OF BALKAN COOKERY

In my opinion it was here, in the Balkans, that all European cookery began about 8,000 years ago.

Man has lived in the region for at least 200,000 years, but the early stages of agriculture, plant cultivation and the domestication of animals, cannot be dated earlier than between the seventh and sixth millenniums BC.

There were perhaps about 100,000 people, scattered in small settlements across the peninsula. Many were real villages of up to thirty houses. Archaeology tells us these had one or two rooms, and were simple constructions of chaff and clay plastered thickly on to a frame of poles and plaited twigs resting on clay floors; exceptionally cool in summer and warm in winter.

Self-sufficient farming families grew wild, indigenous one-seeded einkorn wheat, the cultivated einkorn wheat, the larger-grained emmer wheat, a six-row naked barley and common millet (*Panicum miliaceum*, which appears to have been domesticated in the Balkans), as well as, in the later neolithic period, the more advanced hexaploid bread wheat.

Using long, open-ended saddle querns, they ground the grain into flour, which was scraped up with the help of a spatula carved out of a blade-bone of the wild bull. The flour was converted into bread dough, which was baked in igloo-shaped ovens built on the same principle as the houses themselves, conserving heat better than some modern sophisticated ovens.

Remains of oven floors together with the lower parts of the walls have been uncovered in many settlement sites in Greece and Macedonia, Vinča in Serbia, and in Bulgaria. More recently, small clay models of bread ovens—perhaps the oldest anywhere in the world—were unearthed at Vinča, Valac in Kosovo, and Stara Zagora in Bulgaria. Radio-carbon analysis dates these to between 4,500 and 4,250 BC. Strangely, there are no early examples of such ovens anywhere south of Macedonia. In Crete, for instance, none have been discovered older than about 1,500 BC. Such is the continuity of life in the Balkans that clay ovens, closely resembling these very ancient structures, are still in use in country districts.

At a site called Bereket near Stara Zagora, archaeologists have even unearthed

*1. Thracian gold cup and bowl, from the hoard found at the village of Vulchitrun, near Pleven in northern Bulgaria, c. 13th-12th century BC, in the National Archaeological Museum, Sofia.*
*2. Coin of the Thracian king Remetalk I, c. 16 BC–14 AD, in the Municipal History Museum, Nova Zagora, southern Bulgaria.*
*3. Thracian rhyton (drinking cup, usually in the shape of a horn) from the gold treasure dug up at Panagyurishte in southern Bulgaria, dating from between the 4th and the beginning of the 3rd century BC, in the Archaeological Museum, Plovdiv, southern Bulgaria.*

a clay model of a loaf, which astonishingly seems to date from about 5,100 BC. No flat unleavened loaf, but plump, with holes pricked in the top surface suggesting the porous structure of a fermented dough (a natural sourdough, not a modern yeasty loaf), is this Europe's earliest leavened bread?

In addition to cereals, the communities reared stock and pursued hunting and gathering for supplementary foods. Meat was roasted over a fire or boiled into kinds of soups or pottages in clay pots, perhaps with herbs, seeds and grains.

On available evidence, it seems that the first milking of domestic animals took place as early as 6,500–5,000 BC in Thrace and Macedonia and possibly elsewhere too. Milking was soon followed by cheesemaking; perforated fragments of conic clay pots used for draining cheese have been discovered among household debris in Razgrad, Bulgaria. The Balkan kitchen was already in place.

## THE PEOPLE AND THEIR CROPS

The Balkan peoples are descendants of an extraordinarily rich mixture. Among the earliest inhabitants we can name were the Thracians—powerful groups of related tribes of Indo-European origin—who form an identifiable group from the second millennium BC. It is still unclear whether they had always lived in the Balkans or were invaders. These mysterious Bronze Age warriors occupied the eastern half of the peninsula and are one of the three ancestors of present-day Bulgarians, the other two being the Bulgar-Turks (known to the Bulgarians as proto-Bulgars) and the Slavs.

To the west were the Illyrian tribes, most likely another autochthonous people. In the south, the earliest known Greeks, the Mycenaeans (Homer called them Achaeans), arrived in Greece around 2,000 BC. In the south-west, the Macedonians, possibly another Illyrian tribe, also appeared quite early, but were first identified under their present name in the seventh century BC (from the Greek *makednós*, meaning tall, big, robust, stalwart).

Then, in the third century BC, there was a wave of conquest as Celts, pushing eastward along the Danube, traversed the Balkans. Some settled briefly in the east, but more mixed with western, Illyrian tribes, such as the Albanoi. Modern Albanians are descendants of this dual parentage, hence related to the Scots, Irish, Welsh, Breton, and Manx peoples.

These communities were predominantly agrarian. They grew millet and improved strains of barley, three kinds of wheat including bread wheat, vegetables such as white cabbage, lentils, black winter radish, onion and garlic, and cultivated several varieties of fruit trees. This cereal-fruit-vegetable complex of the ancient Thracians, Illyrians and Greeks has hardly been modified through the centuries. Bread and wheat flour are still the bedrock of the Balkan diet, supplemented by milk, cheese, yoghurt and large quantities of fruit and vegetables. Like most East Europeans, the Balkan peoples could be defined as grain-eaters, in contrast to westerners who are predominantly meat-eaters.

The Christian era marked the beginning of three new developments; bread wheat was increasingly grown at the expense of primitive einkorn and emmer; rye was taken into cultivation; and sourdough bread became more common. The

Romans did not introduce any new crops. Quite the contrary: their conquests led to the dispersal of many Balkan plants, including bread wheat, the cultivated grape vine and the walnut, as well as the craft of making leavened bread, to other parts of Europe.

During the dark centuries which followed the fall of the western Roman Empire, the Balkans suffered further series of invasions and incursions from nomadic tribes and nations spilling out of Asia. First Ostrogoths, Huns and Alans; then Avars, who were in turn displaced by Slavs who poured across the Danube in the sixth and seventh centuries AD and penetrated all parts of the peninsula. To the north-west went the Slovenes; to the west—the Serbo-Croat group of tribes; to the east—the Bulgarian South-Slavonic group, so called because the Bulgar-Turks, a branch

*Damask rose is a shrub up to 1.8 metres tall, armed with hooked spines and prickly bristles. Five leaflets, downy underneath; hips pear-shaped, long and thin. Reddish-pink flowers, very fragant, sweet tasting, produced in large clusters from the end of May until mid-June.*

of Turkic tribes (meaning belonging to the Turkic race—a large Central Asian family of peoples) who overran the area in the seventh century, later fused with the Slavs whom they had conquered. In the south-west, however, the Illyrian-Celtic tribes escaped slavonicization; and the Eastern Roman Empire subjected and assimilated the Slav masses that had settled in Greece proper and the islands, though Slav-speaking communities survived in southern Greece until the end of the middle ages. With these exceptions, most of the central and northern parts of the Balkans became Slavonic in language and culture.

## THE EMPIRE IS DEAD, LONG LIVE THE EMPIRE

While in the beginning the 'barbarians' came down from the north, the expansion of the Turks into the Balkans was from the south after their seizure of Gallipoli in 1354. Thereafter, the Ottoman Empire encompassed the whole of the peninsula until its gradual dissolution from the end of the nineteenth century.

Historiography has emphasized time and again the negative aspects of this domination which some say delayed cultural and economic development by five centuries. But for the cook, if not the nationalist, there were many advantages to Ottoman rule. The Turks introduced many new food plants and aromatics, particularly from south-west and south-east Asia as well as Africa. There were improved grape varieties for the table, and for the production of currants and sultanas. There was the red oil-bearing Damask rose, introduced in the seventeenth century, and soon an important agricultural crop and cottage industry. At present, the 'Rose Valley' which extends for nearly a hundred kilometres south of the Balkan Mountains, is the world's major source of attar - the 'liquid gold' distilled from the rose petals. Other new crops were okra, filberts, spearmint, flat-leaved parsley, aubergine, durum wheat, improved forms of chick-peas, and more.

The Ottoman invasion may have been the last significant movement of peoples within the Balkans, but that never meant that foodstuffs and ingredients stayed as they were. A Turkish document dated between 1498 and 1513 mentions for the first time a stranger from across the Atlantic, the common bean, which soon became a significant supplementary staple. Other early arrivals, noted in 1542, were the winter pumpkin (*Cucurbita maxima*) and the sweet cushaw pumpkin (*C moschata*), as well as the common pumpkin and vegetable marrow (*C pepo*). The great American staple, maize, was introduced in the seventeenth century via Egypt then moved north into Romania and Hungary. In Western Europe it was initially known as 'Turkey wheat'.

Potatoes took a long time to make the journey from the Americas. They were finally introduced in the nineteenth century by Bulgarian market-gardeners working in Romania where the potato had already arrived via Germany, Albania and Czecho–slovakia. Another route of dispersal was from Italy into Dalmatia and Albania.

Commercial market gardening abroad was a strange Bulgarian phenomenon which accounted for the spread of many Turkish imports from their first foothold in the Balkans to Austria, Hungary, Germany, Czechoslovakia, Romania and Russia. Market gardening originated with the need to provide fresh vegetables for the Turkish garrisons located in the conquered territories. A little later, from the end of the seventeenth century, professional Bulgarian gardeners in their thousands, organised in co-operative 'companies', hired or bought vacant land round large European towns and started the cultivation of green beans, onion, chilli peppers, cucumbers and cabbage. These 'Gardeners of Europe', as Hungarian-born George Lang calls them, brought with them their own improved varieties of vegetables, their own terms and methods. Their influence is possibly best seen in Hungary: paprika, that most characteristic seasoning of the Hungarian kitchen, got its name from the Bulgarian word *piperka*, meaning pepper, the fruit of the capsicum plant, which was corrupted into peprika, and, eventually, into paprika.

Columbus brought a few varieties of the hot type of pepper to Spain from Mexico and Guatemala where it was first domesticated. In the sixteenth century, the Ottoman Turks brought the small hot pepper (*Capsicum annuum* ssp *microcarpum*) to the Balkans from Spain, possibly by way of Egypt. Production of the hot culinary powder made from the dried ground pod began soon after its introduction. But the large, sweet pepper for stuffing (*Capsicum annuum* ssp *macrocarpum* var *grossum*) and the long sweet pepper for salads (*Capsicum annuum* ssp *macrocarpum* var *longum*) began to feature in Balkan cookery much later—as late as the beginning of this century.

Two more recent additions to the Balkan larder have been tomatoes, which came around the middle of the nineteenth century and were first eaten in their green state, and the sunflower, which was introduced at the turn of our own century. The manufacture of sunflower-seed oil started in the 1920s and north of Greece and Turkey, this is the oil now most widely used in cooking.

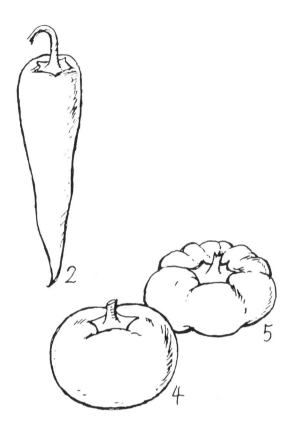

*1. Kapiya, with thick, juicy flesh, is the sweet pepper particularly well suited to grilling and frying because it lacks the grooves of the stuffing pepper, so cooks more easily. It can be eaten green, or fully ripened and deep red.*

*2. Sivriya sweet peppers are shorter, with thinner flesh, which is ideal for drying in the open air and storing for the winter, or grinding into red paprika pepper.*

*3. Chilli: the small, fiery green or red pepper which practically eliminated ginger and black pepper from the Balkan peasant kitchen.*

*4 & 5. Pickling peppers, kambi, look very much like large 'beef' tomatoes and can be smooth or deeply grooved. They are only picked when fully ripe and red, otherwise they taste bitter.*

# CHAPTER II

# A Cook's Tour

The next few pages are devoted to a country by country tour, an overview of styles and approaches to food.

ALBANIA is the smallest and least known Balkan state. They call it Shqipëria, 'Land of Eagles'—appropriate for a country two-thirds mountain. Its language, sole survivor derived from ancient Illyrian, is like no other, although now packed with Turkish, Slavonic and Italian loan words, especially culinary. Albanians are no xenophobes: on my visits I was met with smiles and lively interest. Quite a few spoke English and, with help from two guides and a dictionary, I collected numbers of recipes.

The coastal plain is clothed with wheat and golden maize, grapes and other kinds of fruit, tobacco, cotton and rice, and miles of plastic-covered tunnels filled with early vegetables. The Riviera is lushly beautiful with palms and flowering evergreens, citrus, olive and fig plantations, and boasts copious marine life. Fish recipes are prominent. Freshwater fish inhabit all kinds of inland ponds and lakes and fast-running mountain rivers. In lake Ohrid, for example, there are brown trout, wels or sheat-fish, plus a non-migratory race of salmon, a dwarf relict from the last Ice Age. In the forests, capercaillie, quail, pheasant and black grouse lurk up the hills, and wild boar can still rush you in the thickly wooded valley below the Gllava Pass.

Albanian cookery has evolved under the influence of Turkish food, ritual and culinary practice since the Ottoman occupation in 1500 AD. The exceptions are the far south, which has persisted in more ancient ways, and the coast, where the lure of Italy kept people eating pasta.

Bread, pasta, cheese and yoghurt are valued staples. The standard loaf is made of unbleached, high-extraction flour—dark beige, on the heavy side, with a slightly sour flavour but very satisfying. In hotels, foreigners get white bread which is not half so tasty. Four cheeses are widely available: a white, brine cheese similar to feta, a whey cheese with only 18 per cent fat, and the yellow, full fat cheeses *Djathë Kaçkavall* and *Djathë Kasher*.

Sheep's, cow's and occasionally water-buffalo milk is also turned into yoghurt called *kos*. Its taste, consistency and make-up are similar to Bulgarian yoghurt, but it also contains the lactic yeast *Oidium lactis* and a few moulds.

Pasta, *makaronash*, is very popular. Scores of types are served in dozens of different ways—as a main-course dish for lunch or supper or as a starter, or *antipastë* (from Italian *antipasto*). A regular restaurant *antipastë* is *kanelloni alla toskana*, which sounds familiar but in fact consists of a couple of pancakes stuffed with minced veal (Albanian 'veal' is immature beef) and given a gratin finish. Another national antipastë is *byrek me djathë* (from the Turkish *börek*), a triangular pasty filled with white cheese and eggs.

Like the Bosnian Muslims, the Albanians' love of good eating and drinking has meant a relaxation of Islamic law prohibiting intoxicants. In *High Albania*, the classic account by Edith Durham, she recounts a lively gathering of Albanian men round a meze table, drinking raki and nibbling bite-sized pieces of sheep's cheese, boiled eggs, fruits and sweetmeats: 'Many Albanians indeed prefer this part of an entertainment to the meal that it precedes.'

The meze ritual and various other features of Turkish cookery have been preserved despite the weakening of the Ottoman legacy by education and industrialization. They are still strong among the older generation, as well as reinforced by isolation in the Albanian villages of Yugoslavia—in Kosovo, Montenegro, and the town of Tetovo in Macedonia. Sadly, even in those parts women's emancipation and the slow dismantling of the extended family, are leading to the disappearance of traditions.

> The principal food of these people is wheaten or barley bread, or cakes made of boiled or roasted maize, cheese made of goats'-milk, rice mixed with butter, eggs, dried fish, olives, and vegetables. On holidays kids and sheep are killed, and fowls, of which there are great plenty everywhere; but the proportion of animal food is considerably less than that of the other part of their diet. They drink wine, both Mahometans and Christians, as also an ardent spirit extracted from grape husks and barley, called rackee, not unlike whisky. It is but seldom that they spare any milk from their cheeses. Indeed, cold water is what they chiefly drink, and of this they take large draughts, even in the heats of summer, and during the most violent exercise, without experiencing any inconvenience from the indulgence. Coffee is to be met with in many houses, and now and then the rossoglios of Italy, and the liqueurs made at Cefalonia and Corfu.
> 
> John Cam Hobhouse (Lord Broughton), *Travels in Albania and Other Provinces of Turkey in 1809 & 1810*, new edition 1858.

BULGARIA's capital Sofia stands at the heart of the peninsula, approximately equidistant from the Adriatic and Black Seas, from Istanbul, Athens and Tirana. To the north stretches the great Danubian plain, where water buffalo, cattle and pigs are reared among fields of wheat and maize and orchards of apricots, apples, pears, cherries and quinces. Along the Black Sea coast grow almonds, figs and chestnuts. Rice and lentils are confined to the warmer regions of the south. There are, however, no olives or citrus fruits. These apart, few foods are imported; the Bulgarians prefer home produce and rejoice in a certain culinary conservatism.

This is borne out in their attitude to fish. Bulgarians' intake used to be one of the lowest in Europe. In 1960, annual consumption was only 2 kilos per person, despite the Black Sea and streams and rivers rich in fish, luxuries in other parts of Europe. The Danube alone provides more than 60 species including pike-perch, wels or sheat-fish, the valuable sterlet and sturgeon.

Many Bulgarians eat fish, *riba*, only in the months with an 'r', and most, including myself, are biased against eating fish with milk or yoghurt at the same meal, believing the combination detrimental to health. This long-standing prejudice has roots in the works of Avicenna, the Arab philosopher and physician (*c.* 980—1037 AD), who thought milk should not be consumed together with sour foods, fish, or poultry. His *Canon* was the greatest collection of medical knowledge in the medieval world, and influenced European as well as Balkan medicine and dietetics.

Bulgarians eat a lot of yoghurt. They love it. Two-thirds of the milk output is sold as plain yoghurt. If they won't eat fish in the same meal, it follows their fish-eating window is going to be tiny.

Of all yoghurts, thick sheep's yoghurt is preferred. Balkan sheep are milch breeds; meat and wool have always been secondary. Dr K. Katrandzhiev of the Agricultural Academy of Sciences states: 'the Bulgarian sheep's milk yoghurt ... can claim an ancestry at least as early as Thracian times.' Whether or not the Thracians made yoghurt is still open to question, but it is certainly true that in the seventh century AD—that is, seven centuries before the Ottomans—the Bulgar-Turks (who had nothing to do with the Ottoman Turks, but were one of Bulgaria's earliest tribal societies, originating from somewhere deep in central Asia) used a starter-culture of spontaneously fermented sheep's milk, or sheep's cheese creamed with water and mixed with the warm milk. Called *katuk*, this kind of yoghurt is still made in highland dairies and rural areas towards the end of the ewes' lactation period. The milk is thickened by protracted simmering, then poured into sheep-skin bags, large preserving crocks or wooden firkins and allowed to cool. Brined sheep's cheese (*ovcho salamoureno sirene*) is stirred in to provoke fermentation. The yoghurt is stored for the winter under a protective layer of sheep's butter.

Although the name is derived from the Turkish *katık*, meaning 'anything eaten with bread as a relish', the same term appears in the Bashkir, Uzbek and Tartar Autonomous Republics of the former USSR—a fact which points to an all-Turkic origin of yoghurt on the steppes of central Asia, in a century now long forgotten.

Another national delight probably inherited from the Bulgar-Turks, who used crushed red rock or red clay mixed with red wine as a curative, is a fondness for red-coloured foods and drinks. They are considered healthy and invigorating; red apples are preferred to green or yellow; and folk songs eulogize red wine—but never white. When peppers were introduced in the sixteenth century and the cottage production of ground chilli pepper began, stews took on a crimson glow. A Bulgarian stew, *yahniya* (from Turkish *yahni*), can be meatless, or with meat and vegetables, but it is always red, and always cooked with lots of onion, or to use an old village expression, 'with a lidful of chopped onions'. This 'lidful of onion' puzzled me until I realized that the traditional village tinned-copper stewpan *bakurena tendzhera*, has a domed lid rising about a third of the depth of the pan, and is often used as a measure. Long, slow cooking allows the onion to melt and thicken the juices, giving the stew distinctive flavour.

Minimum frying is an attribute of old Bulgaria. Before the Turkish conquest, frying was almost unknown in the villages, probably because clay dishes could not withstand high temperatures, and copper pans were few and expensive. *Zapruzhka*, a small stew-enrichment sauce based on fried onion and flour, only dates from the last hundred years or so, and nearly all fried dishes of current cookery are adoptions from Greece, Turkey and Central Europe.

Sunflower oil is used in preference to animal fats, replacing walnut and sesame oils of the past, as well as olive oil. Lard or butter are sometimes used in stews and pastries, but beef fat is avoided to such an extent that in many households in Sofia and other towns, minced beef is de-fatted, then cooked with sunflower oil.

The seasons dominate the cooking, determining what goes with what, and when. Meat from older animals or poultry goes with pulses, cabbage, sauerkraut, potatoes, or almost any winter fruit: prunes, dried apricots or chestnuts. Young flesh is combined with spring onion and green garlic, spinach, young broad bean pods or tiny peas. Something like lamb with haricot beans or dried okra would be an inadmissible blunder.

The ancient Bulgarian solar calendar calculated the new year from the shortest day (day zero)—22 December is day one. Consumption of meat was initiated with the sacrificial slaughter of the seasonal animal: on day one of the first month, a pig; on day five of the fifth month, a lamb; on day seven of the seventh month, a chicken; on day ten of the tenth month, a calf; and on day twelve of the twelfth month, fish or game, and so on. This translates in practice with lamb starting in April, on St George's Day; young chickens roasted for the first time on St Peter's Day in June; baked carp stuffed with walnuts served in December on St Nicolas' Day; roast pork at Christmas; and goose or cock on the first of January.

Summer is the time for vegetables served in their own right rather than as accessories to meat or fish, and the time for salads, uncooked tomato or yoghurt soups, ice-cold yoghurt drinks, unsweetened compotes, and fresh fruit. Cherries, strawberries, grapes and peaches are brought home from the market in their wooden crates; melons and watermelons, by the cartload, are piled in the cellar, joined later by a couple of barrels of sauerkraut—one containing whole cabbages for raw salad and *sarmi*, the other with shredded cabbage for cooking—and at least one huge barrel with home-made wine from the family vineyard.

Bulgarian wine goes back to the Thracians who made it from the native wild grape. During the Middle Ages, Bulgarian wines had a high reputation and the Soungourlare wine reached the court of Charlemagne. A good deal of wine is still exported, some of the best of eastern Europe.

*Rakiya* (fruit brandy) is an institution everywhere. It was first produced at the end of the Middle Ages, and by the end of the last century a wide range of richly-scented plum or grape brandies were prepared in private houses in their own stills, as well as in many small commercial distilleries. *Gyulovitsa*, short for *Gyulova rakiya* (from the Turkish *gül*, rose), was brandy double-distilled with the addition of petals of the attar rose. *Anasonliya rakiya* (from the Turkish *anason*, aniseed) was flavoured mainly with pounded seeds of the anise plant, though other aromatics—mastic, dried orange rind, juniper berries, lemon balm and onion—were often added. *Sakuzliya rakiya* (from the Turkish *sakız*, mastic) was re-distilled with added mastic and frankincense. Another kind called 'Aromatic brandy' was perfumed with cloves, nutmeg, cinnamon, angelica, wild mint and lemon balm. 'When this is supplemented in the still by ambergris and musk', wrote P. R. Slavejkov in 1870, 'it becomes the Elixir of life, or what the Turks call *iksir hayat.*' Monks' Herbal Brandy contained an extract of 16 different herbs and spices macerated in ethyl alcohol. The most highly prized (especially by ageing men) was the *amberliya* fruit brandy (from the Turkish *amber*, ambergris), which had reputed aphrodisiac and restorative qualities.

Regrettably, these brandies are no longer made either in the home or at distilleries, except for *mastika*, which is a spirit similar to *rakiya* but flavoured with anethol (the essential oil of anise).

Every village, almost every cottage, has fruit orchards, hop gardens, clinging [grape]vines and strings of red and green peppers round it, every district is celebrated for something, usually something to eat. Bulgaria is one big salad bowl, if you take the trouble to explore it; fruit salad and vegetable salad.
Leslie Gardiner, *Curtain Calls,* 1977.

ROMANIA was born of the union of Wallachia and Moldavia (Moldova). The majority of its population are ethnic Romanians, descendants of Romanized Geto-Dacian tribes (a North Danubian branch of the ancient Thracians) and Roman colonists who settled there after the Roman conquest in 106 AD. Even today, Romanian fondness for piquant spices is a legacy from those first legionaries who coated most of their meat and fish dishes with highly-flavoured sauces, often heavily spiced with pepper.

The country is still overwhelmingly agricultural, despite rushes to industrialization. Maize was the bed-rock of the diet. The grain is, or was until recently, milled into fine powder for *mămăligă*, or ground coarsely for *păsatul*—two kinds of thick porridge which become firm when cool. These are eaten mixed with cheese, soured cream or butter, or as a substitute for bread. Nowadays there is a shift to wheat, especially in the towns: no more the heavy maize bread, *turtă de mălaiu*.

The most colourful crops are the opium poppy and sunflowers. Ripe poppy seeds are not narcotic, and are used freely on bread dough, or as filling for *cozonac*—the traditional yeast cake baked on Good Friday. They also can be cold-pressed for a cooking oil. Generally, sunflower oil is the cooking medium, and gradually replacing animal fats.

Vegetables—beans, peppers, aubergines, tomatoes, marrows and asparagus—are grown in abundance. The Romanians have a long tradition of vegetable cookery—of special importance during Lent and the many fast days.

Fruits make up a significant part of the diet: cherries, quinces, grapes and apples are cultivated in higher areas, especially in the foothills of the Carpathians; the bulk of the grape crop is used for making wine, much of which is exported. Plums abound; they distill a brandy called *Tuică (rachiu)* from the large, sweet, blue-skinned sort—it's the national drink.

Dairy cows graze the plains, water buffalo the low-lying regions of the Danube, and sheep are confined to the hills and mountains. The white brine cheese *telemea*, made from cow's, sheep's or water-buffalo milk, takes first place in the list of Romanian cheeses; it is often spiced with aniseed. Plain *telemea* tastes very much like feta; in fact, in northern Greece, feta is known locally as *telemés*.

*Cașcaval*, as old as the Romans who probably introduced it, is a hard, yellow, full-fat cheese made from sheep's milk. *Brînză*, too, is a sheep's cheese, pale yellow and rather crumbly. It may be packed into sacks made of the tanned skin of sheep or goat or into cylindrical containers made of spruce bark.

Wallachia takes its name from *Walh*, a Germanic word for foreigner (as does Wales). Chaucer gives it early mention in *The Book of the Duchess*, shortly after the appearance of the Wallachian state in the fourteenth century.

> Ne sende men in-to Walakye,
> To Pruyse and in-to Tartarye
> To Alisaundre, ne in-to Turkye,

Chaucer's Wallachia lacked today's oil wells and intensive agriculture of wheat, maize and barley, with rice in the far south. Bucharest, the capital, lies in this region.

Integrated life during Ottoman domination has helped shape Wallachian cookery in the Balkan mould: *baclava*, *chiftea* (burger), *ciorbă* (soup), *dulceață* (fruit preserved in heavy syrup), *ghiveciu* (mixed vegetable casserole), *iahnie* (stew), *rahat* (Turkish delight), *musaca*, *pilaf*, *sarmale*, *mezelic* and more are obviously derived from Turkish and Greek sources.

Many Romanians still live all over the Balkan peninsula. They are known as Vlachs, Koutsovlahs, Tsintsars or Karakachans, and speak Aroumanian, a Romanian dialect. Some Vlachs are shepherds following their flocks into fresh, highland grazings; others inhabit towns and villages in Albania, Bulgaria, Macedonia, Yugoslav Vojvodina, and northern Greece.

After the First World War, a large number of Vlachs settled in Dobrogea, Romania's only maritime province, which already had a motley mixture of Turks, Tartars, Ukrainians and Romanians. The food of Dobrogea is based on the land itself, much of which is ploughed for maize and wheat; the sea which yields a good, though not spectacular harvest; and the delta where the best fish are to be caught. Fishermen, many of whom are of Ukrainian descent, spit-roast or grill their catch over wood embers, or cook a Russian-Ukrainian fish soup called *uha*. In contrast to the Wallachian *ciorbă*, this soup is not acidulated.

Leslie Gardiner described the province in his book *Curtain Calls* (1977):

> When last we voyaged in Dobrudja, it was hard to tell where the Black Sea ended and Romania began. The Danube was spread from horizon to horizon and the redbrick cottages sailed on the delta like flotillas of Noah's Arks.

This time, in autumn, the waters are back where they belong, between the towpaths, turning the odd grain-mill which is anchored in midstream, pushing the odd caviare boat down to Sulina and the sea ... a land of fishermen ('Sea Cossacks') and marshfowlers.

Half an hour downstream ... is where some of the big ships come to take on caviare, sturgeon and herring for the western world.

Meanwhile we shall sit on the verandah of this tavern and taste this caviare (red, thirty pence the pound) and drink what is known as English tea—black, scalding hot, with a slice of lemon. The custom of the delta, as demonstrated by the man on the corner bench, is to sip from the saucer and let the steam invigorate the pores of your cheeks. He finishes his tea and wipes a thick horseshoe-shaped beard. He is the nearest thing we have seen to an Old Believer [*Raskolniki*, in Russian] and I stop fumbling for my cigarettes and decide to do without.

The food in the northern province of Maramureş, which borders on the Ukraine, also shows Russian influence. Local specialities include *borş*, which is beef soup with beetroot and other vegetables; *kaşa*, porridge made with food grain; *găluşti* or dumplings, called in Russian *galoushki*; and *rasol*, a dish of boiled beef, its name derived from the Russian word for brine, *rassol*. Beef is at the heart of Maramureş cooking, and that of the neighbouring province of Moldavia, whose national emblem is the head of an aurochs, the wild bull, ancestor of all modern cattle, as if to underline to the long history of cattle rearing in the region.

Further south and west, Transylvanian cooking is quite different. Three national cuisines meet and cross-pollinate here: Romanian, Hungarian and German.

In the thirteenth century AD, seven towns developed from settlements founded by Saxons (German colonists from the Rhineland—hence the German name for Transylvania, *Siebenburgen* or 'Seven Strongholds'). Saxon cookery has retained its original character in dishes like *Auflauf*, baked pudding; *Knödeln*, dumplings; *Gewürzküchlein*, embossed spiced biscuits; *Rosenkranz*, a rich ring-shaped yeast cake; and *Bratwurst*, beef or pork frying sausage.

A distinct racial group in south-eastern Transylvania are the Sekels (Székely)— Bulgar-Turks who had entered the region with the Magyars in the ninth century AD. Sekel food is considered by many the true, indigenous, Hungarian cuisine. *Székely qulyás*, for example, appears to be of much older parentage than the modern goulash, because it is cooked with Old World ingredients like cabbage in place of the much later potato.

Some very interesting sheep's cheeses are prepared by Romanian and Sekel shepherds such as: *Saitperec*, Hungarian cheese ringlets, about 10 cm in diameter; *Kaskavál-sajt*, which is mainly smoked; *ömlesztett füstölt sajt*, shaped in sculptured wooden moulds; and unique, stylized cheese dolls, known as *bábsajt* in Hungarian or *păpușă de caș* in Romanian, which are ordinarily smoked and offered as gifts.

YUGOSLAVIA was created in 1918 as a union of the Southern Slavs. It broke up, bloodily and irrevocably in 1992 when Croatia, Bosnia-Hercegovina and Slovenia won their battle for recognition. Yugoslavia today is made up of two federal republics, Serbia and Montenegro, and two autonomous provinces, Kosovo and Vojvodina, each with its own background and culinary heritage.

Serbian is the most widely spoken language. The inhabitants of Kosovo and Vojvodina use the Latin script, the Serbs and the Montenegrins, the Cyrillic, so throughout the country, books and menus can be written in either.

Yugoslav food is based on several traditions—old Slavonic, Ottoman, Mediterranean and Central European. Its distinguishing features are a general preference for composite dishes of several different meats, the abundant use of fresh fruit and vegetables, and the consumption of bread with every meal.

Few foreigners experience real Yugoslav food, which is mainly to be had in small local restaurants offering traditional menus, rather than in the tourist hotels with their nondescript fare. In Belgrade (meaning 'White City), the capital of Yugoslavia and also of Serbia, traditional charcoal-grilled specialities such as *ćevapčići* (skinless sausages—from the Turkish *kebap*), *pljeskavice* (burgers), *ražnjići* (shish-kebab) are to be found mainly in small brasseries, grillrooms, open-air stalls and in the bohemian quarter of Skadarlija—the gastronomic centre of the capital.

Serbian cuisine evolved from Slavonic traditions modified by Rome, Byzantium and Turkey. It is characterized by such ingredients as *kajamak*, fresh or salted and briefly ripened clotted cream; *sir*, a generic name for various semi-hard porcelain-white cheeses made from sheep's milk and kept in brine; *kačkavalj*, one of the 'drawn-curd' cheeses, similar to the Italian *caciocavallo* (the curd is heated, stretched and worked to a malleable paste); and two types of yoghurt: liquid *jogurt* from cow's milk, and *kiselo mleko*, the very best, luxury, sheep's milk yoghurt.

*Slatko*, a popular Serbian syrupy conserve, is made with every conceivable fruit or baby vegetable, fruit peel or flower petals. In more traditional households it is still offered to the afternoon visitor with a glass of water and a cup of Turkish coffee, followed by brandy or liqueurs.

The huge plum belt of nearly fifty million trees shared between Serbia and Bosnia provides *šljivovica*, the national drink. There is a widely diffused belief among the Serbs that their brandy, whether taken internally or used as an embrocation, is the original panacea, the water of life, the elixir for curing all ills. (Some claim there are more types of brandy in the country than ailments.) It varies from region to region, from distillery to distillery, the finest, double-distilled plum brandy, *prepečenica*, coming from the Gračanica monastery in southern Serbia. Conversely, *komovica*, an inferior spirit, is distilled from grape marc, and is used principally in cooking and preserves. Serbia also produces almost half the nation's wine—mostly white.

> All day long the bread-roll man runs in and out [of the hotel] with his basket; or two or three bread-roll men, if there is much company. The Servians rarely seem tired of eating rolls, and eat them all day long. Next in frequency to the bread man is the salad man, with a tray of lettuces and a big bunch of onions. The cake man does good trade in the afternoon. But the oddest of all is the hot-stew man. He appears in the evening, with a large tin drum slung around his neck, in which is an enamelled iron soup tureen. Such a cloud of steam rolls out when he lifts the lid that I think there must be heating apparatus in the drum, but he wears it next his stomach and does not appear unduly warm. The pockets of his white apron are full of not over-clean plates, and a formidable array of knives and forks bristles about the drum's edge. His customers take a plate and clean it with their handkerchiefs, serviettes or the tablecloth, and then select tit-bits from the pot, and the man returns later and removes the plate, knife and fork, when done with. If you do not care for stew, there is the hot-sausage man, whose wares look singularly unattractive; and, lastly, there is a man who sells very dry nuts. Except for wine and beer, you can get your whole meal from wandering caterers. ... Servian food and cooking, I may here note, is on the whole very good. It is peppery and flavoursome; mint, thyme, and other herbs, and the very popular 'paprika' (a mild variety of red pepper), are largely used, and the soups are meaty and nourishing. A fourpenny plate of kisela chorba (soup with lemon juice in it) often includes half a fowl, and is enough for a meal.
> M. Edith Durham, *Through the Lands of the Serb*, 1904.

The province of Vojvodina lies north of Belgrade across the Danube and the Sava, sharing a border with Hungary and Romania. It is settled by Serbs and other Slavs, plus Hungarians, Romanians, Slovaks and Ruthenians, all speaking and reading their own tongues. The Novi Sad TV station broadcasts in five languages. It is the granary of Yugoslavia, as well as its main sugar supplier and stockbreeder for beef and pork. Here also, in the canals and by-channels of the Danube, are the richest freshwater fishing grounds in Europe, yielding pike-perch, tench, wels or sheat-fish, carp and sterlet.

It follows that the cuisine of Vojvodina is many-sided. Furthermore, long connections of the region with Hungary, and later with the Austro-Hungarian monarchy, have accentuated Central European influences, particularly in cakes and pastries.

South of Belgrade, the cooking of Kosovo is entirely different. Much of the population is Albanian. The region was under Turkish rule until 1913, and Turkish, Albanian and Serbo-Croat are the official languages. Large areas are given up to viticulture, orchards, wheat, maize, sunflower and soya bean. In the plains, cattle and water buffaloes are reared for milk and meat. From mountain pastures comes lamb unsurpassed in succulence and flavour; naturally it plays a large part in the local cookery.

Many Albanian families in Kosovo still live in patriarchal communities of between fifty and ninety members, where food is cooked and bread baked collectively, and eaten in intimate commensality. Meals are served out of a huge cooking pot (*tenxhere*) or baking pan (*tavë*) on low, round tables (*sofër*). A feature of both Albanian and Turkish cooking in Kosovo is that they have retained their national character virtually intact.

Montenegro lies between Serbia and the sea. Its Venetian and Serbian names both mean 'Black Mountain', in token of the awesome ranges which constitute the greater part of the republic. Montenegrins are of Serbian stock and profess the Orthodox faith. However, they have had a different political past from the Serbs and like to think of themselves as a separate nationality.

Less than five per cent of Montenegro is touched by the plough. Along the Adriatic, the mountains are skirted by vineyards, citrus orchards and olive groves, some of the olive trees being over 3,000 years old. But in the highlands, cultivation is limited to isolated pockets of fertile soil yielding a reluctant harvest mainly of maize and potatoes.

Sheep are of greater importance than cattle and, as of old, the summer surplus of milk is converted into cheese, butter, yoghurt, and ripened salted clotted cream, *kajmac*. The two most common Montenegrin cheeses are *Njeguški sir*—hard, yellow and shaped into flat cylinders, and *Mješinski sir* (goatskin cheese), which, like the Romanian *Brînză de Burduf*, matures in specially prepared goatskin sacks.

Lamb as well as beef and mutton, are favoured, but most Montenegrins find pork disagreeable. Local specialities include *pršuta*, smoked mutton, the counterpart of the Bosnian smoked fillet of mutton or goat.

As I see it, Montenegrin food falls into three categories: the Dalmatian type of the coastal zone; international, as found in the extensive tourist complexes such as 'Sveti Stefan'—an islet and old fishing village converted into a cluster of restaurants and hotels—and the traditional cuisine of the hinterland, which is not unlike that of Serbia but much less rich, and lacking the sweet confections and pork dishes so popular with Serbs.

Some time ago, while gathering recipes in Yugoslavia, I was able to confirm what I had only sensed on my journey through Montenegro. A tight-lipped woman from Kolašin, whose face held no key to her age, after describing for me her way of making cornmeal porridge, added, 'And then we eat it for breakfast, lunch or supper, supplemented with cream or white cheese—if we have any.'

I thought her remark a fair summary of the centuries-long struggle to coax a living from the sparse soil of their harsh mountainous home.

> Life up at Kolashin is mainly a struggle to get enough to eat and a roof overhead. In the lamb season meat is cheap and plentiful. Corn comes chiefly from the lower plains, and there is often lack of bread; in the winter folk fare very hardly. Even in fat times milk and maize-flour boiled in olive oil form the staple food of the peasantry.
> M. Edith Durham, *Through the Lands of the Serb,* 1904.

BOSNIA-HERCEGOVINA declared independence in 1992 and is now suffering the most appalling civil war. The first half of the name derives from the Bosna river where South Slavs settled in the seventh century AD; the second from the title of its fifteenth-century ruler, Duke (*Herzog* in German) Vukčić. Most of the Slavs converted to Islam during the Turkish occupation, but Bosnian Serbs remained Orthodox, and the Croat section of the population, Catholic.

The Bosnian Muslim food and way of life which I write about here are the ones I encountered and recorded a few years before the tragedy of the fratricidal and bloody civil war taking place today. I would like to leave my notes unchanged since I do not wish the traditional way of life and culture of the Bosnians (or indeed anyone else's) to be swept under the carpet of oblivion.

Many Ottoman cookery traditions linger—including those of the Muslim aristocratic caste. In the days of vast banquets, guests were feasted on spectacular preparations served on gold and silver plates. One such, *dolalma*, despite its Turkish name and probable origin, illustrates the South-Slavonic fondness for several sorts of meat in one dish. A young calf was stuffed with a lamb which was stuffed with a chicken stuffed with a raw egg in the shell; or an ox was stuffed with a wether stuffed with a cock, stuffed with an egg. The whole was roasted on a spit. The meat was judged done when the egg was cooked. Such multiple stuffings exist in other countries, of course, for example the ox featured in a sixteenth-century manuscript described by George Lang in *The Cuisine of Hungary*.

Another combination of meats on a less grandiose scale is the Bosnian shish kebab, *Bosanski šiš*, of young mutton, veal and lamb—but not pork, taboo for Muslims.

Bosnians have never been enthusiastic observers of the Islamic prohibition of alcohol, and practically never gave up wine and their beloved *šljivovica*. Drinking was more or less open, with an emphasis on moderation, without public opprobium. Indeed, a favourite pastime to this day, is the evening gathering called *akšamluk* (from the Turkish *akşamlatmak*, to entertain for the night), where men would gather for pleasant conversation, enlivened with brandy, sustained by meze dishes. When the spirits rose, they would softly sing passionate love-songs—the famous *sevdalinke*—to the gentle strains of a small gipsy band.

There is a long tradition of good restaurant food. The first inn with a cook, Isabey's *musafirhana*, was recorded in *c.* 1462, and a list of nearly 200 dishes served at the end of the last century in eating houses of Sarajevo, was given by Ali efendi Numanagić in 1939. Mr Numanagić noted sadly that many of the dishes had already disappeared from menus, and time has even swallowed some of the traditional drinks, including *ramazanija*, a spirit distilled from grape juice, so potent it could easily 'knock a person down'.

Bosnians like to taste their way through a menu, and it is an old restaurant practice to serve small amounts of six or more complementary dishes side by side. *Baščaršijski šahan* (High-Street platter) may consist of one skewer of *šiš ćevap*, a stuffed onion, green pepper and tomato, a few fried tiny meatballs, and stuffed vine or cabbage leaves which are called *sarma* in Bosnia, or *japrak* in Hercegovina. The juices from the saucepans are mixed together and poured over the food, the whole dish garnished with spoons of yoghurt.

CROATIA embraces the old district of Slavonia and the littoral province of Dalmatia. It became independent in 1992. Nationalism has a longer past however, and its revival in the nineteenth century included a lively interest in Croatia's own gastronomic past, reflected today in the boom of reprints of old recipe books.

There is a distinction between inland and coastal cookery, due to historical development as well as climate and location. Croatia proper is Central European in character after 800 years under Hungarian rule; Dalmatia, on the other hand, was Venetian, and not united with Croatia until this century. Not surprisingly, Dalmatian cookery takes after southern Italy and the Mediterranean, though it uses more meat, especially smoked meat, and much less garlic and olive oil.

Fruit is grown widely in Croatia, with grapes, figs, olives, marasca cherries and citrus fruit predominating on the seaboard. The sea itself abounds with infinite variety: Dalmatians boast they could eat a different sort of seafood every day of the year.

Croatia also produces some of the finest wines in the Balkans. One of these, the sweet and fruity Dalmatian *Prošek* is particularly interesting in that it is made, like the wines of ancient Greece, from grapes left to shrivel on the vine to concentrate their sweetness.


MACEDONIA is the ancient name of the region between the Grámmos mountains (the Greek-Albanian border) to the river Strimónas in the east, and from Bitola and the Nidže mountains down to Olympus and the Halkidiki peninsula. Under Ottoman rule, the area included the Turkish *vilayets* of Salonica and Kosovo, but at the beginning of this century Macedonia was partitioned between Serbia and Greece, with a small portion allocated to Bulgaria. In 1992 Macedonia left the Yugoslav federation to become an independent state. Here, living side by side, are Turks, Greeks, Gipsies, Albanians, Jews, Vlachs, Serbs and Macedonians—also known as Macedo-Slavs—who form the greater part of the population. The mixture has given rise to the French term *macédoine*.

The long hot summers herald the Mediterranean climate found further south; the mild springs boost the production of early fruit and vegetables. Apart from raising quantities of wheat and maize, the area is also a great centre for grapes and other fruits, rice, sunflower, sesame, anise and opium poppy. Sheep breeding is the main object of livestock farming.

The Macedonians hold dear their exquisite sheep's milk yoghurt, *ovcho kiselo mleko*, especially that made by shepherds in alpine dairies. I was en route from Ohrid to Lake Mavrovo one summer when I had a chance to taste it. I had stopped to slake my thirst and have a bite at a small roadside eating house. The yoghurt, I was told, had just been brought in by the shepherds from the nearby mountain, Bistra. It was presented together with a bowl of freshly cooked cornmeal porridge, *bakrdan*, glistening with sheep's milk butter. This mountain yoghurt was one of the finest that I have ever eaten—thick, rich and delicately flavoured under its pale-golden crust of cream.

Macedonian food is typically Balkan and old Slavic dishes mingle freely with adaptations from Greece and Turkey, though supplemented with hot red chillies or chilli powder which give country fare its fiery tang.


SLOVENIA was once the most northerly, and richest republic of Yugoslavia. It declared independence in 1992. It is predominantly alpine, with less than 20 per cent arable land under the plough—though little suitable for wheat—but this lack is redeemed by extensive livestock breeding and fruit growing, with viticulture in the valleys of the rivers Sava and Drava, and in the short coastal zone.

The Catholic Slovenes have shown astonishing determination in preserving their language, customs and cuisine regardless of Habsburg domination from the Middle Ages until the First World War. Many dishes, such as *kaša*, drawn from the ancient pan-Slavonic pool have survived into the present. Likewise *žganci* and *močnik* (known in Istria as *skrob*), types of porridge made from buckwheat, rye, maize or wheaten flour, run the gamut from almost solid to liquid mixtures. *Žganci* in solid form is served in individual scoops or crumbled, moistened with hot fat.

*Kolač* is the oldest Slavonic ritual leavened bread, and can be round, or ring-shaped and often elaborately decorated. *Juha*, another ancient Slavic dish, is a meat or vegetable soup and an intrinsic part of the Slovenian meal. *Ded* and *vratnik* are conserves of chopped pork, packed into a pig's stomach, bladder or large casing, poached or smoked or just air-dried. *Ded* means grandfather in Slovenian and is apt reflection of the wrinkles of the dehydrated meat. *Vratnik* is from *vrat* or neck—the part of the animal used in its preparation.

*Štruklji*, the pride of the Slovenian kitchen, was derived from the Austrian *Strudel*, but through the centuries the Slovenes have developed, modified and transformed the prototype. Baked, steamed, or boiled like an English pudding, *štruklji* can be made with stretched or rolled pastry, with yeast-raised dough, or a lightly enriched dough of wheat or buckwheat flour and mashed potatoes. Fillings are amazingly varied: savoury cheese, rice, potatoes, haricot beans, *kaša*, crackling, fresh or smoked meat, pork mixed with eggs and pig's blood; or sweet apples, plums, cherries, pumpkin, bilberries, walnuts, poppy seed or millet. *Štrukeljci* are tiny strudel rolls cut into 10 to 20 cm lengths, while *štrukeljčki* are even smaller, between 2 and 8 cm.

Slovenes are the only European people that I know of that still use millet in their traditional cookery; and who, like the Russians and the Poles, have an everyday liking for buckwheat. The raw materials available to the Slovenes are not as limited now as they were, but people still cling to the old as a metaphor for national identity.


MAINLAND GREECE AND EUROPEAN TURKEY are the southernmost Balkan lands, blessed by the Mediterranean, where the warm earth brings forth citrus fruits, figs, almonds, pomegranates, grapes and olives. These crops, together with cereals, and sheep and goats as the dominant animals, give Balkan Mediterranean agriculture its character. As you travel northwards in mainland Greece, you see more wheat, and cattle assume a greater role than flocks. Thessaly, Macedonia and Thrace are the bread baskets of Greece.

While Greek food is obviously Mediterranean, Greek Macedonia and Turkish Thrace do have long-standing culinary connections with their northern neighbours.

Balkan Mediterranean cuisine is dominated by the use of olive oil (and also, nowadays, by margarines based on olive oil) and ingeniously combines native raw materials with plant introductions from the New World. As in most hot countries, meat has little relish in the summer, and cookery is, in general, grain-centred, with lots of fish and vegetables.

Turkish cuisine, briefly described, is an enchanting blend of Greek, Persian, Arab and Ottoman traditions.

Long domination of the Balkans left permanent relics in many aspects of life, but none more than in the kitchen. Indigenous dishes were forgotten, were cloaked in Turkish names,or superseded by the food of the Turkish ruling class, whose gastronomic standards were set by the Sultan's kitchen at the Topkapı Palace in Istanbul. By the end of the eighteenth century, native dishes survived in isolated mountain tracts of country; in outlying regions of the Empire which were occupied but not freely settled by the Turks; and in areas north of the Danube-Sava line of demarcation—like Slovenia—which had never been in Turkish hands.

The very first Bulgarian cookbook was published in Istanbul by the novelist Petko R. Slavejkov in 1870. Its title was *Cookbook, or Instructions for All Kinds of Dishes Prepared after the Manner of Istanbul, and Other Household References.* Indeed, dishes 'prepared after the manner of Istanbul' were considered the paragon of culinary accomplishments and entered the Balkan repertoire.

The original glories of this manner are dwelled upon in Lady Mary Wortley Montagu's descriptions in her letters home from Turkey during the early eighteenth century.

I went to see the Sultana Hafife, favourite of the last Emperour Mustapha. …She gave me a Dinner of 50 dishes of meat, which (after their fashion) was plac'd on the table but one at a time, and was extremealy tedious, but the magnificence of her table answer'd very well to that of her dress. The Knives were of Gold, the hafts set with di'monds, but the piece of Luxury that greiv'd my Eyes was the Table cloth and napkins, which were all Tiffany embrodier'd with silks and Gold in the finest manner in natural flowers. It was with the utmost regret that I made use of these costly Napkins, as finely wrought as the finest handkercheifs that ever came out of this country. You may be sure that they were entirely spoilt before Dinner was over. The Sherbet (which is the Liquor they drink at meals) was serv'd in China Bowls, but the covers and salvers, massy Gold. After Dinner water was brought in a Gold bason and towels of the same kind of the napkins, which I very unwillingly wip'd my hands upon, and Coffée was serv'd in China with Gold soûcoupes.

*Complete Letters of Lady Mary Wortley Montagu*
(written in 1718, 1965 ed.)

## 'THE BALKAN DIET': FOOD FOR LONGEVITY

Our rapid survey of the Balkans and its cookery may have established lines and boundaries, character and national traits, but if any specific group were to be singled out then it would have to be the centenarians of Smolyan—those remarkably long-lived Bulgarians from high mountain valleys who appear to defy the ageing process, and whose secret seems to lie in their frugal diet—a diet encapsulating the early peasant cookery traditions of the Balkan lands before the onset of industrialization and international exchange and trade.

Bulgaria is, or was until recently, one of the few countries in the world with a very large proportion of centenarians, though the latest figures show a national decline. The percentage remains very high—probably the highest in Europe—in the district of Smolyan, in the central Rhodope mountains, with an average altitude of 1,230 metres. Here, about 4 people per 1,000 population are over 99 years old. In the United States, in 1990, the figure was less than 1.5 per 100,000.

Dr Argir Hadzhihristev of Smolyan District Hospital has kept track of the health of nearly 500 local people who were over the age of 90 at the start of his research. His findings were disclosed at the National Congress of Gerontology held in the town of Smolyan in 1986, and provide an insight into their way of life and their eating patterns.

Most centenarians are mountain-dwellers; more live in villages than towns. There are more female centenarians than male. The majority of both sexes have been employed in agriculture, with an average working day of 12 hours, but without undue stress or mental tensions. All have been married and have had many children, themselves coming from large families. All centenarians have enjoyed a good state of health (one 90-year-old woman, on meeting Dr Hadzhihristev, had asked to be photographed with him as she had never before seen a doctor), all are physically active and possess a great zest for life and a much younger biological age.

Their food is simple—a bulky, frugal diet based primarily on cereals, milk and dairy products, fruits and a few vegetables. First and foremost, coarse bread made from wholegrain wheat is consumed in vast quantities until the age of 80, though reducing after that. Wheat is also converted into *boulgour*, or cooked as *kasha*—a thin porridge, which at its simplest contains no more than wheaten flour (or a combination of maize meal and wheat, rye or barley flour) plus salt and water, but is often fortified with milk, cheese, butter, *tahan* or sauerkraut, and eaten with bread as a main-course dish. *Ovesena kasha*, oatmeal porridge, is cooked for children, 'so they can grow faster and stronger'.

A typical Smolyan speciality is *klin* (a pan-Slavonic word meaning 'wedge', in reference to the way the pastry is cut for serving) which, in English terms, might be 'pie'. It is prepared with a substantial filling of spinach, mashed potato or rice and nettles, with pumpkin, or with cooked boulgour or semolina, plus eggs, whey cheese and sometimes yoghurt. (When made with raw grated potato the dish is known as *patatnik*.) The filling is sandwiched between two buttered sheets of dough arranged in a large, round pan of tinned copper. *Klin* and *patatnik* are traditionally baked in the hearth, directly on the embers and covered with an inverted copper pan of the same size, so that the pastry can be turned over when the underside is cooked.

Another staple cereal is maize. Most often it is ground into meal for making *kachamak*—a sort of thick porridge, or for wheaten bread bulked out with fine maize meal or potato.

An interesting maize product made in the home is *misirena trahana*—dried maize kernels are first lightly roasted, ground in special handmills into grits, then sifted through a coarse grade of mesh to remove the larger particles of grain, and then bolted to separate the grits from any powdered bran or endosperm.

Yoghurt, dried beans and potatoes are served at practically every meal. *Gyozhe* (from the Turkish *göce*) for example, is a bean stew cooked with onion, paprika, and maize grits.

This recurrent combination of pulses, grains and potato in the diet is now generally regarded as an adequate source of protein, and may be the secret weapon of the centenarian. None of these people are vegans or vegetarians; however meat is consumed in modest proportions, often just once a week.

Sheep's milk provides much of the animal protein; in addition, the small Rhodope Shorthorn cattle, well adapted to mountainous terrain and sparse grazing, provide milk as well as beef. *Roupsko sirene* (from *Roupets*, an inhabitant of the central Rhodope) is a local cheese made from skimmed goat's milk. In the past this has been the staple of Rhodope woodcutters. White sheep's cheese, *sirene*, similar to the Greek feta, and sheep's milk yoghurt appear daily at table, except at Lent and other fast days when meat, eggs, milk and animal fats are prohibited by the Bulgarian Orthodox Church. Fasting, which took up intermittently nearly half the days of the year, has been observed by the Smolyan centenarians throughout their lives.

It was the Bulgarians' regular consumption of yoghurt which led Professor Metchnikoff, head of the Pasteur Institute in Paris, to connect yoghurt intake with longevity. However, he never maintained that yoghurt was the elixir of life, nor the panacea against senescence, but simply one of many factors which helped delay ageing. Sheep's milk yoghurt, mostly made at home, is consumed for breakfast or lunch, or sometimes as the only dish for supper teamed with bread and raw garlic.

An original yoghurt product described by Professors Pejchev and Penev is the Rhodope *brano loudouvano mlyako*, 'gathered mad milk' prepared in late August when the milk is exceptionally rich and thick. Yoghurt made from this milk is drained to the consistency of semi-soft cheese, packed in wooden firkins and sealed with a layer of melted sheep's butter. It is called 'mad' because the yoghurt undergoes a phase of violent fermentation, and 'gathered', because the firkin is filled up with yoghurt prepared from several milk yields. This is the only Bulgarian yoghurt product which contains, in addition to the normal yoghurt bacteria, also four natural lactic yeasts: *Saccharomyces lactis, S cartilaginosis, S casei* and *Torula sphaerica*.

Grapes do not grow readily in Smolyan, but hazelnuts, and wild fruits—pears, gages, blackberries and mulberries—are abundant and well liked. These and other fruits such as sloes, crab apples, rose hips, cornelian cherries and mountain cranberries (*Vaccinium vitis-idaea*) are turned into a pleasant, slightly acid, low alcohol drink by steeping in water—together with some mustard seed, but no sugar—in a large wooden barrel for about a month before consumption. (Mustard seed is included because it slows down fermentation and inhibits bacteria.)

Mountain cranberries also provide the basis for the weak local brandy called *langer* or *lyangyur*. While most centenarians are abstainers, the small percentage who drink do so moderately. None of the women in the survey have been smokers, and only 20 per cent of the men were moderate cigarette smokers.

Sugar, spices, tea and coffee are almost non-existent. Honey or concentrated fruit juice, *petmez*, are the main sweeteners figuring in the exceedingly few local desserts. *Mangafish*, a simple preparation of pumpkin pieces stewed with dried fruits and honey is an example.

Generally, the Smolyan centenarians enjoy a varied diet eaten in small quantities; and what they eat dates from an age when there were no commercial convenience foods or surrogates. The diet is surprisingly similar to that of other strongholds of longevity: the Caucasus, Vilcabamba in Ecuador and Hunza in Kashmir, and essentially mirrored by the wholefood scene in the West. It seems significant that none of the people who have lived to extreme ages have succumbed to the radical changes in diet brought about by the food revolution, which started in the 1920s in the Balkans as a result of the industrialization of wheat milling and the refining of oil, fat and sugar.

*A Croatian peasant kitchen from the beginning of the nineteenth century.*

# CHAPTER III

# Pots and Pans

The way something is cooked, or the utensil used, will often give a dish its name, or lend its own particular value to taste and texture. For instance, dishes such as *lonac*, *güveç*, *tava* and *tavche* have acquired the name of the baking crock or copper pan in which they are cooked and served. This chapter illustrates the pots, pans, and methods of heating, frying, baking and roasting through the Balkans.

From the dawn of time, the essential has been an open fire, indoors or out. Shepherds, herdsmen and woodcutters still make primitive outdoor hearths between two large stones to carry the pots, while Hungarian shepherds in Transylvania construct a rather more elaborate square hearth with slabs on three sides for shelter from winds, leaving the front open for stoking. A more permanent fireplace can be achieved by digging a round hearth in the ground, with vertical sides, a flue to admit a controlled flow of air, and a rectangular pit in front for raking out the fire.

When roasting is the thing, hunters and fishermen often cook their catch spitted on straight, non-bitter tasting green sticks, or bake them wrapped in vine or sorrel leaves, cased in clay and buried in hot coals. Ukrainian fishermen living on the Black Sea coast of Romania, simmer a fish soup called *uha* (from Slavonic *yuha*, soup or stock) in a cauldron hung on a wooden tripod over an outdoor fire; and the Hungarian herdsmen and shepherds of Transylvania stew their *qulyás* in the same way, in the traditional round-bottomed copper cauldron or *bogrács*.

Not so long ago, countrymen who brought their grain to the local watermill cooked a soup from fish caught in the millpond, while waiting—often for several days—to get their wheat ground. A vivid description in Tsani Ginchev's novel *Gancho Koserkata* (the name of the chief character) tells how a pot-hook was improvised from a bough driven into the ground at the side of a fire of dry willow and a tinned copper cauldron called *kotel* was half-filled with water and suspended over the flames. Chopped onion, mint and parsley, salt, black pepper and red winestone (the tartaric deposits from the sides of winecasks, called *trigya*) were dropped into the boiling water, followed by the cleaned and cut up fish consisting of twenty large barbels, four breams and the heads of three wels or sheatfish. (The wels themselves were to be baked in the miller's oven dug into the river bank.) The soup was judged ready when the eyes of the wels turned white. 'This is what I have learnt from my father,' remarks the hero. 'Cook fish until its eyes whiten—or it will turn your own eyes white.'

When it comes to cooking meat, roasting over a wood fire is still the most popular. Many Greeks spit-roast whole lambs for Easter over a long pit lined with olive-wood embers; and in various highland regions of Serbia and Macedonia lamb, kid or pig is cooked speared on an iron rod. In Bosnia-Hercegovina, a lamb is sometimes roasted between two fires set about 2 metres apart. As the cooking progresses, the embers are gradually drawn nearer until right under the meat.

A useful contrivance for spit-roasting was recorded by the Turkish traveller Evliya Çelebi, who visited Bosnia in the 1760s. This was the hydro-spit (or *hidoražanj* in modern Serbo-Croat), then known as *čekrk*—a winding wheel which rotated the spit by a pulley system utilizing water power.

In this land of hot, dry summers, cooking over a fixed fireplace in the 'summer kitchen' next to the house, or on a portable brazier, is nigh-on universal. Small charcoal stoves have been used in Greece and Crete for nearly five thousand years; the modern-day Greek earthenware *foufoú*, and the tin rectangular *magkáli* (from the Turkish *mangal*), are reminiscent of the braziers used in ancient Minoan palaces.

Most Balkan movable stoves are nothing more than four-legged tin boxes or pedestalled clay bowls that contain the charcoal, though some more refined models may be made of copper, brass or cast-iron. They could have grates or vents near the bottom to permit air flow beneath the coals, and even a narrow shelf along one side of the box or around the charcoal bowl (as in the Bosnian *mangala*) on which cups and jars can be placed when coffee or mulled brandy is being prepared to welcome relatives and friends.

The small black *mangal*, or brazier, which was used outdoors in the summer kitchen of my father's house, was made of tinplate and lined with firebrick for heat retention, and there was a drawer underneath the grate to remove the ash. Ordinarily, domestic braziers have no racks to place the food on during cooking. Chestnuts, aubergines and long sweet peppers are roasted directly over the glowing embers, and skewers of meat, or fish enclosed in double-sided wire racks, are balanced across the top rim.

Pavement grill-stands and restaurant charcoal grills are to be found almost everywhere. The appliance for roasting the famous Istanbul speciality *döner kebab*—a vertical spit packed with the meat of a whole lamb or ewe—is just a stack of four or five charcoal braziers in front of the spit. *Doner-čevab* was also a favourite restaurant food in Bosnia until the end of the last century. According to Gerim Hilmo, manager of the restaurant 'Daire' ('Tambourine') in Sarajevo, the Bosnian version was made from veal, young beef, lamb, mutton and boned chicken legs. Its popularity was evident in the presence of three doner spits in a restaurant inventory from Sarajevo dated 1770.

Indoor fireplaces trace their history to the Stone Age when man kept a fire for warming his cave and probably for some simple cooking too. In Balkan Neolithic settlements, a fire for heating, cooking and parching grain was built directly on the earthen floor, in the centre of rectangular, single-room gabled cottages made of wattle, clay and stone. Central fireplaces were also the rule in the partially sunken houses of the South Slavs, who baked their bread in earthenware dishes over rectangular stone hearths, or in cupola-shaped clay ovens built in their courtyards. In later times when the dwellings became more sturdy, the fireplace was moved into a corner, or contained within a semi-cylindrical recess let into the wall. More often than not, the hearth was sunk into the floor, occasionally to a depth of 50 cm, the base levelled with beaten clay and bordered with stone slabs. This deep hearth was necessary to house a thick layer of glowing coals and ash, into which earthenware pots were half buried to cook a meat stew, to bake beans, or simmer a dried-fruit compote. The depth of the fireplace also allowed a sufficient amount of embers to be banked up with ashes and kept alive until the next day.

In bigger houses, there could be several fireplaces, as well as one next to the oven in the summer bakehouse. Years after the advent of electricity, home cookery still meant hearth cookery, because in most regions wood was abundant.

If a hearth was built level with the floor, an earthenware stew-pot was surrounded with live embers raked up around its sides. On the same hearth—which could be as much as three metres wide—a second fire was started to replenish the embers when the heat around the pot diminished. In later years, a well-tinned copper cauldron (*kotel*) was suspended from a pot-hook or chain over the fire, or set on a trivet to produce soups, stews or gruel.

Bread is still baked directly in the hot ashes, but the more common method is to enclose the dough in a stout circular earthenware pan (*ponicë*, Albanian; *podnitsa*, Bulgarian; *hljebna crepulja*, Bosnian), ready heated on a trivet, lowered on to the hot ash and covered with a handled convex lid made of tempered clay or sheet iron. Slow-burning fuel (wood embers mixed with ashes) is piled round and over the lid and the dough is left to cook undisturbed for about an hour. By this means the bread is baked with top and bottom heat. In Balkan countries, this principle has been continued in modern domestic electric ovens which have heating elements in the top and under the floor that can be operated independently. The majority of western ovens, by contrast, have elements positioned at the sides.

The portable convex lid-oven, a relic of a far simpler age, is variously known as *vërshnik* in Albanian, from the Slavonic, *vrushnik* in Bulgarian, *vrshnik* in

Macedonian, *vršnik* in Serbo-Croat and *test* in Romanian. It is used if only one loaf is needed or a single dish has to be baked and saves the need to fire the whole oven. Meat, fish, poultry and many kinds of leaf pastry are all baked in this way. The Romans borrowed the Balkan lid-oven, improved it, and diffused it as far west as the British Isles where it became a popular contrivance for baking meat and bread in lowland Britain. It was known there as *clibanus*.

The similarity between present-day clay igloo-shaped ovens and those built some seven or eight thousand years ago is remarkable. In 1955 I watched the construction of such an oven in a vineyard near the town of Vratsa in north-western Bulgaria. First they built a hollow brick base, attached to an outside wall of the summer cottage, open at the front for storing wood. Next, a large round-bottomed wicker-basket, tightly packed with straw, was inverted over it. Tempered clay— mixed with tow, shoddy, chaff and goat's hair to help the clay withstand the strain of firing without cracking—was worked with bare feet and then spread evenly over the basket to a thickness of about 10 cm, leaving a rectangular space for the oven mouth, and a small unplastered outlet on top for the smoke. Finally, a few fire bricks were used to make a decorative border around the mouth—to the selfsame design as on the neolithic oven. A few days later, when the clay was dried hard by the sun, the straw inside was set alight and allowed to burn down together with the basket, and the ashes raked out. This oven baked beautifully, and was still in operation when I re-visited the vineyard in 1985.


You can have a million fires, braziers and ovens, but no soup, stew or braise will come without the use of pots and pans. The list which follows gives a brief account of some of the traditional cooking utensils and tableware still in common use.

> *Basan* (Bulgarian, from the late Latin *bacca*, tub): a round-bottomed untinned copper pan for beating egg whites and fondant. In the beating process a chemical reaction takes place which gives the egg whites added stiffness and reduces the risk of graining.

> *Filzhan* (Albanian), *findžan* (Bosnian), *fildzhan* (Bulgarian), *flytzáni* (Greek), *fildžan* (Macedonian), from the Turkish *kahve fincanı* or *filcan*, in turn from the Arabic: a small cup for serving Turkish coffee, in gilded porcelain or decorated earthenware. It has no handle and usually no saucer, but nowadays is often available with a tiny matching saucer instead of the traditional, brass or silver, cup-shaped holder called *zarf* (Turkish, from the Arabic).

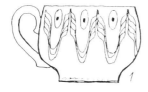

*1. Coffee cup (fildzhan) from Troyan in Bulgaria with characteristic 'feathered' decoration, like feathered icing on a cake.*
*2. Bosnian coffee cup (findžan). The star and moon decoration is sometimes found inside, on the bottom of the cup.*
*3. A Balkan earthenware casserole.*

*Glineni lonac* (Bosnian, Serbo-Croat): a heat-resistant, round-bellied stew-pot made of soft, low-fired terracotta, with one or two side-handles and a tight-fitting lid with a knob on top. Its capacity can vary between 2 and 10 litres. Originally designed for slow braising in embers, the Bosnians of today cook their renowned *Bosanski lonac* by placing the pot in a very slow oven, then serve it either in *lončiće*—smaller, individual-sized replicas of the big stew-pot—or in deep, tinned copper plates with lids (see *sahan*).

*Gyuvech* (Bulgarian), *giouvétsi* (Greek), *djuvec* (Serbo-Croat, from the Turkish *güveç* or *güvec*), meaning earthenware casserole. It is also called *tavë e argjiltë* (Albanian), *zemljana tava* or *crepulja* (Bosnian), *zemjena tava* (Macedonian), meaning in all three languages earthenware baking pan. This is a fairly shallow casserole with a large surface area allowing maximum evaporation. It comes round or oval, lidless and sometimes earless, most often with vertical sides, though in the round version the sides could slope to a small flat base. The outside is normally unglazed because it was originally designed for cooking directly over embers. When glazed on both sides, the casserole is meant for oven cooking only. The common family size is about 30 cm long and 9 cm deep, but dimensions can vary. This is also the term for many things baked and served in the dish. In the Dobroudzha district of Bulgaria, *gyuvech* made with the flesh of game birds is cooked in a narrow, boat-shaped baking dish much like a small Viking ship. The resemblance is heightened by two upright handles in the form of bird's heads facing each other from each end.

*Gyuveche*, the diminutive form of *gyuvech*, is an individual-sized earthenware bowl similar to British stoneware soup bowls, but unglazed on the outside, so it can be used over charcoal or under the grill as well as in the oven. The bowl measures about 8 cm at the base, and 14 cm at the top, and occasionally has a domed lid topped with a knob.

*Havan* (Bosnian, Bulgarian), *avan* (Macedonian, Serbo-Croat) from the Turkish *havan* (originally from Persian) is a mortar for pounding. It is called *goudí* in Greek and *piuliță* in Romanian. There are three traditional sorts—each with pestles made of the same material. The first is a handsome, deep, heavy brass vessel with two knobs to lift it, engraved on the outside, used for pounding sugar-candy, lump sugar, rusks and spices. A heavy porcelain bowl is preferred for pounding minced meat, walnuts, almonds and such like. And finally there are mortars made out of hardwoods, usually apple, cherry, pear or cornel. This group includes small bowl-shaped mortars reserved exclusively for garlic, larger ones for processing wheat grains for bulgur and boiled wheat, and a further type for beating tarama.

*1. Small wooden mortar for pounding garlic.*
*2. Heavy brass mortar, handed down in my family from generation to generation.*

*Ibrik kafeje* (Albanian), *kahveni (kafeni) ibrik* (Bosnian, Serbo-Croat), *ibrik pentru cafea* (Romanian), from the Turkish *kahve ibriği*, which originates from the Persian for coffee pot, is a tall, slender, narrow-waisted vessel reminiscent of an hour-glass, with a long teapot-shaped spout and curved handle, the flat or domed lid having a towering ornamental grip. Sometimes pots are in the shape of a tankard, in which case they have a short beak-spout, straight handle and a domed lid with an elongated knob. Customarily made of brass or tinned copper, the coffee pots of the Bosnian Muslim aristocracy were plated with—or made of—gold or silver, and topped with a precious stone.

*Bosnian brass coffee pot with incised ornament, similar to Turkish, Persian and Arab pots.*

*Kotel* (Bulgarian, Macedonian, Slovenian), *kotao* (Serbo-Croat), *căldare* (Romanian): a tinned copper cauldron, round-bellied, lidless, with a hoop handle. As well as being useful for boiling water or cooking food, two cauldrons can be slung from a yoke across the shoulders for carrying water from the village fountain. This Balkan vessel is of particular interest because it seems to be the original of all cauldrons—taken up by the ancient Greeks, then copied by barbarian cultures as distant as the Celtic Britons. In Greek mythology, Medea's cauldron was the one in which the sorceress, daughter of the king of Colchis, 'boiled the old into youth again' (Ovid, *Metamorphoses* vii, 251–349). Cauldrons of rejuvenation are common both in Greek and Celtic mythology. There is a lovely Greek amphora in the British Museum depicting Medea and her rejuvenating cauldron with the ram inside.

As the etymology indicates, the Slavonic cauldron (*kotel* or *kotao*) is cognate with the Anglo-Saxon *cetel*—an iron cauldron, which has given rise to the modern word kettle—both derived from the Latin word *catillus*, meaning a small deep bowl. The Romanian *căldare* and the English cauldron, on the other hand, are parallels of a rather later date, both terms stemming from the late Latin *caldaria* or stew-pan.

*Kuzi-tendžera* (Bosnian), literally, lamb-pan: a tall, gradated Bosnian utensil made of tinned copper, specially designed for braising a whole lamb which was placed vertically inside it. Twice as wide at the base than the rim, the pan has side-handles and a relatively shallow, tight-fitting domed lid.

*Okllai* or *petës* (Albanian), *tochilka* (Bulgarian), *sukalo* (Macedonian), *sul* or *tăvălug* (Romanian), *oklagija* (Serbo-Croat and Slovenian), *oklava* (Turkish): a long, thin rolling pin, indispensable for making leaf pastry. It is normally made of hardwood, 70–90 cm long, 1–2.5 cm diameter. The thinner pins are used to make thinner pastry sheets. Wooden dowels, cut to the desired length, make adequate substitutes.

*Sach* (Bulgarian), from *sac* or *saç* (Turkish): griddle—a round sheet-iron plate with a slightly domed surface, prepared for cooking by heating on a trivet over wood or charcoal. The *sach* was brought to the Balkans by the Ottoman Turks. Like the earlier Bulgar-Turks, the nomadic Ottomans had no ovens for making bread; instead, they baked thin unleavened sheets of dough on portable griddles. From the beginning of this century, the popularity of the *sach* seems to have waned with the diminished influence of Turkish cookery, though earthenware griddles called *tikli* are still sold in Sliven and a few other towns in Bulgaria. In Turkey itself, however, baking flat bread and sheets of dough on a griddle is—today no less than in the past—a common technique.

Sahan, *the Bosnian lidded plate made of tinned copper, decorated on the outside with sgraffito.*

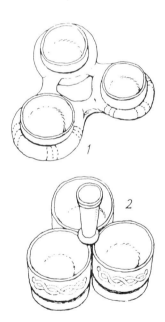

*Seven thousand years separate the prehistoric salt cellar (1) from the one used today (2), yet they share a mutual identity.*

*Sahan* (Bosnian, Bulgarian, Macedonian, Serbo-Croat, Turkish, from the Arabic): a deep, ornate plate or serving dish of tinned copper, with a flat, plain or scallop-edged rim, complete with a gradated domed lid topped by a knob or star-shaped ornament. Both plate and lid are often embellished on the outside with sgraffito—a pattern scratched through the tin to reveal the copper body.

*Solnitsa* (Bulgarian): salt cellar. I could not resist mentioning the traditional Bulgarian wooden salt cellar because of its similarity with a prehistoric one found in 1974 during Dr Henrietta Todorova's excavations near the village of Ovcharovo in Turgovishtko. This has been dated to about 5,000 BC. It comprises three tiny bowls of hand-moulded clay, joined like a clover leaf round a small central opening. The set had been glazed black, ornamented by short incised lines. Today's country salt cellar has the same trefoil arrangement, but the wooden bowls are often decorated with poker-work and attached to a central tooth-pick holder. It is brought to the table filled with salt, paprika salt, and spiced salt (*sharena sol*)—which is salt pounded together with dried winter savory, spearmint, cumin, fenugreek, chilli powder and/or black pepper.

*Tavë* or *tepsi* (Albanian), *tava* or *tepsija* (Bosnian, Macedonian, Serbo-Croat), *tava* or *tepsiya* (Bulgarian), *tavá(s)* or *tapsí* (Greek), *tavă* or *tipsie* (Romanian), from Turkish *tava* and *tepsi*: a circular metal pan of Turkish origin—and the shallowest Balkan ovenware—for baking bread, pastries, biscuits, vegetables, and roasting meat or poultry. In Albania, Bosnia and Macedonia, *tava* can also be made of china or earthenware. The dual terms are interchangeable except in Turkish where *tava* means frying pan. Traditionally made of tinned copper (nowadays of aluminium) and always with vertical sides, measurements vary from 25 to 60 cm diameter and 2.5 to 10 cm depth, but for baking *baklava* and *kadaif* the pans can be up to 1 metre across and, in Bosnia and Istanbul, have an ornate scalloped rim. Unlike the rim of the English pie tin, this is purely decorative.

*Tavche* (Macedonian), the diminutive form of *tava* and short for *zemjena tava* meaning an earthenware baking dish. It comes in many sizes—from small round pots for individual baking and serving, to large, fairly shallow, circular or oval dishes about 30 cm long and 3 to 5 cm deep. All have slightly sloping sides and two ears on the side, but no lids. Like the Turkish *güveç*, most of them are glazed on the inside only and can be used over charcoal or on top of the stove (with a mat underneath as a precaution), as well as in the oven. Macedonian baked beans, *Gravche Tavche*, are baked in this vessel.

*Tenxhere bakëre* (Albanian), *bakurena tendzhera* (Bulgarian), *hálkinos téntzeris* (Greek), *bakrena tendžera* (Serbo-Croat), *bakır tencere* (Turkish): copper pan. A large, fairly deep, tinned vessel of Turkish origin, usually with sloping sides and without handles, for stewing and braising on top of the stove, and also for cooking pilaf. The lid—always domed and inset—can rise as high as the pan is deep, except in the old Turkish *tencere* for cooking *tencere kebabı* (lamb kebab) where the pan has a flat inset lid on which embers are piled. These copper pans are now mostly replaced by straight-sided stew pans with handles and flat lids. The best are made of enamelled cast iron, stainless steel, flame-proof glass or porcelain.

*Vodenitsa za kafe* (Bulgarian, Macedonian), *mýlos kafé* (Greek), *mlinac za kavu* (Serbo-Croat), *râşniţă de cafea* (Romanian): coffee mill. A tall, cylindrical, brass hand-mill with a folding handle, for pulverising coffee beans: in this respect, more efficient than the modern electric coffee-grinders which can rarely achieve the fine powdery consistency necessary for making a good cup of Turkish coffee.

*Xhezve* (Albanian), *dzhezve* (Bulgarian), *džezve* (Macedonian), and *džezva* (Serbo-Croat) come from the Turkish *cezve*. *Mpríki* (Greek) derives from the Turkish *kahve ibriği* or *ibrik*. This is a pot for making Turkish coffee, with a long handle and a pouring lip. Its shape—round and wide at the bottom narrowing to the neck, and then opening out again to the rim—helps the formation of froth prized by connoisseurs. The vessels come in various sizes—from single cup ones to huge containers for making 20 cups. Like the coffee pots of the former Muslim nobility, they were once plated with, or made of gold or silver. Nowadays, however, besides the traditional brass or tinned copper ones, they are generally made of aluminium, stainless steel or brightly coloured enamelled cast iron—the stainless steel and the enamelled iron being best because they do not impart a metal aftertaste.

*Collapsible hand mill of Turkish origin. It is usually held in the lap for grinding. The ground coffee is collected in the bottom half.*

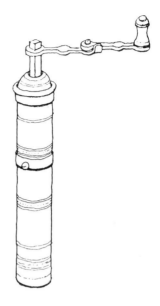

Pots for making Turkish coffee, drawn from those I have collected during travels in the Balkans.
1. Albanian three-cup pot, xhezve. Enamelled cast iron. (Serbian coffee pots are similar.)
2. Bulgarian dzhezve without a spout. It serves five or six. Brightly coloured and decorated enamelled cast iron.
3. A two-cup stainless steel dzhezve from Bulgaria.
4. A Macedonian one-cup džezve of tin-plated copper. Ohrid, the town where it was made, is engraved on the handle in Cyrillic script.

# CHAPTER IV

# Unfamiliar Ingredients

Nearly all the ingredients I suggest in my recipes are widely available in supermarkets, or healthfood and ethnic stores in Britain. For the few that may be difficult to obtain I have given appropriate substitutes.

The next few pages describe the most characteristic ingredients and specialities of Balkan cookery.

*Aguridhë* (Albanian), *yagorida* (Bulgarian), *aguridă* (Romanian), from the Greek *agourítha* (*ágouros*, unripe); *koruk* or *kuruk* (Turkish): sour grape. There are three types of sour grape growing in the Balkans of which the wild vine (*Vitis vinifera* ssp *sylvestris*) is particularly interesting because it is a relict of the indigenous European grape vine that did not survive the Ice Age in central and northern parts of the continent. Similar to the Italian agresto grape (from the Latin *agrestis*, wild, uncultivated), and the Turkish *yabanasması* (wild vine), this survivor still grows in southern areas. Up to the end of the nineteenth century it was gathered, when ripe, by the countryfolk in Bulgaria with prescribed ceremony and celebrations. The juice of the tiny, black berries was used to make vinegar, and to give a crimson glow and bouquet to home-made wine.

The second type of sour grape is the feral form of *Vitis vinifera* ssp *vinifera*, the cultivated vine, which has escaped from cultivation and gone wild.

The third most common kind, is simply unripe grapes from the cultivated varieties, picked in early summer (or at the end of a bad season) when still green.

Sour grapes, or their juice—known in English-speaking countries as verjuice—are used in Balkan cookery instead of vinegar or lemon.

*Babek* (Bulgarian, Macedonian, from *bàba*, meaning grandmother or old woman) or *starets* (Bulgarian, Macedonian, meaning old man), *ded* (Slovenian, meaning grandfather), is so named because the surface of the finished product is wrinkled like the face of an old person. It is a meat conserve prepared during the winter slaughtering of pigs. It is made of chopped pork mixed with finely diced back fat, spices and seasoning, cured in the pig's stomach bag, pressed, and then air dried. It is served sliced like salami, either as it is, or fried with scrambled eggs.

## Unfamiliar Ingredients

*Bollgur* (Albanian), *bungur* (Bosnian), *boulgour* (Bulgarian), *pligoúri* (Greek), *bulgur* (Macedonian, Romanian), derives from the Turkish *bulgur*, coming in turn from the Persian; in Slovenian it is *bela zdroba*. A high quality cereal containing the embryo germ of the wheat, it is made up of irregular fragments of hard-wheat grains from which the uppermost layers of bran have been removed. The manufacture of bulgur involves initial steaming to split the outer layers of the bran, making them easier to remove. This process also diffuses part of the bran nutrients into the endosperm or white, starchy bulk of the grain.

Bulgur wheat is available outside the Balkans from wholefood shops and some supermarkets in several grain sizes. The name on the packets is often misspelt as 'bulgar'. The best quality coarse bulgur imported into Britain comes from France.

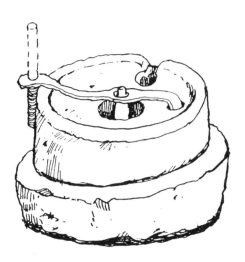

*Rotary stone hand-mill or quern dating from approximately the fourth century AD, found near Turnovo in Bulgaria. Such querns are still in use in country districts for grinding wheat into* bulgur.

*Bozë* (Albanian), *boza* (Bulgarian, Bosnian, Macedonian, Serbian), from the Turkish *boza*, originally from the Persian, is called *bragă* in Romanian. It is a popular Balkan drink of great antiquity, normally prepared from boiled, yeast-fermented millet, rice, bulgur wheat, rye, malted meal or, in Albania, from maize. At present it is the only product made from millet on a commercial scale in Europe.

Similar drinks have been fermented for centuries in Central Asia and the Caucasus as well as in Egypt and aboriginal America. In the Balkans it was first prepared by the Paeoni, an ancient Illyrian tribe which occupied the territory west of the river Strouma in western Bulgaria. They boiled millet and let it ferment naturally, in much the same way as the Incas brewed their potent maize beer *chicha*. Unfortunately, the ancient Illyrian name of this drink has been lost and superseded by the Turkish.

On average, millet *boza* contains between 80 and 90 per cent water and the rest is largely starch, with some vegetable protein in the form of amino acids, fat, sugar, traces of minerals and micro-elements, and a high concentration of vitamins (primarily of the B group). It is practically non-alcoholic.

In Albania, Bulgaria and Macedonia, this thickish, slightly effervescent drink is widely sold in pastry shops, kiosks and by street vendors. It is usually served ice-cold in summer or at room temperature in winter—on its own, or as accompaniment to halva and baklava.

Buckwheat is a quick-growing herbaceous crop from Central Asia, suitable for cool climates and the poorest soil, whence its vernacular name 'Poor man's bread'. The flour, grey in colour and deficient in gluten, can be milled from whole grain, in which case it is flecked with black specks of husks, or from husked grain. Porridge made from buckwheat flour has an unusual sweetish aroma, not to everyone's liking, but this flavour is less pronounced when the dish is cooled.

Carob is the fruit of the evergreen carob tree (*Ceratonia siliqua*), also known as the locust bean or St John's bread. It is native to the eastern Mediterranean and widely grown in the southern Balkans. The fruit is a capsule of intensely sweet, high-pectin pulp containing 30 to 50 per cent natural sugars, a row of up to 12 hard seeds or beans, and a sweet, edible dark brown pod enclosing the whole. Its Turkish name, *keçiboynuzu*, 'goat's horn', refers to the shape of the pods. These are eaten raw when fully ripe—fresh or dried—in the popular belief that they promote virility; or simply because they make a pleasant *pasatempo* snack especially beloved by children. Roasted carob beans are occasionally used as a caffeine-free alternative to coffee, while the roasted pulverized pulp is sometimes substituted for cocoa powder.

Carob beans are exceptionally uniform in weight and size. The weight of one such bean (0.18 g) is said to have been the original of the carat unit formerly used by goldsmiths, jewellers and apothecaries.

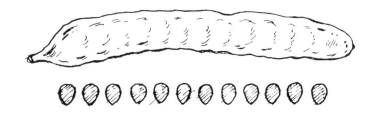

*The carob pod*

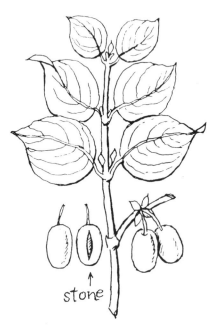

*The Cornelian cherry. Each fruit is about 2 cm long and 12 mm wide. The stone is spindle-shaped. The fruits ripen irregularly from August to November. Overripe cherries lose some of their tartness and can be eaten raw.*

Cornelian cherry (*Cornus mas*) is a large shrub or small tree, indigenous to central and south-eastern Europe, and long cultivated in Britain, originally as an orchard tree. In the Balkans it grows in woodlands to an altitude of 1300 m and is occasionally grown in private gardens. The blood-red stone fruits, approximately the shape and size of a small olive, were at one time pickled in brine as a substitute for olives. Now they are better valued for jams, jellies and fruit butters because of their high pectin level—higher than that of cooking apples and crab apples—and the pulp is exported in considerable quantities. Cornelian cherries also make excellent preserves (either dried or in syrup), and a potent eau-de-vie with a slightly scented taste is distilled from the over-ripe fruit. Dried, they give a pleasant additional flavour to winter dried-fruit compotes such as *oshav*.

*Féta* (Greek) is the most popular, national Greek white cheese, with an ancestry that stretches at least as far back as Homer. Comparable types of cheese throughout the Balkans, variously named according to language, may be even older in origin. Commercially produced feta is generally made from pasteurized, pre-ripened sheep's milk, the milk of cows or goats, or a mixture of any of the three. It is a piquant, slightly sour, semi-soft cheese which ripens naturally in its own whey mixed with brine and does not develop a rind. The salt and fat content of sheep's feta is rather high; on average it contains 4 per cent salt, and between 45 and 60 per cent milk fat. Because of its demand, feta, and its Bulgarian counterpart *sirene*, is exported worldwide, including Britain, and can be bought at most Greek shops and delicatessens.

Feta gives pastries and sauces a flavour unmatched by any other cheese. Out of its brine, it can be kept up to three weeks in a refrigerator—in a plastic box or in cling film—but it does not freeze well. For longer storage it should be put into a covered glass or china container and immersed in brine strong enough to float a raw egg (approximately 200 g of cooking salt to each litre of water, boiled for 5 minutes). Stored like that in a cool cellar or refrigerator, it will keep six months or more. Before use, soak in fresh water for about 2 hours to remove the saltiness.

*Gjevrek* is a ring-shaped roll which, like the bagel of Jewish cookery, is first briefly poached, then baked. It is sold from the basket or shoulder-strapped tray of street vendors and eaten in the street.

Bulgarian *gevrek* is a baker's speciality, impossible to reproduce at home without a purpose-built oven. The dough is yeast-leavened, then shaped into thin rings about 15 cm in diameter, giving large surface-to-volume ratio for more crust than crumb. The crispness and appearance of the crust is achieved by underproving the dough (which causes high crust colour and chewy texture), by poaching the dough rings briefly in a special solution of 5 tablespoons of liquid glucose to 5 litres of water (a secret disclosed to me by a friendly baker in Sofia), then starting the baking in the oven with a burst of steam, which coagulates the carbohydrates on the surface of the dough to give it a glossy-brown crackly crust.

In Belgrade, Zagreb and Sarajevo, *djevrek* is the same shape, but made from a lightly enriched dough raised with baking powder. The dough, of course, is not poached before baking.

For green garlic, young garlic plants with thick, fleshy, succulent stems and underdeveloped cloves are grown from a selected form—with very large cloves— of common garlic. The name of this form, 'black garlic', is presumably due to the greyish-white papery skin of the bulb, streaked with a darker grey, which makes it easy to distinguish from the common white-skinned variety.

In April and May, green garlic is sold in bunches throughout the Balkans and in Romania. It is easy to grow from the outer ring of cloves which are planted individually in well manured soil at the end of autumn. Green garlic is used in exactly the same way as spring onion.

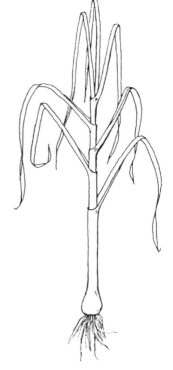

*Green garlic. The edible parts are the bulb and stem up to the first leaf. The rest is too coarse to eat.*

Halva is perhaps the most celebrated sweetmeat of the eastern Mediterranean. In the Balkans, two kinds are produced commercially.

The first is called *tahan-halvasi* (Albanian), *tahan halva* (Bosnian, Bulgarian), *tahíni halvás* (Greek—the best being manufactured in Salonica under the brand name 'Makedonikós halvás', Macedonian halva), *taan alva* (Macedonian), deriving from the Turkish *tahan* or *tahin helvası*. As the name indicates, it is based on sesame-seed paste (*tahan*), but in Bulgaria, it is also made with sunflower oil or peanut butter and often enriched with vitamins. *Tahíni halvás* may be plain, or peppered with nuts—such as pistachios—and even streaked with chocolate.

North of Greece, it is traditionally accompanied by *boza*, but can be served with tea, coffee, fresh fruit juice, or a glass of spring or mineral water.

*A label for 'Special Macedonian Halva', produced in Thessaloniki from sesame-seed paste.*

The second type is called *hallvë e bardhë* (Albanian)—meaning white halva, *byala halva s orehi* (Bulgarian), *bela halva sa orasima* (Serbo-Croat)—white halva with walnuts, *kos halva* (Bosnian), or *kos alva* (Macedonian), from the Turkish *koz helvası*—walnut halva. This resembles brittle nougat: so hard it has to be cut or broken with a heavy knife or hammer. It is made with an infusion from the root of the wild 'spinach' of the hedgerows, Good King Henry, which acts as a natural emulsifier. A few days before the onset of Lent (the severe forty-day fast imposed by the Orthodox Church), halva sellers would set up their stalls in many of the larger towns, as it was customary to eat halva on the eve of Lent.

There is a curious ritual still widely performed in Macedonia and Bulgaria to mark the beginning of the fast. A piece of white halva is suspended from the ceiling above the dining table and swung around for all the members of the family to try to catch with their mouths. This is called 'swinging the halva' and in earlier times was done with a peeled hard-boiled egg or a piece of white cheese.

*Hórta* or *ágria hórta* is the Greek for wild greenery for the table as opposed to cultivated kinds (*ímera hórta*). Indigenous leaves which grow throughout mainland Greece and Crete may include the Mediterranean wild carrot (*Daucus carota*), wild celery (*Apium graveolens*), wild lettuce (*Lactuca scariola*, syn *L serriola*) and wild asparagus (*Asparagus officinalis*). These have been gathered since Neolithic times and, like the olive and the vine, have pre-Hellenic names. *Hórta* are normally picked before the plants start to flower. They are boiled and served as soup or as a salad dressed while warm with olive oil and lemon juice; or the greens may go into savoury pastries and meat stews.

In Dalmatia, similar dishes are prepared with *divlje zelje*—wild herbs and greens which abound near the Adriatic coast.

*Kajmak* (Albanian, Bosnian, Macedonian, Serbo-Croat), *kaimáki* (Greek), *caimac* (Romanian), from the Turkish *kaymak*, is clotted cream skimmed from scalded cow's, sheep's, or water-buffalo's milk, slightly salted to prevent fermentation, then weighted and briefly ripened. In composition it resembles butter, though richer in milk protein. In Serbia it is often used instead of butter, especially when frying fish. Stored in a cool place, salted *kajmak* will keep for up to a year.

Fresh, unsalted clotted cream, similar to that traditionally associated with Devon and Cornwall in England, is termed *mladi kajmac* (young clotted cream) or *skorup* in Serbo-Croat and Bosnian, and *kajmac* in Bulgarian. According to a Bosnian document of 1531, travellers were welcomed in guest-houses with bread and *skorupača*—a dish of fresh clotted cream drizzled with honey.

Oil is not often used, but butter.
> John Cam Hobhouse (Lord Broughton), *Travels in Albania and Other Provinces of Turkey in 1809 & 1810*, new edition 1858.

*Kaša* is the Slovenian and Serbo-Croat term for dried husked grains, except those of wheat, that are either ground coarsely to produce grits (for example, barley grits, *ječmena kaša*), or left as whole seeds (millet grains, *prosena kaša*, or buckwheat groats, *ajdova kaša*).

The term is also applied to various porridges made by simmering *kaša* in milk, stock or water, then enriched with cream, butter or lard.

Maraschino liqueur is made from the small black sour marasca cherry (*Prunus cerasus* var *marasca*), a hybrid between the morello and Duke cherries, which grows on the Adriatic coast around the town of Zadar. The liqueur, dark red in colour and with a beautiful bouquet, enhances many Dalmatian cakes, creams, ice creams, fruit salads and preserves. Maraschino liqueur is produced in the 'Maraska' distillery in Zadar, as well as in Albania and Italy.

Mastic (from Greek *mastíha* or *mastíhi*) is a valuable fragrant resin obtained from the small evergreen mastic (lentisk) tree *Pistacia lentiscus*, which grows in the Greek archipelago, especially on the island of Chios. The resin is exuded from incisions made in the bark in the form of drops which harden into glassy, amber-coloured pellets. These have been used for centuries as the original chewing gum—to sweeten the breath and strengthen the teeth—usually supplemented by a few shavings of candle beeswax to give the resin a softer texture and to make it easier to chew. (Stearin or paraffin-wax candles will not do—they tend to stick to the teeth.)

Mastic is much used in Balkan cooking: pulverised, it imparts a delicate perfume to lamb dishes, creams and pastries, Turkish delight, ice cream and fondant.

The resin is also the essential flavouring agent of an exclusive type of spirit, the Greek *mastíha* and its Turkish counterpart *mastika* (alternatively known as *sakız rakısı*). Both can be sweet or dry, and are drunk neat, with water or over ice. However, the Albanian *mastikë*, the Bulgarian, Macedonian, and Serbo-Croat *mastika*, and the Romanian *mastică*, like the French pastis and the Greek ouzo, get their flavour chiefly from anethole, the active principle of the volatile oils of aniseed and fennel seed. (Aniseed oil contains 80-90 per cent anethole; fennel seed oil, up to 60 per cent.) With the addition of ice cubes or water, or when chilled, anethole turns miraculously white.

*Neblebi* (Albanian), *leblebiya* (Bulgarian), *stragália afráta* (Greek), *leblebija* (Bosnian, Macedonian, Serbo-Croat), *leblebi* (Turkish) are made from the skinned whole seeds of the chick-pea plant which are lightly toasted in a special oven fitted with a stirring device. They are a popular snack food sold by street vendors or at kiosks and supermarkets throughout the Balkans. Toasted chick-peas are pale yellow in colour and have a very pleasant nutty flavour; they can be unsalted, lightly salted or—Istanbul style—even sugared. The Greeks have a second type, *stragália sklirá*, which are frosty white, salty and very hard.

*Paprika* (from the Hungarian *peprika* or *paprika*, which in turn derives from the Bulgarian *piperka*, pepper pod) is bright lobster-red seasoning powder made from the dried pods and seeds of the sweet pepper plant. Greek and Serbian paprika may be mildly hot, and sometimes even fiery, due to the inclusion of varying proportions of ground chillies.

Chillies and chilli powder have been the most popular agents for imparting colour, flavour and heat to many Balkan dishes—especially to soups and casseroles—since the latter half of the sixteenth century when hot chillies were first introduced as an alternative to ginger and black pepper.

The use of sweet paprika, on the other hand, is a comparatively recent development, as the sweet pepper plant has only been in cultivation in the Balkans since the beginning of this century.

The seeds of all varieties of peppers contain solanine (also found in sprouting potatoes, green tomatoes and aubergines), as well as other alkaloids, and can be toxic if used in quantity. While home-made paprika or commercial powders of the first quality do not use too many of the seeds from the dried fruit, some Hungarian paprikas may consist of up to 40 per cent ground seeds to 60 per cent ground flesh.

Paprika and chilli powder will keep for at least a year if stored properly in well-filled, tightly-closed, dark coloured glass jars, in a dark dry place.

Parsley is called *majdanoz* (Albanian), *peršun* or *majdonos* (Bosnian), *magdanoz* (Bulgarian), *magdanos* (Macedonian), *pătrunjel* (Romanian), *peršun* (Serbo-Croat), *petersilj* (Slovenian), from either the Greek *petrosélinon* or Turkish *maydanoz* or *maydonoz*. Two varieties of cultivated parsley are used in Balkan cookery and pickling.

Leaf parsley (*Petrosilenum sativum* var *foliosum*) is flat-leaved with small, branching out roots and largish, strongly aromatic leaves. The curly-leaved sort familiar to the British is less flavourful and grown only occasionally in Balkan gardens as a decorative plant. Both evolved from the wild, plain-leaved parsley indigenous to the Mediterranean.

Root parsley, *Petroselinum sativum* var *tuberosum*, a flat-leaved variety with smaller, less aromatic leaves, and an edible root with a hard core closely resembling a parsnip in shape. There are several thick, fleshy sorts of roots of which 'Berlin Root' (known in the UK as Hamburg Parsley) is the thinnest and the most common. Because of its strong flavour, it is never served on its own but is the invariable constituent of a group of vegetables known as 'soup aromatics' or 'soup roots' (the other four being celeriac, parsnip, onion and carrot). These are nearly always present in winter soups and, in the late autumn, are often sold (without onion) at greengroceries, tied in little bunches.

*Pekmez* (Albanian, Bosnian, Macedonian, Serbo-Croat), *petmez* (Bulgarian), *petimézi* (Greek), from the Turkish *pekmez*, is a natural sweetener, a survivor from an age that had no refined sugar. It is made from the juice of dessert grapes which are first cleared and de-acidified with calcium carbonate or 'white soil'—a local form of kaolin (china clay)—and then boiled to the consistency and colour of black treacle. To the taste, pekmez syrup is mildly sweet and reminiscent of malt extract. The French have a similar preserve which they call *raisiné simple*.

When fruit is cooked in pekmez syrup, the preparation is then known as *reçel* (Albanian), *rachel* (Bulgarian), *retséli* (Greek), *recelj* (Serbo-Croat), from the Turkish *reçel*. Among the more common fruits used are small green figs, tiny immature aubergines, pieces of quince and cubes of sweet, firm-fleshed pumpkin. For crispness, the pumpkin cubes are first soaked in lime water (a dilute solution of calcium hydroxide or slaked lime) for a couple of hours, then washed and cooked.

Poppy seeds come from the opium poppy, a native of the eastern Mediterranean where it has been raised since antiquity, but is now cultivated worldwide in warm climates. In Macedonia and Bulgaria, as well as in Turkey, Hungary and Romania, it is grown under government control for poppy straw—as the plant's ripened, dried-on-the-stem seed capsules are called.

Poppy straw does not yield opium, only a concentrate extracted from the empty capsules which is subsequently converted into morphine, a potent pain-killer, and codeine, used mostly in cough syrups.

Poppy *seeds* are opiate-free. The brown sorts are normally cold-pressed for high-quality cooking oil and margarine. The more expensive greyish-blue seeds are mainly used for sprinkling on bread, buns and bagels, though strudel and some rich cake-breads may contain a sweet filling of ground poppy seeds.

Three main species of pumpkin have been grown in the Balkans since the sixteenth century.

There is the common pumpkin or summer squash (*Cucurbita pepo*), with orange skin, and watery, fibrous orange flesh, which was first domesticated in northern Mexico and the lowlands of North America. The variety 'Hundredweight' is well known in the UK.

Sugar pumpkin or winter (turban) squash (*Cucurbita maxima*) is a white-skinned species from South America, with firm chestnut-like flesh. It grows well in many warm and dry parts of temperate Europe.

Fiddle-back pumpkin or cushaw squash (*Cucurbita moschata*) is indigenous to the sunny lowlands of Mexico, but may originally have been more widespread in South America. It thrives only in climates with hot dry summers. I grow it easily in our unheated greenhouse in Oxfordshire.

The words *raki* (Albanian), *rakiya* (Bulgarian), *rakí* (Greek), *rakija* (Macedonian, Serbo-Croat), *rachiu* or *țuica* (Romanian), derive from the Turkish *rakı*. The Slovenes use the noun *žganje* which is from the verb *žgati*, meaning to distil ardent spirit. *Raki* is distilled spirit obtained from the fermented pulp of over-ripe fruits such as

*1. This home-grown winter pumpkin weighed 5.5 kg. It contained 250 g of thick-skinned, pale brown seeds which I salted and roasted to serve as* pasatempo. *The stalk is cylindrical and lightly grooved.*
*2. The cushaw squash can be identified by its shape and its stalk, which is wide at the base and five-sided. The seeds are pale brown or nearly white, smaller than the winter pumpkin's and unsuitable for roasting. With me, it varies in weight from 450 g to 1.5 kg.*

pears, cherries, apricots and quinces, wild cornelian cherries and, most often, the Balkan variety of large, sweet, blue-skinned plums.

Besides these, several different kinds of grape brandy are also made. One, like Cognac, is distilled from wine; another (rougher) brandy from wine marc (the refuse from pressed grapes); a third from lees (sediment of wine). The alcoholic content of these brandies varies between 36 and 50 degrees.

Fruit brandy is the national drink of all Balkan countries, and even today, many householders take the produce of their orchards to be processed at small distilleries found in most larger villages and towns.

In Macedonia and Bulgaria, by tradition, fruit brandy sweetened with sugar, honey or *petmez* is, or was until recently, offered to visitors on the morning after the nuptial night as a sign of the bride's chastity.

The best commercial product available today is double-distilled plum brandy, matured in mulberry or oak barrels for at least three years. It is this wood, and the period of ageing, which impart to the clear spirit its mellowness and warm amber colour.

Fruit brandy is served straight, chilled to between 10° and 15°C.

'Have you seen how *țuică* is made? Come with me and I will show you.'

So we went down together, the doctor knocking the plums from the trees and filling my hands with them. In a barn were eight enormous barrels about ten feet high, standing on their ends. A gentle sizzling came from them, the air was filled with the scent of fermenting plums.

'When I make *țuică* I do not make it straight from the fruit off the trees as the peasants do. I fill these barrels and let the plums lie there fermenting for about six weeks. After that I put them in the *fabrică* (factory). That is in the other shed. There are some there now.'

I had no idea that *țuică* could be made so simply. On a brick furnace stood a large copper, a long pipe from it led through a barrel and from the pipe's end fell drop by drop the *țuică* into a container.

'It is primitive, is it not? The fermenting plums are put in the copper, the vapour passes through the pipe. In that barrel is water which is always cold because a stream from the hill flows through it. So the vapour is condensed and there is *țuică*. So simple, eh?'

D.J. Hall, *Romanian Furrow*, 1933.

*Salep* (Albanian, Bosnian, Bulgarian, Macedonian), *salépi* (Greek), from the Turkish *salep*, originally from the Arabic, is the name given to a number of wild indigenous orchid species valued for their nutritional and medicinal qualities. They include: *Orchis morio*, the common (green-winged) orchid, *O mascula*, early purple (masculine) orchid, *O maculata*, heath spotted orchid, *O militaris*, military orchid, *O latifolia*, march orchid, *Anacamptis pyramidalis*, pyramidal orchid, and *Platanthera bifolia*, lesser butterfly orchid.

Each orchid (salep) plant has two tuberous roots—one old and wrinkled which feeds the plants, and a young tuber which will feed next year's plant, and which, when gathered, dried and powdered, provides the salep of commerce—for making drinks and ice cream.

In herbal therapy, hot salep drinks have the reputation of curing dry coughs and bronchitis, especially when mixed with ginger and candy-sugar crystals.

*Tahan* (Albanian, Bosnian, Bulgarian), *tahíni* (Greek), *taan* (Macedonian), from the Turkish *tahan* or *tahin*, from the Arabic, is a thick oily paste obtained from the finely ground, toasted seeds of the sesame plant (*Sesamum indicum*), cultivated in the southern Balkans, including the Thracian plain, Macedonia and parts of Greece.

In former times, making *tahan* was a local trade rather than a household concern. The seed was washed, mechanically hulled and toasted in wood-fired ovens (similar

*Two species of orchis, fairly common in the Balkans, where they are known as salep plants.*

*1. Orchis morio, Green-winged or Common Orchis, has rounded tubers and unspotted veined leaves. The flowers are wine-red, the top three petals forming a hood or helmet.*

*2. Orchis maculata (syn Dactylorchis maculata), Heath Spotted Orchis, has veined spotted leaves, violet-red or pinkish flowers and slightly flattened, long-fingered tubers.*

to country bread ovens), then ground between two large millstones, the upper being made to rotate over the flat base by a blindfold horse moving in a fixed circle. These sesame mills closely resembled ancient Roman flour mills, except that those were bigger and turned by several slaves or a team of mules and horses. The old method of grinding sesame was retained until late in this century when it was all but replaced, quite satisfactorily, by industrial processes.

The best commercial paste is manufactured in Salonica (Thessalonica) and the town of Larisa in Thessaly, Greece. Top quality paste is light beige with a tinge of grey and the fragrance of roasted sesame. It is mild in taste, yet with a hint of bitterness. When stored it tends to separate—sesame oil on top, thick paste at the bottom. The oil can be stirred in, or poured off and used in salads. It has a pleasant scent reminiscent of cold-pressed sunflower oil, and has no bitterness whatsoever. Once opened, *tahan* should be kept refrigerated, though does not easily go rancid.

Brown sesame paste can be a low-grade by-product of sesame oil extraction, or a paste ground from whole (unhulled) roasted sesame seeds. Both taste quite bitter and there is hardly any visible separation in the jar. They are of limited culinary value.

The water buffalo (*Bos bubalus*) is called *buall* in Albanian, and *bivol* in Bulgarian, Macedonian, Romanian, Serbo-Croat, and Slovenian. The name comes from the Greek *boúbalos*. In Turkish it is *manda* or *camus*. The buffalo of the Old World, a docile draught-animal more powerful than the ox, is well adjusted to a hot climate. It is reared in most of Asia, India, North Africa and parts of Southern Europe, including the Balkans.

Domesticated in India some 5,000 years ago, its migration westward was very slow; the first Balkan record that mentions buffaloes is a peace treaty of 815 AD between the Byzantine Emperor Leo V and the Bulgar-Turkic Khan Omourtag, according to which each Byzantine warrior that had been captured in a stronghold was to be exchanged for a couple of water buffaloes. The animals were, no doubt, wanted by the Khan principally for transporting battering-rams and for building. The inscription on a stone column in Turnovo shows the Khan to have been of philosophical bent. It reads: 'Even if he lives well, man dies and another one is born. Let him who is born later, on reading these lines, remember him who made them. The name of the ruler is Omourtag, Khan *Yuvigi* [Great], may God let him live a hundred years.'

Since that time, successive generations of farmers have been breeding water buffaloes over most of the Peninsula because of their ability to exist on forage unpalatable to cows such as spent heads of sunflower and threshed corn cobs, as well as their general freedom from disease, extreme hardiness and strength as working animals—all in addition to the milk and meat they provide. Patrick Leigh Fermor described his first encounter with the beast in Transylvania during his walk across Europe in 1934: 'The water-meadows that lay about the river [Mureşul] were wallows for buffaloes; lustrous as seals, or caked in dried mud as armour against insect, they were sometimes only to be spotted in the slime and the swamps by bubbles or an emerging nostril.'

The milk output of the local buffalo-cow is substantially lower than that of the dairy cow, but the milk itself is richer in proteins, fat, milk sugar and vitamins. Moreover, the milk can be consumed fresh and untreated since they do not carry diseases such as tuberculosis or brucellosis.

In 1962, high-yield Indian buffaloes called 'murrah' were imported into Bulgaria and cross-bred with local stock. By 1987, 90 per cent had been replaced by the new, upgraded buffalo-cow, which produced almost 2,000 litres of milk per annum, with an average fat content of 7.5 per cent. The milk is used for making quality yoghurt, butter, thick fresh cream, sour cream and *kaymak* (clotted cream), as well as various cheeses, such as the Romanian brine cheese *telemea* and a soft unripened cheese similar to Italian mozzarella.

The flesh of older animals is tough and little used in the kitchen. Buffalo-calf meat, on the other hand, is tender, sweet and tasty—tastier in fact than veal, and contains more proteins, phosphorus and iron. It can be cooked in any manner suitable for veal.

In the Balkans, a number of dried all-meat sausages are made either from buffalo veal alone, or mixed half-and-half with pork. Another buffalo-meat product, the so-called 'beef' *pastırma* is normally prepared from the fillet of an older, plump and fatted buffalo calf.

# CHAPTER V

# Meze and Zakouski

> Dyado Liben calls his youngest daughter-in-law and whispers in her ear: 'Go, young woman, and fill a small bottle of the best *rakiya*. Then pour some in a coffee pot, mix it with some honey…, an adequate amount, and heat it on the fire, but very gently… Then tell your mother [-in-law] to take out one head of sauerkraut [from the barrel] and to sprinkle it with [hot] red pepper, but, you know, not too much pepper… Bring also some figs and dried grapes! Grill then a little lamb's liver and slice some *loukanka* [dried, raw, all-meat sausage]… very thinly… And see what else there is for meze and bring it here. We… must regale Hadzhi Gencha like a special guest, because… he is to me a precious person.'
>
> Karavelov, *Bulgari ot Staro Vreme*, 1867

*Meze* (Albanian, Bosnian, Bulgarian, Macedonian, Serbo-Croat), *mezés* (Greek), *mezea* (Romanian), from the Turkish *meze*, meaning a snack to go with a drink or drinks, was first introduced by the Turks as an accompaniment to coffee, fruit juices and sherbets. Over the centuries, however, meze has become inseparable from distilled spirits, wine and beer, and their prime complement, pleasant, lively conversation. Someone from the Balkans would rarely, if ever, drink without having a bite to eat, if only to counteract the effect of the alcohol. Meze and drinks can be offered at any time, day or night, to welcome guests or celebrate a special occasion. The custom is to down a small glass of alcohol, then take some food immediately.

*Zakuski* (Russian, Serbo-Croat, Slovenian) or *zakouski* (Bulgarian, Macedonian) is another word for meze—much favoured by the Balkan Slavs. When served as a first course to a formal meal or feast (with or without strong spirits) meze or zakuski have been re-named starters: *predyasiya* (Bulgarian), *prejela* (Bosnian, Serbo-Croat), *predjed* (Slovenian), *antipastë* (Albanian), or, in popular nomenclature, appetizers: *razyadki* (Bulgarian), *orektiká* (Greek).

A well-composed mixed Balkan meze, usually served on a flat dish divided into sections, includes a choice of at least seven or eight complementary items such as feta cheese; kashkaval or another firm cheese; cold meats or chicken; salami or raw dried sausage; grilled peppers; fresh tomatoes, pickled vegetables or Russian salad; black and green olives; sliced boiled eggs and fish or shellfish. The range of such foods is infinite, but I have written notes on those most often encountered, and put them down here as a list. I have also made a note where there is a more detailed recipe later in the book. All these foods go wonderfully with plum brandy or, for that matter, with any other pure-fruit or grain spirit, wine or beer.

> Brawn, from sheep's or pig's trotters and knuckles, calf's feet, ox cheeks or veal shins, makes a cold jellied mould. Pig's head 'cheese', another variety of brawn, is stuffed into a pig's stomach bag, boiled, pressed between two boards, then sliced and served plain.

> Canapés may be topped with any kind of meat, liver, fish or cheese spread, eggs, salami, dried sausage, salted pork back fat, anchovies, sardines, *garozi* (p. 127), *lakerda* (p. 128), *aýgotárahon* (p. 124), puréed black olives (p. 95), vegetable 'caviar' ( p. 65), tarama 'caviar' (p. 67), and for special occasions, real black or red caviar.

> Caviar, black (beluga) or red (Keta) caviar (p. 125) is served well chilled, immediately after opening the container. This is embedded in crushed ice and accompanied by wafer-thin strips of toast, chilled unsalted butter and Russian vodka, plum brandy, ouzo or Champagne.

> Cheese is the item most often served. It might be presented as a selection of sliced firm cheeses, or cubed feta sprinkled with vegetable oil and paprika, or in small bowls as potted cheese (p. 117). Another way is to offer it hot, as melted cheese (p. 114) or wrapped in greaseproof paper or vine leaves and served bubbling from the grill. Alternatively, slices of hard cheese are battered or crumbed and fried in butter (p. 116).

> Cream. A favourite Bosnian meze is *skorupača sa jagodama*, which is two parts fresh clotted cream mixed with one measure of wild or garden strawberries (and no sugar or honey). Sometimes, *kajmac* (salted ripened clotted cream, p. 50) is cut into cubes and used on the meze board instead of butter.

> Cracklings, bits of crisply fried pork fat, well salted, served hot, are popular.

Fish is served in a variety of ways: as slices of uncooked salt fish, *lakerda* (p. 128), or as a salad of grilled, dried, mackerel called *chiroz* (recipe p. 73). Tiny sea or river fish are crisply fried, or simmered in a marinade. Steaks of mackerel, swordfish or beluga can be poached or fried, then also marinaded.

Only sweet fruits, dried or fresh, such as grapes, musk melon, cherries, peaches, strawberries and figs, are traditionally served with spirits. One exception is the Bosnian *Limun-meze* which consists of peeled lemons, sliced into semi-circles and sprinkled with sugar to taste. (My mother used to prepare the same dish but with unpeeled lemon as an occasional treat for the children).

In summer, dishes of fresh fruit are arranged on a bed of crushed ice not just to keep them cool, but for looks as well. A watermelon is served just chilled or, for special occasions, injected through the rind with *mastika* and served with a glass of the same spirit. That was how I had it at Sozopol, a Bulgarian Black Sea resort.

Ham is commonly included and most Serbs and Croats would consider a meze spread incomplete without their local *pršut(a)*, (from the Italian, *prosciutto*), matured smoked ham, which in Bosnia-Hercegovina and Montenegro is prepared from goat or mutton, in Serbia and Croatia normally from pork, while in Slovenia *pršut* could be dry-salted, unsmoked ham, air-dried for ten or eleven months. *Pršut(a)* is also the Serbo-Croat name for cured and smoked fillet of beef. The Albanian *proshutë mish viçi* is cured veal ham, often served with plum brandy.

*Keşkek* (Turkish) is a winter meze dish of wheat cooked with chicken or turkey to form a thick paste and served hot (recipe p. 212).

*Köfte* (*Kyufteta*), tiny meat balls fried in oil and served on cocktail sticks (p. 153) are a favourite everywhere.

Cold poached or roast meat (beef, pork or mutton) makes a good winter starter sliced and arranged on a large dish in overlapping rows.

Freshly roasted, salted almonds, chick peas, walnuts, peanuts and pistachios are a welcome accompaniment to alcohol.

Large black olives, which have been stored in olive oil with bay leaf, strips of lemon zest or a sprig of oregano, can be served plain or stuffed with black or red caviar.

*Pastërma* (Albanian), *pastrma* (Bosnian, Macedonian, Serbo-Croat), *pasturma* (Bulgarian), *pastourmá* (Greek), *pastramă* (Romanian), from Turkish *pastırma*, is dry-salted, air-dried fillet of beef (in Turkish *bel pastırma*), or fillets taken from lamb, goat, calf or young water buffalo, cut into the thinnest possible slices and eaten uncooked or lightly grilled as meze. A speciality of the town of Kayseri (Caesarea of Roman times) in Anatolia, is pasturma coated with a paste of paprika, fenugreek or cumin and salt which protects and adds piquancy to the meat. The American pastrami, the cured, smoked underside of beef, is from the same linguistic root.

Diminutive savoury pastries have also been the fashionable thing for many keen home-cooks: cheese straws raised with yeast or baking powder; small shortcrust pastries made with cracklings, lard or butter; puff-pastry turnovers filled with mushrooms, cheese or meat; minute choux puffs; and a great variety of leaf-pastries, either baked, fried or (in Slovenia and Croatia) boiled.

Fruits and vegetables preserved in vinegar are standard companions to plum brandy, but not to wine. A colourful mixed dish may comprise crisp white cauliflower florets and infant heads of onions and garlic; amber cubes of pumpkin; long fleshy yellow peppers; fancy shapes of carrot; red and green salad peppers or tiny grilled chillies with their charred skins left on; crimson beetroots and blood-red morello cherries, green bunches of grapes, baby aubergines, courgettes and gherkins, and many others. The pickles are served dressed with a little sunflower oil or olive oil. Nothing else.

Pork back fat, dry-salted, the outside painted red with paprika, is sliced thin and usually consumed raw.

Shining, bite-sized rolls of vine leaves wrapped round a rice and onion mixture, called *sarma od lozov list so oriz* in Macedonia, are cooked all over the Balkans (recipe p. 98). They are classic meze fare served nowadays at nearly all big gatherings, official banquets and receptions, stand-up parties and other formal social functions, as well as in the home.

Sauerkraut makes a popular winter salad (p. 72), on its own or chased by a glass of plum brandy.

Fresh thin sausages, made of pure pork, beef or venison, are fried or grilled, often twisted into a tightly-wound spiral, and served hot. Uncooked, air-dried or smoked sausages, round-shaped or pressed flat, are quality products, made of the best cuts of meat. They are usually served in thin overlapping slices, decorated on top with a fine lace of piped butter. Blood sausage, is a traditional home-made delicacy prepared during the annual winter slaughter of pigs. It is an anticipated treat offered with a glass of wine or spirit when relatives and friends come to offer their good wishes for Christmas and the coming year.

There is a popular conserve of fatty lamb, mutton or kid, sometimes young beef or water-buffalo, called *sazdurma* in Bulgarian (from the Turkish *sızdırma*), *susma* (Bosnian) from the Turkish *sızmak*, (meaning to cause [the fat] to ooze out), and *kolloface dhënsh* (in Albanian). The flesh is cut small, then cooked for a long time in its own juice and fat to get rid of the moisture before packing into the traditional casings (gut or stomach) and pressing. After it has dried, it can be sliced fairly thick and served cold, or hot with scrambled eggs.

Shellfish are considered delicious meze or beginning to a meal, and Balkan cooks have scores of ways of preparing molluscs (such as snails, oysters, scallops, mussels, cuttlefish, octopus and squid) and crustaceans (shrimps, prawns, scampi, crawfish, crayfish, crab and lobster).

Tripe used to be a favourite meze, but no longer except perhaps in some country districts, where it may come plain—just sprinkled with salt, vinegar and paprika—or in a potato salad, or occasionally re-boiled in rich wine and onion sauce.

Yoghurt is not generally thought a happy combination with strong spirits; nevertheless, in Greece, a cucumber salad called *tzatzíki* is dressed with thick garlic-flavoured yoghurt and traditionally partners ouzo; and in Bosnia-Hercegovina, a grated cucumber mixed with crushed garlic and sheep's milk yoghurt, is offered with plum brandy as *teretur-meze* (from the Turkish *tarator*). It has the consistency of thick cream and is usually drunk—the only drinking salad there is. The Turks have something similar called *cacık*, which can be either sipped or eaten as a cold soup in the middle or the end of a meal. If the yoghurt is thick and undiluted, and the cucumber sliced instead of grated, *cacık* is served as a salad or meze (p. 68).

## SALTED WALNUTS
Serves 4–6 as an accompaniment to drinks

*Arra me kripë* (Albanian), *soleni orehi* (Bulgarian), *slani orasi* (Serbo-Croat)

100 g walnut halves • 1 1/2 teaspoons coarsely ground sea-salt

Rinse the walnuts under cold running water, and while still wet, spread them in one layer on a baking tray. Sprinkle with the salt.

Roast the walnuts in a preheated 160°C/320°F/gas 3 oven for 13–15 minutes at the most, without stirring—but watch them carefully as they burn easily. The walnuts are ready when they give out their unmistakeable aroma and are tinged a very light brown. Serve them straight from the oven, or cooled.

Salted almonds and hazelnuts can be similarly prepared, except that they are usually salted after toasting.

In the Balkans proper, north of the olive belt, the word caviar is also used for various purées and pastes based on grains, nuts, pulses or vegetables such as potatoes, aubergines, peppers, dried broad beans or chick-peas. All these relishes are known collectively as 'Vegetarian caviar' and sometimes as 'Poor man's caviar'.

## SEMOLINA CAVIAR
Makes about 150 ml relish

*Hajver ot gris* (Bulgarian); *ajvar od griz* (Macedonian)

1/4 teaspoon salt • 1 teaspoon tomato paste diluted with a little water • 2 tablespoons semolina • 50 ml sunflower or olive oil • 2 tablespoons lemon juice • 1 teaspoon finely grated onion

Heat 125 ml water with the salt in a small non-stick saucepan. Add the tomato paste and bring to a boil. Sprinkle in the semolina gradually, stirring all the time, and cook over a medium heat until it forms a thick, solid mass, about 3–5 minutes. Transfer to a mixing bowl and cool. Beat in the oil by driblets, then beat in the lemon juice and the grated onion. Season to taste. Pile the caviar in a deep serving dish and refrigerate. Just before serving surround it with a garland of olives, lemon wedges, sliced eggs and parsley, and present it with thin unbuttered strips of toast.

# AUBERGINE CAVIAR
Serves 4

*Havjar me patëllxhan* (Albanian); *hajvar od patlidžana* (Bosnian); *ajvar od patlidžan* (Macedonian); a*jvar od patlidžana* (Serbo-Croat); *zelen hajver* (Bulgarian, 'green caviar'). In Greece and Turkey this purée is known as aubergine salad: *melitzanosaláta* (Greek) and *patlıcan salatası* (Turkish), and also as *kyopoolou* (Bulgarian), *kiopolo* (Macedonian), from Turkish *köpoğlu*, meaning scoundrel

It is best to grill the aubergine and the pepper over wood or charcoal. It gives them a delicate smoky flavour, and the intense heat of the coals minimizes the browning of the aubergine flesh.

1 aubergine weighing about 300 g • 1 medium-sized green pepper • salt •
2–3 garlic cloves, peeled and pounded to a cream with a pinch of salt •
50 ml vegetable oil • 1 teaspoon vinegar
*Marinade*
1 litre cold water, 30-40 g salt, 30-40 ml wine vinegar

Make four cuts the length of the aubergine and place it, together with the green pepper, over a glowing fire, or under a grill set at its hottest. Turn at intervals until the flesh is soft to the touch and the skins charred and blistered, then put them in a saucepan and cover.

Putting the cooked aubergine on a tilted plate, press it with a potato masher to help release its bitter juices, then peel it quickly while still hot and drop it immediately into the cold marinade. To prevent browning, leave the aubergine to macerate for at least an hour, or preferably longer; then drain it thoroughly, cut off the end piece with the stalk, and process or mash the flesh to a purée in a mortar. Transfer it to a mixing bowl.

Meanwhile, peel and seed the pepper and chop it up finely—but do not process—the caviar needs to have a somewhat grainy texture. Add this to the bowl together with the garlic. Beat in the oil, a little at a time as for mayonnaise, then beat in the vinegar. Continue beating for a further 5 minutes or so, as this will improve the colour of the mixture. Taste, and heighten any of the seasonings.

Heap the purée into a deep serving dish, sprinkle the top with a little chopped parsley and decorate with tomato rounds and olives. Serve on the day you make it, at room temperature with crusty bread.

To make an aubergine and walnut caviar, pound 75–100 g of walnuts to a paste in a mortar and add them to the aubergine purée before beating in the oil.

# RED PEPPER RELISH
Makes two 400 g jars

*Lyutenitsa* (Bulgarian, meaning hot relish); *ajvar ljuti od paprika* (Serbian, meaning hot caviar of peppers)

---

'This isn't *shop*'s [*shop* means a peasant from the villages round the Bulgarian capital, Sofia] *lyutenitsa*, brother Kiro; *shop*'s *lyutenitsa* is even hotter... made with hot chilli peppers, raw onion and the juices of *kachamak* [polenta]—all pounded together to a paste and so hot that it can set you on fire... But the *shopi* villagers are used to it and dip their *kachamak* in it, and even the children eat it without batting an eyelid'.

Ginchev, *Gancho Koserkata*, 1889

For today's children Bulgaria produces a mild red-pepper relish, without chilli peppers. Serbian varieties are also not too hot: in a Belgrade supermarket I found two kinds—one with fried vegetables, *Uprženi ajvar*, and another, *Neupržen ajvar*, prepared without frying, as below.

1 kg fleshy sweet red peppers, grilled, peeled, seeded and minced or processed into coarse purée • 2 (or more) raw chilli peppers, seeded, well-pounded or processed into pulp • 100 g tomato purée • 1 teaspoon salt • 100 ml sunflower or olive oil • 1–2 garlic cloves, peeled and pounded in a mortar with a pinch of salt

Put all the ingredients (except the oil and garlic) into a thick-based or non-stick saucepan and cook, stirring, for about 10 minutes. Gradually stir in the oil, then add the garlic. Simmer for a minute or two, until the sauce is just thick enough to hold a trail. Cool, then refrigerate. The relish will keep well for a few days.

You can also pot the hot relish into two clean jars, warmed in the oven. Protect it with a layer of oil poured, then tightly cover. It should keep about a month. If you want to keep it longer, pot the hot relish into two hot jars, leaving about 2.5 cm headspace. Screw on the hot lids, and place them on a thin board or crumpled cloth in a deep pan. Fill the pan with hot water to the level of the relish in the jars. Bring slowly to the boil and simmer very gently for 40 minutes with a lid on the pan. Lift the jars out of the water and cool upside down.

Serve as a starter with bread and butter, or with beef, game or poultry.

# TARAMA
Makes about 300–350 g relish

*Tarama hajver* (Bulgarian, meaning salted hard roe caviar); *taramosaláta* (Greek, meaning salted hard-roe salad), from the Turkish *tarama* meaning both salted hard roe and the relish prepared from it; *ajvar od ikre* (Serbo-Croat, meaning fish-roe caviar)

Some Balkan people add bread or mashed potato and onion to the recipe below, but then the relish has a short storage life and should be eaten the day it is made. The Serbs prepare their fish-roe caviar with freshly salted hard roe.

100 g salted tarama roe • 1 tablespoon lemon juice • 250 ml olive oil, or a mixture with salad oil (you may need a little more for a stiffer consistency) • 15 g onion, finely chopped or coarsely grated and rinsed under cold running water, well drained • 25 ml soda water or water

Peel off the outer membrane of the roes, if any, and mash them to a pulp. Using a balloon whisk, an electric hand beater or a food processor, whisk in the lemon juice and then the oil, first almost drop by drop, as if you were making a mayonnaise, then a spoonful at a time, until the mixture thickens and forms stiff lumps. Then beat in the onion (if you are using the tarama the same day), and the water (if you prefer a softer mousse-like consistency). Turn on to a serving plate or a bowl, and decorate with olives and lemon or tomato slices. Serve with small wedges of bread or toast, accompanied, if you like, with beer.

Ten brothers in one white shirt. Who are they?
[The cloves in a bulb of garlic]

*Balkan riddle*

## BLACK OLIVE STEW
Serves 8–10 as a buffet dish

*Jahni me ullinj* (Albanian), *yahniya ot maslini* (Bulgarian)

In Bulgaria, this dish is served on Christmas Eve when black olives, imported from Greece or Turkey, are available. It also makes an unusual cold-table dish for help-yourself parties.

400 g black olives, soaked in several changes of hot water for 3–4 hours • 800 g onions, finely chopped • 400 g tomatoes, peeled and chopped • 1 generous tablespoon tomato purée • 1 large lemon, peeled, quartered and thinly sliced, pips removed • salt (if necessary) and freshly ground black pepper • lemon juice • 2–3 tablespoons finely chopped parsley

In a large saucepan, sweat the onions in the oil over low heat, covered, for about 45 minutes, or until soft and melting.

Meanwhile, drain the olives, cover them with cold water and cook for 15 minutes, then drain them again and rinse under the cold water tap to remove excess saltiness.

Stir the tomatoes and purée into the onions, and cook for a minute or two. Then add a little water and the drained olives and simmer for 35–45 minutes. Once the liquid has evaporated and the onion sauce is glistening with the oil, drop in the sliced lemon and remove the pan from the heat. Add salt, pepper and lemon juice to taste. Serve chilled or at room temperature, sprinkled with the parsley, with soft rolls or bread.

## CUCUMBER AND YOGHURT SALAD
Serves 4–5

*Sallatë me krastavec dhe kos* (Albanian); *salata ot krastavitsa i kiselo mlyako* (Bulgarian); *tzatzíki* (Greek); *salata od krastavitsa so kiselo mleko* (Macedonian); *salata od krastavaca s kiselim mlekom* (Serbo-Croat); *mlečne kumare v solati* (Slovenian); *cacık* (Turkish)

In her *Turkish Cuisine*, Nevin Halıcı gives two recipes for *Cacıc*—a thick garlic-flavoured yoghurt sauce which enhances either a cucumber salad, *salatalık cacığı*, or a salad of cos lettuce hearts, *marul cacığı*. Her formula is 1 kg thick yoghurt beaten with five pounded cloves of garlic and some salt. Three peeled and diced cucumbers or finely shredded cos lettuce hearts are tossed in this sauce, and served sprinkled with chopped dill and drizzled with a tablespoonful of olive oil.

Such salads may be found almost anywhere in the Balkans, and even in neighbouring regions to the north. They are almost the same—except in Slovenia, where a modest quantity of soured cream is usually blended with the yoghurt. As to the salting (or not salting) of cucumber ahead of time, this is a matter of taste. The Turks invariably salt in advance, then drain and squeeze dry. Most Balkan people, on the other hand, prefer the crispness and juiciness of freshly sliced, unsalted cucumber—as in the Balkan version of *cacık* below.

A 20 cm length of cucumber, peeled, halved lengthwise, then thinly sliced across or diced • 250 ml thick sheep's milk yoghurt (or drained plain cow's milk yoghurt), lightly beaten with a spoon • 1 clove garlic (or more if you like), pounded to a pulp with a pinch of salt • 1 teaspoon vinegar • 1 tablespoon dill or mint, chopped • salt and white pepper

Combine all the main ingredients in a salad bowl, and serve immediately, drizzled with some olive oil and given a scattering of paprika.

## WINTER BLACK RADISH SALAD
serves 4–6

*Crna rodakva na salatu* (Bosnian); *salata ot cherna ryapa* (Bulgarian); *salata od povrtnice or rotkve* (Croat); *črna redkov v solati* (Slovenian); *turp salatası* (Turkish)

200 g winter black radish, peeled, finely grated, seasoned with a little salt and sugar, let stand, then drained of the hot-tasting juices—or use undrained •
200 g carrots, scraped and finely grated • extra salt, if necessary
*Dressing I*
1 tablespoon vinegar or lemon juice (or 6–8 tablespoons thick, plain yoghurt) •
3 tablespoons pumpkin-seed oil, sunflower oil or olive oil
*Dressing II*
1 tablespoon lemon juice • 6–8 tablespoons sour cream or clotted cream

Pour the chosen dressing over the vegetables in a bowl, toss well and garnish with black olives. Serve at once with fried pork chops or beefburgers, or as an accompaniment to a meatless haricot bean stew.

## COS-LETTUCE SALAD
Serves 4–6

*Sallatë marule* (Albanian); *maroúlosaláta* (Greek); *marul salatası* (Turkish); all meaning cos-lettuce salad; *zelena salata* (Bosnian, Bulgarian, Macedonian, Serbo-Croat); *zelena solata* (Slovenian); *salată verde* (Romanian), all meaning green salad

Cos-lettuce, originating in the Greek island of Kos, is one of the oldest varieties of cultivated lettuce, and the favourite salad vegetable among Balkan people.

1 large cos-lettuce, as fresh as possible •
1 small bunch of spring onions, cleaned and finely chopped •
6–8 round all-red radishes, halved or quartered
*Dressing*
1 1/2–2 tablespoons wine or cider vinegar • 6 tablespoons salad oil or olive oil • salt

Put all the dressing ingredients in a salad bowl and beat with a fork until emulsified.

Separate the leaves, wash them one by one under running water, then pat dry with a clean cloth (as excess moisture will dilute the dressing) and chill in the salad compartment of the refrigerator for at least one hour. When cold and crisp, shred into fine ribbons (do not just tear them into small pieces) and place on top of the dressing, together with the onions and the radishes. Refrigerate until needed.

Just before serving, in the kitchen or at the table, toss the salad with the dressing, then garnish it, if you like, with quartered hard-boiled eggs or olives.

## GRILLED PEPPER SALAD
Serves 5

*Sallatë me piperka të pjekura* (Albanian); *salata ot pecheni piperki* (Bulgarian); *salata od pecheni piperki* (Macedonian); *salată de ardei* (Romanian); *salata od pečenih paprika* (Serbo-Croat); *biber salatası* (Turkish)

10 long, green or yellow salad peppers • salt • 1 garlic clove, peeled •
5 tablespoons sunflower or olive oil • 5 medium tomatoes • wine vinegar •
1 medium onion, sliced into thin rings • freshly ground black pepper

Grill the peppers over glowing charcoal or under a very hot grill close to the heat, turning them frequently, until the skins are blistered and charred evenly all over, but without burning the flesh. Wrap them immediately in several sheets of newspaper or put them in a saucepan with a tight-fitting lid. Leave them to sweat for 20–30 minutes, then peel the skin. Discard the tops, cores and seeds. Sprinkle the peppers with salt and leave them at room temperature for 4–5 hours.

Meanwhile, pound the garlic clove with a pinch of salt to a purée and blend with the oil; reserve until needed.

To serve, slice each tomato into 6 rounds, discarding the rounded ends. On each of the 5 salad plates arrange 4 tomato rounds in a straight row down the centre and sprinkle them with salt. Then pour a little vinegar into a shallow bowl and dip each pepper in it. Put a pepper on each side of the tomatoes, their tips pointing in opposite directions. Scatter a few of the onion rings on top and dribble the garlic oil over the lot. Season with a generous grind of black pepper.

Serve as accompaniment to cold meats or as a starter.

# GRILLED PEPPER AND TOMATO SALAD, AS IN PRILEP

Serves 6–8

*Pindžour na Prilepski nachin* (Macedonian)

1 kg fleshy, green, red or yellow peppers, grilled (as in the preceding recipe), skinned, seeded and finely chopped • 500 g ripe tomatoes, grilled whole, skinned and finely chopped • 1 or 2 cloves of garlic crushed in a mortar with a pinch of salt • salt • 100 ml sunflower oil

Combine the vegetables in a bowl and season with salt. Heat the oil and pour it over. Mix, transfer to a salad bowl and serve.

You can grill, skin and chop an aubergine and add it to this salad if you want.

## MIXED SUMMER SALAD
### Serves 5

*Sallatë e përzier* (Albanian, meaning mixed salad); *shopska salata* (Bulgarian, meaning salad of the *shopi*—the inhabitants of villages around Sofia); *horiátki* or *exohikós* or *theriní saláta* (Greek, meaning peasant, or rural, or summer salad respectively, and known in the USA as *'Ellinikí saláta*, or Greek salad); *mešana* or *Srpska salata* (Serbo-Croat, meaning mixed or Serbian salad); *mešana solata* (Slovenian, 'mixed salad'); *coban salatası* (Turkish, meaning shepherd's salad)

---

One of the most popular of Balkan salads, usually served as a starter. The proportions of the ingredients can vary according to national preferences. In Albanian restaurants the oil and vinegar are served separately.

5 large, ripe tomatoes (peeled, if thick skinned), cut into chunks • half a cucumber, peeled and diced • 1 large green or yellow pepper, raw, or grilled, skinned, seeded and cut into short strips • 1 medium, preferably red, onion, thinly sliced into semi-circles • salt (feta cheese is very salty) • vinegar (some tomatoes can be very sour) • 50 ml salad oil or olive oil

*To finish*

150 g feta cheese (or White Stilton), crumbled or diced • 2 or 3 tablespoons finely chopped parsley • 2–3 small, hot, chilli peppers, grilled but not skinned • black olives

Mix gently all the salad ingredients together in a salad bowl. Pile the cheese over the top and sprinkle with the parsley. Decorate, if you wish, with chilli peppers and olives. Once assembled, serve as soon as possible.

## SAUERKRAUT SALAD
### Serves 10

*Salata ot kiselo zele* (Bulgarian); *salata od kisela zelka* (Macedonian); *kislo zele v solata* (Slovenian), all meaning salad of sour cabbage; *kiseo kupus kao predjelo* (Serbo-Croat, meaning sour cabbage as a starter)

---

For a salad, sauerkraut must be in whole heads—not shredded and canned which is unsatisfactory for eating raw. Serve the salad as a starter or as an accompaniment to a simple dish of haricot beans baked with onion and tomato, or grilled sausages and fried potatoes.

1 small, firm head of sauerkraut (p. 318), weighing about 1.2 kg, drained of brine •
1 tablespoon paprika •
100–150 ml walnut, sesame or pumpkin seed oil (but not olive oil) •
black olives

Quarter the cabbage and remove the core. Shred it as finely as possible, then sprinkle with the paprika and the oil, and toss well, giving a final tossing at the table to ensure that every shred is pink and glistening with oil. Serve immediately, with a scattering of black olives.

## DRIED-FISH SALAD
Serves 6–8 as meze with beer or brandy

*Salata ot chirozi* (Bulgarian); *tsirosaláta* (Greek); *çiroz salatası* (Turkish; a speciality of Istanbul)

The Greeks' deep fondness for dried mackerel is illustrated by the old Bulgarian saying '*Chirozi* are to a Greek what nettles are to a Bulgarian'.

4 dried spring mackerel (see the description of *chiroz* on p. 126) •
1 tablespoon unobtrusive oil, such as corn oil or sunflower •
1 tablespoon vinegar or lemon juice • 4–6 tablespoons dill leaves, finely chopped

Moisten the fish with water, then beat them lightly with a wooden mallet to tenderize the flesh. Grill them briskly on either side in a ridged grill pan or on an electric hot plate; alternatively, you could enclose the fish in a double-sided wire basket and grill them over ash-covered embers of a fire or over a spirit burner, until the skin blisters and their bellies turn a deep golden colour.

While still hot, remove the skin, cut off the fins, heads and tails and bone them quickly; then pull the flesh apart into long thin shreds. If these are to be kept for any length of time, wrap them in a warm cloth which has been dampened with a mixture of hot water and vinegar, and leave them in a warm place. If they are to be eaten immediately, arrange the warm fish shreds on a serving dish, sprinkle them with the oil, vinegar (or lemon), a tablespoon of water and scatter the chopped dill on top.

# CHAPTER VI

# Soups

The long makeshift tables of oak planks were covered with multicoloured hand-woven cloths...The candles were lit, the tables laid out with spoons, salt and pepper and chunks of soft, freshly-baked bread from the family's own wheat... The helpers placed upon the tables bowls of hot, sour, chicken chorba which has been previously brought to the house in a big cauldron and reheated...

The tantalising aroma of the sour chorba and the parsley in it filled the air...

Ginchev, *Povesti*, 1887

*Corbë* (Albanian); *čorba* (Bosnian, Serbo-Croat); *chorba* (Bulgarian, Macedonian); *ciorbă* (Romanian), for long associated in the West with sour soup, means simply soup—a term derived from the Turkish word, *çorba*, which in turn comes from the Persian. As a sour soup, *chorba* figures prominently in pan-Balkan cookery; its foundation can be stock from meat, poultry, offal, lamb or veal trotters, giblets, fish or vegetables. When based on meat or poultry, sour soup is invariably a starter to nearly all Balkan festive meals—except in Bosnia where it is served at the end, before coffee. The sour element is usually vinegar, lemon juice or citric acid, but sauerkraut liquor, verjuice or freshly squeezed juice of cooking apples is sometimes used. In wine-growing regions, winestone (the tartaric deposit in winecasks) is considered the best acidifier for fish soups.

Apart from the sour soups, there exists a great many *chorbas* and *soupas* which are by tradition never acidulated, comprising all broths thickened with pasta, trahana, whole or crushed grain (barley, maize, millet or wheat), bulgur, semolina, dumplings, mashed bread, blood or flour. *Juha*, another Balkan name for soup or stock, is an archaic survival from the Old Slavonic, retained in Slovenia, mainland Croatia and along the Adriatic coast.

# SOUR LAMB SOUP
Serves 4–5

*Corbë e thartë me mish gëngji* (Albanian); *kisela janjeća čorba* (Bosnian); *kisela agneshka chorba* (Bulgarian); *kisela jagneshka chorba* (Macedonian); *corbă acră cu carne de miel* (Romanian); *kisela jagnjeća čorba* (Serbo-Croat)

---

1 half shoulder (blade-end) of lamb, excess fat and surface membrane trimmed off, boned and cut into medium-sized cubes; bones reserved •
about 1 litre cold bone stock or water • 1 teaspoon salt • 1 teaspoon paprika •
1 teaspoon whole peppercorns • 1 each of onion, carrot, piece of celeriac or celery stalk, parsnip, continental parsley root (if available), all cut into large chunks •
3–4 whole peeled garlic cloves

*Finishing sauce*

2–3 egg yolks (or 2–3 tablespoons sour cream or thick strained yoghurt) •
2–3 tablespoons lemon juice or vinegar • freshly-ground black pepper •
fresh dill or fennel, finely chopped • fresh parsley, finely chopped

*Topping*

paprika butter (p. 347) prepared with 25 g butter, melted with 1 teaspoon of paprika, or carrot butter (p. 348) prepared with 25 g butter and 25 g grated carrot

Put the bones on the bottom of a medium-sized pan, add the cubed meat and pour on stock or water to cover the meat completely. Bring slowly to a simmer, skimming any scum that rises; season with the salt, paprika and peppercorns. Simmer gently for about an hour.

Now add the prepared vegetables and cook for a further hour, until the meat is tender. Strain into another pan, discard the bones, vegetables and peppercorns, return the meat to the stock and simmer for another 5–10 minutes; then keep hot.

Just prior to serving, prepare the finishing sauce. In a small basin, cream the egg yolks (or sour cream or yoghurt) with the lemon juice or vinegar and season with black pepper. Add a ladle of hot—but not boiling—soup and stir well. Continue to add more soup in small quantities, then stir the sauce into the soup together with the herbs. Reheat, stirring continuously, but do not allow to boil again. Check the seasoning.

To serve, ladle the soup into a hot tureen or individual hot bowls and dribble the red paprika butter or carrot butter over the top. Serve with thick chunks of hot garlic bread. Do not reheat.

## SOUR SOUP OF LAMBS' TONGUES
Serves 2 as a main course

*Kisela chorba ot agneshki ezitsi* (Bulgarian); *kisela chorba od jagneshki jazitsi* (Macedonian); *kisela čorba od jagnjećih jezika* (Serbian)

---

400 g lambs' tongues, washed, soaked in salted water for 1–2 hours, then washed again •
1/4 teaspoon salt • 1 medium-sized onion, finely chopped • 1 carrot, diced •
1 small piece celeriac, or 1 stick celery, chopped, or 1 small parsnip, diced •
a little mint, fresh or dried • freshly ground black pepper •
1/2 quantity egg-and-lemon finishing sauce (p. 349), or wine vinegar, or sour cream

Put the tongues in a saucepan with the salt, and add water to barely cover. Bring to the boil, skim, and poach over a very low heat—adding hot water when necessary to keep them covered—for 2 1/2–3 hours, or until you can peel the tongue's skin with your fingers without the help of a knife. Lift the tongues out and refresh them under running cold water. Reserve the stock. Then skin and trim the tongues, and cut them into small pieces.

In another saucepan, put the vegetables with a little of the reserved stock, and simmer until tender. Add the remaining stock, the tongues and the mint, and continue cooking for a further 5–10 minutes. Check the seasoning. Off the heat, enrich the soup, if you wish, with the egg-and-lemon sauce, or simply acidulate it with vinegar or sour cream to taste. Serve hot, sprinkled with black pepper.


## SAUERKRAUT SOUP WITH PORK
Serves 4–5

*Chorba ot kiselo zele* (Bulgarian); *savanyúkáposztaleves* (Hungarian); *cirobă de varză acră* (Romanian); *supa od kiselog kupusa* (Serbo-Croat)

---

400 g shredded sauerkraut, home made or bought in jars, plastic packs or loose (from the barrel) • 250 g thick belly of pork, cut into 2.5 cm cubes •
2 tablespoons lard or vegetable oil • 1 medium-sized onion, finely chopped •
2 tablespoons flour • 1/2 teaspoon paprika •
250 g smoked pork sausage, skin removed and cut into 4–5 equal-sized pieces •
salt and freshly ground black pepper • 125 ml sour cream

Put the sauerkraut in a colander placed over a bowl and press it down with a wooden spoon to extract the juice. Add cold water to the juice to make up the quantity of liquid to 1 litre and pour into an enamelled or stainless steel saucepan. Bring the liquid to the boil, add the sauerkraut and the pork, and cook over a low heat for about 30 minutes.

Meanwhile, fry the chopped onion in the hot fat until soft, then add the flour and cook until it turns a light golden colour. Away from the heat, add the paprika and a ladleful of the boiling soup. Return the frying pan to the heat and stir the mixture until smooth, then pour it into the soup, stirring. Drop in the sausage pieces and season the soup with salt and pepper to taste. Continue cooking a further 30 minutes or until the pork is tender and the sausage heated through.

Ladle the soup into warmed earthenware bowls and keep hot. Just before serving, dot the surface of the soup with teaspoonfuls of the soured cream. This soup is just as good reheated.

*Soup from a Nail*
A demobbed soldier on his way home from the wars decided to stay overnight in a small village. Tired and hungry, he knocked on the door of a nearby cottage. The door was opened by an old woman who, at his request, offered him a bed for the night. As he entered the house, the old woman—who had a reputation for being rather stingy—apologetically told the soldier that she could not offer him food as she had already eaten.

'Never mind,' he said, 'I know how to make soup out of a nail.'

'Out of a nail!' exclaimed the woman. 'Please, show me how it's done!' she added, leading him into her kitchen.

'It's easy enough. First, put a pot of water on the stove, and when it come to the boil drop in a nail. Then throw in a chopped onion And a few cloves of garlic; add a couple of dried peppers—from those hanging on the wall, and a large handful of lentils, one or two carrots and some celeriac from the basket in the corner. Then pour in a spoonful or two of olive oil. When it is all cooked, season it with salt and beat in a little vinegar.'

'Now,' he said, rubbing his hands in anticipation. 'Let me remove the nail and eat the soup while it is hot.'

*Balkan folk-tale*

# TRIPE SOUP
## Serves 4

*Paçe plëndësi* (Albanian); *škembe čorba* (Bosnian); *shkembe chorba* (Bulgarian, Macedonian); *patsás soúpa* (Greek); *ciorbă de burtă* (Romanian); *čorba od škembića* (Serbian); *vampova juha* (Slovenian); *işkembe çorbası* (Turkish)

Tripe soup, strong-flavoured, garlicky and sour, is still offered at any of the scores of small unpretentious tripe restaurants, descendants of the earliest cheap Balkan urban catering. These restaurants might be approximated to the English tripe parlours once common in the industrial north. In the past, tripe soup was considered working-class fare. These days, though, tripe eating places are frequented by labourers, and many families, office workers, intellectuals and artists who enjoy the piquancy of the soup.

The Turkish author Miss Nevin Halıcı mentions in her *Turkish Cookbook* that, 'in Turkey, tripe soup is usually drunk late in the evening. In large towns there are tripe restaurants—*işkembeci*—which remain open all night. People who have been out drinking make a final call at the tripe house before returning home.'

That alcohol was not entirely forbidden in the more fiercely Mulsim pre-revolutionary Turkey is noted by Lady Mary Wortley Montagu in a letter of 1717:

> Achmet Beg ... made no scruple of deviateing from some part of Mahomet's Law by drinking Wine with the same freedom we did. When I ask'd him how he came to allow himselfe that Liberty, he made Answer, all the Creatures of God were good and design'd for the use of Man: however, that the prohibition of Wine was a very wise maxim and meant for the common people, being the Source of all disorders amongst them, but that the Prophet never design'd to confine those that knew how to use it with moderation.

Beef tripe requires longer cooking than that of veal, but it makes a more flavourful foundation. It was often, and still is, taken by householders in sealed earthenware pots to the local baker's and left overnight to cook in the oven after the bread has been taken out.

400 g dressed, uncooked, beef tripe • 1 teaspoon salt • 250 ml milk • egg-and-lemon finishing sauce (p. 349) prepared with lemon juice or wine vinegar • 1/2 quantity red paprika butter (p. 347) • garlic vinegar (p. 348), or 4 cloves of garlic, crushed and mixed with 50 ml wine vinegar

Put the tripe into a cooking pot and add enough cold water to cover it by about 5–6 cm. Put the lid on and seal it with a strip of flour-and-water paste. Place the pot in an oven on the lowest setting and cook for 8–10 hours, or until the tripe is done. Alternatively, put the tripe into a saucepan, cover it with cold water, cover the pan, and boil over a moderate heat for 5–7 hours, adding extra boiling water from time to time to maintain the original level. Season with salt at the end of the cooking time when the tripe is tender. Lift out and leave to cool. Strain the cooking liquid and top it up with the milk, and extra water or beef stock if necessary, to measure 750 ml. Chop the tripe with a cleaver, or slice into thin short strips and set aside. Prepare the egg-and-lemon finishing sauce. Whisk in gradually a ladleful or two of the cooking liquid, then pour this back into the pan still whisking. Add the tripe, bring the soup to simmering point and simmer for about 5 minutes.

Serve the soup in hot soup bowls. Dribble the red paprika butter over the top for a decorative effect. Pass round the garlic vinegar.

## COLD SAUERKRAUT SOUP
Serves 4–5

*Armeya chorba* (Bulgarian, meaning soup with sauerkraut liquor); *hladna čorba od rasola* (Serbian, meaning cold soup with sauerkraut liquor)

In Bulgaria, this soup, accompanied by a bowl of grilled chilli peppers, is eaten on Christmas Eve. Served without the peppers, it is known as *Chorba Bismark*—after the Prussian statesman, founder of the German Empire. From the recipe, you will see that using tinned sauerkraut is not really feasible, but you can find barrelled sauerkraut in some delicatessens.

1 litre freshly-drawn sauerkraut liquor •
1 leek, the white part only, finely chopped •
250 g piece of crisp sauerkraut from the barrel, sliced thinly
(shredded or pasteurised sauerkraut is unsuitable) •
2 tablespoons olive oil • 1–2 teaspoons paprika • 4 dried chilli peppers, lightly grilled

Pour the sauerkraut liquor into a soup tureen or large bowl. Slide in the leek and sauerkraut. Add the olive oil and stir. Sprinkle with the paprika. Serve at room temperature, with the chilli peppers on a side plate.

## PORK KNUCKLE SOUP
Serves 4

*Paçe derri* (Albanian); *soupa-pacha* (Bulgarian); *piktí soúpa* (Greek); *pacha* (Macedonian); *pihtija* or *pače* (Serbo-Croat); from Turkish *pıhtı*, coagulated liquid, and *paça* —a dish made from sheep's head and trotters.

A nourishing soup cooked by lengthy poaching; when cold it will set into a thick jelly similar to English brawn. The best pork soup is considered to be one made from the Yorkshire breed of pigs, known in Serbia as the *engleza*.

Beside knuckle, other gelatinous cuts, such as pig's trotters, head (without the brains), tongue, snout and ears, can all be used for the soup—but not the tail which is too fatty. In areas inhabited by Muslims, this soup is prepared with sheep's or lamb's head and trotters, or calf's head, feet or knuckle bones sawn into pieces.

1 knuckle of pork, singed over a flame, then well washed • 2 pig's trotters, cleaned by the butcher • 1/4–1/2 teaspoon salt • 1 medium onion, peeled and quartered • 4–5 cloves of garlic, unpeeled • 2–3 carrots and 1 parsnip, peeled and cut into rounds • 150 g piece of celeriac, cut into chunks; or 2–3 sticks of celery, in short lengths • 1 teaspoon black peppercorns • 1/2 quantity egg-and-lemon finishing sauce (p. 349) • freshly ground black pepper • 2 tablespoons chopped parsley, or 1/2 quantity red paprika butter (p. 347) • garlic vinegar (p. 348); or 6–8 garlic cloves, crushed and blended with 2 tablespoons vinegar; or a sauce made by mixing 2 tablespoons grated horseradish with 2 tablespoons vinegar

Over a low heat, bring the knuckle, trotters and about 850 ml cold water to the boil in a pan just large enough for them. Skim until no more scum rises, add the salt, then cook at a bare simmer for 3 hours, or until the meat begins to fall from the bone. Strain the stock into a bowl, then cool and refrigerate. Remove the meat from the knuckle and cut into very small pieces. Scrape the fat from the skin and cut the skin into tiny dice. Mix with the meat and refrigerate. Discard the trotters.

Next day, remove the fat from the surface of the jellied stock, discard it, and return stock to the pan. Add the vegetables and peppercorns and cook on a low heat for 35 minutes, until the vegetables are soft. Strain through a sieve, pressing down lightly on the vegetables with a wooden spoon to extract maximum flavour. Discard the vegetables. If less than 750 ml stock remains, make it up to this amount with water. Return the meat and simmer for 10 minutes. Prepare the egg-and-lemon sauce and combine it with the soup. Cook gently for 5 minutes, then taste for seasoning. Serve hot, sprinkled with black pepper and the parsley or red paprika butter. Pass the garlic vinegar or horseradish sauce separately.

# MEATBALL SOUP (WITH VEGETABLES)
Serves 4

*Supë me kokëla të mishi* (Albanian); *uvalaci-čorba* (Bosnian); *soupa s topcheta* (Bulgarian); *giouvarlákia soúpa* (Greek from Turkish *yuvarlak*, ball, marble); *supa od koftinja* (Macedonian); *ciorbă de perişoare de carne* (Romanian); *čiorba od ćufteta* (Serbo-Croat); *kulak çorbasi* (Turkish), all meaning meatball soup

1 litre meat or chicken stock • 1 small onion, finely chopped • 1 carrot, sliced • 1/2 celeriac, peeled and diced (or 2 sticks celery) • 50 g frozen peas (if fresh, blanched for 5 minutes, then refreshed with cold water) • 50 g young green beans (fresh or frozen), cut into bite-sized pieces • 2 peeled tomatoes, chopped • 1/2 red pepper, cut into small squares • 1 lemon slice, unpeeled, diced small • 1 medium-sized potato, peeled and diced • 1/4 teaspoon each salt and pepper

*Meatballs*

200 g minced lamb or beef, or a mixture • 25 g round grain rice • 1/4 teaspoon salt • large pinch freshly ground black pepper • 1 tablespoon finely chopped parsley • a little stock or water to obtain a mixture of soft consistency, and a little plain flour for coating

Bring the stock to the boil in a large pan. When bubbling vigorously, add the remaining ingredients (apart from the meatballs) and cook over a gentle heat for about 20 minutes. Leave to cool.

For the meatballs, pass the meat through a mincer a couple of times, add the rest of the ingredients (except the flour) and beat with a spoon to form a smooth mass. Or you can put the ingredients (except the flour and rice) through a food processor, then stir in the rice. Shape the mixture into small balls, the size of cherries, dipping your hands in water whenever necessary.

Coat them with flour, drop them into the cooled soup and simmer for a further 30 minutes, until the rice grains start sticking out and the meat is tender. Taste and heighten the seasoning, if necessary.

This soup can be finished with an egg-and-lemon sauce or egg-and-yoghurt sauce. For this, omit the tomatoes from the recipe and cook the soup until the vegetables are practically disintegrating. Strain the soup and discard them. Cook the meatballs in the strained soup until done—about 25–30 minutes. Off the heat, enrich the soup with 1 egg yolk beaten with 1 tablespoon lemon juice (or 3–4 tablespoons plain yoghurt) and 1 tablespoon plain flour.

Children love this soup. It is not too salty, the meatballs with rice needles sticking out look like little hedgehogs. They are soft and fun to eat.

# FISH SOUP
Serves 7–8

*Corbë peshku* (Albanian); *chorba ot riba* (Bulgarian); *riblja juha* (Croat); *psarósoupa* (Greek); *chorba od riba* (Macedonian); *ciorbă de peste* (Romanian); *čorba od ribe* (Serbian); *ribiška juha* (Slovenian); *balık corbası* (Turkish)

In winter, Bulgarians like to add sauerkraut liquor instead of wine to the soup, especially when it is prepared with the fatty head of a large Danubian wels or sheat-fish (*Silurus glanis*).

600 g fish, such as turbot, sterlet, flounder, wels or red scorpion fish (*Scorpaena scrofa*), skinned, gutted, washed and cut into portions • salt • 2–3 tablespoons sunflower oil or olive oil; or 25 g butter • lemon juice • 1–2 tablespoons chopped parsley • lemon wedges
*Balkan court bouillon*
1 carrot, peeled and sliced • 1 leek, white part only, thinly sliced • 1/4 celeriac, peeled and diced, or three sticks celery, diced • 1 medium onion, chopped • 3 cloves of garlic, unpeeled • 2–3 parsley roots, or 1 parsnip, peeled and thinly sliced • a few strips of lemon zest • 5 sprigs of parsley • 1 sprig of thyme • 2 sprigs of fennel, or 5 sprigs of dill • 1/4 bay leaf • 1 teaspoon black peppercorns • 10 g coarse sea salt • 250 ml dry white wine

Season the fish lightly and refrigerate it while you make the court bouillon. Put all the ingredients, except the wine, into a pan, add 1 litre water, bring to the boil and simmer over a low heat for 30 minutes. Then add the wine and simmer for a few more seconds. Remove from the heat and allow to cool.

When you are ready to cook the soup, strain the court bouillon through a sieve with a light pressure to extract as much flavour as possible. You should have at least 1 litre bouillon. If not, make up with water. Add the oil or butter, the fish and lemon juice to taste. Poach the fish with the lid on over a very low heat—so that the liquid just trembles—for 10–15 minutes (depending on the type of fish and thickness of your portions), or until the flesh just begins to flake.

Serve the soup hot, sprinkled with parsley. Hand around lemon wedges separately.

For fish soup flavoured with egg-and-lemon sauce, make up the recipe above omitting the lemon juice. Prepare a double quantity of egg-and-lemon sauce (p. 349) using the strained liquid of the fish soup, then pour the mixture back into the soup. Simmer for 1–2 minutes without stirring to avoid breaking up the fish.

## VEGETABLE SOUP
Serves 4–5

*Supë me zarzavate* (Albanian); *čorba od povrća* (Bosnian, Serbian); *juha od povrća* (Croat); *chorba od zelenchuk* (Macedonian); *gradinarska soupa* (Bulgarian, meaning Gardeners' soup)

A midsummer soup prepared with nearly all the vegetables of the season; their variety provides a wholesome start to a light summer lunch or supper.

2 tablespoons vegetable oil • 1 medium-sized onion, chopped •
150 g cabbage, shredded thinly • half red pepper, diced small •
100 g green beans, cut into bite-sized pieces • 50 g shelled peas •
1 carrot, coarsely grated • 1 parsley root coarsely grated •
50 g piece of parsnip, diced small • 25 g piece of celeriac, diced small •
100 g courgettes or young vegetable marrow, diced small •
2 medium potatoes, peeled and diced small • 150 g peeled tomatoes, chopped •
1/2 teaspoon paprika • 1 teaspoon salt • black pepper
*Garlic sauce*
3–5 peeled garlic cloves • a pinch of salt • 1–2 tablespoons chopped mint leaves •
1 tablespoon vegetable oil • vinegar or plain yoghurt

Place a thick-based enamelled pan with a lid over a low heat. Pour in the oil, then add the vegetables in the order given, peeling, washing and cutting or grating them one after the other as they go into the pot. After each addition, stir, then cover the pan to allow them to sweat in their own juices. Season with the paprika and salt, and when the vegetables are quite soft, pour in 500 ml boiling water and cook for a further 10 minutes or so. Remove the pan from the heat and grind in some pepper.

Keep the soup hot while you prepare the garlic sauce. For this, pound the garlic in a mortar with a pinch of salt, then add the chopped mint and pound the mixture to a paste. Stir in the oil and a little vinegar (or yoghurt), then stir the sauce into the hot soup. Taste and add a little more seasoning, if necessary.

Serve in hot soup-plates or bowls with a tablespoon or two of grated Parmesan, kashkaval or kasher cheese heaped on top, and plenty of good bread.

## MONASTERY BEAN SOUP
Serves 5–6

*Monastirska bobena chorba* (Bulgarian)

'Now we shall eat a bean soup made from the sins of father Nikodim,' Father Sisoj confided, and explained to the company that the beans were found hidden in a crock in the late monk's cell. A small piece of paper, on which had been written a sinful thought that had occurred to the monk, had been wrapped around each bean: around a black bean—an unpardonable thought, around a white one—a less sinful, perhaps pardonable thought...

'At this moment, the kitchener...brought a large bowl of steaming, aromatic soup speckled with white and black beans.

'There it is, the bean soup of Father Nikodim's sins,' father Sisoj said. 'And with the wine, which is now cooling, we will drink a toast for the peace of the good monk's soul.'

Elin Pelin, *Under the Monastery Vine Arbour* (1936)

A steaming, aromatic bean soup was served to me one early spring during Lent at the Monastery of the Transfiguration near the town of Turnovo. The soup was prepared with haricot beans grown in the monastery grounds and included dried chilli peppers which added flavour as well as tremendous heat. It was cooked in a huge earthenware bean-pot which had a hole in the lid to allow the steam to escape.

250 g white haricot beans, preferably a large variety, soaked overnight and drained • 2 tablespoons sunflower oil • 1 large red pepper, cut into small pieces, or two whole dried red peppers • 1 (or more) chilli pepper, lightly grilled • 1 large onion, finely chopped • 2 carrots, sliced into rounds • 100 g celeriac or parsnip, diced small • 2–3 garlic cloves, peeled and crushed • 1 teaspoon paprika • freshly ground black pepper • 4–5 sprigs each of mint and parsley, tied together in a bunch • 1 teaspoon salt • 4 tablespoons olive oil • fresh parsley leaves, finely chopped • fresh mint leaves, finely chopped

Put the soaked, drained beans into a pan and pour over plenty of cold water. Bring to the boil, skimming, and boil fast for 10 minutes. Drain and discard the cooking liquid.

Transfer the beans to a large pan or fireproof bean-pot; add the sunflower oil. Pour in 1 litre boiling water. Simmer gently for an hour (or longer, if the beans are more than a year old). When they are soft but still intact, add all the other ingredients except the salt, oil and chopped herbs, and cook for a further 30 minutes, or until the vegetables are tender, and the beans soft and creamy. Season with the salt and cook for another five minutes.

Remove from the heat and discard the bunch of herbs. Taste for seasoning. Pour the soup into a tureen, stir in the olive oil and chopped herbs to taste, and serve with bread. Pass round vinegar and olive oil to sprinkle extra if you want.

# TOMATO SOUP
### Serves 4–6

*Supë domatesh* (Albanian); *domatena soupa* (Bulgarian); *juha od rajčica* (Croat); *tomatósoupa* (Greek); *supa od domati* (Macedonian); *čorba od paradajza* (Bosnian, Serbian); *domates çorbası* (Turkish)

---

1 kg very ripe tomatoes, fresh or canned, chopped • 1 tablespoon concentrated tomato purée or ketchup • 3 tablespoons vegetable oil, or 50 g butter • 3 tablespoons plain flour • 1/2 teaspoon paprika, 1 bay leaf, or 1 large pinch of ground mace or nutmeg or a pinch or two of dried mixed herbs • 1 teaspoon sugar • 1/4 teaspoon salt • freshly ground black pepper • a little meat or vegetable stock, or white wine, or water

Simmer the chopped tomatoes for 30 minutes, covered, until they are practically disintegrating. While still hot, rub them through a fine nylon sieve to make a very thin, watery tomato paste; if it lacks flavour (which is likely if the tomatoes were not fully sun-ripened outdoors), add the concentrated tomato purée or ketchup, then leave to cool. Discard the skins and seeds left in the sieve.

In a heavy-based pan, heat the oil or butter, then blend in the flour. Cook for a minute or so, without colouring, stirring all the time. Still stirring—or beating with a wire whisk—slowly pour in the cooled tomato liquid, then add the chosen flavouring (paprika, bay leaf, nutmeg, mace, or mixed herbs), sugar, salt and black pepper to taste, and simmer for 4–5 minutes, until the soup thickens. Thin the soup down with stock, wine or water to a coating consistency and bring back to the boil. If you have used a bay leaf, discard it now.

Serve in heated soup bowls. Sprinkle with 100–125 g of crumbled cheese such as sirene or feta, or float a spoonful of thick cream on top of each portion.

For an uncooked soup, mix 1 litre chilled tomato juice with 100 g crumbled white brine cheese and some finely chopped parsley. Season with salt and pepper to taste. Serve in soup cups, sprinkled with a little sunflower oil. This serves 4 or 5.

# NETTLE SOUP WITH WALNUTS OR CHEESE
Serves 4–5

*Chorba ot dzhourkana kopriva* (Bulgarian, meaning soup made from nettles mashed with a wooden mallet, *dzhourlyak*), *chorba od kapriva* (Macedonian, nettle soup)

600 g young top shoots of nettles, well washed • salt • 50 g plain flour •
50 g butter, or 3 tablespoons sunflower oil •
50 g shelled walnuts, finely ground or pounded; or 75 g white brine *sirene* cheese (or white Stilton ), crumbled • garlic vinegar (p 348)

Sweat the nettle tips, sprinkled with a little salt and water, in a lidded pan until just limp. Pound them in a mortar or purée them in a processor. Fry the flour in the oil or butter until pale golden. Off the heat, add the nettles and gradually stir in about 1 litre of hot water. Simmer for a minute or two, adding more salt or water, if necessary, until the soup is smooth and creamy but not too thick.

In a heated soup tureen, place the crushed nuts or crumbled cheese; pour over the boiling soup and stir everything together. Hand round the garlic vinegar separately.


Montenegrin nettle soup (*Crnogorska čorba od kopriva*). For this soup add 50 g of round-grain rice and 2 diced potatoes instead of the flour and butter mixture, as well as a bunch of spring onions, coarsely chopped. Serve with 50 g of *kajmak* (clotted cream) in the tureen instead of the walnuts or cheese, and omit the vinegar.


Serbian nettle soup (*Srpska čorba od kopriva*). Fry the flour plus a small bunch of chopped spring onions in 50 g of lard. In place of the cheese or walnuts, enrich the soup with 2 beaten egg yolks or a few tablespoons of thick plain yoghurt.

# ICED CUCUMBER SOUP
Serves 5–6

*Teretur* (Bosnian), from Turkish dialect *teretor*; *tarator* (Bulgarian, Macedonian), from Turkish *tarator*, a walnut and garlic sauce, from the Persian; *tzatzíki soúpa* (Greek), from Turkish *cacık*, cucumber and yoghurt salad

This summer soup is based on the Turkish walnut and yoghurt sauce (p. 346). The Croatian *hladna žetelačka supa*, 'cold harvester's soup', is similar but without yoghurt. The Greek *tzatzíki soúpa* is also related but lacks walnuts. For the best result, the garlic and walnuts for the soup are pounded to a paste in a mortar, not ground in a food processor.

4–5 cloves of garlic, peeled • at least 1/2 teaspoon salt • 75 g shelled walnuts •
35 g crustless, day-old bread, moistened, excess water then gently squeezed out •
2 tablespoons sunflower or walnut oil •
400 ml thick, fresh cow's-milk or sheep's-milk yoghurt, chilled •
25 cm length of cucumber, peeled • 125 ml mineral or spring water, chilled •
2–3 teaspoons cider vinegar or lemon juice • ice cubes

*To finish*
35 g shelled walnuts, coarsely crushed • 5–6 teaspoons vegetable oil •
4–5 teaspoons finely chopped dill leaves • 2 lemons, quartered

Pound the garlic in a large mortar with the salt, reducing it to a thin cream, then pound in the walnuts, little by little, followed by the bread. When the mixture is a thick, smooth paste, start adding the oil, a little at a time, stirring steadily. Transfer the mixture to a large bowl; beat in the yoghurt. Cut the peeled cucumber into tiny dice and drop into the bowl; alternatively, carefully chop the cucumber holding it vertically in one hand, chopping downwards into the face forming a criss-cross pattern of cuts to a depth of about 2.5 cm. Then, holding the cucumber horizontally over the soup, slice downwards across the chopped end allowing the pieces to fall into the soup. Repeat the process until the cucumber is used up. Stir in the chilled water and vinegar or lemon juice to taste.

Serve the soup over ice in individual soup bowls with crushed walnuts, vegetable oil and chopped dill sprinkled over the top. Pass round the quartered lemons separately at the table.

# CHAPTER VII

# The Garden Crop

The Balkans have a long tradition of good vegetable cookery. People enjoy them for their own sake, not just on fast days, but every day of the week. Some meatless dishes do also have traditional associations with feast days and holidays. The Orthodox Christmas Eve supper, for example, will be based entirely on the garden: a thick red stew of haricot beans, a plateful of dried red peppers stuffed with fragrant rice or beans, or a dish of small rolls of rice and raisins wrapped in sauerkraut leaves, all perhaps to be followed by a pumpkin-layered pastry or baked pumpkin smothered in ground walnuts and honey. The dishes served may vary from place to place, but the meal itself is always opulent, the table laden with fruits and vegetables of the land.

Some simple recipes grew out of the life of the farming population; others, more sophisticated, came originally from Greece and Turkey, but underwent their own evolution. From the whole crop I have provided a selection of those that have stood the test of time and have gained particular—and a few of them international—renown.

## SPINACH PURÉE WITH FRIED EGGS
### Serves 4 as a light lunch or supper

*Pure spinaqi dhe vezë të ferguara* (Albanian); *pyure ot spanak s purzheni vajtsa* (Bulgarian); *pire od spanaḱ so prženi jajtsa* (Macedonian); *pire od spanaća s prženim jajima* (Serbo-Croat)

---

700 g fresh spinach, cleaned weight, meticulously washed, or 600 g frozen spinach leaves; coarsely chopped • salt • 100 g spring onions, trimmed and chopped • 25 g butter, or 1 1/2 tablespoons vegetable oil • 2 cloves of garlic, chopped • 25 g plain flour • 175 ml milk or pouring cream • 4 eggs • 50 g unsalted butter • a large pinch of paprika

Pack the spinach, sprinkled sparingly with salt, into a saucepan. Cover tightly and sweat over a low heat in the water clinging to the leaves, for about 20 minutes until most of the juices have evaporated and the spinach is tender. Drain, pressing it with a wooden mallet to extract any remaining moisture, then chop it up.

In a heavy-based saucepan or large frying pan, fry the spring onions in the butter. When they start to soften, add the garlic and cook for a few more seconds only. Stir in the flour and continue cooking for a further minute or so without colouring. Off the heat, add the spinach, then pour in the milk or cream. Bring the mixture to a simmer and cook gently for 3–4 minutes until it thickens.

Transfer the spinach purée to 4 dinner plates or small earthenware bowls. Keep warm in a very slow oven while you fry the eggs in hot butter (covered with a plate or lid) until the whites are set and the yolks done to your taste. Alternatively, poach the eggs.

To serve the purée, place a fried egg on top of each portion. Add the paprika to the butter left in the pan, pour the clear butter over the eggs and spinach; discard the sediment. Serve immediately with bread or warm bread rolls.

# NETTLE PURÉE
Serves 4

*Pure hithre* (Albanian); *pyure ot kopriva* (Bulgarian); *pire od kopriva* (Macedonian, Serbo-Croat), from the French, *purée*

Nettles are a traditional early-spring dish believed to purify the blood after a winter of self-indulgence in meat and fatty foods.

Nettle purée can be prepared in the same way as spinach purée or, as below, without a thickening of flour. Only young nettles, picked in the spring before they start to flower, are suitable for cooking; in June the nature of the plant changes and the leaves become too coarse to eat. Avoid being stung by wearing gloves to pick and wash them. Once cooked, they are harmless.

1 kg top young shoots of nettles, well washed but not allowed to soak • salt • 50 g unsalted butter • 50 g shelled walnuts, coarsely ground or pounded • 150 ml thick-set plain yoghurt, or 100 ml sour cream

Sweat the nettles, lightly seasoned with salt, in a closed pan, with no more water than that left clinging to the shoots after washing. Cook for 5–6 minutes until limp and tender, then pound them in a mortar with a pestle, or purée them in a food processor. Return to the pan, add the butter and cook, stirring, for a few more minutes, until the purée thickens. Serve sprinkled with walnuts, with a tablespoon or two of yoghurt or sour cream on the side of each plate.

## LEEKS COOKED IN WHITE WINE
Serves 6 as a starter

*Praz varen v byalo vino* (Bulgarian); *praziluk kuvan u belom vinu* (Serbo-Croat)

700 g trimmed leeks (white parts only), well washed and cut into 5 cm lengths • salt •
50 ml sunflower or olive oil, or a mixture • 100 ml dry white wine •
freshly ground white pepper • 4 cloves of garlic, peeled and chopped •
3 lemons, quartered • black olives • 2–3 tablespoons chopped parsley

Blanch the leeks in a lightly salted boiling water for 2 minutes and drain. Arrange them in a wide and shallow enamelled pan, preferably in 1 layer. Add the oil, wine, scant 1/2 teaspoon of salt, pepper and garlic. Cover, bring to the boil and simmer for 1 hour until the leeks are very tender (but still hold their shape) and most of the liquid has evaporated. Remove from the heat and allow the leeks to cool in the cooking juices. Serve with lemon wedges, olives and chopped parsley.

## GREEN BEAN STEW
Serves 4–5

*Jahni me fasule të njoma* (Albanian); *zelen fasoul yahniya* (Bulgarian); *zeleni grah (mahuna) kuhani* (Croat); *zelena boranija kuvana* (Serbian)

1 kg stringless, young, green beans, fresh or frozen, topped and tailed, cut into 2.5 cm lengths • 50 ml sunflower oil • 2 large onions, finely chopped •
400 g ripe, peeled tomatoes, fresh or canned, chopped; or 2 rounded tablespoons tomato purée • 1 teaspoon paprika • 1 teaspoon salt • 6–8 large cloves of garlic, peeled and crushed with a pinch of salt • 2 tablespoons chopped parsley

Put the green beans into a saucepan, pour over hot water to cover and simmer, covered, for 25 minutes to soften slightly.

Meanwhile, heat the oil in a frying pan with a lid and sweat the onions until golden—about 25 minutes. Add the tomatoes, or purée, the paprika and salt, cook briskly for a while, then stir this into the beans. Add more hot water, if necessary, to cover the beans, then simmer for a further 35 minutes, until the beans are very tender. Remove from the heat and stir in the garlic and the parsley.

This dish may be eaten hot or cold, with a spoonful or more of thick yoghurt. Otherwise, only bread—to mop up the tasty cooking juices.

## ALLELUIA
Serves 6–8 as a side dish

*Aleluja* (Slovenian)

Today few young Slovenes would have heard of Aleluja, a dish of fresh or dried turnips thickened with flour or *kaša* (p. 50) and enriched with cream or pork cracklings. But in the sixteenth century, the population of Slovenia survived during the great famine caused by the Turkish invasions by eating slices of dried turnip cooked to a kind of purée or porridge without any fat. Until the beginning of World War One, Aleluja was still a common dish, and country women sold dried turnips in the open-air market of Ljubljana. This simple version comes from the town of Ribnica nearby.

Pork cracklings are a by-product of lard making—well fried scraps of pork fat.

100 g millet • 400 ml hot meat stock–preferably one in which ham or gammon has been cooked • 1 kg turnip (or swede, if you prefer), thinly sliced • salt and pepper • pouring cream or crackling to garnish

Simmer the millet in the stock for about 30 minutes or until soft and all the stock is absorbed. Separately, cook the turnip (or swede) in slightly salted simmering water for about 30 minutes until tender. Drain and mash or purée in a food processor. Combine with the millet, season to taste, and cook the mixture for a further 2–3 minutes. Serve with pouring cream or cracklings on the table to hand around.

## BORANI: TOMATOES WITH RICE
Serves 4 as a main course, or 9 as a cold table dish

*Domate me oriz* (Albanian); *domati s oriz* (Bulgarian); *tomatórizo* or *mpouraní* (Greek); *domati so oriz* (Macedonian); *paradajz* or *rajčice s pirinčom* (Serbo-Croat)

*Borani* is an old Persian dish of fried aubergines, though nowadays the word describes a composition of raw or boiled vegetables mixed with yoghurt. It is thought to have been named after Purandokht—daughter of the Sassanid king Khusru Parviz, and the first woman to rule Persia, albeit for a short time (AD 629–631).

Early in its history the dish spread into the Muslim world, and meat was added to the recipe. The Turks brought it to the Balkans, and they further developed it by adding rice or home-processed bulgur wheat. The names attest its spread: *buranija* in Bosnian, *bouraniya* in Bulgarian, *mpouraní* in Greek, and *borani* in Turkish.

Once in the Balkans, however, due to a confusion of words, *borani* was restored to a purely vegetable dish; the name was taken to mean something made with green or other edible plants since *bouren*, *bouryan* or *bouran* in most Slavonic tongues designates a weed, herb or vegetable. *Bouraniya* seems to have been a familiar dish in Bulgaria because it appears in the 1905 volume of Najden Gerov's *Dictionary* where it is defined as a 'thick vegetable purée' and 'a dish of cabbage or a leafy vegetable cooked with rice'. The name is still preserved in a few Balkan country districts and in Greece, though today, it is simply called spinach, or sauerkraut, or tomatoes (but not aubergine) with rice.

The Bosnian *buranija* is entirely different and much closer to the Persian original. Prepared from a single vegetable (except aubergine) by baking or frying, it contains no rice and is served with yoghurt often flavoured with crushed garlic.

400 g onions, finely chopped • 1 green or yellow pepper, diced small •
2 tablespoons sunflower oil • 2–3 cloves garlic, finely chopped • 2 teaspoons paprika •
600 g fresh or tinned peeled tomatoes, finely chopped (and, if you wish, passed through a sieve to remove the seeds) • 200 g round-grain rice • 1 teaspoon salt •
1 teaspoon freshly ground black pepper •
2 tablespoons each finely chopped parsley and dill leaves (or 1 teaspoon dried mint) •
2 tablespoons olive oil • 1 teaspoon melted butter or oil

Put the onion and pepper into a heavy-based saucepan with the oil to cook slowly, covered with a lid, until softened but not coloured. Add the garlic and paprika, then stir in the tomatoes and cook the mixture for 5 minutes. Add the rice and 250 ml water and simmer over the lowest possible heat for about 30 minutes or until all the liquid has been absorbed and the mixture is very thick. Add the salt about 5 minutes before the end of the cooking time, when the rice is already tender. Remove from the heat and mix in the ground pepper, herbs and olive oil. Taste for seasoning.

Transfer the mixture to a 20 cm square dish or stainless steel pan, lightly oiled, and spread it out evenly. Bake in an oven preheated to 190°C/375°F/gas 5 for about 35 minutes, until browned on top. Remove and brush with melted butter or oil to make the surface shiny. Leave to cool and firm up, then cut into diamonds or squares. Serve cold, with a scattering of parsley sprigs and black olives.

## COURGETTES WITH RICE

Serves 4 as a main course, 8 as a vegetable accompaniment, or 12 as a cold-table dish

*Tikvichki s oriz* (Bulgarian); *tikvichki so oriz* (Macedonian); *tikvice s pirincem* (Serbo-Croat)

This recipe also belongs to the Balkan *borani* group.

300 g onions, finely chopped, or spring onions, chopped (including the green parts) •
2–3 cloves garlic, finely chopped, or 2–3 spring-garlic plants, chopped (green leaves discarded) • 2 tablespoons sunflower oil • 2 teaspoons paprika •
400 g fresh or tinned peeled tomatoes, chopped •
1.2 kg courgettes (peeled or scraped only if they are too large), sliced into rounds •
1 teaspoon salt • 200 g round-grain rice • a good grinding of black pepper •
2 tablespoons each of chopped dill leaves and parsley • 2 tablespoons olive oil •
1–2 teaspoons melted butter or vegetable oil

Soften the onion and garlic in oil, add the paprika and tomatoes and simmer for about 5 minutes. Then stir in the sliced courgettes, season with the salt and cook gently for 10–15 minutes to draw out their juices. Add the rice and simmer over the lowest possible heat, stirring often, for about 45 minutes, until the rice is tender and the mixture thick. Remove from the heat and stir in the pepper, dill, parsley and the olive oil. Spread the mixture out in a thick layer in a baking dish or pan and bake in a preheated oven (190°C/375°F/gas 5) for about 35 minutes, or until pale brown. Brush with melted butter or oil and leave to cool. Serve warm or cold, garnished with dill and olives. Thick, plain yoghurt goes well with this dish.

> Out in the big open spaces, in a glory of golden light, were piled tons of grapes, peaches, melons, pumpkins, gourds, glowing heaps of scarlet and orange tomatoes, shiny paprikas, yellow, green and red, black purple patajans (aubergines), long green bamias, cabbage, lettuces, beans, in Arabian Nights profusion.
>
> M. Edith Durham, *High Albania*, 1909.

## RICE AND POTATO CASSEROLE
Serves 4–5 as accompaniment to cooked meat, or 2–3 as a main course dish with salad

*Piryan s kartofi* (Bulgarian)

The Bulgarian word *piryan* (*pirjan* in Bosnian and Serbo-Croat), derived from the Persian word *biryan,* designates many kinds of thick stews made with rice and vegetables. *Biryan* reached the Balkans probably during the late Middle Ages, but grew away from the highly spiced Persian prototype and, in Bulgaria, disposed of meat altogether. In Bosnia and Hercegovina the stew is supplemented by meat, poultry or lights and liver. The meatless versions are acidulated with garlic-flavoured vinegar and often finished off in the oven to make them even thicker.

This casserole is found in Smolyan in the Rhodope Mountains and the eastern part of the Danubian Plain. Bulgarians who like a pronounced garlic flavour use 5 or more crushed garlic cloves, mixed with the vinegar, diluted with a tablespoon of water, and poured over the dish about 5 minutes before baking is complete.

There are two related dishes: the Macedonian *tavche so kompiri* (potato casserole), and Albanian *tavë me patate dhe oriz* (casserole with potatoes and rice).

3 tablespoons sunflower oil • 300 g onions, chopped • 250 g potatoes, peeled and cut into 1.5 cm dice • 100 g round-grain rice • 1/2 teaspoon salt • 1 teaspoon paprika • 1 clove garlic, peeled, crushed with a pinch of salt in a mortar • 1 teaspoon wine vinegar • 250 g tomatoes, 2 sliced into thin rounds, the remainder chopped finely • 1 tablespoon finely chopped parsley • freshly ground black pepper • 15 g butter

Heat the oil in a saucepan, stir in the onion and cover. Keeping the heat fairly low, leave the onion to sweat, stirring from time to time, until it is soft and just beginning to colour. Stir in the potato, rice, salt and paprika, and add 375 ml warm water. Simmer for 20 minutes, until the rice and potatoes are tender but slightly firm to the bite. Remove from the heat and adjust the seasoning to taste.

Now stir in the crushed garlic mixed with the vinegar, the chopped tomatoes, parsley and a good grinding of pepper. Pour this mixture into a greased baking dish of about 20 cm diameter, smoothing the surface with the back of a spoon. Place a slice of tomato in the centre and arrange the remainder in a circle around the edge of the dish. Dot the surface with butter. Bake in a preheated oven (200°C/400°F/gas 6), on a high shelf, for about 45 minutes, until the tomatoes are lightly browned and all the liquid has been absorbed. Serve warm or cold with cold meats, beefburgers or a salad.

## SHEPHERD'S CASSEROLE
Serves 4

*Choban gyuvech* (Bulgarian), from the Turkish *çoban*, shepherd and *güveç*, casserole; *ovcharska tava* (Macedonian)

100 g spinach, or any edible wild greens such as Good King Henry (*Chenopodium bonus-henricus*), fat hen (*Chenopodium album*), purslane (*Portulaca oleracea*) or orach (*Artiplex hortensis*) • 50 g butter • 100 g fine rusk crumbs •
150 g sirene (feta) cheese, soaked for about 2 hours, drained, coarsely crumbled •
5 eggs • 250 ml strained, full-fat yoghurt, freshly made or pasteurized • 250 ml milk

Slice the spinach (or wild greens of your choice) into strips and cook in 25 g of the butter, covered, until limp, then chop it up. Put it into a round 23 cm baking dish greased with 15 g of the butter, and stir in the rusk crumbs and the cheese.

In a bowl, beat the eggs lightly, then beat in the yoghurt and milk. Pour this over the spinach mixture, dot with the remaining butter and bake in a preheated oven (180°C/350°F/gas 4) for about 50 minutes, or until set and golden brown on top. Allow to cool a little in the oven with the heat switched off and the door open, then serve warm with bread and salad.

## BLACK OLIVE PURÉE
Serves 4

*Pyure ot maslini* (Bulgarian); *pire od crnih maslina* (Serbo-Croat)

This piquant purée is used as an accompaniment to fried vegetables, poached fish, cold meats, baked beans, or spread on buttered bread or toast.

100 g black olives, well washed, stones removed (with a cherry stoner) •
25 g crustless bread, moistened with wine or water and squeezed dry •
25 g unsalted butter(or 1 tablespoon olive oil) • 1/2 medium onion, finely chopped •
2 teaspoons lemon juice

Pound to a paste the olives and bread in a mortar, then pound in the butter —or the oil, drop by drop, as if for mayonnaise. Stir in the chopped onion and then lemon juice to taste. A quicker way is to blend all the ingredients in a food processor. If you are using oil rather than butter, add it through the feeder tube drop by drop. Store, covered, in the refrigerator.

## BAKED BROCCOLI WITH EGGS AND CHEESE
This is right for a single serving; to make more, increase the ingredients proportionately.

*Zapekanka ot brokoli* (Bulgarian); *koh od brokola* (Serbo-Croat, from the German *kochen*, to cook)

Broccoli is little grown in the Balkans; when available, it is considered a delicacy.

125 g fresh or frozen broccoli florets, cooked in boiling salted water for 4–6 minutes, or until slightly underdone, then drained • 15 g unsalted butter, melted •
50 g white cheese, such as Cheshire or Lancashire, finely diced or crumbled
*Batter*
1 egg • 1 tablespoon plain flour • 2 tablespoons milk or thin cream • 1 large pinch salt • freshly ground black pepper
*Topping*
15 g hard cheese, such as Cheddar, coarsely grated • a small knob of butter

Butter an individual ovenproof bowl of about 350 ml capacity. Put the broccoli in it, stir in the melted butter and the white cheese. Separately, lightly beat the egg with a spoon, then blend with the flour, milk or cream and season with salt and pepper. Pour this batter over the broccoli mixture. Top with the grated cheese and dot the surface with flakes of butter.

Bake in a preheated oven (180°C/350°F/gas 4), on a shelf set reasonably high, for 30 minutes or until golden brown. Serve warm or hot, but not piping hot.


## AUBERGINES STUFFED WITH ONION AND GARLIC: IMAM BAYILDI
Serves 4 as a first course

*Imam bajaldë* (Albanian); *imam bajildi* (Bosnian, Macedonian); *imam bayaldu* (Bulgarian); *imám baildí* (Greek); *imam baildi* (Serbian); from Turkish *imam bayıldı*

The Turks allow no priest between themselves and Allah, and an imam is simply a leader in public worship rather than a priest. Whether he fainted (*bayılmak*, meaning to faint or swoon) because he gorged himself to repletion, or whether he was just passionately fond (*bayıle*) of this dish is still open to question. However, one thing is certain: this unique Turkish dish has become part of the national tradition of all Balkan countries.

2 long, thin aubergines, about 300 g each (round, plump ones are unsuitable) • salt •
100 ml sunflower oil or olive oil, or a combination of the two
*Filling*
300 g onions, peeled and halved, then finely sliced into semicircles •
100 g carrots, finely shredded •
100 g piece of celeriac or parsnip, peeled and finely shredded •
50 g garlic, peeled and thickly sliced •
200 g ripe, peeled tomatoes, fresh or tinned, chopped • salt and pepper •
1–2 tablespoons finely chopped parsley
*Topping*
2 tomatoes, cut into 8 thin slices, with skin on • 2 tablespoons sunflower oil or olive oil

Cut off the green leaves or sepals round the stem of each aubergine, but leave the stems on. Peel lengthwise strips of skin at intervals, then halve each vegetable lengthwise through the stem. Make a deep slit on the cut surface of each half, leaving a bit of uncut flesh at both ends. Sprinkle generously with salt and leave the aubergines to sweat for at least 4–5 hours or overnight to allow the bitter juices to drain away. Rinse in cold water, drain and squeeze them dry with your hands.

Heat the oil in a frying pan and brown the aubergine halves on both sides. Drain them on absorbent kitchen paper.

In a covered pan, gently fry the onions, carrot and celeriac in the remaining oil until soft (about 25 minutes), then add the garlic and cook without the lid until the vegetables are slightly coloured. Add the tomatoes and a little salt and continue cooking, until all the tomato juice has evaporated. Draw off the heat and stir in pepper and the parsley.

Arrange the fried aubergines, cut-side up, in a baking dish just large enough to contain them side by side. Cover each one with a quarter of the filling, piled into a smooth dome. Place two tomato slices on each. Spoon over the two tablespoons of oil, and pour a little hot water in the dish.

Bake the aubergines in a preheated oven (200°C/400°F/gas 6) for 25–30 minutes, or until the tomato slices are slightly browned round the edges. Alternatively, arrange the aubergines in a wide and shallow pan and stew them over a moderate heat in two tablespoons of oil and a little water until done—about 45 minutes. Serve them at room temperature, rather than chilled, with soft buns or bread.

## VINE-LEAF ROLLS WITH RICE
Makes 40–45 rolls

*Dollma me fletë hardhije me oriz* (Albanian); *lozovi sarmi s oriz* (Bulgarian); *sarma od lozov list so oriz* (Macedonian); *sarmale cu frunziş de viţă cu orezi* (Romanian); from the Turkish *yaprak sarması*, meaning (vine) leaves wrapped around a filling, and *yaprak dolması*, meaning stuffed leaves. *Lozova jalan sarma* (Bosnian), and *ntolmathákia gialantzí* (Greek), come from the Turkish *yalancı sarma*, meaning false rolls because they are meatless

These little rolls of rice, nuts and raisins wrapped in tender vine-leaves are the jewel of the family of meatless dishes. The first Turkish recipe for them printed in English appeared in London in 1864. Its author was Turabi Effendi (Türâbi Efendi), a learned person who, besides Arabic, had a good knowledge of Turkish, English and French. His recipes were translations, though unacknowledged, from the earliest printed Turkish-language cookery book (*Melceü't-Tabbâhın*, 'Refuge of Cooks', printed in Istanbul in 1844).

Modern Greek cooks supplement the faint acidity of the vine leaves with lemon juice—which masks their delicate aroma; Turabi Effendi, on the other hand, recommends the inclusion of unripe, sour plums, or a small bunch of unripe grapes instead of lemon. He adds, 'they are preferred to lemon when they are in season.'

A variation was published in 1908 in *Prakticheska Gotvarska Kniga*: the sourness of the leaves is reinforced by dry, white wine and under-ripe morello cherries.

When vine leaves are not available, other edible leaves are often used. These include beetroot tops, green cabbage, savoy cabbage, cos lettuce, young hazelnut leaves gathered from the end of May to the middle of June, kohlrabi tops—particularly those of the larger Balkan variety, young tender leaves of the broad-leaved lime tree, leaves of the mallow plant, and of the marshmallow, spinach, sweet dock, and Swiss chard. In contrast to vine leaves, all these benefit from having lemon juice in the cooking liquid.

In our Oxfordshire garden we have planted a hardy *Triomphe d'Alsace* vine flat against a south-facing stone wall. Its foliage is disease-resistant (so it needs no spraying), and we gather young leaves for *sarma* all through the summer months.

If you are using fresh vine leaves you have not grown yourself, before blanching, soak them for a few minutes in a bowl filled with water and a few tablespoons of vinegar to remove any possible chemical spray.

If fresh leaves are not available, substitute 200 g vine leaves preserved in brine. Blanch them in boiling water. Drain and discard the water. Place the leaves in a bowl of cold water and set aside until needed.

50 fresh vine leaves, about 12–13 cm wide, the stems snipped off • salt
*Filling*
150 g long-grained rice, washed and drained in a fine sieve •
350 g onions or spring onions (including the green parts), very finely chopped •
25 g pine nuts or hulled sunflower seeds •
25 g currants or sultanas (or 1–2 teaspoons sugar) • 2 tablespoons mint leaves, chopped •
4 tablespoons parsley leaves, chopped • 6 (or more) tablespoons dill leaves, chopped •
3/4 teaspoon freshly ground black pepper • 1 teaspoon salt •
50 ml olive oil or sunflower oil
*To add after the vine leaves are stuffed*
50 g sour plums, morello cherries, sour grapes or gooseberries (or lemon juice) •
50 ml olive oil or sunflower oil

Wash, then blanch the leaves for less than a minute (or until limp) in boiling water that has been salted to taste. Drain and reserve the water.

Place the blanched leaves in a bowl of cold water to float, so that you can separate them easily. Meanwhile, mix all the filling ingredients together.

To roll the vine leaves, lay each leaf, dull side up, on a flat surface (or the palm of one hand). Put a heaped teaspoon of the filling across the leaf at the stalk-end to take up about half the leaf's width, then fold over the two base lobes and the sides to enclose the filling. Roll the leaf up tightly from the base to form a thin neat roll.

Cover the bottom of a wide and shallow saucepan with a few torn vine leaves. Arrange the rolls, loose end down, in the pan closely packed in circles. If there is to be a second layer, you could cover the one below with a few leaves. Now scatter the dish with the sour fruits (or sprinkle them with lemon juice) and pour over the oil and some of the reserved water which should not quite cover all the rolls. Then place an inverted plate on top to keep the rolls in place. Cover the pan with a tight-fitting lid and simmer until all the liquid has been absorbed, about 50 minutes. Serve them cold as meze, garnished with lemon wedges and parsley, or with yoghurt as the first course of a meal.

## PEPPERS STUFFED WITH RICE
Serves 4

*Speca të mbushura me oriz* (Albanian); *piperki pulneni s oriz* (Bulgarian); *piperki polneti so oriz* (Macedonian); *paprike punjene sa pirinčom* (Serbian)

4 medium stuffing peppers, about 750 g in total • plain flour
*Stuffing*
2 large onions, about 600 g in all, finely chopped • 2 tablespoons vegetable oil •
150 g long-grain rice • 50 g pine nuts or sunflower seeds •
50 g sultanas (or 1 teaspoon sugar) • salt and freshly ground black pepper •
2–3 tablespoons chopped parsley •
1 teaspoon chopped fresh savory (or 1/2 teaspoon dried savory) •
1–2 teaspoons chopped mint leaves (or 1/2 teaspoon dried mint) •
1–2 tablespoons chopped dill
*Cooking liquid*
125 ml tomato juice • 1/2 teaspoon paprika • 2 tablespoons vegetable oil or 25 g butter •
1/4 teaspoon each salt and pepper
egg-and-lemon finishing sauce (p 349)

Cut the tops off the peppers and discard. Remove the cores, seeds and ribs.

To make the stuffing, heat the oil in a saucepan over a low heat and cook the onion, covered, until golden—about 25 minutes. Stir in the rice, then the pine nuts or sunflower seeds and sultanas and add 150 ml water. Cover the pan and simmer for 10–15 minutes, keeping the rice slightly underdone. Season with salt and pepper to taste, then add the herbs.

Arrange the peppers in a saucepan that will hold them upright. Stuff the peppers up to their tops, then dip their tops momentarily in the flour to seal them (the rice mixture will not fall out). Return the peppers to the saucepan, add the tomato juice and paprika, if you like, the oil or butter and enough water to come a third of the way up their sides. Season with the salt and pepper. Simmer for about half an hour or until the rice is tender.

Prepare the egg-and-lemon finishing sauce using the cooking liquid of the peppers—making it up to 500 ml with warm water, if necessary. Pour the sauce mixture around the peppers in the pan and simmer for 1–2 minutes without stirring.

Serve warm, rather than hot. Most people will not want to eat the skin of the pepper, they should leave it on the side of their plate.

# CELERIAC STUFFED LIKE ARTICHOKES
Serves 4

*Tselina kato anginari* (Bulgarian); *telină ca anghinara* (Romanian); *celer kao artišoki* (Croat); all meaning celeriac like artichokes

Like all vegetables cooked in olive oil, this celeriac is excellent when prepared in advance and served cold as a first course. My grandmother would prepare this dish in late autumn when celeriac appeared in the shops. If the root is stuffed with the same filling as an artichoke, it is supposed to taste like artichokes.

4 medium celeriac, each about 200 g • juice of 1 lemon • salt • 125 g good olive oil
*Stuffing*
4–5 (or more) cloves of garlic, peeled and finely chopped • 1/4 teaspoon salt •
1 teaspoon peppercorns, finely crushed • 3–4 tablespoons finely chopped parsley

Peel the celeriac and immerse immediately in water acidulated with lemon juice to prevent discoloration. Scoop out most of the flesh, leaving a 1 cm shell. Chop this flesh finely and mix with all the stuffing ingredients. Season the insides sparingly with salt. Arrange them in a stewpan large enough to hold them upright, and pack them with the stuffing. Add the oil and enough of the acidulated water to barely cover. Simmer over a gentle heat until the celeriac are tender and most of the liquid has been absorbed. Serve warm or cold, in their juices, garnished with wedges of lemon.

## VEGETABLE MACÉDOINE TO SERVE WITH ROAST BEEF
Serves 4–6

*Mešano povrće kao dodatak pečenom mesu* (Serbo-Croat)

25 g butter • 3 medium carrots, cut into 5 mm dice •
2 medium potatoes, cut into 1.5 cm cubes • 1 large celeriac, cut into 1.5 cm cubes •
100 g frozen peas (blanched fresh peas if available) • 1/2 teaspoon salt •
freshly ground black pepper

Melt the butter in a large frying pan over a low heat. Add all the vegetables, and the salt and pepper to taste. Stir the vegetables together, put on a tightly fitting lid and sweat over the lowest possible heat, without browning, for 20 minutes, or until the vegetables are just soft enough to eat but have not lost their firmness. Taste for seasoning and spoon them into an oven-to-table serving dish. Keep warm.

To serve, pour off most of the fat from the pan in which your beef has been roasted. Drizzle the beef pan juices over the vegetables and serve very hot.

## MIXED BRAISED VEGETABLES
Serves 4–6

*Zadoushen smesen zelenchouk* (Bulgarian); *dinstuvan meshan zelenchuk* (Macedonian); *pirjanjeno mešano povrće* (Serbo-Croat)

This and French ratatouille are closely allied.

250 g onions, finely chopped • 50–100 ml sunflower oil or olive oil •
250 g aubergines, peeled, cut into 2 cm cubes, salted, left to stand for 1–2 hours, rinsed and gently squeezed dry •
250 g courgettes, peeled and sliced, salted, left to stand for 1–2 hours, then drained and wiped dry •
250 g red peppers (2 large peppers), seeded and cut into small squares •
3–4 tomatoes, peeled and chopped • 4 cloves garlic, finely chopped •
salt and freshly ground black pepper • 1–2 tablespoons finely chopped parsley

Cook the onions gently in the oil in a large, covered pan for about 20 minutes until they are soft. Add the aubergines, courgettes and peppers and fry them for a further 10 minutes, without the lid, until the vegetables are slightly browned. Stir in the tomatoes and garlic, salt lightly, cover the pan and simmer over a low heat until all the vegetables are tender, and the vegetable juices are reduced to the consistency of thick syrup.

Serve the dish hot, warm or cold, sprinkled with pepper and the parsley. Accompany with hot garlic bread.

## BAKED WHITE CABBAGE
Serves 3–4 as a vegetable

*Byalo zele na fourna* (Bulgarian); *sladak kupus u pećnicu* (Serbo-Croat)

1 tablespoon vegetable oil • 600 g firm white cabbage, finely shredded, core finely chopped • salt • 125 g peeled chopped tomatoes; or thick seeded tomato juice • 1 teaspoon paprika • freshly ground black pepper
*Topping*
2–3 tomatoes, thinly sliced • 1 tablespoon vegetable oil • salt and pepper

Heat the oil in a large frying pan with a lid. Stir in the cabbage, season with a little salt, cover, and cook slowly for 10–15 minutes, stirring occasionally, until the cabbage is limp. Add 2–3 tablespoons water, cover again and continue cooking for about 15 minutes, then mix in the tomatoes. Remove from the heat, season with paprika, a good grinding of pepper and a little more salt, if necessary.

Transfer the mixture to an enamelled casserole, about 21 cm across and even the surface with a spoon. Arrange the sliced tomatoes on the surface, sprinkle them lightly with salt and pepper and dribble the oil over. Bake on a top shelf in a preheated oven (180°C/350°F/gas 4) for 40–45 minutes, or until shreds of the cabbage and the tomato slices are charred around the edges. When cooked this way, the natural sugars of white cabbage caramelize, and give it an appetizing glaze. It is just as tasty cold as hot.

For baked cabbage flavoured with a red pepper, cook the cabbage as above, adding a red pepper cut into squares together with the tomatoes.

For baked cabbage with haricot beans, add 500 g boiled beans (p 105) together with the tomatoes and bake as above. This will serve 4 people as a main course.

## MIXED VEGETABLE CASSEROLE
Serves 4 as a main course, 6–8 as a cold table dish

*Gjuveç pa mish* (Albanian); *tyurlyu gyuvech* (Bulgarian); *tourloú or mpriáni* (Greek); *turli tava* (Macedonian); *ghiveciu cu zarzavaturi* (Romanian); *djuveč bez mesa* (Bosnian, Serbo-Croat); from Turkish *türlü* (*güveç*)

Found throughout the region, this famous dish has many local variations. The Turkish word *türlü* means of all sorts and refers to the mixture of vegetables; *güveç* is the earthenware casserole in which the vegetables are baked; *tava* in Turkish designates a frying pan, but has come to mean a baking pan or dish in Balkan languages.

1 medium aubergine, unpeeled, cut into cubes, sprinkled with salt and left to drain in a colander for 2–3 hours, rinsed and squeezed gently to remove excess moisture •
100 g young okra, stalks carefully pared off without cutting into the pod •
250 g frozen peas (if fresh, pre-cooked in boiling water for 10 minutes) •
250–300 g young green beans, fresh or frozen, trimmed and cut into bite-sized pieces •
4 medium-sized courgettes, unpeeled, sliced into rounds •
2 medium-sized onions, finely chopped •
400 g potatoes, peeled and cut into small chunks •
400 g peeled fresh or canned tomatoes, chopped •
1 large green pepper, seeded and cut into squares •
1 large bunch parsley, chopped • 2–3 teaspoons salt • 2 teaspoons paprika •
5–6 tablespoons vegetable oil • 4–5 tomatoes, sliced into rounds (for topping)

Keep the sliced tomatoes on one side, but put all the other vegetables and the parsley in a large earthenware casserole or terrine, about 30 cm in diameter and about 9 cm deep. Season with salt and paprika and pour over 4 tablespoons of the oil.

Mix all the ingredients thoroughly. Arrange the tomato rounds on top. Sprinkle with the remaining oil and smooth the surface with the back of a spoon.

Bake in a pre-heated oven (190°C/375°F/gas mark 5) for about 60 to 75 minutes, until the tomatoes on top have browned. There should be only a little sauce left in the casserole. Serve in the cooking dish either hot or cold, with a cucumber salad and fresh bread.

*The Garden Crop*

# MACEDONIAN BAKED BEANS
Serves 4–5

*Tavche gravche* (Macedonian)

If you were to visit Macedonia and stroll around an open-air market, as I did in Ohrid a few summers ago, you would be sure to hear over the bustle the mysterious sing-song chant of a village seller: 'Tavche za gravche...Tavche za gravche...' (Baking dish for beans...Baking dish for beans...). Among the warm-brown earthenware spread on the ground are lidless casseroles, straw coloured on the inside, unglazed outside, in which this national dish is cooked.

This version comes from the town of Tetovo—renowned for the production of the best dried haricot beans in Macedonia.

> 500 g large white haricot beans, not more than a year old (the nearest to the Tetovo varieties of dried beans are the Italian cannellini) • 1 red chilli pepper, fresh or dried
> *Enrichment sauce*
> 500 g onions, finely chopped • 3 tablespoons vegetable oil • 1 teaspoon paprika • 2–3 peeled garlic cloves, chopped • freshly-ground black pepper • 1 teaspoon salt • 1 teaspoon (or more) mint leaves, chopped
> *Topping*
> Tomato rounds • 2–3 long, red salad peppers, fresh (or dried, soaked for a few hours) • 1 teaspoon flour • 2 tablespoons vegetable oil • flat parsley and mint, finely chopped

Soak the beans overnight in plenty of cold water. Drain and cover with fresh water. Boil rapidly for 10–15 minutes, skimming. Drain again and discard the cooking liquid. Empty them into a heavy pan, add the chilli pepper and just enough boiling water to cover the beans. Simmer until the beans are soft but still intact—about 45 minutes to 1 hour, depending on their age. Transfer to a larger casserole, about 24 cm in diameter. Discard the chilli pepper.

In a large covered frying pan, sweat the onions in the hot oil, until soft; uncover, and cook them until lightly browned. Off the heat, stir in the paprika, chopped garlic (if you are fond of it), pepper, salt and mint, and add a little hot water to make a sauce. Pour the sauce over the beans and mix them together carefully.

Arrange the topping of tomatoes and peppers in a pattern on the surface. Sprinkle all over with the flour, and then with the oil. Bake in a preheated oven at 160°C/325°F/gas 3 for at least one hour. If the beans dry up before the end of the cooking time, add a little more hot water. Serve from the casserole, with chopped parsley and mint sprinkled over the top, accompanied by a side dish of pickled red peppers or gherkins, and bread.

## BAKED COURGETTES
Serves 2–3

*Kungulleshka të pjekura* (Albanian); *tikvichki pecheni* (Bulgarian; Macedonian); *tikvice pečene* (Serbo-Croat)

3 large courgettes (or young marrows), each weighing about 400 g, lightly scraped and cut into 5 mm slices •
salt • 2 tablespoons fine rusk crumbs (or fine Matzo meal) • 1/2 teaspoon paprika •
1 1/2 tablespoons vegetable oil, or 25 g unsalted butter, melted •
yoghurt and garlic sauce (p. 347)

Sprinkle the sliced courgettes lightly with salt and leave to drain in a colander for 3–4 hours. Arrange in an oiled shallow pan, about 30 cm across, overlapping each other, in concentric circles working from the centre outwards. Combine the crumbs with the paprika and sieve over the courgettes, then dribble oil or melted butter.

Bake in a preheated oven (240°C/475°F/gas 9), on a high shelf, for 60 to 90 minutes, or until browned. Halfway through, press them down lightly with the back of a spoon to help extract the juices. Check the seasoning.

Serve cold (or warm, if cooked in butter), with the yoghurt and garlic sauce.

## PANCAKES STUFFED WITH VEGETABLES
Serves 6 as a starter, 3 as a main course

*Vegetarianska drob-sarma* (Bulgarian, meaning vegetarian lamb's pluck parcels); *palačinke nadevene povrćem* (Serbo-Croat, meaning pancakes stuffed with vegetables)

6 pancakes, lightly fried then stacked to keep soft (p. 254)
*Mixed vegetable stuffing*
15 g butter • 50 g onion, finely chopped • 50 g carrot, peeled and diced to the size of a pea •
25 g piece of celeriac, or 1/2 a parsnip, peeled and diced to the size of a pea •
50 g green beans, fresh or frozen, cut into julienne strips the size of matchsticks •
25 g frozen peas (blanched if fresh) • 1/2 teaspoon salt • 25 g round-grain or risotto rice •
300 g potatoes, peeled and cut into 1 cm cubes • 1 tablespoon vegetable oil •
1/2 tablespoon each of chopped mint or dill and parsley; or 1/4 teaspoon dried sage •
a little freshly ground black pepper • a little paprika • 15 g melted butter for brushing the tops
*Cheese sauce*
Half the quantity of the recipe for all-in-one cheese sauce on page 342

First prepare the pancakes and set them aside. Next, make the stuffing. Heat the butter in a heavy-based saucepan with a tight-fitting lid. Add the vegetables (except the potatoes) in sequence to the pan, at about 3 minute intervals, cooking gently over a low heat. Then add 2 tablespoons of water and the salt and simmer until the vegetables are tender. Remove from the heat.

Meanwhile, boil the rice in water for about 10 minutes, then drain and add to the vegetables. Fry the cubed potatoes in the tablespoon of oil, preferably in a non-stick frying pan, then stir them, together with the herbs and black pepper, into the vegetable and rice mixture.

To stuff the pancakes, place each one in a small bowl or soup ladle, put a sixth of the stuffing in, and wrap the edges of the pancake over the stuffing to make a neat, round parcel.

Butter a baking dish of a size to just contain them. Pour a little of the cheese sauce to barely cover the bottom of the dish, then arrange the filled pancakes, with the folded edges downwards, over the sauce. Sprinkle a little paprika over their tops and brush them with the melted butter. Bake the pancakes in a preheated oven (150°C/300°F/gas 2) for 15 minutes until light-brown. Pour over the remainder of the cheese sauce and continue cooking at the same temperature for a few more minutes until the surface starts to bubble. Serve immediately.

Pancakes stuffed with mushrooms are called *vegetarianska drob-sarma s qubi* in Bulgarian, meaning vegetarian lamb's pluck parcels with mushrooms. They are made in the same way as the preceding recipe except they are stuffed with mushrooms, not mixed vegetables.

*Mushroom stuffing*
15 g butter • 50 g peeled onion, finely chopped • 200 g mushrooms, chopped •
15 g round-grain or risotto rice • 100 g potato, peeled, cut into 1 cm cubes •
1 tablespoon vegetable oil • 1/4 teaspoon each of salt and black pepper

To prepare the stuffing, sweat the onions and mushrooms in butter, covered, for about 10 minutes before adding the rice. Then continue cooking over a slightly higher heat for another 20–25 minutes until nearly all the juices have evaporated and the rice is tender. Remove from the heat. Fry the cubed potato in the oil then stir it into the mushroom mixture. Season with salt and pepper to taste.

In the *ograten ot razni zelenchoutsi* (Bulgarian), or *gratinirano mešano povrće* (Serbian), both terms meaning gratinated mixed vegetables, from the French *gratin*, mixed vegetables are cooked in just the same way as they are for stuffing pancakes, but they are simply spooned into a buttered baking dish, cheese sauce is poured over them and then they are topped with 25 g fresh breadcrumbs mixed with 25 g grated cheese before grilling to a toast-brown gratin crust.

You can add other vegetables, such as red or green peppers, tomatoes, artichokes, and even boiled pasta to the vegetable medley with good results.

## THRACIAN TOMATO CASSEROLE
Serves 4–5 as a vegetable dish

*Trakijski gyuvech* (Bulgarian)

This comes from Thrace in southern Bulgaria. It is eaten as a main course at harvest-time and also during the three hottest days of the year—known by the farming population as *goreshnitsite* (15th, 16th, and 17th July).

2–3 tablespoons chopped parsley •
1.2 kg ripe tomatoes, unpeeled, cut into thin slices, discarding the first and last slices •
1/4 teaspoon salt • 1 teaspoon sugar •
50 g rusks, ground into coarse crumbs • 40 ml sunflower oil • 1/2 teaspoon paprika

Lightly oil a roasting pan or ovenproof dish handsome enough to be shown at table, measuring about 55 by 37 cm, and scatter the parsley over the bottom. Arrange the tomato slices over the parsley in one layer, slightly overlapping each other, in rows. Sprinkle with the salt and sugar.

Put the rusk crumbs in a small bowl, add oil and the paprika, if you are using it, and mix thoroughly with a fork. Scatter the crumb mixture over the tomatoes. Bake in a preheated oven (200°C/400°F/gas 6) for about 50 minutes, or until most of the tomato juices have evaporated and the crumbs are lightly browned.

Serve it cold as an accompaniment to cold meats, game or poultry.

# FRIED COURGETTES
Serves 7–8 as a starter, 5–6 as a main course

*Kungulleshka të skuqura* (Albanian); *purzheni tikvichki* (Bulgarian); *kolokithákia tiganitá* (Greek); *prženi tikvichki* (Macedonian); *pržene tikvice* (Serbo-Croat); *kabak tavası* (Turkish)

If you like them better, you can substitute aubergines for the courgettes. Using two frying pans reduces the time spent frying and prevents the oil from browning too much.

1 kg medium-sized courgettes or young marrows no more than 18 cm long, lightly scraped and cut either lengthwise into strips, or crosswise into rounds 4 mm thick •
plain flour for dredging •
yoghurt and garlic sauce (p. 347), or walnut and garlic sauce (p. 346) •
a few sprigs of dill, finely chopped

Sprinkle the sliced courgettes with salt and leave to drain in a colander for a few hours, then rinse out under running cold water. Drain, but do not wipe them dry—a slight moistness helps the coating to adhere.

Dredge the courgettes with flour. Heat enough oil in two frying pans to cover their bases well and fry the courgettes in a single layer over no more than medium heat so that they colour lightly and evenly on either side without burning.

Arrange the fried courgettes, overlapping, on individual plates, spoon across them a band of either yoghurt and garlic or walnut and garlic sauce, dribble over the top a little of the aromatic oil in which the courgettes were cooked, and sprinkle all over with a little of the chopped dill.

Serve at room temperature, with bread.

## FRIED PEPPERS STUFFED WITH CHEESE
Serves 2 as a light lunch or supper dish

*Piperki pulneni sus sirene* (Bulgarian); *piperki polneti so sirenje* (Macedonian); *paprike nadevene sa sirom* (Serbo-Croat)

4 long single-tipped salad peppers without grooves, baked under a hot grill until the skins are charred, wrapped in a plastic bag or newspaper and left to stand for an hour
*Filling*
1 small egg (or one large egg yolk), beaten with a fork • 75 g feta cheese (or another white cheese such as Lancashire or Cheshire) mashed with a fork to a paste •
1–2 tablespoons chopped parsley
*Coating*
plain flour, spread out on a plate •
1 small egg, beaten with a fork and poured on to another plate

Peel the grilled peppers and, with a sharp knife, slit each one lengthwise on one side, and spread it open like a book. Remove the cores and seeds, but leave the stalks intact.

Blend the filling ingredients together and spread a quarter over one half of each pepper. Fold the other half over the top, then brush the outsides with water. Dip them first in the flour, then in the beaten egg and finish the coating by dipping them again in the flour.

Fry the stuffed peppers over a low heat, in enough mixed butter and oil to generously cover the bottom of the pan. Cook until the filling has set. Serve either hot, perhaps with fried potatoes, or cold with a cucumber and tomato salad.

## FRIED PEPPERS WITH TOMATO SAUCE
Serves 4

*Panirani pecheni piperki* (Bulgarian); *pohuvani pecheni piperki* (Macedonian); *paniranje pečene parike* (Serbian); all meaning roasted peppers fried with a coating, deriving from the French term *pané*—coated with breadcrumbs before frying

8 long, fleshy salad peppers, grilled and skinned, stalks left on, each pepper slit on one side and seed core carefully cut out • 3 eggs • plain flour • 50 g any white cheese, crumbled with a fork • quick tomato sauce made with tinned tomatoes (p. 345)

Beat the eggs lightly with a fork in a soup plate. Spread the flour on a large sheet of greaseproof paper. Holding each pepper by its stalk, dip into the beaten egg and then lay it on the flour. With the help of the paper, roll the pepper to and fro to coat it completely. Then finish the coating by slipping the pepper into the egg again.

Heat enough oil or clarified butter to cover generously the bottom of a large frying pan. Arrange the peppers with their tips towards the centre, their stalks sticking out of the pan, and fry them over a moderate heat until golden brown on both sides. Pour any remaining egg into the centre of the pan, sprinkle the cheese over the egg and cook for a few moments longer until the egg is set. Serve immediately directly from the pan. Hand round the tomato sauce separately.

## SPINACH CAKES
Makes 8

*Qofte me spinaq* (Albanian); *kyufteta ot spanak* (Bulgarian); *chiftele de spanac* (Romanian); *ćufteta od spanaća* (Serbian); from Turkish *köfte*, fried meatball, from the Persian

Other vegetables, such as Swiss chard, cabbage and cauliflower, can be prepared in the same way.

500 g spinach or perpetual spinach beet, cleaned weight, sliced into strips, stalks chopped finely • pinch salt • 1 large or 2 small eggs, unbeaten •
15 g fine toasted breadcrumbs •
15 g kashkaval, mature Cheddar or Gruyère cheese, diced small, or Cheshire cheese, coarsely crumbled • freshly ground black pepper

Cook the spinach with a tablespoon of water in a pan with the lid on until tender, then drain well, squeeze out the excess water and chop it finely.

Combine the spinach, the unbeaten egg or eggs, toasted breadcrumbs, cheese and a little black pepper in a bowl. Divide the mixture into 8 small mounds, roll each one into a ball, then flatten into a round. Fry the spinach cakes over a moderate heat in oil until brown on both sides. Serve hot or at room temperature with yoghurt flavoured with a little crushed garlic, and fresh bread.

To reheat the cakes, arrange them in a buttered roasting pan, place a small thick slice of cheese over each one and bake in a preheated oven (150°C/300°F/gas 2) for 7–8 minutes, until the cheese just melts and the cakes are heated through.

## SPINACH AND POTATO CAKES
Serves 3–4 as a light main course

These are a popular variation on spinach cakes.

200 g peeled potatoes, cut into chunks • 15 g butter • 300 g spinach or perpetual spinach beet, sliced into strips, the stalks chopped finely • 1 large egg, beaten • 75 g white cheese, such as Cheshire or Lancashire, crumbled, or 50 g feta, crumbled • 1 tablespoon flour • freshly ground pepper • salt

Boil the potatoes in lightly salted water until tender. Drain well, add the butter and mash together to a thick purée. Leave to cool.

Meanwhile, put the prepared spinach into a saucepan, cover and cook without adding any water, until tender. Drain, chop roughly and squeeze out excess moisture.

When the spinach is completely cold, add the mashed potato, beaten egg, cheese, flour, pepper and a little salt. Mix thoroughly and refrigerate until needed.

Just before serving, shape the mixture into 12 thin, flattened cakes. Dip each one in flour. Fry the cakes over a moderate heat, in batches, in enough oil to generously cover the bottom of the pan, until well browned on either side.

Serve the cakes immediately, or keep them hot in a slow oven until ready to serve. Plain yoghurt or a salad and hot garlic bread are the best accompaniments.


## POTATO CAKES
Makes 8–12

*Qofte patatesh* (Albanian); *kartofeni kyufteta* (Bulgarian); *Koftinja od kompiri* (Macedonian); *ćufteta od krompira* (Serbian); *patates köftesi* (Turkish)

500 g peeled weight, baked potatoes • 25 g butter • salt • 1 egg • about 150 g plain flour

Mash the hot potatoes with the butter and salt to taste, then mash in the egg. Stir in the flour gradually and knead to form a stiff yet pliable dough. Refrigerate until you are ready to cook the cakes. Divide the dough into 8–12 pieces. Pat each one into a flat, thin round with floured hands. Heat a little oil in a large frying pan, and fry the potato cakes, a few at a time, until browned on both sides. Keep hot.

Serve the potato cakes with a tomato sauce, meat sauce, gravy, or the cooking juices of a pot roast.

# CHAPTER VIII

# Cheese and Eggs

## MELTED CHEESE: PASTORAL FOOD FROM ALPINE PASTURES

Tradition and traditional cookery have survived far longer in the mountains, insulated from change to a greater extent than the more prosperous lowlands. Some of the most interesting milk dishes are made by shepherds during the summer, when the flocks are driven to high pastures above the tree line. They live there during the ewes' lactation—from May into October, and sustenance consists mainly of dairy products and bread or cornmeal porridge.

Melted cheese is one of these mountain dishes, but as a town child I had always associated it with 'Dyado' (grandfather) Dimitrov—an elderly agronomist, my father's friend of many years standing, who was then head of the Russe agricultural research station Obraztsov Chiflic (which was known in Turkish times as *Nümune Çiftliği* or Model Farm).

On one of our visits Dyado Dimitrov brought out as a treat a plateful of melted cheese produced in the station's experimental kitchen. The yellowish cubes were unlike any we had ever tasted before—chewy, salt free, with an elusive edge of sweetness; very tasty. It came as a surprise to learn that this cheese bore the strange name of *Byal Muzh*, literally 'White Man'. I can remember puzzling over the name, for there was nothing to suggest the shape or colour of a man.

Years later I tumbled to the fact that it was really a corruption of *balmoush* or *belmush*; and that, on philological grounds, *balmoush* appears to have been a Turkic dish brought by the Bulgar-Turks in seventh century AD from the heartland of Asia—long before the Ottomans reintroduced it after their conquest of the Balkans.

*Balmoush*, also known as *oshmara* (Turkish *hoşmerim*) is traditionally prepared by shepherds in the Rhodope on St Peter's Day, 29th June, or as a treat to welcome any passing traveller. It is made from fresh unsalted sheep's cheese, melted and thickened with a little maize or wheat flour. It can be sweetened or lightly salted, and may be served hot, or shaped into a slab and cut into pieces when cool. This is similar to the Hungarian *bálmos* and the Turkish *belmuş*, while the cornmeal *balmoş* or *balmuş* of rural Romania is a mush-like variation enriched with sheep's milk and sheep's milk butter.

The melted-cheese recipes which follow resemble also another mountain food—the Swiss fondue; but Balkan versions are served individually in small heated earthenware bowls—not in one pot. They can be offered as a first course or as an impromptu supper along with tea or dry white wine, and fresh warm rolls. Melted cheese is usually eaten with a spoon, but if you prefer, pieces of bread can be speared on a fork, dipped into the bowl and eaten fondue-fashion.

## BOSNIAN FONDUE
Serves 5

*Karacoca*

*Kara* in Turkish means black, Coca is a Bosnian and Macedonian woman's name. This recipe is from the southern mountains of Bosnia. You can substitute white Stilton, white Cheshire or Lancashire for the feta. The dish can be served with hot rolls but it is also delicious poured over pasta or baked potatoes.

50 g unsalted butter, cut into pieces • 500 g *sir* (feta) cheese, crumbled •
125 ml double cream

Heat 5 small earthenware bowls in a slow oven at 130°C/250°F/gas 1/2. Meanwhile, put the butter, cheese and cream into a heavy saucepan and melt over the lowest possible heat, stirring continuously. Do not allow the mixture to boil or the cream may curdle. Serve immediately in the bowls.

## SLOVENIAN MELTED CHEESE WITH BACON
Serves 5

*Friko* (Slovenian)

From pastoral villages nestling deep in the Julian Alps, comes this simple supper dish made with local cheeses such as *skuta*—an unsalted whey cheese and/or *tolmins*, a hard cheese of the Emmenthal type. Ricotta, white Cheshire or Emmenthal can be used instead.

400 g streaky bacon, rind removed •
500g *skuta* or *tolmins* cheese, cut into small cubes; or a combination of the two.

Cut the bacon into small dice and fry in a dry pan over low heat until the fat runs and the bacon is crisp. Pour off the fat and add the cheese. As it melts, stir continuously, scraping the pan to keep the mixture from sticking. Serve immediately spooned over hot polenta (p. 216) or bread dumplings (p. 228).

## BULGARIAN MELTED CHEESE
Serves 4 as a supper dish, 5 as a snack

*Sindirme*

This is a simple dish, cooked in a matter of minutes, that is found in the villages around Plovdiv in southern Bulgaria. White Cheshire, white Stilton, Wensleydale or Caerphilly may be used instead of feta, and Cheddar in place of kashkaval.

75g unsalted butter •
250 g sirene (feta) cheese, crumbled, or kashkaval cheese, cut into small cubes •
125g plain flour

Melt the butter in a thick-based saucepan over a low heat. Add the cheese, and when completely melted, stir in the flour. Pour in 250 ml water and continue to cook, stirring constantly, for 2-3 minutes until it is thick and porridge-like. Serve hot in small, heated, earthenware bowls, with hot rolls or wholewheat bread.

I have a little barrel half full of red wine, half full of white wine, yet the wines don't get mixed together. Guess what this is.
[An egg]

*Balkan riddle*

## CHEESE GRILLED IN PAPER PARCELS
Serves 2

*Sirene pecheno v hartishka* (Bulgarian); *sir pečen u hartiju* (Serbian)

This can be served as an accompaniment to drinks, or with tea and toast for breakfast.

150 g sirene or feta cheese, cut into 2 thick slices • 25 g unsalted butter, melted • paprika

Place one slice of cheese on a sheet of greaseproof paper, about 25 x 20 cm, or large enough to wrap it. Brush cheese and paper with some of the melted butter. Make a neat parcel. Repeat with the second slice. Cook the parcels under a preheated grill for about 3 minutes, turning once, or barbecue about 10 centimetres above a bed of ash-covered embers. However you do it, the paper should be well branded by the hot bars of the rack, but not burnt.

When cooked, open the parcels and toss each slice on to a small heated plate. Sprinkle with the remaining butter heated with a pinch or two of paprika and serve immediately with hot rolls or toast.

## FRIED CHEESE SLICES
Serves 6–12

*Kaçkavall djathë pane* (Albanian), *kashkaval pane* (Bulgarian), from the French *pané*, coated with breadcrumbs; *kasséri tiganitó* (Greek); *pohovan kačkavalj* (Serbo-Croat)

The cheese for this recipe can be any that holds its shape on heating, such as Gruyère, processed cheese, Cheshire or mature Cheddar. It can be served as a hot starter for 12 people, or as a light luncheon dish for 6, accompanied by a crisp green salad.

About 600 g cheese, rind removed, cut into twelve 1 cm thick slices • plain white flour •
2–3 eggs, beaten • fine, pale-toasted bread crumbs (or fine Matzo meal) •
clarified butter, or equal quantities of oil and unsalted butter, for deep frying

First rinse the slices of cheese under cold running water, then dip them in flour, then beaten egg, and coat them with bread crumbs or Matzo meal. Repeat this procedure to make a rather thick protective coating. Heat enough fat to immerse the slices in one layer, then fry them in batches, over a high heat (180°C or 350°F) for 1 minute on each side, until golden brown. Drain on kitchen paper and keep warm. Serve them very hot, with bread.

## MECHKA

*Mechka* (Bulgarian, meaning female bear); *Urs* (Romanian, meaning male bear)

Generations of Bulgarian children have been fed on bread and cheese as a mainstay. To make the combination more appealing, a small cube of *sirene* cheese was wrapped in a piece of crustless bread and shaped into a bite-sized ball. In 1899, Najden Gerov defined *mechka* in his great dictionary as 'the soft crumb of bread shaped into a round morsel with sirene cheese in the centre'. The Bulgarian-German dictionary of Weigand and Dorich (published in 1939), describes it as 'bread and cheese shaped into a small ball'.

The Romanians have a similar preparation which is called *Urs*, but instead of using bread, the cheese is inserted into *mămăligă*, cornmeal porridge (p. 216), formed into a ball and baked in a moderate oven until browned.

## HOME-MADE LIPTAUER CHEESE
Serves 4–6 as a snack or starter

This potted cheese is manufactured in most countries along the Danube. It is also prepared at home and served as a spread with drinks or as a first course. The recipe comes from Serbia and Croatia. The Slovenian *sirček* is a rather similar preparation made with sour cream instead of butter.

150 g lightly drained quark or fresh, unsalted white cheese • 75 g unsalted butter, at room temperature • 1 teaspoon finely grated onion • 2 hard-boiled eggs, peeled and halved • 1 teaspoon prepared mustard • 1/2 teaspoon finely ground or pounded caraway seed • 1/2 teaspoon paprika • 1/2 teaspoon salt • a good grinding of pepper (preferably white)

Combine all the ingredients and either whizz to a smooth cream in a food processor, or force through a sieve. Serve chilled, with wholewheat or rye bread.

*Cheese and Eggs*

## POACHED EGGS WITH YOGHURT
Serves 4

*Jajtsa s ovcho kiselo mlyako* (Bulgarian), *jaja na čimbur* (Croat), *jajtsa so ovcho kiselo mleko* (Macedonian), *jaja s kiselim mlekom* (Serbian), all meaning eggs with sheep's milk yoghurt; *yoğurtlu yumurta* or *çılbır* (Turkish), meaning eggs with yoghurt

Poached eggs can also be served on a bed of spinach, fried onions or crumbled feta as a satisfying main-course dish for a family meal.

8 eggs • 2 tablespoons vinegar • salt • double quantity yoghurt and garlic sauce (p. 347) • red paprika butter (p. 347)

Prepare the yoghurt sauce and divide it equally between 4 ovenproof bowls. If you wish, place them in a low oven to warm the yoghurt slightly while you poach the eggs. In a large frying pan, bring 500 ml water with the vinegar (but no salt which toughens the whites) to a steady boil. Carefully break the eggs into a saucer and slip them, one at a time, into the boiling water. You may need to cook the eggs in at least two batches. Cover the pan, lower the heat and poach the eggs for 2–3 minutes or until set to your liking. Put 2 eggs in each bowl on top of the yoghurt and season with salt. Prepare the paprika butter and pour it evenly over the eggs and yoghurt. Serve while the eggs are still hot.

## SCRAMBLED EGGS WITH PEPPERS AND TOMATOES
Serves 4 as a light lunch or supper

*Mish-mash* (Bulgarian, Macedonian), from the German *Mischmasch*, a mixture

1 small onion, finely chopped • 4 large red peppers, roasted, skinned, seeded and cut into small pieces • 50 g butter • 4 tomatoes, peeled and chopped • salt and pepper • 4 large eggs, lightly beaten • 50 g white brine cheese, sirene or feta, crumbled

Fry the onion and peppers in the butter until the onion is soft and golden, and the peppers tender. Add the tomatoes, salt and pepper to taste and cook for a few more minutes until most of the juices have evaporated. Pour in the eggs and cook over a low heat—stirring to scramble. When softly set, place the mish-mash on heated plates. Sprinkle with the cheese and serve hot with a tomato salad and bread.

## SCRAMBLED EGGS WITH MINCED MEAT
Serves 4–5

*Kajgana s mlevenim mesom* (Serbo-Croat), from the Turkish *kıymalı kaygana*, mincemeat omelette

15 g butter • 1 small onion, finely chopped • 1 small red pepper, seeded and finely chopped • 500 g lean minced lamb, beef or pork, or a mixture • 1 teaspoon salt • freshly ground black pepper • 4 medium eggs, beaten

Lightly brown the onion and pepper in the hot butter. Add the meat and stir-fry for about 15 minutes, or until most of the juices have evaporated. If the mixture appears to be drying out too quickly, add a little water—the cooked meat should be just moist. Season with salt and plenty of pepper. Reduce the heat to the lowest possible setting and stir in the eggs. Continue cooking for a few more minutes until the eggs are well scrambled. Add more salt and pepper if necessary. Serve with plain boiled potatoes, rice, pasta, or a salad.

## BAKED EGGS AND CHEESE
Serves 4

*Pecheni yajtsa sus sirene* (Bulgarian); *pečena jaja sa sirom* (Serbo-Croat)

This recipe may be varied by using salami, frankfurters or sausages for the cheese.

400 g feta, soaked for 2 hours in cold water to rid it of salt, then crumbled; or a less salty white cheese such as Lancashire or Cheshire, crumbled •
50 g butter, or *kajmak* (thick, ripened clotted cream), diced •
8 medium eggs, lightly beaten • 100 ml milk, single cream or thick plain yoghurt •
4 fresh green or red chilli peppers • paprika

Butter 4 deep ovenproof bowls, each of about 425 ml. Distribute the cheese evenly and add half the butter or kajmak. Mix the milk, cream or yoghurt and the beaten eggs well together. Pour the mixture into the bowls, add the chillis, if you like them, dot the remaining butter or kajmak on top, and sprinkle with a pinch of paprika. Bake in a preheated oven (180°C/350°F/gas 4) for about 35 minutes, or until puffed up and the tops are a deep copper brown. Serve hot, with warm crusty bread.

# CHAPTER IX

# Milk, Yoghurt, Cream and Butter

Milk is one of the main constituents of the daily diet in the Balkans. Mostly cow's, but sheep's, goat and water buffalo milks are used as well. Much is converted into cheese, yoghurt, other cultured milks, sour cream or lactic butter by deliberately adding ripening cultures. The main products, other than cheese, that can still be found in the Balkans may be summarised as these:

> The sheep's milk condensed by long slow simmering over a wood or charcoal fire called *kourtmach* or *korkmach* (from the Turkish dialect word *koyurtmaç*) is particularly interesting. It is usually prepared by shepherds in late August and consumed as it is, without allowing it to ferment, or left to ferment spontaneously in earthenware pots or kegs, then sealed with melted sheep's butter and stored for winter use. *Kourtmach* is most often eaten with bread, or used as a substitute for cream, sometimes mixed with fruit and sugar, jam, melted chocolate or coffee.

> *Koumiss* (from the Tartar) is an ancient alcoholic drink of the Turkic nomadic tribes (including the proto-Bulgars) who wandered the vast spaces of Asia. Prepared from fermented mare's milk, it is still consumed in the former Soviet Asiatic republics, but no longer in the Balkans.

> Yoghurt is milk fermented by the action of benevolent bacteria—*Lactobacterium bulgaricum* and *Streptococcus thermophilus*, both found naturally in the Balkans and in other parts of the world. In the case of the Albanian yoghurt *kos*, the lactic yeast *Oidium lactis* is present as well. Yoghurt made with *Lactobacterium acidophilum* is not yet manufactured in the Balkans.

> *Ayran* (Turkish) is a refreshing summer drink made from low-fat or skimmed yoghurt mixed with tap, soda or mineral water (recipe p. 339).

> Strained yoghurt, which has many local variations depending on the type of milk and its fat content, is popular all across the Balkans and in Turkey. It is made by draining thick, natural yoghurt through a fine cheese cloth for 24 hours or overnight, to allow the whey to run out (recipe p. 123).

Cream and sour cream are used quite freely in Romania and the Balkans, though more sparingly in Albania and Bulgaria. Clotted cream, *kaymak* (Turkish), is renowned for its distinctive flavour acquired from scalding during processing. In Bosnia there are several varieties of *kajmak*, among them the smoked *romanijski kajmak*. An old fashioned clotted cream speciality, once popular but now rarely seen, is *kaymak* prepared from water-buffalo milk and rolled into finger lengths. The rolls are, or were, usually dusted with a little sugar.

Butter was churned from fresh cow's milk or from spontaneously soured milk or yoghurt. It is still made in country districts. The production of butter from fresh or ripened cream (sweet butter and lactic butter) is a recent commercial development dating from around the beginning of this century.

Sheep's butter, made from fresh sheep's milk or whey, does not store well so it is usually clarified to improve keeping. Because of its rather odd, thick odour, sheep's butter is used principally for frying and in stews.

Buffalo butter, porcelain white and mild to the taste, is also made—though less so now than a few decades ago. It is used both for cooking and at table.

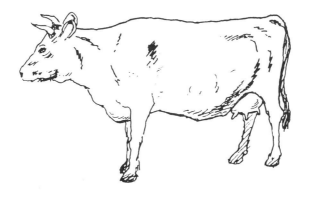

## BALKAN YOGHURT
### Makes about 1 litre yoghurt

*Kos* (Albanian), *kiselo mlijeko* (Bosnian, Croat), *kiselo mlyako* (Bulgarian), *kiselo mleko* (Macedonian, Serbian), *kislo mleko* (Slovenian)—literally 'sour milk' which, in Serbia, Montenegro and the former Yugoslav republics, refers solely to thick yoghurt made from sheep's or water buffalo's milk. *Jogurt* (Bosnian, Macedonian, Serbo-Croat, Slovenian, applies to thin cow's milk yoghurt only), *giaoúrti* (Greek), and *iaurt* (Romanian), come from the Turkish *yoğurt*

---

The ideal milk for yoghurt is sheep's milk, but sterilized, canned or homogenized full-cream cow's milk can also be used successfully. Skimmed milk makes a thin yoghurt, so it is sometimes thickened with dried milk before boiling to improve the consistency. One important point: make sure your pots and utensils are spotlessly clean and rinsed with boiling water to prevent any undesirable bacteria.

1.25 litres fresh full-fat cow's milk, raw or pasteurized • 1 tablespoon natural commercial yoghurt (unpasteurized), or yoghurt reserved from a previous batch, at room temperature

Choose a wide, shallow, heavy-based pan, preferably of enamelled iron, fire-proof glass or with a non-stick inner surface. Rinse with cold water and set over a flame-proof mat or heat-diffuser. Pour in the milk, bring to a bare simmer and continue, uncovered, over a very low heat (the temperature of the milk should be 90°–95°C or 194°–203°F) for 30 minutes, or until the milk is reduced by about one fifth.

Remove from the heat and either pour the milk into an electric yoghurt-maker container to cool, or leave it in the pan until cooled to 46°C (115°F) on a thermometer. At this temperature the outside of the pan or container will be rather warm, while a spoonful of the milk, dribbled on your tongue, will feel pleasantly warm, not hot.

Cream the yoghurt starter in a little bowl, with a spoon, and dilute it gradually with a few tablespoons of the milk until the mixture is quite runny, pour it back into the milk and stir briefly to combine. Cover with the lid and either put the container into the yoghurt-maker and leave undisturbed for 6–8 hours, or wrap the covered pan with a sheet of plastic, overwrap with a thick cloth or fur, and leave in a warm place for the same length of time or overnight.

Unwrap the set yoghurt and, without shaking, transfer it to the refrigerator. After 4 hours it will be ready to serve; stored for more than three days, it becomes progressively sourer.

*Milk, Yoghurt, Cream and Butter*

# STRAINED YOGHURT
Yields about 225 g depending on the loss of whey

*Smisa-kiselo mlijeko* (Bosnian), *tsedeno kiselo mlyako* (Bulgarian), *tsedeno kiselo mleko* (Macedonian), *süzme yoğurt* (Turkish), all meaning strained yoghurt; *torba yoğurdu* (Turkish, meaning bag yoghurt)

In Ottoman times, thick strained, sheep's-milk yoghurt was exported from the Bulgarian town of Samokov to the Sultan's palace in Istanbul.

500 g low- or full-fat plain yoghurt, freshly made or pasteurised • paprika or olive oil

Drape a tea-towel, cheese cloth or double layer of muslin over a mixing bowl. Tip the yoghurt into the cloth. Gather up the four corners and tie them together, then suspend the pouch with the yoghurt over a bowl to allow the whey to drip overnight or for 24 hours.

Next day, give the pouch a twist, then continue to tighten the twisted ends to squeeze out the remaining whey. Transfer the yoghurt to a small jar or cup, cover and refrigerate until needed. Serve as a first course of a meal, sprinkled with a little paprika or olive oil, or as a light supper dish for one along with bread and fried egg or salad.

# CHAPTER X

# Fish and Shellfish

> Mesolonghi was formerly the seat of a pasha. ... The inhabitants ... subsist chiefly on the fishery, where grey mullet is taken in quantities sufficient to supply many parts of Roumelia and the Morea with the boutaraga made from their roes.
>
> John Cam Hobhouse (Lord Broughton), *Travels in Albania and Other Provinces of Turkey in 1809 & 1810*, new edition 1858.

It is impossible to underestimate the importance of fish to many of the communities living in the peninsula, even if Bulgarians, as I mentioned before, are less enthusiastic than some. Because descriptions can be confusing and names may vary from place to place, I have attempted a short catalogue of the most popular species, as well as a description of some specialities such as caviar and tarama.

*Asp (Aspius aspius)* is a valuable fish which lives in shoals in larger rivers such as the Maritsa, Tundzha, Arda, Struma, the Danube and its tributaries. It grows up to 4 kg with specimens recorded up to 12 kg. The flesh, especially that of winter catches, is very palatable; it is usually fried, grilled or casseroled.

*Aýgotáraho(n)* is a famous Greek delicacy. Whole hard roes of grey mullet (*Mugil cephalus*) are salted, put in the sun to dry, then wrapped in a thick coat of beeswax to preserve them further. Expensive, but with an exquisite flavour, the roe is served thinly sliced—after removing the wax and skin—accompanied by good bread.

Beluga sturgeon (*Huso huso*) occurs along the Black Sea coast as well as in the lower reaches of the Danube (as far west as the Iron Gates) and, rarely, in the Adriatic. It can weigh more than 1000 kg and live for 200 years. The fish is of enormous economic importance because it provides the best caviar. Its flesh has good flavour, a relatively high fat content, and is well suited to many ways of cooking. In Bulgaria it is often the chief ingredient of *plakiya*. Beluga is sold fresh, salted, dried, frozen, smoked or canned.

Bleak (*Alburnus alburnus*) is a favourite white fish of Macedonians, common in lakes Ohrid and Skadar, and in many slow-moving rivers in central and eastern parts of the peninsula. Small—not more than 40 g—they are good for frying, grilling, smoking and canning, as is the Danube bleak (*Chalcalburnus chalcoides*) which lives in the Danube system and rivers entering the Black Sea.

Bonito (*Sarda sarda*) is met throughout the Mediterranean including the Adriatic, and in the Black Sea. Four different names have been given to bonito according to size: *chiviya* (Bulgarian from the Turkish *çivi*, wedge or nail) are fish up to 15 cm; *tsiganka* (Bulgarian, gypsy woman, from Turkish *çingene*, gypsy)—from 15 to 30 cm; *pallamud* (Albanian), *palamud* (Bulgarian), *palamída* (Greek), *palamida* or *polanda* (Serbo-Croat), all deriving from Turkish *palamut* is the name for fish from 30 to 50 cm; and *torouk* (Bulgarian, from Turkish *torik*) is what they call the biggest, measuring from 50 to 75 cm.

Bonito is truly marvellous. The rich, succulent flesh has exquisite flavour. The smallest are usually fried; the larger sizes (*çingene* and *palamut*) may be grilled, baked, stewed, or put into *plakí* (p. 138) or *brodet* (p. 140). *Torik* and *palamut* are often dry-salted—in which case they are known as *lakerda* (p. 128).

Carp (*Cyprinus carpio*) is an indigenous Balkan freshwater fish. From its original range—the tributaries of the Danube and the rivers of the Black Sea to north-eastern China—it has been spread by man to much of the world. In the Balkans it lives in lakes, slow-flowing rivers, and even in swampy, brackish waters. In the past, specimens weighing 50 kg have been caught but now fish over 15 kg are rare. Carp is often stocked in fishponds, and transported in tanks to be sold live. The flesh is tasty, especially when baked, but very bony. Improved forms created by fish breeders, such as the Scaly (King) Carp, the Mirror Carp and the scaleless Leather Carp have more succulent flesh and less bones. The silver form from the river Drava and the yellow one from the Danube are reputed the best. In Bulgaria and Macedonia, baked carp stuffed with walnuts is a ritual dish, eaten on St Nikolas' day, or as a sacrifice to a patron saint. It is also the invariable fish served after a funeral.

Caviar (from Turkish *havyar*) is salted hard roe of older females from all the species of the sturgeon family, including the sturgeon (*Acipenser sturio*), the waxdick (*A güldenstädti*), beluga (*Huso huso*), sevruga (*A stellatus*) and the sterlet (*A ruthenus*). Of all the kinds of caviar, Beluga caviar, and especially Royal Beluga caviar, are considered the finest and most luxurious, with price correspondingly high.

In the Balkans, the term black caviar refers to sturgeon roe, as distinct from the red (keta) caviar, called *kırmızı havyar* (Turkish) or *syomga* (Bulgarian, from the Russian—which comes from Latin *salmo*): the salted, orangey-red large-grained roe of the North Pacific and Siberian chum salmon (*Oncorhynchus keta*).

*Chiroz* (Bulgarian), *tsíros* (Greek), from the Turkish *çiroz*, is the name for small, lean mackerel (*Scomber scomber*) caught after spawning in the spring. They are usually canned; or they can be gutted through the gills, washed and soaked for 8 hours in an 18 per cent solution of sea salt and water, then strung and dried in the sun for about two weeks until dehydrated and quite hard. Although rather salty, the fish are prized for their distinct aroma, enhanced by a brisk grilling. They are commonly served as meze with beer or plum brandy. The word *chiroz* or *çiroz* is also used half humorously to describe a skinny, dried-out person.

Cod (*Gadus morhua*) are not found in Balkan waters. This North Atlantic fish is too well known in the West to need much explanation, save to mention the Balkan fondness for imported salt cod (which is partially dried), and stockfish (dried cod, often salt-free). Both kinds are soaked overnight to partly desalt or soften the flesh prior to poaching, baking, or stewing.

The warty crab (*Eriphia spinifrons*) is the most valued of all crabs in the Mediterranean. It rarely grows bigger than 400 g in the Adriatic, even smaller in the Black Sea. Commonly served plain or coated with mayonnaise, it is sometimes put in *brodet* to impregnate the fish with its piquant flavour.

Crayfish (*Astacus spp*), the freshwater crustacean, is plentiful along the banks of well oxygenated chalk streams, ponds and lakes throughout the region. It attains an average weight of 60 g, males are sometimes 150 g. Caught mostly at night, crayfish are transported in baskets wrapped in moistened nettles and grass. Greenish-brown before cooking, they turn red when put into boiling vegetable stock, dry white wine or beer.

Crayfish are best served au naturel, or used in *yahni*, soup, or risotto. An interesting preparation is the pale pink crayfish butter made with the dry pounded shells of boiled crayfish.

Dentex (*Dentex dentex*) is a Mediterranean fish that occasionally enters the Black Sea. It may grow as long as a metre and weigh 16 kg. The best part to eat, so I was told in Croatia, is the head with the shoulders. The flesh is tasty and suited to all standard methods of cooking fish, including poaching and making *brodet*.

The Dublin Bay prawn or scampi (*Nephrops norvegicus*) is neither crawfish nor prawn but a close relative of the common lobster. ('Scampi' is the accepted English culinary term for the tail meat).

In the Adriatic, *skampi* (Slovenian), *skampi* or *škampi* (Serbo-Croat) are quite abundant—larger and meatier than their British counterpart—but they are rare in the Aegean. In Dalmatia scampi are often added to *brodet* and risotto; served poached, marinated or fried, they are an excellent meze to go with drinks.

Eel (*Anguilla anguilla*) is a migratory fish found along the coasts of Europe. In the Balkans it spends most of its life in muddy estuarial waters, in the rivers of the Aegean Sea and Sea of Marmora, as well as in a few lakes such as Ohrid which it enters through the river Crni Drim. It is also stocked as pond-fish. The weight of adults can vary between 0.5 and 3 kg. The flesh—firm, fatty and free of bone—is especially suitable for grilling; or it may go into a rice casserole or *brodet*.

Flounder (*Platichthys flesus*) is another Mediterranean species particularly abundant in Adriatic inshore waters, where weights of 1.25 kg have been recorded. It is also present in saltwater lakes and inlets. The Sea of Marmora and the Black Sea sub-species (*P f luscus*) is much smaller, rarely exceeding 150 g. Flounder is not bony. Its flesh is white and good to eat, especially fried or baked; small specimens are commonly put into a fish soup or *brodet*.

*Garozi* (Bulgarian) are livers of autumn mackerels packed in jars with 8 to 10 per cent sea-salt, and covered with a layer of olive or sunflower oil to exclude air. Refrigerated, they have a storage life of 5 to 6 months. *Garozi* are served as meze with beer.

Goby (*Gobiidae*): a small number of this large family are esteemed for their white delicate flesh and flavour. One such from the Adriatic (*Gobius exanthematicus*), seldom exceeding 400 g, is used in *brodet* to impart its inimitable aroma. Another species from the Black Sea, *Mesogobius batrachocephalus*, can be twice as large. It is generally fried.

Grey Mullet (*Mugil cephalus*) is an inshore fish, also found in estuaries and lakes connected with the sea. The largest Mediterranean grey mullet can weigh as much as 6 kg, but they are rarely over 1.8 kg in the Black Sea. It has few small bones, and its fat content is not too high. Best charcoal-grilled, fried, or baked in a plakí, its roe is used for making *aýgotárahon* and tarama (p. 130).

Hake (*Merluccius merluccius*) is not present in the Black Sea, but plentiful in the Mediterranean where weights of 5 kg have been known. A very palatable lean fish with few bones, much in demand especially in Dalmatia and Albania, and one of the prime objectives of the Bulgarian deep-sea fishing fleet, it is excellent steamed, poached or baked. The fillets are often coated in soufflé batter and deep fried. Larger specimens, split open and wind-dried for a day prior to cooking, take on an interestingly piquant flavour. Fried hake liver is considered a delicacy.

John Dory (*Zeus faber*) is a very odd looking Mediterranean species—uncommon in the Black Sea—with a round dark spot surrounded with a halo on either side of its body. The spots are thought to be the thumb-prints of Christ or St Peter, hence the name 'Christ's fish' in Greek and 'St Peter's fish' in Bulgarian and vernacular Serbo-Croat. As to size, Josip Basioli mentions fairly large specimens (of 3 kg) taken in the Adriatic. Ordinarily, John Dory is steamed, or deep fried as batter-coated fillets; it is also in demand for *brodet*.

*Lakerdë* (Albanian), *lakerda* (Bulgarian), *lâkerda* (Turkish), all coming from the modern Greek *lakértha*, itself from the Latin, is a luxury food. It is prepared from large specimens of the bonito which are dry-salted with 15-20 per cent sea-salt. The fish is either left whole or, when it weighs more than 4 kg, is cut into thick pieces. The process draws out some of the juices and changes the nature of the protein (much as cooking with heat would do) so the fish can be eaten without any cooking.

The Greeks also prepare a similar, but less expensive delicacy from tuna fish (*Thunnus thynnus*) called *tónnolakértha*; and in cheap Greek taverns, mackerel slices in oil, extremely salty but with a pleasant flavour all their own, may feature on menus as *lakértha*.

Traditionally, the fish is served in thin slices, garnished with slender rings of red onion and lemon wedges. This, plus good bread, unsalted butter or olive oil and perhaps a glass of wine, is—by Balkan standards—a modest repast or a very pleasant way to begin a meal.

Langouste or spiny lobster (*Palinurus vulgaris*) is one of the largest Mediterranean shellfish—up to 5 kg in weight—and much appreciated for its flavour. In Dalmatia it is sold either live or freshly boiled. The cooked flesh is ordinarily put into *brodet* or risotto, or, for more formal occasions, it is served on its own dressed with lemon juice and olive oil, or mayonnaise.

Mussel (*Mytilus galloprovincialis*) has worldwide distribution, and in the Mediterranean and Black Seas may reach a length of 15 cm and a weight of 30 g.

Mussels are usually sold live, buried in crushed ice. They are cooked in many different ways—as *yahni*, *plakí*, soups, rice casseroles—the simplest and most popular in the Balkans being to boil them in wine-and-vegetable stock until well opened, and then serve them as they are in their shells, set in a bowl of ice.

Nase (*Chondrostoma nasus*) is a Central European river fish, also found in Romania and the north-eastern half of the Balkan peninsula, where it lives in running water and below mountain dams. Rarely over 1.5 kg in weight, it is most often fried or grilled.

Perch (*Perca fluviatilis*) is a freshwater fish found throughout the peninsula except in the south and west. Catches usually weigh no more than 900 g. Perch has white and tender flesh; it is usually poached, braised or baked.

Pike (*Esox lucius*) lives in thickly weeded lakes, dams, in slow waters and brackish river mouths. It can grow enormous, though specimens exceeding 15 kg are rare. Fish for the table are best up to 2.5 kg as larger fish are often rather dry. Its hard roe and flesh—despite the numerous bones—are much sought after. Pike is prepared by frying, poaching, or braising with aromatics in wine.

Pike-Perch or Zander (*Stizostedion lucioperca*) is an East European white fish, now widespread in the Balkans in clean lakes, warm rivers, dams and estuaries. Mature females can run up to 30 kg. The lean flesh has good flavour, with no fat under the skin and very few bones. Generally it is fried, baked, marinaded, or poached in court-bouillon.

The *Mullus surmuletus* is the best and biggest of the red mullets, prized for its succulence and unique flavour. It is easily distinguished by its stripes from the inferior related species (*M barbatus*) which has a muddy taste. Its range is the whole Mediterranean, and is quite plentiful in the Adriatic, where it rarely grows bigger than 1 kg. Many people consider charcoal grilling and frying as the only appropriate cooking methods. However it is also good baked, or cooked in a *brodet*. Another red mullet (*M b ponticus*), belonging to the Black Sea and the Sea of Marmora, has little commercial importance.

Salmon (*Salmo salar*) is not present except as Lake Ohrid salmon—a non-migratory relic from the last Ice Age, spending all its life in fresh water and spawning in the tributaries of the lake. Outside Macedonia, this fish is rarely eaten; however, many Balkan people are extremely fond of keta caviar, the imported salted roe of the chum salmon.

Two species of the sea-bream family are well liked: the gilthead bream (*Sparus auratus*), which can achieve a weight of 10 kg, and the smaller striped bream (*Lithograthus mormyrus*). Both are usually poached in vegetable stock or grilled over a wood fire, the second being a constant element in *brodet*.

Semling (*Barbus meridionalis petenyi*) spends its life in the Danube system, the Sava and most rivers and dams in the peninsula. It is small, rarely exceeding 300 g, has tasty flesh and fewer bones than the related barbel (*Barbus barbus*). Both species are usually fried.

Sterlet (*Acipenser ruthenus*) is a freshwater cartilaginous species which swims the Danube as far as Bavaria. In the Balkans, where this fish is liked for its superb flavour and lack of bone, sterlets of manageable sizes—they can be as heavy as 4 kg—are often poached whole. Before immersion, the cartilaginous (not of real bone) spinal cord is removed to prevent twisting and spoiling the shape when presented, cold, coated with mayonnaise. It can also be baked, fried, marinaded or cooked in a *plakí*.

Swordfish (*Xiphias gladius*) is an ocean species found also in Balkan waters. It can be very big—about 350 kg—in the Adriatic, and even slightly larger (though rarer these days) in the Black Sea. The flesh is firm and said to be most pleasant, especially the younger fish. It is poached, steamed, baked as *plakí*, fried and charcoal-grilled in the form of steaks and shish kebab.

*Tarama* (Bulgarian), *tamará* (Greek), from the Turkish *tarama* are words for hard roes, customarily but not invariably from grey mullet (*Mogul cephalus*), carp (*Cyprinus carpio*) or tuna (*Thunnus thynnus*), dry-salted with 12 per cent sea salt of the roe's weight, and matured for three months in jars or firkins. Commercial tarama usually contains saltpetre—which improves the brick-red colour and inhibits bacteria—so the cured roe can be stored for up to a year. It is used for the preparation of a special kind of stew, fried roeburgers and tarama hors-d'oeuvre (p. 67). Outside the Balkans, though, taramosaláta is usually made with the smoked roe of the North

Atlantic cod and coloured pink—but then, of course, it is no longer quite the authentic dish.

Trout (*Salmo trutta*) occurs in several forms and brown trout (*S trutta fario*) is often thought the best of all freshwater fish. It is a typical cold-water species belonging to the upper reaches of nearly all Balkan rivers, streams and clear mountain lakes. Brown trout is easily distinguished by the vermilion spots on its back and the unspotted tail. It has extremely delicate, clean-tasting flesh, and a good lake trout could weight about 1.5 kg or more. Rainbow trout (*S gairdneri*) has been introduced from California into many dam lakes, reservoirs and ponds, but it arouses little enthusiasm because of its insipid flavour.

Tuna or tunny (*Thunnus thynnus*) is a huge fish of 500 kg and more—plentiful in the Mediterranean, but a rare catch in Bulgarian and Romanian waters. The flesh is firm with a high fat content and well suited to grilling, pickling, baking and braising. Some people count the abdominal part, called *penceta* in Serbo-Croat, the best to eat. It makes excellent *brodet*.

Turbot (*Psetta maxima* or *Rhombus maximus*) is a valuable species found in the Mediterranean as well as the Atlantic and has a fair, 'non-fishy' flavour. It reaches about 10 kg. The bony, button-like protuberances are especially prominent in the Black Sea species (*P maeotica* or *R maeoticus*). Turbot lends itself best to frying, poaching and casserole cooking in the form of *plakí*; or it may go into *brodet*.

Wels or Sheat-fish (*Silurus glanis*) is a native of Central and Eastern Europe and has made its home in many lakes and rivers flowing into the Black Sea and the Aegean. Wels were once among the largest Balkan freshwater catches and in winter, Danubian wels of 100 kg were often taken among thick floes of ice. Nowadays, however, fish over 50 kg are rare. The flesh, free of tiny bones, is white, rich and tasty, especially the rear half of young winter catches. It may be bought fresh, salted, smoked or dried. Wels can be oven-baked as shish kebab, *güvec* or *plakí*, and wels steaks can be fried or stewed as *paprikash*.

## FISH GRILLED OVER EMBERS
Serves 4

*Pechena riba na zhar* (Bulgarian), *pechena riba na žar* (Macedonian), *pečena riba na žaru* (Bosnian, Serbo-Croat, Slovenian), all meaning grilled fish over embers; *psári tis skáras* (Greek), *balık ızgarası* (Turkish), both meaning grilled fish.

The fondness of most Balkan people for grilled fish is seen in the 1895 satirical novel by Aleko Konstantinov called *Baj Ganyu: the Incredible Stories of a Contemporary Bulgarian*. The author describes how the hero, a travelling salesman, grills a whole fish placed on fire-tongs held over the wood embers of a kitchen range. The cooked fish must have been very much to his taste, because the author comments: 'With what words, what interjections, exclamation marks and musical notes is it possible to depict Baj Ganyu's lip-smacking, munching, tongue-clicking, grunting, sniffling and sucking, which accompanied his eating of the fish.'

Large, oil-rich fish like sturgeon, bonito, pike, and swordfish are excellent for grilling, either as steaks or filleted. Equally enjoyable are flat fish such as sole, left whole, or the smaller oily fish like mackerel, sprats or sardines. The best way to grill them is enclosed in a double-sided hinged grilling basket made of wire, which can be turned over without the fish inside it being moved.

4 fish steaks or fillets • salt and freshly ground black pepper • 2 tablespoons lemon juice • 2 tablespoons sunflower or olive oil

Season the fish with salt and pepper and refrigerate for 1–2 hours. Meanwhile, prepare a wood or charcoal fire and let it burn down until the embers are covered in ash.

Mix together the lemon juice and oil. Arrange the fish side by side in a greased grilling basket. Grill over the embers, turning once, for about 10 minutes or until cooked through, basting from time to time with the lemon and oil mixture. Serve hot, sprinkled with dill or parsley and provided with lemon wedges.

## GRILLED TROUT WITH CLOTTED CREAM
Serves 4

*Ohridska pastrmka na kajmaku* (Serbian), meaning Ohrid trout over clotted cream.

---

2 brown or rainbow trout each weighing about 300 g, skinned and filleted •
juice of 1 lemon • 125 g clotted cream •
salt and freshly ground black pepper • 15 g butter

Place the fillets in a close-fitting dish and pour over the lemon juice. Marinate for 2 hours in a refrigerator.

Season the cream with salt and pepper and spread it on the base of a shallow rectangular baking dish large enough to hold the fillets snugly in a single layer. Lay the fillets over the cream, season, and dot with butter.

Grill for 10 minutes at medium heat, then lower the heat and cook for a further 5 minutes, or until the fish flakes easily with a fork.

Serve with buttered peas and fried mushrooms, lemon wedges, and the juices poured over the fillets.


## FRIED WHITEBAIT
Serves 4–6

*Purzhena drebna riba* (Bulgarian), *pržena sitna riba* (Macedonian, Serbo-Croat)

---

600 g mixed small fish, or one kind only, cleaned, but with heads and tails left on, washed in very cold water and dried thoroughly •
plain flour • salt • 2–3 lemons cut into wedges

Put some flour on a large sheet of greaseproof paper and toss the fish in it; then shake the fish in a sieve to remove excess flour.

Have ready a deep pan with very hot, but not smoking, vegetable oil. Heat the frying basket in the oil and fry the fish in small batches for 2–3 minutes until crisp. When all the fish have been fried, return all of them to the basket and re-fry for a few seconds to make them crisper. Drain them well, sprinkle with salt to taste and serve immediately with lemon wedges.

# FISH PARCELS
Serves 5

*Peshk në letër* (Albanian), *riba vo hartija* (Macedonian), *riba u hartiju* (Serbo-Croat), all meaning fish in paper; *keat ot riba* (Bulgarian), from the Turkish *kâğıt*, paper, or *riba v hartiya*, fish in paper.

Balkan fishermen often cook their catch wrapped in layers of paper or leaves. The parcel is tied, damped with water, buried in hot ashes covered with a layer of glowing coals, then left undisturbed for 30–40 minutes depending on thickness.

For this recipe, use strong brown wrapping paper; aluminium foil is unsuitable as lemon juice may react adversely with the metal.

About 1 kg any whole fish (salmon, sea bass, sturgeon, etc) cleaned, head and tail removed • salt and freshly ground black pepper • juice of 1 lemon • 100 g butter, melted, or 4–5 tablespoons vegetable oil • a few sprigs of parsley or fennel

Wash and season the fish inside and out with salt, pepper and lemon juice. Refrigerate for about 30 minutes.

Cut out a double layer of thick wrapping paper large enough to enclose the fish completely, and brush it on either side with some of the melted butter or oil. Place the fish in the centre of the paper and pour over the remaining butter or oil. Place the parsley or fennel sprigs in the body cavity. Wrap the paper loosely around the fish to make a neat, secure parcel. Cook on a grill rack over hot (not glowing) wood coals or charcoal for 30–40 minutes. Alternatively the fish may be cooked in the oven for 20 minutes at 200° C for well cooked fish. There is no need to turn the fish. Serve it with the juices poured over.

*The common carp (Cyprinus carpio) [left] is normally fully scaled. The mirror carp (Cyprinus carpio var.) [right] has irregularly spread scales of varying sizes. Though there are only a few of these, they are large and glitter like mirrors as the fish moves in the water.*

# FRIED HAKE IN BATTER
Serves 4

*Fileto merluc-pane* (Albanian), *purzhena merlouza-pane* (Bulgarian), *pržen pahiran oslić* (Serbo-Croat), from French *pané*, coated with breadcrumbs.

Ever since I first smelt freshly caught hake cooking in bubbling oil in a small Adriatic village, I have been a hake admirer. I also came across fried hake at a tourist hotel in Dubrovnik, and a year later—at the hotel Tiranë in Tirana. In either case, the fillets were wrapped in a fluffy batter, crisply deep-fried and served with chips. The recipe particularly suits flatfish like sole, turbot, brill and flounder.

4 hake fillets, at room temperature, skinned and slightly flattened with a cutlet bat or the palm of the hand
*Batter*
100 g plain flour • 1/4 teaspoon baking powder • a little salt • 150 g white wine, dry cider or water • 1 egg white, beaten until perfectly stiff • extra flour for coating

Sieve the flour with the baking powder and salt into a bowl. Add the wine (cider or water) and beat the mixture to a smooth batter, then fold in the beaten egg white.

Coat the fish fillets first in flour, then in batter. Heat a deep-fat fryer to 150°C (300°F). Place the coated fillets in the fryer without the basket, not more than two at a time to avoid lowering the temperature of the oil. Cook for 7–10 minutes until the coating is crisp and golden and the fish cooked through. Drain on kitchen paper and serve immediately on heated plates.

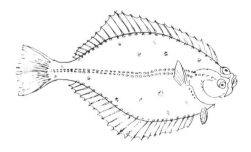

*Flounder (Platichthys flesus). The surest test to distinguish a flounder from other flatfish is to run a fingertip along the lateral line of the fish. The ridge of fine bony scales should feel quite rough.*

# CARP STUFFED WITH WALNUTS
Serves 10–12

*Sharan pulnen s orehi* (Bulgarian), *sharan polnet so orevi* (Macedonian), *šaran nadeven sa orasima* (Serbian)

A very ancient dish, possibly of Slavic origin, traditionally served on December 6th, to mark the feast of St Nikolas, patron saint of fishermen. In Northern Europe, because St Nicholas was protector of seafarers as well as children, it became customary for children to receive small gifts of gilded gingerbread or toys on his feast day. Later the Church associated him with the bringing of presents at Christmas.

In Eastern Orthodox countries huge carp, sometimes weighing up to 15 kg are stuffed and baked for a family gathering in honour of the Saint. It is also customary to serve this dish after a funeral.

Alternatives to carp can be any whole fish such as barbel, pike-perch, or salmon.

1–1.5 kg carp, scaled and gutted (preferably through the gills), roe reserved • salt • 1 tablespoon tomato purée • 2 tablespoons walnut or sunflower oil

*Stuffing*

200 ml walnut or sunflower oil • 1 kg onions, peeled and thinly sliced • 1 teaspoon paprika • 1 knife-tip cinnamon • 1/2 teaspoon freshly ground black pepper • 200 g walnuts, coarsely ground or pounded • 1 tablespoon flat-leaved parsley, finely chopped • 2–3 lemon slices, peeled and roughly chopped • salt

Sprinkle fish inside and out with salt and set aside while you prepare the stuffing.

Heat the oil in a large frying pan over moderate heat, and cook the onion gently until soft and golden. Add the peeled roe, then remove the pan from the heat and stir in the rest of the stuffing ingredients. Use part of the mixture to stuff the fish either through the belly or through the gills. Secure the opening with a few crossed toothpicks. Spread the rest of the stuffing in an oval baking dish big enough for the fish and place the fish on top. Dilute the tomato purée with a little water and pour over, then sprinkle with 2 tablespoons of oil.

Bake in a preheated oven, set at 180°C/350°F/gas 4, for 30–40 minutes, depending on the size of the fish, or until it is well browned.

# FISH BAKED IN A DOUGH JACKET
Serves 5–6

*Ribnik* (Bulgarian), *riba vo koshula* (Macedonian, fish in a shirt)

An old native dish, still current in country kitchens.

About 1 kg wels, beluga or similar fish in one piece; or 1 whole fish, such as grey mullet, carp or other large fish, cleaned and skinned • salt • 100 ml vegetable oil
*Dough*
250 g strong white flour • 1/2 teaspoon salt • 1 egg, lightly beaten (reserve 1/2 for glazing) • 10 g fresh yeast • 50 ml tepid water •
about 50 ml tepid milk • a little extra flour for kneading

Sprinkle the fish with salt and refrigerate for up to an hour

Prepare the dough by combining the flour and salt in a mixing bowl. Make a large well in the centre and pour in half the beaten egg. Dissolve the yeast in the water and add, with enough tepid milk to make a soft, rather sticky dough. Knead it with a little extra flour until smooth but still soft. Divide it into 2 equal portions. On a floured board, roll out thickly to the shape of your fish, only slightly larger.

Choose a baking dish just large enough to accommodate the fish. Pour about a third of the oil into the dish and place one of the dough pieces on the bottom. Brush the edges with water. Put the fish on top and cover it with the other piece of dough. Press the edges firmly to seal. Pour the remaining oil over the fish, then glaze the top with the reserved egg.

While the oven is heating to 180°C/350°F/gas 4, let the dough go through its final proof on the stove-top. Then bake it for 20–25 minutes, until golden brown. Bring to the table in the baking dish.

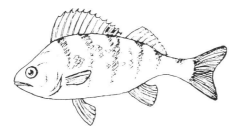

*The perch* (Perca fluviatilis). *Sometimes it has a distinctively striped body, as here.*

# FISH CASSEROLE
Serves 4 as a main course or cold-table dish

*Riba plakiya* (Bulgarian), *riba plakija* (Macedonian), *plachie de pește* (Romanian), *balık pilakisi* (Turkish), from the Greek *psári plakí*

Many Balkan people consider turbot, beluga, sterlet or sturgeon best for this casserole; however, you can use steak or fillets of grey mullet or cod, whole fresh anchovies, sardines, or sprats, and even shellfish, with excellent results.

The Turkish *balık pilakisi* differs from the standard recipe in that the fish is fried and then stewed in the sauce on top of the stove—without browning the dish in the oven.

4 fish steaks, skinned, sprinkled with a little salt, pepper and lemon juice and left to stand for 30–40 minutes

*Sauce*

2 tablespoons sunflower oil or olive oil • 4 medium-sized onions, very finely chopped •
1 teaspoon sea-salt crystals • 4 garlic cloves, finely chopped •
4 medium tomatoes (fresh or canned), peeled and chopped • 1/2 bay leaf •
4 allspice berries • freshly ground black pepper • 1/2 teaspoon paprika • 100 ml dry white wine

*Topping*

50 ml dry white wine • 4 thin lemon rounds, peeled and seeded • a little chopped parsley •
1–2 tablespoons sunflower oil or olive oil

Put the oil, onions and salt into a heavy, shallow saucepan and add 2 tablespoons of water. Cover and cook gently for about an hour, until the onions are practically disintegrating and just starting to colour. Stir in the chopped garlic, cook for a further minute or two, and add the tomatoes, spices and white wine. Cook, still covered, over a somewhat higher heat, until the sauce thickens—about 10–15 minutes. Discard the bay leaf and the allspice.

Now pour most of the sauce into a shallow baking dish large enough to take the fish steaks in one layer. Arrange the fish over the sauce, pour over the wine and the remaining sauce, place a lemon slice on each steak and sprinkle with chopped parsley and the oil.

Bake at the top of a preheated oven (180°C/350°F/gas 4) for 15–20 minutes, or until the sauce thickens a little more, the fish flakes easily and the edges of the lemon slices are coloured slightly.

Serve warm or cold with soft white bread or rolls.

*Fish and Shellfish*

# BAKED FISH WITH ONIONS
Serves 6

*Tavë me peshk* (Albanian), *riba na tava* (Macedonian), both meaning fish casserole

---

1 kg dentex, flounder, wels, or other large fish cut into steaks, skinned and lightly seasoned with salt, pepper and lemon juice • 1 kg onions, peeled and thinly sliced • 3 tablespoons vegetable oil • 2 tomatoes, finely chopped • 2–3 tablespoons chopped parsley • 1/2 teaspoon salt and a little freshly ground black pepper • paprika

*Topping*
plain flour • vegetable oil

Sweat the onions in the oil in a large covered frying pan over a medium to low heat until they soften (about 25 minutes), then cook them without the lid for a further 5–8 minutes to evaporate any moisture. Add tomatoes and fry for another minute or two. Stir in the parsley, salt, pepper and one teaspoon of paprika off the heat.

Choose a baking dish just large enough to hold the fish in a single layer. Spread the onion mixture on the bottom of the dish. Rub the fish steaks with a little paprika and arrange them on top. Sieve over a little flour and sprinkle with little oil from a spoon. Bake in a preheated oven (180°C/350°F/gas 4) for about 30 minutes, until the fish is slightly browned on top.

Serve not too hot, with plenty of lemon wedges or perhaps some mixed pickle.

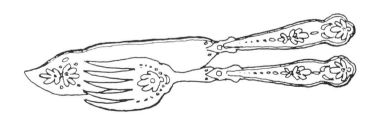

# FISH STEW: BRODET
Serves 8

*Brodet* (Croat, Slovenian), *mpourdéto* (Greek), from the Italian *brodetto*, fish soup, in turn deriving from the word *brodo*, broth or stock.

This Dalmatian speciality, also known in Corfu, was borrowed from the Italian kitchen. The most suitable kinds of fish and shellfish are bonito, warty crab, dentex, eel, flounder, John Dory, langouste, red mullet, scampi, sea bream, tuna and turbot. The tastiest *brodet* is prepared from a medley of the day's catch cooked in a well flavoured fish stock.

*Fish stock*
1 carrot, peeled and sliced • 1/4 celeriac, peeled and diced, or 2–3 sticks celery, diced •
1 small leek, white part only, sliced • 1–2 sprigs of fennel or dill •
1 teaspoon green peppercorns or 1/2 teaspoon black peppercorns •1 tablespoon vegetable oil •
500 g broken-up fish bones, heads (gills removed) and trimmings •
50 ml white wine • salt

*For the brodet*
1 large onion, peeled and finely chopped • 50 ml vegetable oil •
3 cloves of garlic, coarsely chopped • 2 heaped tablespoons tomato purée •
3–4 tomatoes, peeled and chopped • 2 tablespoons wine vinegar •
1 tablespoon coarsely chopped parsley • 1 bay leaf • 1.5 kg fish, either one kind or a mixture, gutted, cleaned, skinned, washed and cut into fair-sized pieces •
extra salt and pepper, if necessary • finely chopped parsley

To make the fish stock, put the vegetables, herbs and peppercorns into a pan with the oil, season lightly , cover and leave to sweat over gentle heat until soft—about 30 minutes. Add the bones, heads and trimmings and 400 ml water. Simmer for no more than 20 minutes to avoid a 'fishy' flavour. Strain through a fine sieve, squeezing to extract the juices. Discard the residue. Season to taste. Add the wine.

To make the brodet, sweat the onion in the oil in a heavy-based pan until pale gold, then add the garlic and cook for a few seconds more. Stir in the tomatoes and purée, then add the vinegar, parsley, bay leaf, prepared fish and enough stock to cover the fish well. Bring quickly to the boil, then turn the heat down and poach the fish, uncovered, for about 30 minutes, or until it just begins to flake readily with a fork, and the cooking liquid is reduced a little and slightly thickened. Shake the pan occasionally during cooking, but do not stir to avoid breaking up the fish. Remove from the heat and check the seasoning.

To serve, put a round of soft bread, or garlic-rubbed bread baked crisp in a low oven, or mashed potato, or polenta (p. 216) into deep plates or bowls. Pour over the cooking juices, then place portions of fish on top and sprinkle with chopped parsley. Eat hot or cool rather than chilled.

## STEWED FAN MUSSELS
Serves 5–6

*Brodet od lostura (periska)* (Croat)

10 large fan mussels (*Pinna nobilis*) • 100 ml vegetable oil • 1 onion, finely chopped • 5–6 cloves garlic • 1 bunch parsley, chopped • a little salt • 2–3 tablespoons tomato purée • 2–3 tomatoes, skinned and roughly chopped • 1 tablespoon vinegar

Scrub the fan mussels with a brush, pull off their tuft of silky filaments or byssus which the Dalmatian fishermen call *papar*. Rinse under cold running water and drain well. Open them by boiling in a little salted water or sea water. As they open, remove the edible muscle, which should be washed thoroughly and cut into pieces. Discard the shells.

Heat the oil in a heavy pan over moderate heat and colour the onion, at which point, add the garlic, mussels, parsley, a pinch or two of salt, tomato purée and tomatoes. Cook over a very low heat, tightly covered, for at least 1 hour, adding a little hot water if it dries out. When the fan mussels are tender, stir in the vinegar and check the seasoning. Serve hot or at room temperature.

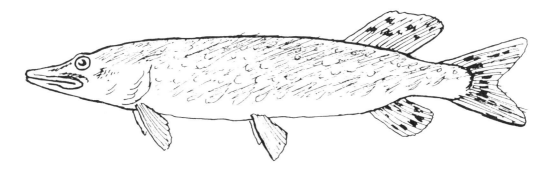

*Pike (*Esox lucius*) is usually yellowish or greenish in colour with mottled yellow spots, and has a large mouth with a great many backward-slanting teeth.*

## STUFFED MUSSELS
Serves 3–5 as a starter

*Midi pulneni* (Bulgarian); *kokošice (crne školjke) punjene* (Croat); *midye dolması* (Turkish)

1 kg live mussels • vegetable oil
*Stuffing*
6 tablespoons bread crumbs • 3 cloves garlic, finely chopped or crushed • 1 tablespoon finely chopped parsley • a little freshly ground black pepper • 2 tablespoons vegetable oil

Scrape the mussels with a knife and allow to soak in cold water for half an hour. Scrub them clean with a stiff or wire brush and wash thoroughly. Then prise the shells open with a blunt knife (so as not to damage the shells). Save the mussel juices. Cut off the beard. Leave each mussel in half shell, discarding the other half. Arrange them in greased baking pan that will just contain them in one layer.

Mix all the stuffing ingredients together; add the reserved mussel juices and mix again. Place a little of the stuffing over each mussel and drizzle a little extra oil over the top with a spoon. Bake in a preheated oven (180°C/350°F/gas 4) for 15–20 minutes or until just cooked, then serve immediately.

## MUSSELS IN WHITE WINE, DALMATIAN STYLE
Serves 4

*Dagnje u umaku od vina, na dalmatinski način* (Croat, meaning mussels in wine sauce, the Dalmatian way)

1 kg mussels, scraped, scrubbed, washed and bearded • 1–2 tablespoons vegetable oil • 2–3 cloves garlic, finely chopped • 1–2 tablespoons fresh bread crumbs • 1 tablespoon finely chopped parsley • 250 ml white wine • freshly ground black pepper • salt

Put the mussels into a large pan to open over a high heat. Let them simmer for 5–10 minutes in their own juices. Once tender, turn them into a serving bowl. Reserve the juices. In another pan, fry the garlic slowly in the oil until pale golden. Stir in the bread crumbs and parsley, and cook for just a few seconds. Pour in the mussel juices and wine, season with pepper and a little salt, if necessary. Bring the mixture to the boiling point, then pour it into a sauce boat and serve separately.

## SCAMPI RISOTTO
Serves 6

*Rižot od škampi* (Croat); *rizoto od škampa* (Serbian), from Italian *risotto*

Risottos are very popular in the Balkans, and risottos with seafood have long been a great favourite along the Adriatic. They are best made with Italian Arborio or Gallo rice often labelled 'Risotto Rice' in supermarkets. In the Balkans themselves, risotto rice is widely grown.

The rice is first fried, then cooked with gradual additions of liquid until the grains are three times their original size and creamy but not mushy.

In Dalmatia, mussels, cockles (*Cardium edule*), limpets (*Patella caerula*), date-shell (*Lithophaga lithophaga*), razor-shell (*Solen vagina*) and crayfish are all cooked the same way as the popular scampi suggested here.

1 large onion, finely chopped • 3 tablespoons vegetable or olive oil •
3–4 cloves of garlic, peeled and chopped • 250 g risotto rice •
200 g shelled raw scampi (thawed, if frozen), deveined •
salt and freshly ground black pepper •
2–3 tablespoons finely chopped parsley and grated Parmesan

Fry the onion in a heavy-based, covered pan over low heat until soft (about 20–25 minutes). Add the garlic and rice and stir over a moderate heat for 3–4 minutes, until the rice is partly translucent but not brown. Add hot water gradually, ladle by ladle, allowing each addition to be thoroughly absorbed before the next. You will need about 875 ml, or by volume, 1 part rice to 3 parts water. Simmer with the lid on, stirring occasionally, until the rice is almost tender. Then stir in the scampi and a little salt and cook for a further 7–10 minutes depending on the size of the scampi. The total cooking time should take about 35 minutes. When done, the rice should be moist but not watery. Stir in the parsley and pepper to taste, add more salt if necessary, and serve with the fresh Parmesan.

Fish and Shellfish

# GRILLED OYSTERS
Serves 4

*Stridha në skarë* (Albanian); *ostrige (kamenice) na roštilju* (Croat)

40 fresh oysters in the shell
(ask the fishmonger to shuck them for you; the oyster juices should be clear, not milky) •
vegetable oil • lemon juice • freshly ground black pepper •
lemon wedges, to garnish

Leave each oyster in its half-shell, discarding the top. Sprinkle with a few drops of oil, lemon juice and a little black pepper, but no salt. Place on a rack about 10 cm above glowing charcoal or wood embers, and grill for 4–5 minutes only. Serve immediately together with lemon wedges.

*Turbot (*Psetta maxima*). The nodules on top of the fish are bony protuberances which are best removed and discarded together with the skin before or after cooking.*

# CHAPTER XI

# Meat

It was the custom on Michaelmas each year to slaughter a young steer or a heifer in front of the church shop, and then people bought whatever cut of the animal they fancied.

In those days, in the town of Lyaskovets, there were many people who would never touch beef, nor would they have it in their houses. But some, who had been working previously in Istanbul at the Sultan's bakeries, or had been sent there as soldiers to pasture the Sultan's horses, knew that beef could be eaten, and urged the others to buy some and cook it with wine and whole heads of onion and garlic.

The populace at that time strictly observed all Wednesdays and Fridays, and some even fasted on Mondays, so few days were left for meat-eating. On non-fast days they consumed: hens, geese, ducks, turkeys and other fowl; after Christmas they ate pork, after St George's Day—lamb and kid, and after Assumption—mutton from ewes and wethers.

Ginchev, *Povesti*, 1887

The broth, being the stewing of a lamb, was excellent, and as my friends greatly preferred the meat with all the goodness boiled out of it, there was plenty for me. On my account there were extra luxuries, and all were pleased. We dipped out of the caldron and offered one another the tit-bits. When the lamb's head was fished up, Monsieur was grieved that I should not have had it, and pulling out the eyes and tongue, offered me them in his hand. In order to make me understand exactly what the morsel was, they put out their own tongues and waggled them about. I said I had had quite enough and thanked him, and they divided the delicacies carefully between them, each taking a bite.

Mary E. Durham, *Through the Lands of the Serb*, 1904.

Lamb has always reigned supreme throughout the Balkans, with mutton next in the hierarchy, except in Greece where mutton is not usually eaten. It maintains that position particularly because lamb continues to be one of the few food animals still free-range.

Pork used to be a 'winter meat' as almost every rural family kept pigs which grubbed around on corn and scraps, and were traditionally slaughtered for Christmas. Nowadays, factory farming has made it available all year round.

Oxen and cows were raised as draught animals rather than for beef. Eating their meat, and veal too, is a taste recently acquired—once agriculture was mechanized. With few exceptions (a case in point is Serbia which produces veal sometimes barely 6 weeks old), Balkan 'veal' is young beef with fully developed flavour and enough fat to ensure succulence, butchered at 10 to 12 months. In some areas the flesh of young water-buffaloes is also used in cooking and preserving.

## ROAST SUCKING PIG
### Serves 6–8

*Gic i pjekur* (Albanian); *pecheno prasentse* (Bulgarian); *pečeni odojak* (Serbo Croat); *pečen prašiček* (Slovenian)

An imposing festive dish associated with weddings and other celebrations. The pig should be roasted soon after slaughtering, without hanging. It is sometimes stuffed with potatoes, or with rice and the chopped pig's haslet. Its flesh is exceptionally succulent, but does not reheat well so needs to be cooked just before serving.

1 small sucking pig weighing about 4.5 kg, head and trotters left on, oven-ready, singed, if necessary, over an open flame; washed, dried, rubbed with salt inside and out, and allowed to stand for 1 hour • lemon juice • 250–300 ml beer

Put an empty pot, cup or bottle into the stomach cavity, skewer or sew up the opening, then lay the pig on its belly, with legs tucked under, on a greased rack (or criss-crossed fruit tree prunings or boiled beech twigs) in a roasting pan. Place a walnut in its mouth to keep it open and to allow the heat to penetrate. Brush the skin with lemon juice. Cover the ears and tail with little cones of aluminium foil or greased paper. Roast in an oven preheated to 180°C/350°F/gas 4, basting periodically with the pan juices mixed with beer and the juice of a lemon until the skin crackles and the meat almost falls from the bone. This takes approximately 3–3 1/2 hours.

When done, remove the vessel from the stomach cavity and the protective coverings from the tail and ears. With a sharp knife, make a deep slit in the back of the neck to allow the steam to escape and keep the skin crisp, then return the pig to the oven for 10 more minutes.

Bring whole to the table. You can either carve it in the usual manner, or, as they do in the Balkans, break off portions of the animal using the edge of a plate as a knife. Serve with horseradish sauce and gravy made from the pan juices.

# WHOLE ROAST STUFFED LAMB FOR ST GEORGE'S DAY
Serves 12–15

*Gergiyovsko agne* (Bulgarian)

In Bulgarian towns young sucking lamb is traditional at Easter, but in the villages lamb is ritually slaughtered and eaten for the first time on St George's Day (May 6th in Orthodox countries).

1 whole very young lamb, about 6 kg dressed weight, feet removed, head left on •
salt and freshly ground pepper • lard, clarified butter or vegetable oil
*Rice stuffing*
use 4 times the quantity of the recipe for rice stuffing given for chicken (p 188),
substituting the lights and liver of the lamb for the giblets, and spring onions for onions.

Season the lamb generously inside and out, and leave to stand.

Prepare the stuffing and spoon it into the stomach cavity of the lamb; sew up the opening. Place the lamb in a roasting pan and smear it all over with lard, warm clarified butter or oil. Cook it in a preheated oven at 180°C/350°F/gas 4 for 3 hours or until well done, turning the lamb over at half-time to brown the other side.

St George's lamb is served very hot, the head split in half to reveal the brain, with boiled new potatoes, young broad beans and crisp spring salads.

## SHISH KEBAB
Serves 4

*Shishqebap* (Albanian), from the Turkish *sis kebabı*, meat cooked on skewers; *shishcheta* (Bulgarian); *souvlákia* (Greek); *raženchinja* (Macedonian); *frigărui* (Romanian); *ražnjiči* (Bosnian, Serbo-Croat), all meaning small skewers

Kebabs on skewers consist of cubes of lean marinated meat alternating with thin squares of fat which baste the meat while it is cooking and keep it moist. Lamb or mutton is traditional, but pork and beef are also used, especially in Romania and Serbia. To vary the taste, pieces of pepper, tomato, onion, mushroom or courgette are often added. However, vegetables do have a slightly drying effect on the meat, though they are delicious and make the meat go further.

As for the cooking of kebabs, nothing can equal a natural fire of wood or charcoal to lend flavour and sear the surface quickly to seal in the juices. Most electric cookers (there are hardly any gas stoves) in Balkan homes come without a grill compartment. Grilling is invariably done over an open fire. If you are constrained by the weather, or your situation, and have to use a domestic cooker grill, remember that they hardly ever get hot enough to exactly replicate the effect of a natural fire. This means the meat is cooked more slowly and hence could be tougher.

600 g lamb fillets, or boned lamb from the leg or loin (alternatively, use pork fillet or loin; chuck, rump or sirloin of beef), trimmed of fat and gristle, cut into 2.5–3 cm cubes •
vegetable oil or olive oil • 1 teaspoon black peppercorns, coarsely crushed •
about 200 g thin rashers of fatty bacon or strips of back pork fat, salt or fresh, cut into squares the same size as the cubes of meat (the Turks use sheep's tail fat) • salt
*To finish*
1 large onion, finely chopped, or a bunch of spring onions, chopped •
1 tablespoon finely chopped parsley • salt

Steep the cubed meat in 3–4 tablespoons of oil and the pepper in the refrigerator overnight, or at room temperature while preparing the fire for cooking.

Thread the meat alternately with back fat or bacon on to 4 large or 8 small, flat-bladed skewers, close together but not too tight. Place the skewers on a greased pre-heated rack close to the embers and cook for about 5–6 minutes, or until done to your taste, basting the meat with oil as it dries. Salt lightly and serve immediately still on the skewers. Onion mixed with parsley and sprinkled with salt just before serving is the traditional accompaniment.

## MEATBALL SHISH KEBAB
Serves 4

*Shishcheta ot smlyano meso* (Bulgarian); *raženchinja so meleno meso* (Macedonian); *ražnjići od mlevenog mesa* (Serbo-Croat); all meaning skewers with minced meat

800 g minced lamb or beef (or a mixture) •
50 g white bread, crusts removed, dipped in water, then excess water gently squeezed out •
1 small to medium onion, peeled and quartered •
1 teaspoon salt • freshly ground black pepper • 1 teaspoon ground coriander (optional) •
1/2 teaspoon ground cumin seed (optional) • 1 tablespoon finely chopped parsley •
8 sharp, flat-bladed skewers • a little oil for basting

Put the minced meat and the quartered onion through the fine disk of a mincer, then add the remaining ingredients. Mash everything together well until a really smooth and rather soft texture is achieved (if necessary, add a few tablespoons of water). This can also be done, in batches, in an electric food processor.

With dampened hands, mould the mixture into 32–40 small balls. Thread 4 or 5 balls, just touching each other, on to each skewer. Brush with oil and grill them over a charcoal fire or under a hot grill for 7–10 minutes, turning and basting them with oil several times during cooking. (Meatballs remain tender if cooked under a conventional cooker grill.)

Place the kebabs, still on the skewers, on warmed plates and serve with chopped onion mixed with parsley, lemon wedges and boiled haricot beans or potatoes.

## MIXED GRILL OF LAMB
Serves 4

*Meshena agneshka skara* (Bulgarian); *mješana janjetina na žaru* (Croat); *mešano jagnjeće meso na žaru* (Serbian)

In April and May, while the sweetbreads of young lambs were still available, this was a dish served in Bulgarian restaurants. Besides thymus or throat sweetbreads, the more highly prized heart sweetbreads from the pancreas are sometimes added for variety.

4 small shish kebabs, made from 300 g fillet or boned leg of lamb •
4 lamb cutlets or loin chops, lightly flattened •
150 g lamb's sweetbreads, washed and blanched in simmering water for 2–3 minutes, then refreshed under cold running water; membrane, fat or vein discarded; divided into serving pieces •
2 lamb's kidneys, surrounding fat eased away and reserved for greasing the heated grill rack, skin removed, cut in half lengthways and cored; soaked for 1 hour in cold water •
4 slices of lamb's liver, about 125 g in all, any vein or gristle removed • sunflower oil •
2–3 tablespoons black peppercorns, coarsely crushed • salt

Lay the meat and offal in a large baking tray or dish, brush liberally with oil and sprinkle with crushed peppercorns. Leave to stand for 2 hours at room temperature, a bit longer in the refrigerator.

Grill the shish kebabs and cutlets or loin chops over glowing charcoal for about 10 minutes, turning and basting frequently with a small bunch of rosemary dipped in oil. Add the sweetbreads, and shortly afterwards the kidneys (both preferably enclosed in double-sided wire-racks for ease of turning) and continue grilling—adding the sliced liver last of all. Cook until all the meats are done to your liking. In the Balkans meat is seldom, if ever, served underdone.

Transfer to a hot shallow stewpot, preferably of ovenproof glass, season lightly with salt, cover, and bring to the table with a plateful of trimmed spring onions and a large tossed green salad.

# CHARCOAL-GRILLED SKINLESS SAUSAGES
Serves 4–6

*Qebap në skarë* (Albanian); *kebapcheta* (Bulgarian); *ćevapčići* (Bosnian, Serbo-Croat), from the Turkish *kebap*, from the Arabic; *mititei* (Romanian); *sucuk köftesi* (Turkish)

These pure-meat sausages (no cereal binding) are as popular and universal in the Balkans as are hamburgers in the West. They can be found in almost every town—in special grill-rooms, self-service bars and beer gardens, but seldom in restaurants. For succulence, the minced meat mixture contains a considerable quantity of fat (25–45 per cent). Besides beef, the sausages can also be prepared with 900 g fatty lamb, or beef and fatty pork in equal quantities—in which case no suet or bone marrow should be added.

> 800 g boneless beef (back rib, skirt or flank), trimmed of gristle and excess fat •
> 100 g beef marrow or fresh beef suet, any membrane peeled away • 1 teaspoon salt •
> 1/2 teaspoon freshly ground black pepper • 1/2 teaspoon ground cumin, optional •
> 1 tablespoon finely chopped onion • suet or pork fat for greasing the rack

With a heavy knife or cleaver, chop the meat and suet finely—first separately and then combined; alternatively, purée them together in a food processor or mince them twice.

In a bowl, mix the meat with the rest of the ingredients and knead thoroughly. Fry a teaspoon of the mixture to make sure that you have the seasoning right. Cover the rest and refrigerate for at least 30 minutes or up to 12 hours.

To shape the sausages, force the meat through the sausage-making attachment of a mincer in approximately 10 cm lengths or extrude it through a piping bag fitted with a plain 2 cm nozzle. Otherwise divide into balls the size of small tomatoes and roll each one backwards and forwards on a table until about 10 cm long. Straighten up the ends. Refrigerate until you are ready to cook.

Prepare a glowing fire, with the rack close to the heat. Slick the bars with a scrap of suet or fat, then sear the sausages on all sides. Move the rack further from the heat and continue to cook for 5–10 minutes until done to your taste.

Serve immediately, on hot plates, with a spoonful of chopped onion and parsley, some pickled red peppers or gherkins, and some grilled fresh chillies. The raw onion permeates the whole dish and gives the sausages their characteristic flavour.

## GRILLED BEEF STEAKS
Serves 4

*Djulbastija* (Bosnian), *kulbastija* (Macedonian), *ćulbastija* (Serbian), from the Turkish *külbastı*, grilled meat, poultry, offal, fish or shellfish

---

4 boneless rump or sirloin steaks, cut across the grain into 1 cm slices • vegetable oil • coarsley crushed or cracked black peppercorns • salt

Rub a little oil into each steak, then press both surfaces into the peppercorns. Cover and leave to stand for 30–60 minutes, or a day in the refrigerator.

Shortly before serving, grill the meat on either side over hot wood or charcoal embers to the desired rareness. Most Serbs prefer their meat well done. Remove the steaks from the grill and season with salt. Serve them with some chopped onion mixed with parsley, and buttered boiled potatoes.

## KYUFTETA, GRILLED PATTIES

*Qofte të skarë* (Albanian); *kyfteta na skara* (Bulgarian); *keftédes tis skáras* (Greek); *Koftinja na skara* (Macedonian); *chiftele la grătar* (Romanian); from Turkish *izgara* or *ızkara köfte*; *pljeskavice* (Bosnian, Serbo-Croat, meaning burgers or patties slapped between the palms of the hands)

---

Prepare the meat in exactly the same way as for the sausages in the recipe on the preceding page, but shape it into patties. Divide it into balls about the size of an egg and flatten each one between oiled palms into rounds about 1 cm thick.

For 'nervous' or fiery burgers, add 1/2 teaspoon of hot chilli powder to the meat mixture.

## FRIED KYUFTETA
Makes 6–8 patties

*Qofte të fërguara* (Albanian); *purzheni kyufteta* (Bulgarian); *keftédes tiganités* (Greek); *pržena ḱoftinja* (Macedonian); *chiftea prăjita* (Romanian); *pržena ćufteta* (Bosnian, Serbo-Croat); from the Turkish *köfte,* from the Persian

In many parts of the Balkans these are made with a pestle and mortar to reduce the meat to a perfectly smooth purée. An electric food processor saves time and gives the same result. The same meat mixture, but seasoned more heavily with salt and pepper, can be shaped into miniature meat balls, the size of hazelnuts or marbles, and deep-fried. These are served on cocktail sticks as a meze with wine, beer or plum brandy.

25 g day-old crustless bread (no need to moisten it with milk or water) • 40 g onion • scant 1/2 teaspoon salt • 1/2 teaspoon freshly ground black pepper • 1/2 bunch parsley, preferably flat-leaved (or 1/2 teaspoon dried crumbled savory or oregano) • 1 egg • 400 g minced beef, lamb or pork (or a mixture of beef and lamb) • flour for coating

Using the metal blade of a food processor, combine the ingredients in the order given, processing thoroughly after each addition. Refrigerate for at least an hour to allow all the flavours to develop. Divide into 6 or 8 equal parts. With dampened hands, form each one into a flattened ball, then coat with flour on either side.

Pour about 1 cm of vegetable oil into a frying pan (for preference non-stick) over a medium heat. Cook in two batches to avoid crowding. Fry for about a minute on either side to brown and seal the surfaces. If the oil is not hot enough they take too long to brown; or they stick if you do not use a non-stick surface. Lower the heat and fry for further 3–4 minutes, turning once, until cooked through. Keep the first batch hot while frying the second; or leave to cool completely and reheat thoroughly in the oven the following day—though they are good cold and make excellent travel food.

To make these by hand, use the same quantities but first soak the bread in a little water, and gently squeeze out the excess. In a bowl, mash the bread with a fork, then chop the onion finely and mash it in together with the salt, black pepper and the fresh or dried herb. Beat the egg into the mixture with a fork. Add the meat and work it in to make a soft, loosely-bound paste. Divide this into 6 or 8. With dampened hands, shape each one into a flattened ball, then coat lightly with flour and fry exactly the same way as before.

Serve with mashed or fried potatoes, boiled haricot beans flavoured with a little fat left from the frying, buttered noodles and pickled gherkins or red peppers. A thin garlic and tomato sauce also goes well (p. 344).

## KYUFTETA BAKED IN YOGHURT CUSTARD
Serves 4

*Mlechen gyuvech s kyufteta* (Bulgarian, meaning dairy casserole with fried patties); *ćufteta u umaku od kiselog mleka* (Serbian, meaning fried patties in yoghurt sauce)

8 lamb or beef *kyufteta*, mixed in a food processor or by hand and fried as in the preceding recipe (they should be well browned, but still pink inside)
*Yoghurt custard*
3 medium eggs • pinch of salt • freshly ground black pepper •
375 g strained, pasteurized (non-sour), or freshly made (slightly sour) full-fat yoghurt

Arrange the fried kyufteta in a buttered baking dish no smaller than 24 cm in diameter. Thoroughly beat the eggs with the salt and pepper. Gradually beat in the yoghurt. Pour the custard round the meat so that a little of the tops are visible, and sprinkle over the surface some of the fat left from frying the meat for added flavour.

Bake on a centre shelf in a preheated oven (180°C/350°F/gas 4) for about 40 minutes, or until the custard is set, puffed up and golden-brown on top. Serve hot.

## MEATBALLS IN TOMATO SAUCE
Serves 4–6

*Qofte me salcë domatesh* (Albanian), *perişoare in sos de roşii* (Romanian), *ćufte u umaku od paradajza* (Serbian), all meaning meatballs in tomato sauce; *uvalaci* or *šakavci* (Bosnian, meaning meatballs that are rolled in the palm of the hand); *toparlak yahniya* (Bulgarian, from the Turkish *toparlak*, round and *yahni*, stew, from the Persian); *giouvarlákia me sáltsa* (Greek, meaning meatballs with tomato sauce, from the Turkish *yuvarlak*, ball or marble)

Follow the recipe for fried *kyufteta*, above, and roll the meat mixture with moistened hands into 24 small balls, then proceed to cook them as you would *kyufteta*. Keep them warm. Make the tomato sauce (p. 345) and cook for 5 minutes to thicken slightly. Drop in the meatballs and simmer to heat through; or reheat them thoroughly if you have made them a day in advance. Taste for seasoning and scatter parsley over the top. Bread, mashed potatoes or buttered noodles are the usual things to eat with these.

# MEATBALLS IN ONION SAUCE
Serves 4

*Qofte me qepë* (Albanian), *ćufte sa lukom* (Bosnian), both meaning meatballs with onion; *souvan kyufte* (Bulgarian, from Turkish *soğan*, onion, and *köfte*, meatball); *ćufte u umaku od crnog luka* (Serbian, meaning meatballs in onion sauce)

Fried *kyufteta* mixture shaped into 16 balls, floured and browned in oil or clarified butter
*Onion sauce*
600 g medium onions or red onions, peeled and cut across into thin slices •
sunflower oil or clarified butter (or a mixture of oil and fresh butter) •
150 ml good meat or vegetable stock • 1/4 teaspoon salt •
a little freshly ground black pepper

First prepare the meatballs and set aside. In a large covered frying pan, sweat the onion slices in a minimum of oil or butter over a low heat until soft. This may take up to 45 minutes. Then take the lid off and continue to cook for a further 15 minutes until the onions form a shiny golden-brown mass. Stir in the stock, salt and pepper. Bring to the boil, drop in the meatballs, and cook over a low heat for 4–5 minutes. Serve hot with bread, rice, polenta or mashed potatoes.

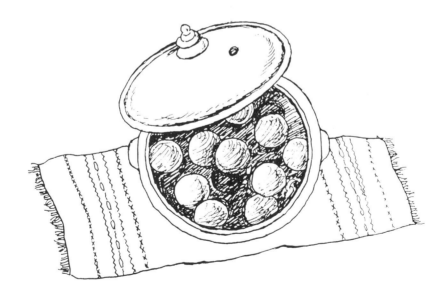

# MEATBALLS IN EGG-AND-LEMON SAUCE
Serves 4

*Zastroeni kyufteta—terbielii* (Bulgarian, meaning meatballs flavoured with a sauce—*terbiyeli* style), from the Turkish *terbiyeli köfte*, sauce-flavoured meatballs; *giouvarlákia mé sáltsa aýgolémono* (Greek, meaning meatballs with egg-lemon sauce) from the Turkish *yuvarlak*, ball or marble

400 g lean minced beef, pork or lamb, pounded to a paste, or puréed in food processor, or passed at least twice through the fine disk of a mincer •
50 g finely grated onion (including its juice) • 50 g round-grain rice •
scant 1/2 teaspoon salt • 1/4 teaspoon freshly ground black pepper •
1 tablespoon finely chopped parsley leaves • flour for coating the balls
625 ml strained meat stock or vegetable stock made with 2 each of onion, carrot and parsnip, quartered, 1/2 celeriac or 2 sticks celery, diced, and salt •
egg-and-lemon sauce (p. 349) • 4 tablespoons red paprika butter (p. 347)

To make the meatballs, combine the meat with the onion, rice, salt, pepper and the parsley and mix thoroughly. Shape the mixture into 24 balls and place them in one layer on a large round tray thinly covered with flour. Sprinkle more flour over the meatballs and roll them in it until coated all over.

To cook them, pour the stock into a wide and shallow pan and bring to the boil. Drop in the meatballs, preferably in one layer, and simmer until the rice grains stick out of each meatball like the needles of a hedgehog—about 35–40 minutes. Remove from the heat and keep warm.

Meanwhile, prepare the egg-and-lemon sauce using the strained cooking liquid, then pour this back into the pan. Simmer the meatballs in the sauce for 1–2 minutes without stirring. Check the seasoning. Serve hot, dribbling some paprika butter over each portion.

These meatballs are sometimes made with rice that has been parboiled for 10 minutes in unsalted water. In that case you can reduce the cooking time of the meatballs to 15 to 20 minutes.

The egg-and-lemon sauce can also be prepared without flour, but then the sauce should not be allowed to simmer or the egg may curdle.

*Meat*

# UNIVERSAL SCHNITZELS
Serves 4

*Kultsan shnitsel, paniran* (Bulgarian, from the French *paner*, to coat in crumbs); *sechkani pohuvani shnitsli* (Macedonian); *faširane phovane šnicle* (Serbo-Croat, from the French *farce*, forcemeat); from the German *Schnitzel*

---

My mother had many kitchen notebooks, where she wrote down all the family recipes—some of which had been passed on from mother to daughter from generation to generation. This is one. It is fairly universal in the region—I would be hard pressed to tell apart those I have eaten in Belgrade or in Skopje.

25 g crustless white bread • 4 tablespoons milk • 1/2 teaspoon each salt and pepper • 400 g finely minced beef, lamb or pork • 100 g clarified butter for frying • 75 g fine, lightly toasted breadcrumbs (or medium Matzo meal) and 2 medium eggs beaten, for coating

Soak the bread in milk, and mash with a fork. Add salt, pepper and the meat, and mix until smooth. Divide into 8 and shape into a slightly elongated, oval escalopes, about 5–6 mm thick. Dip first in crumbs, then in egg, and again in the breadcrumbs. Fry in batches over a moderate heat until golden—about 5 minutes on either side. To test if they are cooked, pierce with the point of a knife and press with spatula to see if the juice runs clear. Serve straight from the pan, with wedges of lemon.

# PLAIN VEAL ESCALOPES
Serves 4

*Shnicel i fërguar* (Albanian, meaning fried escalopes); *teleshki shnitsel natyur* (Bulgarian), *teleshki shnitsli natur* (Macedonian), *şniţel de viţel natural* (Romanian), *natur (naravne) teleće šnicle* (Serbo-Croat), all meaning plain veal escalopes—from the German *Naturschnitzel*

---

Besides veal, pork may be used: the fillet-end of leg, the fillet or tenderloin, or the eye of the loin. You can also flavour the meat by marinating in oil, lemon juice or plain yoghurt and fresh herbs for a few hours.

4 thin escalopes, from the rump or from the topside, lightly flattened to about 5 mm • plain flour for coating • clarified butter, or a mixture of unsalted butter and oil, for frying • dry wine, or meat or vegetable stock • salt and freshly ground pepper • 25 g butter

Coat the escalopes lightly with flour and fry over medium heat, in clarified butter or butter and oil, until well done. Like the flesh of sucking pig and lamb, undercooked veal is not easily digested. To test, pierce an escalope with the tip of your knife; if clear juice appears, it is well done. Transfer the meat to heated plates and keep hot while you prepare a sauce from the pan juices.

Pour off excess fat from the pan, return to the heat and put in a generous splash of wine or stock. With a wooden spoon, scrape to loosen and dissolve the browned meat deposits, then add more wine or stock—there should be about 2 tablespoons of sauce for each serving. Season with salt and pepper. Stir in the butter off the heat. Pour over the meat and serve immediately with buttered pasta and vegetables.

## VEAL ESCALOPES, VIENNESE STYLE
Serves 4

*Skallop viçi vienez* (Albanian, meaning Viennese veal escalopes); *Vienski shnitsel* (Bulgarian, 'Wiener Schnitzel'); *bečki teleći odresci-viner-šnicle* (Serbo-Croat, 'Viennese veal slices—Wiener Schnitzel')

This is found everywhere on Balkan restaurant menus. I had excellent one in the Hotel Tiranë in Tirana. Pork escalopes or boned pork cutlets, tiny lamb cutlets with the rib ends stripped to expose the bone, even fish fillets and flattened poultry breasts can also be cooked in this way.

4 veal escalopes (or small boned cutlets) • black pepper • vegetable oil • salt • plain white flour, 2 eggs, lightly beaten with a fork until the whites just blend with the yolks, and 75–100 g pale crumbs, dried in the oven, for coating

Flatten the escalopes with a meat bat or empty bottle as thin as possible, working in some pepper. Brush with a little oil, stack on a plate and refrigerate until you are ready. Dip each one in flour, then in egg, and finally in crumbs, making sure that they are all well coated. With the dull edge of a knife, lightly criss-cross the coating to prevent it cracking in the cooking. Leave at room temperature for 30 minutes.

Heat a 5 mm layer of fat (clarified butter, oil or lard, or a mixture of unsalted butter and oil) in a large frying pan and fry the escalopes over no more than medium heat so the coating does not brown too much before the meat is cooked. To test, pierce the escalope with a sharp skewer; if the juices run clear, it is done. Season with salt.

Serve very hot, each escalope topped with a piece of butter and a lemon twist.

# ALBANIAN LAMB AND YOGHURT CASSEROLE
Serves 4

*Tavë kosi* (Albanian, yoghurt casserole)

A national dish of Albania. I had this lovely and uncommon dish at the Hotel Adriatic—situated in the seaside resort a few miles south of the city of Durres. The recipe itself was given to me by two ladies from Berat. The Macedonian *Jogurt tava* is related.

If the yoghurt custard is thickened with rice grown near the town of Elbasan—thought the best rice in the country—instead of flour, *Tavë kosi* is renamed *Tavë Elbasani*, Elbasan casserole. The rice is fully cooked before adding to the custard.

800 g half shoulder of lamb, blade end (the knuckle-end will give you less meat), excess fat removed • 1 carrot and 1 small parnsip, peeled and halved •
1/4 celeriac, peeled (or 2 sticks of celery, cut into short lengths) •
1 teaspoon peppercorns • 1/4 teaspoon salt

*Custard sauce*

2 eggs • 2 tablespoons flour •
200 g full fat, strained or thick-set yoghurt, freshly made or pasteurized (thin, low-fat, sour yoghurt will not do) •
400 ml broth in which the meat was poached (if there is less broth, make it up to this amount with water) • 1/4 teaspoon salt

Choose a saucepan of a size just to contain the meat. Pour 500 ml of water into the empty pan, and when it comes to the boil, lower the joint into the water and bring it back to the boil, skimming. When the liquid is clear, add the vegetables and pepper, cover and poach at the barest simmer for about 1 1/2 hours, or until the lamb flesh falls off the bones. Add the salt towards the end of the cooking time.

Lift the lamb out, remove the bones and cut the meat into walnut-sized pieces. Reserve the broth. Divide the meat equally among 4 oven-proof bowls.

To make the custard sauce, strain the broth, discarding the vegetables and peppercorns; leave until lukewarm. In a bowl, beat the eggs then add the rest of the sauce ingredients in sequence, beating after each addition.

Pour the sauce over the meat in the bowls, and bake in a preheated oven (180°C/350°F/gas 4) for 20 minutes until the custard sets lightly. Avoid longer cooking which will make the custard too firm. Either bring the bowls themselves to table, or turn them out on to fresh hot plates.

## ALBANIAN LAMB STEW WITH PARSLEY
Serves 2

*Mish shqeto* (Albanian, 'meat cooked without vegetables'); *janjeće meso sa majdanosom* (Bosnian); *jagneshko so magdanos—shketo* (Macedonian)

This centuries-old recipe is still current. It attests the ingenuity of housewives who create delectable food from the simplest ingredients. Flat-leaved parsley, not curly, is indispensable for authentic flavour.

700 g half-shoulder of lamb, the blade end: thoroughly trimmed, deboned, bones reserved, meat cut into 3.5 cm cubes •
25 g clarified butter (or the same amount of fresh butter with 1 tablespoon oil) •
scant 1/2 teaspoon salt • 2 bunches flat-leaved parsley, the thick parts of the stem removed, the sprigs finely chopped • freshly ground black pepper

Put the reserved bones in a pan, pour over 250 ml of water and bring slowly to the boil. Meanwhile, heat the butter in a frying pan, and fry the meat pieces briskly to sear on all sides. As they brown, transfer to the pan with the boiling water. When they are all in, pour over some of the frying pan juices, add salt, cover and simmer for about 1 3/4 hours or until the meat is tender. Stir in the parsley and simmer for a further 10 minutes. Season generously with black pepper. Spoon the meat on to warm plates and pour over the juices remaining in the pan. The dish is eaten with a spoon and the only accompaniment is bread.

## PORK AND RICE CASSEROLE
Serves 3

*Slavyanski gyuvech* (Bulgarian, 'casserole of the Slavs')

This casserole, which in Bulgaria is traditionally made with pork, has acquired its name owing to the fact that the early Slavs were the first people in north-eastern Europe to domesticate the wild boar, *Sus scrofa*, the ancestor of the European pig.

500 g lean, boneless pork, trimmed weight, cut into 4 cm cubes • 15 g lard •
1 medium onion, chopped • 1 teaspoon paprika • meat or vegetable stock or water •
1 green pepper, seeded, cut into small squares • 1/2 teaspoon salt • 100 g round-grain rice •
4–5 tomatoes, peeled, sliced into rounds and lightly salted • a little oil for brushing the tomatoes • 1 tablespoon parsley leaves, finely chopped

Brown the meat on all sides in the lard. Transfer to a heavy saucepan, using a slotted spoon. Lightly brown the onion in the fat remaining in the frying pan, add to the meat, stir in the paprika and pour over enough hot stock or water to cover completely. Simmer, covered, for up to an hour, or until the meat is tender, then add the green pepper and the salt. Cook for 10 minutes more, then stir in the rice and cook for 10 more minutes to allow the rice to absorb most of the liquid.

Transfer the contents of the saucepan to a medium casserole and add some more hot stock or water if the rice seems rather dry. Arrange the sliced tomatoes on the surface to cover and protect the top grains of rice from hardening in the oven. Brush with a little oil, then bake in a preheated oven (160°C/325°F/gas 3) for 30 minutes, until the tomatoes are slightly tinged with brown. Scatter chopped parsley on top and serve straight from the casserole.

## BOILED BEEF
### Serves 10–12

*Mish kau i zier* (Albanian); *vareno govezhdo* (Bulgarian); *vareno govedsko* (Macedonian); *kuvana govedina* (Serbo-Croat); *kuhana govedina* (Slovenian); *sığır eti söğüşü* (Turkish); *rasol* (Romanian) from the Russian *rassol*

2.5 kg topside or silverside of beef, trimmed of fat and tied into a compact shape •
1 teaspoon black peppercorns • 4 allspice berries • 1 bay leaf • 2 cloves • 15 g salt •
1 medium celeriac, quartered • 3–4 carrots, peeled and halved •
1 parsley root or parsnip, peeled and halved • 250 g pickling onions, peeled

Place the meat in a large saucepan or stock-pot, with just enough water to cover, then lift the meat out and bring the water to the boil. Carefully lower the meat into the boiling water and cook it over medium-high heat, uncovered, for 10–15 minutes to seal the meat, removing any scum that rises to the surface.

Add the spices, cover and reduce the heat until the water barely simmers. For well-done beef, cook the joint for 2 1/2 hours; for medium rare about 2 hours, and 1 1/2 hours for rare, adding the salt and vegetables some 30 minutes before the end.

Remove the meat from the stock, cut off the trussing strings and let it stand for about 10 minutes to make carving easier. Slice the beef thinly across the grain, arrange the slices on a large heated serving dish and keep warm. Strain the stock and place the cooked vegetables round the meat; discard the spices. Pour a little of the hot stock over the meat.

## BEEF KEBABS BAKED IN PAPER PARCELS
Serves 4

*Qebap viçi në letër* (Albanian); *teleshki kebap v hartiya* (Bulgarian); *teleći ćevap u hartiju* (Serbo-Croat); from the Turkish *kağıt kebabı*, paper kebab

In the past, small pieces of meat or game were baked in hot ashes wrapped in vine or sorrel leaves or the leaves of an ear of maize. Larger cuts or small whole birds were given an outer wrapping of clay and roasted in embers until the casing fell apart. Meat cooked in this way has come to be generally known as 'Guerilla kebab': *hajdoushki kebap* in Bulgaria and *hajdučki ćevap* in Vojvodina and Serbia. The leaf-and-clay wrapping methods are still followed in many country districts.

500 g piece of beef with a fine marbling of fat (such as back-rib fillet, i.e. the fillet to the first 4 ribs after the blade-bone), cut into cubes 2 cm square • 50 g butter •
400 g spring onions, trimmed weight (including the green parts), thinly sliced •
5–10 mint leaves, chopped • 2–3 tablespoons parsley, finely chopped •
salt and freshly ground pepper •
4 sheets of greaseproof paper, approximately 30 cm square, well buttered or oiled on both sides

Lightly fry the meat in the butter. Remove from the heat and stir in the spring onions and herbs. Season sparingly with salt but generously with black pepper. Divide this, including the juices, between the four sheets of paper. Fold the top and bottom edges to cover the meat, then fold over the ends of the rectangle to make a neat square. Place on a greased baking sheet with the loose ends down, sprinkle with a little water and bake in a preheated oven (160°C/ 325°F/gas 3) for 45 minutes. The paper should be a shade darker, but not brown or burnt.

To open the parcels, place them on individual hot plates and make a cross cut with scissors or small sharp knife from end to end, then fold the paper back to form a diamond-shaped opening, displaying the contents.

This kebab is eaten with a spoon. Accompany with a baked potato and a tossed green salad.

# LAMB STEW WITH SPRING ONIONS
### Serves 4–5

*Kapama* (Albanian, Bosnian, Bulgarian, Macedonian, Serbian), *kapamá* (Greek), from the Turkish *kapama*

---

1.5 kg shoulder or middle neck of lamb, cut into serving pieces • 600 g spring onions, including the green parts • 100 g spring garlic, including the green parts, or 4 garlic cloves chopped finely • salt • mint or dill leaves, chopped • freshly ground black pepper

Trim the 'beards' from the onion and garlic and any damaged or withered leaves. Chop roughly into 1 cm pieces and put them into a large, shallow stewpan. Add the meat, some salt and a little boiling water. Cover and simmer for an hour or so, until the onion and the garlic have almost melted into the sauce and the meat is falling away from the bones. Stir in the mint or dill leaves. Take the pan off the heat and remove any loose bones. Sprinkle black pepper over the dish and check for seasoning. Serve in heated earthenware bowls, with boiled potatoes or bread.

If you prefer, you can fry the meat and onions in lard, which is the Serbian way, or oil—as they do in Macedonia—before stewing.

# LAMB STEW WITH PEAS
### Serves 4–5

*Mish qëngji me bizele* (Albanian); *agneshko meso s grah* (Bulgarian); *jagneshko meso so grashok* (Macedonian); *jagnjeće meso sa graškom* (Serbian)

---

600 g lamb, weighed after large bones have been removed • 50 g clarified butter, or 3–4 tablespoons vegetable oil (or a mixture of fresh butter and oil) • 2–3 onions, finely chopped • 2–3 tomatoes, peeled and chopped • 1/2 teaspoon paprika • 1 teaspoon salt • 400 g young shelled peas, fresh or frozen • 2–3 tablespoons chopped dill leaves

Cut the meat into 2–3 pieces per portion, without removing the smaller bones. Brown in butter or oil, then reserve. Prepare a small enrichment sauce by gently frying the chopped onion in the same fat until soft and golden-brown. Add the tomatoes, and when the sauce has reduced considerably, stir in the paprika. Return the meat to the pan; pour in about 200 ml warm water and simmer gently until half-cooked. Add the salt and fresh peas (if frozen, add them when the lamb is almost ready), and continue cooking until all is tender. Serve hot, sprinkled with chopped dill leaves, and a little yoghurt as accompaniment.

## LAMB STEW WITH SPINACH
Serves 4

*Jahni* or *jani me mish qëngji dhe spinaq* (Albanian); *janjeća jahnija sa špinatom* (Bosnian); *agneshka yahniya sus spanak* (Bulgarian); *jagneshka janija so spanak* (Macedonian); *jagnjeća janija sa spanaćem* (Serbian); *janjetina sa špinatom* (Croat)

600 g boned shoulder of lamb, in portions • 50 g butter or lard (or 3–4 tablespoons oil) • 150 g spring onions, sliced (including the green parts) • 1 tablespoon tomato purée • 1/2 teaspoon paprika • about 100 ml hot meat stock or water • 1/2 teaspoon salt • 600 g spinach, trimmed weight, coarsely chopped, or the same quantity frozen spinach

In a heavy pan, lightly brown the meat in the hot fat, then add the spring onions and cook until these are just soft. Stir in the tomato purée and, off the heat, the paprika. Pour over the hot stock or water and add salt. Simmer over a mere thread of heat, adding a bare amount of hot liquid when necessary so that the meat will not fry. When the meat is tender (about an hour), slide in the spinach and cook for a further 15–20 minutes until the spinach is done. Check the seasoning and serve hot with a tablespoon or two of plain yoghurt at the side of each plate.

## LAMB STEW WITH GREEN BEANS
Serves 4

*Jahni (Jani) me mish qëngji dhe fasule të njoma* (Albanian); *janjeća jahnija s mladim grahom* (Bosnian); *agneshka yahniya sus zelen fasoul* (Bulgarian); *janjetina s mladim grahom (mahuna)* (Croat); *jagneshka janija so boranija* (Macedonian); *jagneća janija od zelene (mlade) boranije* (Serbian)

This stew is just as good with chuck steak, braising steak or shin of beef

400–600 g lean boned lamb, cut into serving pieces • 2 tablespoons vegetable oil • 1 medium onion, finely chopped • 1 tablespoon tomato purée • 1/2 teaspoon paprika • meat stock or water • 800 g young, stringless green beans, fresh or frozen, cut into bite-sized pieces • 4 unpeeled garlic cloves • salt and freshly ground black pepper • 2–3 tomatoes, quartered • 25 g butter or 2 tablespoons olive oil
*To finish*
4 or more garlic cloves, pounded with a pinch of salt, then blended with 1 tablespoon of oil • thick set plain yoghurt

Brown the meat on all sides in the oil and transfer to a saucepan. Fry the onion in the same oil, stir in the tomato purée and the paprika. Add a little warm water, then combine this small sauce with the meat. Pour over enough stock or water to come to the level of the meat and simmer over a low heat until the meat is half-cooked. Drop in the beans and the whole garlic cloves and continue cooking for another 25–30 minutes. At the end of the cooking there should be enough juices left in the pan to come halfway up the sides of the stew; if not, add a little more hot stock or water.

Remove the stew from the heat, discard the garlic cloves, then stir in the butter or olive oil. Serve hot with bread. Pass round separately a small bowl with pounded garlic and another one with yoghurt so that everyone can help themselves.

## LAMB STEW WITH POTATOES
Serves 4

*Jagnjeća kalja sa krompirom* (Bosnian, Serbian), *kalle ot agneshko s kartofi* (Bulgarian), via the Turkish *kalle* and *kalya*, itself from the Arabic *qalya* or *qaliyya* which comes ultimately from the Latin *caulis*, cabbage, stalk of a plant

An ancient dish, originally prepared with cabbage, mentioned in the fifteenth-century *Divan* (a Persian collection of verse of Bushaq of Shiraz). In the Balkans it is always made with meat and either cabbage, turnip or potato. When cooked with potatoes and onions, it is similar to Irish stew—and very tasty.

4 middle-neck fillets of lamb or mutton, sliced into serving pieces •
1 large onion, chopped • 1 kg potatoes, peeled and cut into chunks • 1/2 teaspoon salt •
1 teaspoon paprika • 1/2 teaspoon black peppercorns, coarsely crushed

Put the meat and onion into a stew-pan and pour in enough hot water to come half way up the meat. Cover and simmer for 1 hour, until tender. Stir in the potatoes, salt, paprika and peppercorns, and add a little more hot water, if necessary—there should be enough cooking liquid to serve as a sauce. Cook the stew for another half an hour, or until the potatoes are soft. Taste for salt and pepper and serve hot.

## PRIEST'S STEW
Serves 5–6

*Papazjanija* (Bosnian, Macedonian, Serbian), *popska yahniya* (Bulgarian), from the Turkish *papaz yahnisi*, meaning stew of an Eastern Orthodox priest; *stufat* (Romanian), from the Greek *stifádo*

---

A dish of Greek origin, re-named 'Priest's stew' by the Turks—Eastern Orthodox priests were known as connoisseurs of good food and wine. The French *boeuf bourguignonne* is similar, though with no link to the church.

In the Balkans this is a winter dish traditionally made with equal quantities of beef (or game) and pickling onions. The meat is either browned in oil before cooking or dropped into a mixture of boiling wine and water to seal in the juices. There is also a meatless version.

1 kg lean beef, chuck or topside, cut into 5 cm cubes • 2–3 tablespoons sunflower oil •
1 medium onion, finely chopped • 1–2 tablespoons tomato purée • 1 teaspoon paprika •
250 ml dry red wine • 2 tablespoons red wine vinegar • 1 1/2 teaspoons salt •
5 allspice berries • 1 bay leaf • freshly ground black pepper •
1 kg pickling onions, blanched in boiling water, then topped, tailed and peeled, but left whole •
5 or more whole garlic cloves, peeled • 1 1/2 tablespoons lightly roasted flour (p 340)

Fry the meat in the oil, a few pieces at a time, until nicely browned. Lift out and reserve. Fry the chopped onion in the same oil until it colours, then stir in the tomato purée and paprika, and pour in the wine, vinegar and 250 ml water. Bring the mixture to the boil and add the meat, salt and spices. Cover and simmer gently for about 50 minutes, or until the meat is tender.

Add the onions and garlic, and continue to cook for a further 45 minutes or until the onions are soft but not disintegrating. To add body to the stew, blend the roasted flour gradually with a ladleful of the hot cooking juices. Pour this back into the stew and cook for 2 more minutes, shaking the pan rather than stirring, to avoid breaking up the onions. Once cooked, remove the bay and allspice and check the seasoning. Serve on heated plates with some mashed potato.

## BEEF STEW WITH PRUNES
Serves 6

*Yahniya sus suhi slivi* (Bulgarian); *janija so suvi slivi* (Macedonian); *janija od suvih šljiva* (Serbo-Croat); from the Turkish *Erik yahnisi*

A winter dish of Arabic provenance, commonly prepared in the Balkans with pork, mutton, hen or rabbit. It is exceptionally tasty if instead you use equal quantities of beef brisket and topside. Besides prunes, other winter fruits that often go into the pot are quinces, chestnuts or dried apricots.

900 g boned beef, cut into 4 cm cubes • 3–4 tablespoons vegetable oil or clarified butter •
1 large onion, finely chopped • 2 tablespoons tomato purée • 1 teaspoon paprika •
hot stock or water • 1 small stick cinnamon or 2 bay leaves or 1–2 teaspoons mixed spice •
1/2 teaspoon salt • freshly ground black pepper • 3–4 tablespoons sugar •
600–700 g prunes, not soaked in advance • 1 tablespoon plain or roasted flour (p. 340) •
250 ml dry red wine

Brown the meat on all sides in the oil or clarified butter. Transfer to a saucepan with a well-fitting lid. Fry the onion in the same fat, then stir in the tomato purée and paprika. Tip this over the meat, pour in hot stock or water to come to the level of the meat and add the cinnamon, mixed spice or bay leaves. Cover the pan and simmer for about 1 1/2 hours, or until the meat begins to soften, then stir in salt and pepper to taste.

Dissolve the sugar in 3 tablespoons water and cook until the sugar turns a golden-brown. Once this happens, pour the hot caramel over the meat, then add the prunes, stir, and continue to simmer for another 40–45 minutes, until the meat and fruit are tender but not disintegrating.

Blend the flour with the wine, pour it into the pan and cook for a further 10 minutes. Discard the cinnamon or bay leaves and check the seasoning. The stew should have sufficient sauce just to cover the meat and prunes. Serve immediately or reheat thoroughly the following day: the dish will only gain in flavour.

# BEEF STEW WITH RICE, LEEKS AND POTATOES
Serves 2

*Pirjan sa prasom* (Bosnian, Hercegovinian), from Persian *biryan*

Though Persian in origin, this modest Bosnian and Hercegovinian family stew of meat, rice and vegetables bears little likeness to *biryan*—the spicy meat and rice dish of medieval Persia.

200 g minced or finely chopped beef • 600 g leeks, white part only, cut into 1.5 cm thick rounds • 1/2 teaspoon salt • paprika • 50 g round-grain rice • 1 medium potato, peeled and diced • freshly ground black pepper • red paprika butter of 15 g butter and paprika

Fry the meat in its own fat until it just turns colour. Add the leeks, salt, 1/4 teaspoon paprika, the rice, potato and 5 tablespoons warm water. Mix together delicately, without breaking the leek rounds. Simmer gently, shaking the pan occasionally, for about 30 minutes, until everything is tender and the liquid absorbed. Remove from the heat. Add pepper to taste and season with extra salt, if necessary. Spoon on to well heated plates and keep hot. As a last touch, heat the butter in a small pan. Off the heat, stir in 2–3 large pinches of paprika, and dribble the clear, red liquid over each portion. Serve immediately.

# VINE LEAF ROLLS WITH MEAT AND RICE
Serves 4

*Lozova sarma* (Bosnian), *sarmi s lozovi lista* (Bulgarian), *sarma od japraka* (Croat), *japrak* (Hercegovinian), *sarma od lozov list* (Macedonian), *sarmale cu frunziș de viță* (Romanian), *sarma od vinovog lišća* (Serbian), from the Turkish *yaprak sarması*, 'vine leaves wrapped around a filling'. *Dollma me fletë hardhije* (Albanian), *ntolmádes* (Greek), come from the Turkish *yaprak dolması,* meaning leaves or vine leaves stuffed with a filling—which is now regarded, even in Turkey, as incorrect since the leaves are not stuffed, but wrapped around a filling.

Although cabbage, spinach, sauerkraut and other leaves can be used for this dish vine leaves have a gentle acidity and aroma unmatched by any other.

As minced lamb can be fatty, you may wish to de-fat the meat before using it. Once cooked, rolls with rice in the filling are never left to stand in either sauce or cooking liquid lest the rice should go mushy.

200 g packet or jar of vine leaves preserved in brine, drained, stem ends snipped off; or an equal quantity of trimmed young fresh vine leaves

*Filling*

400 g finely minced lean lamb • 2 tablespoons vegetable oil or melted butter •
2 medium-sized onions, very finely chopped • 50 g round-grained rice •
1 teaspoon paprika • 3 tablespoons chopped parsley, or 3 teaspoons dried parsley •
3 tablespoons chopped fresh or frozen dill (if available) •
2 tablespoons chopped mint leaves, or 1 teaspoon dried mint, crumbled •
1 teaspoon chopped fresh savory or oregano, or 1/4 teaspoon dried • 3/4 teaspoon salt •
1/2 teaspoon freshly ground black pepper • a little meat stock or water

*Finishing sauce*

250 ml plain yoghurt or thin cream (or the juice of 1 lemon) • 2 egg yolks •
2 tablespoons plain flour • salt and pepper

Blanch the leaves in boiling water—this will take 1–2 minutes for young fresh leaves, longer if the leaves are brined. Drain, then float them in a bowl of cold water to separate them easily.

Mix all the filling ingredients together, moistening them with a little stock or water.

To shape the rolls, lay each leaf vein-side up on a flat surface. Spoon a rounded tablespoon of the stuffing on to the stalk end, spreading the stuffing into sausage shape. Fold over the stalk end then the sides, to enclose the stuffing. Roll up the leaf tightly towards its tip to make a neat roll.

Oil the bottom of a large shallow saucepan and cover it with a few torn leaves. Arrange the rolls, loose-end down, in the pan—in a single or double layer, closely packed in circles. Invert a plate over them to keep them in place and pour over enough water to just cover it. Put on the lid and simmer gently for 90 minutes, or until the rolls are perfectly tender and can be cut across with a fork.

Combine the cream, yoghurt, or lemon juice with the egg yolks in a small pan. Sprinkle over the flour, season with salt and pepper and stir well. Drain off the cooking juices from the vine leaves into a measuring jug. This is a hot and hazardous procedure that needs an oven glove to hold the plate down while you tip the pan. Top up the juices in the jug with water to make 300 ml and add this to the yoghurt mixture. Stir the sauce over a low heat until it starts to bubble and thickens enough to coat the spoon—this takes about a minute. Remove from the heat and check for seasoning, then pour equal amounts of the sauce on to 4 heated plates. Arrange the rolls on the sauce then drizzle with any sauce that remains. Keep warm until served. A basketful of hot dinner rolls and hearty red wine are fine accompaniments.

# CABBAGE-LEAF ROLLS WITH MEAT AND RICE
### Makes 12–16 rolls

*Sarmi s pryasno zele* (Bulgarian), *sarma od lisja od sveža zelka* (Macedonian), *sarma od slatkog kapusa* (Serbian), from the Turkish *lahana sarması* 'cabbage wrapped round a filling'

---

1 medium sized savoy cabbage (tightly-packed white cabbage is unsuitable) •
1 tablespoon each of oil and lemon juice

*Stuffing*

400 g lean minced beef • 1 large onion, very finely chopped • 2 tablespoons vegetable oil •
50 g round-grain rice • 1 tablespoon tomato purée • 1 teaspoon paprika • 3/4 teaspoon salt •
black pepper • 1/2 tablespoon fresh mint, chopped, or 1/2 teaspoon dried mint

*Finishing sauce*

1 tablespoon plain flour, toasted in a dry frying pan • 25 g butter • salt and pepper

Separate 20 outer leaves of the cabbage and pare the protruding part of the thick central rib of each leaf. Simmer in slightly salted boiling water for 5–10 minutes until soft and pliable, then drain.

Mix the stuffing ingredients together, moistening with a little water. Stuff the cabbage leaves in the same way as the vine leaves of the preceding recipe. Arrange in a wide and shallow saucepan, sprinkle over the tablespoons of oil and lemon juice and cover with an inverted plate. Pour in enough water to cover the top of the plate. Put the lid on, and simmer gently for 75–90 minutes, until tender.

Strain the cooking liquid into a small pan and sprinkle in the toasted flour. Stir, adding the butter, salt and pepper, and cook for a few more seconds. Pour over the rolls, or pass it round separately. Serve with lemon wedges and hot garlic bread.

# SAUERKRAUT ROLLS WITH MEAT AND RICE
### Makes 12–16 rolls

*Sarmi s kiselo zele* (Bulgarian); *sarma od kisela zelka* (Macedonian); *sarmale cu varză acră* (Romanian); *sarma od kiselog kupusa* (Serbian)

---

Sauerkraut rolls are known as 'white rolls' since they contain neither paprika nor tomatoes. The pleasant sourness and saltiness of the sauerkraut leaves and liquor make the addition of salt scarcely necessary.

20 outer sauerkraut leaves, the protruding part of the thick central rib pared away •
2–3 tablespoons sauerkraut liquor • 1 tablespoon vegetable oil
*Stuffing*
400 g half and half mixture of beef and pork, finely minced •
1 onion, very finely chopped • 2 tablespoons vegetable oil • 50 g round-grain rice •
ground black pepper

Prepare the sauerkraut rolls in the same way as the cabbage rolls. Simmer them in a mixture of sauerkraut liquor and water, mellowed with 1 tablespoon oil, for about 2 hours or until tender and most of the liquid has been absorbed. Serve hot on heated plates.

## PORK POT WITH WHITE CABBAGE
Serves 4

*Svinjska rebra sa slatkim kupusom* (Serbo-Croat); *svinjska rebrca z zeljem* (Slovenian), both meaning pork rib chops with cabbage

1 kg white cabbage, cored and sliced into 2 cm chunks •
1 large red pepper, halved, seeded and cut into 2 cm slices • 1 teaspoon paprika •
1 teaspoon salt • about 250 g chorizo, or other paprika-flavoured pork sausage, peeled and sliced into rounds •
4 pork loin or spare-rib chops, about 700 g altogether, lightly rubbed with salt •
1 teaspoon cornflour • 125 ml single cream

Combine the cabbage, pepper, paprika, salt and sausage in a large bowl and mix well. Using a heavy stewpot, place the cabbage and pork chops in alternating layers of cabbage, a pair of chops, cabbage, the second pair of chops, then a top layer of cabbage. Pour in 150 ml water.

Cover and cook over a low heat for 90 minutes, until all the liquid in the bottom of the pan has evaporated, the cabbage is practically disintegrating, and the meat is fork-tender.

Finish this with a teaspoon of cornflour slaked with the cream stirred in at the last minute. Bring the mixture back to the boil and allow to simmer for a few moments. Adjust the seasoning with salt and serve with hot rolls.

## PORK WITH SAUERKRAUT
Serves 3–4

*Svinsko s kiselo zele* (Bulgarian); *svinsko so kisela zelka* (Macedonian); *porc cu varză acră* (Romanian); *svinjetina s kiselim kupusom* (Serbo-Croat)

A classic winter dish sometimes enriched with sour cream, or cooked with a little boiled rice and fried onion.

400 g lean, boned shoulder of pork, cubed •
75 g lard or raw pork fat, chopped, or 75 ml oil •
400 g shredded sauerkraut, home-made or bought in a jar (not canned), rinsed briefly under running water and drained (or leave unwashed if you prefer a more acid taste) •
1 1/2 teaspoons paprika • 1 fresh or dried chilli pepper • salt and pepper

Lightly brown the meat on all sides in the hot fat. Transfer the meat to an enamelled saucepan or one made of fireproof porcelain or glass that is not affected by acidity. Briefly fry the sauerkraut in the remaining fat, season with paprika, and tip into the saucepan with the meat. Stir everything together and bury the chilli in the middle, if you are using it. Cover and cook over a low heat for 60–90 minutes, adding a spoonful of water when necessary, until all is tender, and the liquid evaporated. Towards the end of the cooking time, discard the chilli, and season to taste.

## POT-ROASTED SILVERSIDE OF BEEF
Serves 4–6

*Zadousheno govezhdo ot vajsbrata* (Bulgarian); *pirjanjena bela govedja pečenica* (Serbian)

I think beef braised in the simple traditional manner with spices and wine rather than stock or water is one of the nicest ways. Besides silverside, this method works admirably for other large cuts—especially when they are marbled or interspersed with thin layers of fat (such as thin rib or brisket) which bastes the meat from within and keeps it moist.

As the name suggests, the meat is 'roasted' in a piece in a pot on top of the stove, not in the oven. It is ideal for the shared occasion—because the larger the cut, the juicier and therefore the better the meat should be. Like so many Balkan dishes this is also excellent when cooked a day in advance and re-heated thoroughly in its gravy.

1.3 kg silverside of beef, external fat removed, the joint re-tied to a neat shape •
oil, lard or dripping • 1 tablespoon red wine vinegar • dry red wine •
1 teaspoon black peppercorns • 1 bay leaf • 5–6 allspice berries • 5–6 cloves •
7–8 garlic cloves, unpeeled •
10 cm length of leek, sliced • 1/4 head celeriac, diced (or 1 stick celery, sliced) •
1 small carrot, sliced • 1/4 teaspoon salt • 1–1 1/2 tablespoons plain flour

Brown the meat on all sides in the hot fat to seal in the juices; discard the fat. Put the meat in a saucepan just large enough to hold it snugly, pour in the vinegar and red wine to come no more than a third of the way up the sides of the meat. Add the spices and tuck the prepared vegetables around. Cover with a tight-fitting lid, bring to the boil and simmer gently for up to 4 hours. Half-way through the cooking transfer the meat to a smaller pan that just fits its reduced size and add the salt.

When it is ready, remove the meat and keep it warm. Strain the cooking juices, discard the spices and vegetables and return the liquid to the pan. Pour in the flour blended with a little water and stir over a low heat until the gravy thickens. Carve the meat, moisten with some of the gravy and serve the remainder separately, with mashed potatoes, peas and noodles.

## BOSNIAN POT WITH MEAT AND VEGETABLES
Serves 4–5

*Bosanski lonac*

*Lonac* in Serbo-Croat signifies pot, stew-pan or saucepan. *Glineni lonac* is a deep earthenware stewpot which has given its name to the mixture of meats and vegetables which is cooked in it. The dish itself has undergone considerable changes since its inception during the Middle Ages as a miner's one-pot meal.

Bosnia is an ancient mining region, rich in ores. According to the scholar Alija Lakišić, medieval miners assembled the few ingredients they brought with them into large communal clay pots, *glineni lonci*, which were marked on the outside with the symbol of each group of workers to differentiate one vessel from another. The pots were luted, that is sealed tight with dough, and left to cook for hours buried in the embers of an outdoor fire while the men toiled in the open-cast mines. The dish that bears the name today uses mainly seasonal ingredients and can vary from month to month, family to family. It is at its best when prepared in large quantities and baked really slowly.

800 g lean braising steak, chuck or shoulder (or a mixture of beef, pork and lamb), cut into 7 cm cubes • 600 g waxy potatoes, peeled weight, quartered or left whole if small • 3 medium onions, sliced • 1–2 carrots, sliced • 6 tablespoons chopped parsley • 4 tablespoons chopped celeriac leaves (or 1–2 sticks of celery, cut into pieces) • 3/4 teaspoon salt • 75 g fresh pork back fat, diced small • 2 teaspoons black peppercorns, 2–3 cloves, 2–3 allspice berries, and 50 g whole unpeeled garlic cloves (in a muslin bag) • 100 ml wine, or 75 ml water plus 2 tablespoons wine vinegar

In a large earthenware or stoneware stewpot (4 litre capacity), layer the meat with the vegetables (which have been previously mixed with the herbs, salt and diced pork fat), starting and finishing with the vegetables. Bury the spice bag in the centre of the pot, then pour over the wine or water mixed with vinegar. Cover and seal the lid with a strip of flour-and-water dough. Place the pot in a preheated oven at 220°C/425°F/gas 7 for 30 minutes, then reduce to 125°C/250°F/gas 1/2, and leave for another 4 hours. When the time is up, discard the spice bag and serve straight from the pot.

# HERCEGOVINIAN POT WITH MEAT AND VEGETABLES
Serves 6

*Hercegovački lonac*

1 kg lean lamb on the bone, cut into 12 pieces • 3–4 medium (red) onions, chopped • 1 whole bulb of garlic, topped. tailed, the loose outer skin peeled • 1 teaspoon salt • 1 teaspoon black peppercorns, coarsely crushed • 3–4 green or yellow peppers, seeded, sliced into bite-sized squares • 500 g tomatoes, peeled and chopped • 4–5 potatoes, peeled and cut in chunks • 100 g fresh shelled peas, parboiled for 5 minutes; or the same quantity of frozen peas • 50 g butter or lard, melted • 250 ml stock or water

Mix all the ingredients together and put them into a large earthenware or stoneware stewpot or casserole. Add 250 ml stock or water, cover and place in an oven preheated to 220°C/425°F/gas 7 for 30 minutes; then reduce the heat to 125°C/250°F/gas 1/2 and leave to cook for a further 5 hours, or until the meat is tender. Remove from the oven and discard the garlic bulb. Check the seasoning and serve immediately in earthenware bowls, with wholemeal bread and a cucumber salad.

# SHEPHERD'S LAMB KEBAB
Serves 4

*Kavurma-kebap po ovcharski* (Bulgarian, meaning fried kebab shepherd's style), from the Turkish *kavurmak*, to fry, and *kebab*, itself from Arabic; *kavurma-jelo* (Serbian, meaning fried-meat dish)

---

600 g fillet of lamb, in bite-sized pieces • 2–3 tablespoons sunflower oil •
1 medium onion (or bunch spring onions), chopped •
2 medium tomatoes, peeled and chopped • stock • 1/2 teaspoon salt •
1 tablespoon chopped parsley • freshly ground black pepper
*Topping*
125 g sirene or feta cheese, soaked in cold water for 2 hours, then drained and coarsely crumbled • 50 g unsalted butter

Brown the lamb in oil in a heavy pan. Transfer to a plate. In the same oil, fry the onion, then add tomatoes, a spoonful or two of stock and the salt, and cook for a few minutes. Return the meat to the pan, cover and simmer for 10–15 minutes, until tender. Remove from the heat and stir in parsley and black pepper to taste.

Divide the kebab among 4 ovenproof dishes. Sprinkle the crumbled cheese over the top and dot with pieces of butter. Flash under a hot grill until golden brown then serve immediately.

> Every reader is sufficiently acquainted with the Turks to know the sort of viands usual at their tables: but I must say of them, that many are very palatable to an English taste, much more so, indeed, than those to be met with in Portuguese or Spanish cookery. There is a dish of chopped mutton, rolled up with rice highly seasoned, called yaprák, and a large thin pasty of fowl, or spinach sprinkled with sugar; both of which are very commendable.
> John Cam Hobhouse (Lord Broughton), *Travels in Albania and Other Provinces of Turkey in 1809 & 1810*, new edition 1858.

## SWEET KEBAB
Serves 8–10

*Sladki ćevab* (Bosnian)

This is one of the obligatory dishes at Bosnian and Hercegovinian feasts. Served usually at room temperature, it makes a unique dish for a cold table.

> 1 kg boneless beef or mutton (any cut so long as not too fatty) in bite-sized cubes •
> 500 g prunes, soaked in water overnight •
> 500 g each of dessert apples and hard, cooking pears, peeled, cored and sliced into wedges •
> 50 g sultanas, soaked in water overnight • 8–10 each of dried figs and stoned dates •
> 2–3 sticks cinnamon, broken but not powdered (to avoid clouding the juices) •
> 4–5 whole cloves • 400 g sugar

Braise the meat in a little hot, unsalted water with some of the sugar until completely tender, adding more hot water if and when necessary. Transfer the meat to a clean saucepan. Strain the cooking liquor through a cloth and pour over the meat. Cover and keep warm in slow oven.

Separately, cook the prunes in a little water until just soft, drain them, remove the stones and add to the meat. Their cooking liquid is not used so that the juices of the finished dish may remain clear.

Prepare a thick syrup with the rest of the sugar and about 100 ml water. Cook the apple slices in the syrup until just soft, lift them out and add to the meat. In the same syrup cook the pears until soft and translucent; add to the meat. Poach the sultanas, figs and dates in the remaining syrup and add, together with the syrup, to the meat.

In a small saucepan, cover the cinnamon sticks and the cloves with cold water, bring to the boil and reduce a little. Strain the liquid through a cloth and pour it over the meat mixture. Discard the spices.

Now bring everything to the boil over a moderate heat and cook for 2–3 minutes, shaking the pan several times to mix the ingredients and ensure even cooking. Serve warm or at room temperature with no accompaniment, other than perhaps wine or mineral water.

# BOWL KEBAB
Serves 6

*Tasqebap* (Albanian), *tas-kebap* (Bulgarian), *taś-kempap* (Greek), *taz-ćevap* (Serbian), from the Turkish *tas kebabı* (*tas* meaning a bowl)

Of the many dishes that reached the Balkans from Istanbul, this one is a perfect illustration of a dish which has retained the name of its prototype, but has changed beyond recognition. Turkish *tas kebabı* is a simple stew of lamb or mutton which is cooked then placed under an inverted bowl in a fresh pot. Rice and the cooking juices of the meat are poured around the bowl, the pot covered and put on top of the stove. When the rice is done, the bowl is removed for serving.

The Balkan version, on the other hand, has disposed of the *tas* altogether, but gained wine, garlic, and spices. It can also be prepared with pork, beef or mutton.

1 kg shoulder or leg of lamb, boned weight; meat trimmed of excess fat (fat reserved), and cut into 2.5 cm cubes • 2 medium-sized onions, chopped • 50 ml dry wine • 2 teaspoons wine vinegar • 1 teaspoon black peppercorns, crushed • 1 bay leaf • 2 cloves • 3 allspice berries • 4 garlic cloves, unpeeled • salt

Fry the cubed meat in batches in the reserved fat until well browned on all sides. Lift it out with a perforated spoon into a saucepan. Pour off most of the fat from the frying pan, add the chopped onions and cook them until they start to colour. Combine the onions with the meat, then pour in the wine, wine vinegar and a little hot water. Simmer over a low heat for about 90 minutes, or until the meat is tender, adding small quantities of hot water if and when this is necessary. A few minutes before the end of the cooking time, season with salt to taste. Serve with rice, noodles or mashed potatoes.

> Old mother, beautiful daughters, mischievous grandson. Who are they?
> [Grape vine, grapes and wine.]
>
> *Balkan riddle.*

## MOUSSAKA

Although this celebrated dish is always considered Greek, its name comes from the Turkish *musakka*, in turn of Arabic provenance. The dish itself is a layered assemblage of meat and vegetables—usually cooked ahead of time. It was most likely originally made with lamb or mutton and aubergines, Old-World ingredients, though today beef, pork and other vegetables, such as leeks, courgettes, green beans, asparagus, lettuce, spinach, potatoes and even vine leaves, cabbage and sauerkraut are also used, especially in the Balkan meatless versions.

North of Greece, moussaka is much less oily and contains fewer layers so it keeps its shape better when sliced for serving. The traditional topping is not the French béchamel, now commonly employed in Greece, but a light custard of eggs and milk or yoghurt which penetrates the layers to hold them in place.

## AUBERGINE MOUSSAKA
Serves 4

*Mousaka s patladzhani* (Bulgarian), *musaka so modri patlidžani* (Macedonian), *musaka od modrih patlidžana* (Bosnian, Serbo-Croat), from the Greek *melitzánes mousaká*

500 g aubergines, peeled lengthwise at intervals, leaving narrow strips of skin, then cut into long slices 1 cm thick • salt • plain white flour • vegetable oil for frying •
300 g potatoes, peeled and cut into very thin slices

*Meat mixture*

500 g minced lamb, beef, pork, or a mixture, briefly fried in its own fat, then drained of the fat • 2 medium-sized onions, finely chopped • 1 tablespoon vegetable oil •
1 rounded tablespoon tomato purée • 1/2 teaspoon paprika • salt •
1/4 teaspoon ground cinnamon or a little freshly grated nutmeg (optional) •
freshly ground black pepper • 1 bunch parsley, finely chopped • 1 egg, beaten

*Topping*

half the quantity of the all-in-one sauce given on p 342, whisked into 1 beaten egg; or 2 eggs lightly beaten with 4–5 tablespoons plain yoghurt or thin cream and seasoned with salt, pepper, and paprika •
50 g grated cheese such as kashkaval, Gruyère, Parmesan or Cheshire •
a little freshly grated nutmeg (optional)

You may, if you wish, substitute extra aubergines for the potatoes—but potatoes do give additional taste and body to the dish. Alternatively, all the aubergines may be replaced by courgettes, which you need not peel or salt before frying.

You can cook most of the ingredients in advance, refrigerate them until the following day and then quickly assemble them for baking.

Sprinkle the aubergine slices with salt and leave them to sweat for at least 3 hours or overnight. Rinse thoroughly under running cold water, then gently squeeze dry with the hands. Dip the slices in flour and partially cook them in the oil. Drain them on paper towels. Alternatively, arrange the unfloured aubergine slices on a grill rack and brush with oil to cook under a very hot grill until light brown on one side. Turn them over, brush with oil and grill as before. (Treated in this way they absorb much less oil.)

To prepare the meat mixture, fry the onions in the oil until soft and yellow, then stir in the tomato purée, paprika, the de-fatted mince, a little hot water and some salt to taste, keeping in mind that the aubergines will be salty. Add the cinnamon, nutmeg or oregano, if liked, and simmer over a low heat for about 30 minutes. Take the pan off the heat, cool slightly, and add a good grinding of pepper, the parsley and the beaten egg.

Grease a large baking dish 24 cm round or 20 cm square, and at least 5 cm deep. Arrange alternating layers of potatoes, meat and aubergines in the dish, starting and finishing with a layer of potatoes. Sprinkle 1 tablespoon of oil and a little salt over the top and bake in a pre-heated oven at 190°C/375°F/gas 5 for 30 minutes. Remove from the oven, pour over the chosen topping, sprinkle with grated cheese and the nutmeg if you like it, and bake for a further 25 minutes, until golden brown.

Slice into portions and serve on heated plates with some yoghurt.

## MOUSSAKA WITH POTATOES
Serves 4–5

*Mousaka s kartofi* (Bulgarian), *musaka so kompiri* (Macedonian), *musaka od krompira* (Bosnian, Serbian), from the Greek *patátes mousaká*

---

600 g minced lamb or beef, fried in its own fat, then drained of the fat •
4 tablespoons sunflower or corn oil • 250 g onions, chopped • 1 tablespoon tomato purée •
1 teaspoon paprika • salt • 1 teaspoon freshly ground black pepper •
4–5 tablespoons finely chopped parsley, preferably the flat leaved variety •
600 g peeled potatoes, sliced in approx 3 mm thick rounds, sprinkled lightly with salt
*Topping*
3 eggs • 75 ml top-of-the-milk (otherwise thin cream, milk or yoghurt) •
50 g grated cheese, such as kashkaval, Gruyère, Parmesan or Cheshire

In a heavy saucepan, fry the onions in 2 tablespoons of the oil until they turn golden. Stir in the tomato purée, paprika and drained mince. Season with 1/4 teaspoon of the salt, pour in a little hot water, and simmer gently for 20 minutes. Remove from the heat and mix in the pepper and parsley.

To assemble the moussaka, arrange one third of the sliced, lightly salted potatoes in the bottom of an oiled baking dish (20 cm square). Layer half the meat mixture over the potatoes and cover with another third of the potatoes. Layer the remaining meat mixture over them. Finish with a top layer of potatoes, and sprinkle on the rest of the oil. Press down the top with the back of a spoon. There should be just enough liquid to appear on the surface and colour the potatoes; if there is not, add a little warm water or the moussaka will be rather dry.

Bake in an oven set at 190°C/375°F/gas 5 for about 50 minutes, or until the potatoes are soft and all the liquid has been absorbed. Remove and allow to cool for 20 minutes.

Make the topping by beating the eggs in a bowl, adding the top-of-the-milk and whisking briefly to blend. Pour over the moussaka and, using a long-pronged fork, pierce down through the layers, all over, to help the topping to penetrate the entire dish. Scatter the grated cheese on top and return to the oven for a further 15–20 minutes, or until the topping mixture has set and the surface of the dish is golden brown.

Leave to cool for 5–10 minutes before slicing into portions. Serve on heated plates with some plain yoghurt.

## MIXED VEGETABLE CASSEROLE WITH MEAT
Serves 6

*Gjuveç me mish* (Albanian), *turlu-tava* (Bosnian), *tyurlyu gyuvech s meso* (Bulgarian), *turli tava so meso* (Macedonian), *ghiveciu cu carne* (Romanian), *djuveč od raznog povrća* (Serbo-Croat), from the Turkish *sebzeli etli güveci*, meaning vegetable and meat casserole, and *türlü güveç*, mixed casserole

As with the meatless version on page 104, the dish has acquired the name of the vessel, *güveç* or *tava*. The reason for using earthenware, not metal, is that it transmits heat slowly and evenly, and retains it for a good while when brought to the table. Sometimes two or three whole chilli peppers or a handful of unripe, green grapes or greengages are cooked together with the meat and vegetables to add piquancy.

1 kg boned beef (such as chuck or blade steak), or stewing lamb, pork or mutton, cut in approx 4 cm cubes • lard or oil • 1 medium onion, chopped • 1 medium aubergine, cut in cubes, salted and drained • 100 g young okra, stalks pared off • 100 g frozen peas (if fresh, pre-cooked) • 250 g young green beans, fresh or frozen, trimmed and cut into bite-sized pieces • 4 medium courgettes, unpeeled, in rounds • 400 g potatoes, peeled and cut in small chunks • 300 g peeled fresh, or canned drained tomatoes, chopped • 1 large green or yellow pepper, seeded and cut into squares • 1 bunch of parsley, chopped • 1–2 teaspoons salt • 2 teaspoons paprika • 1/2 teaspoon chilli powder or 2 whole chillies (optional) • 3–4 tablespoons sunflower oil • 2 eggs, lightly beaten with 2 tablespoons of milk or yoghurt, for topping

Heat a small quantity of fat in a frying pan. Brown the meat in batches and transfer them to a lidded saucepan. Fry the onion lightly in the same fat, then add to the meat. Add hot water (about 5 mm in the bottom of the pan) and simmer until it has absorbed most of the liquid and is almost tender.

Grease a large earthenware casserole (at least 35 cm in diameter). Arrange the meat pieces in a single layer on the bottom. Mix the remaining ingredients together with your hands and place them to cover the meat completely. Pour over any cooking juices remaining in the saucepan.

Bake in a preheated oven at 180°C/350°F/gas 4. After 45 minutes, press the top of the vegetables with the back of a wooden spoon to level the surface, and continue cooking until everything is perfectly tender and all juices absorbed—a total of approximately 75 minutes. Pour the topping evenly all over and bake for a further 20 minutes until golden brown. Serve directly from the casserole. This dish is just as enjoyable if left for a day, then covered and reheated thoroughly.

Ivan Vazov's *Under the Yoke* was first published in a collection of folklore, science and literature sponsored by the Ministry of Public Education in Sofia in 1889. He writes there of *gyuvech*:

> This lonely meadow, so pleasantly nestling among the foothills of Stara Planina [The Balkan mountains]. ... Its seclusion, loveliness and freshness has for several years ... attracted those who have a taste for merrymaking and feasting; and there were many such....
>
> A flask of wine, drunk in the cool shade of the willows by the babbling crystal-clear river, makes you forget thraldom; *gyuvech*, baked with red tomatoes, fragrant parsley and hot peppers, eaten on the grass under the overhanging branches, ... is a kingdom in itself, and, if there are also fiddlers, it is the height of earthly bliss. Enslaved peoples have their own philosophy which reconciles them to life. An irretrievably ruined man sometimes ends with a bullet in his brain, or in the noose of a rope. A people enslaved, no matter how hopelessly, never commits suicide; it eats, drinks and begets children. It makes merry.

## PEPPERS STUFFED WITH MEAT
Serves 2–4

*Speca të mbushura me mish* (Albanian); *pulneni piperki s meso* (Bulgarian); *piperiés gemistés mé kimá* (Greek); *polneti piperki so meso* (Macedonian); *punjene paprike sa mesom* (Serbo-Croat); *etli biber dolması* (Turkish)

This dish of baked peppers stuffed with an aromatic mixture of minced meat and rice or bulgur is justly regarded as one of the masterpieces of the Balkan kitchen. Besides peppers, it is also common to stuff and bake other fruits and vegetables such as apples, quinces, tomatoes, onions and potatoes, though stuffed leeks, courgettes and celeriac are best simmered on top of the stove in a small amount of stock or water.

It is not usual to eat the skin of the peppers. To eat this dish, therefore, slit each pepper from top to bottom and open it out. Then scoop up spoonfuls of the stuffing mixed with a little cream or yoghurt and pieces from the pepper's flesh, leaving the skins intact on the plate.

4 medium-sized stuffing peppers, weighing about 650 g, of equal height and, for visual effect, of different colours: green, yellow, orange and red

*Stuffing*

400 g minced lamb or beef, or a mixture • 2 medium-sized onions, finely chopped •
2 tablespoons vegetable oil • 25 g round-grained rice or bulgur wheat •
2 tablespoons tomato purée • 1 teaspoon paprika • 1/2 teaspoon salt •
2 tablespoons chopped parsley • 2 tablespoons chopped mint leaves •
4 tablespoons chopped dill sprigs • 1/2 teaspoon freshly ground black pepper

*To finish*

250 g tomatoes: 1 tomato sliced into 4 thin rounds, the remainder peeled and very finely chopped • 1 extra tablespoon vegetable oil • a little extra salt and pepper

To prepare peppers for stuffing, slice off the stalk ends neatly and discard, pull out and discard the seeds and pith. Drop the peppers into slightly salted boiling water and blanch for 6–7 minutes; this will make it easier to separate the skin from the flesh at the table. Drain them by leaving them upside down on a plate.

Fry the mince in its own fat until lightly browned. Transfer it with a slotted spoon to a saucepan, allowing all the fat to drain away; discard the fat. Add 150 ml of hot water and cook very gently for 30 minutes.

Brown the chopped onions in the oil, add the rice and stir continuously until well coated. Stir in the tomato purée, paprika and salt and mix this with the meat in the saucepan. Cover the pan and cook the meat and rice mixture, just barely simmering, for 15 minutes or until the rice is partially cooked and all the liquid has been absorbed. Remove from the heat and stir in the herbs and black pepper.

Choose an ovenproof dish that will hold the peppers snugly. Stand the peppers upright in the dish and spoon a quarter of the stuffing into each pepper. Cover their tops with a tomato round and pour the chopped tomatoes plus 4 tablespoons of water around the peppers. Smear the tomato rounds with a tablespoon of oil and sprinkle a little salt and pepper all over the dish.

Bake on a shelf above the centre of an oven preheated to 190°C/375°F/gas 5 for 1 hour, or until the tomato rounds have charred round the edges—a sign that the dish has been properly cooked.

Serve the peppers on heated plates with a tablespoon of sour cream or plain yoghurt. Hand round bread separately.

## QUINCES STUFFED WITH BEEF OR VEAL
Serves 4

*Dyuli pulneni s meso* (Bulgarian), *dunji polneti so meso* (Macedonian), both meaning quinces stuffed with meat, from the Turkish *ayva dolması*, 'stuffed quince'

4 medium, ripe quinces, carefully wiped to remove the down •
hot beef or veal stock, or hot water • 200 g tomato juice •
2–3 teaspoons sugar • a little salt • 25 g butter
*Stuffing*
50 ml oil, or 50 g butter • 1 medium onion, finely chopped •
200 g lean beef or veal, finely minced • 1–2 teaspoons sugar • 1/2 teaspoon paprika •
3/4 teaspoon ground cinnamon, or 1 teaspoon ground coriander seeds •
a little salt and freshly ground pepper

Cut the stalk-ends off each fruit for lids, then scoop out the core and seeds, leaving a cavity large enough to contain the stuffing.

Fry the onion in oil or butter until soft and golden, then add the rest of the stuffing ingredients. Stir-fry the mixture until most of the pan juices have evaporated. Taste and adjust the seasonings. Fill the quinces with this mixture, put their lids on, and place them upright in an ovenproof dish or saucepan large enough to hold them in a single layer. Pour enough hot stock or water to reach one-third up their sides, then add the tomato juice, sugar, salt and butter.

Cook the dish either on top of the stove, covered, over a medium heat for about 30 minutes; or bake in a preheated oven at 180°C/350°F/gas 4 for about 45 minutes. The quinces are ready when soft but not disintegrating and the pan juices have reduced to less than half their original volume.

## PORK SAUSAGES
Makes about 1 kg fresh sausages

*Kolloface derri* (Albanian); *svinski nadenitsi* (Bulgarian); *loukánika* (Greek); *svinski kolbasi* (Macedonian); *cîrnaţi de carne de porc* (Romanian); *svinjske kobasice* (Serbo-Croat)

In the first half of this century, winters on the Danubian plain were much colder than today, and temperatures of minus 30°C were not uncommon. The lower reaches of the Danube used to freeze over, forming a mile-wide bridge of glittering ice between Romania and Bulgaria.

Each Sunday, crowds of people from the town of Russe on the Bulgarian bank crossed over the river on foot, on skates, or in two-horse sleighs, the harness bells filling the crystal air with their merry jingle.

On Romanian soil, near the town of Giurgiu (where pipelines brought oil from the wells around Ploeşti), my father invariably bought *ţuică*, the fiery Romanian plum brandy, and the most delicious fresh pork sausages, *cîrnaţi*, from the pedlars, which tasted out of this world after our excursion over the ice!

These all-meat sausages are made without the meat preservative saltpetre (sodium or potassium nitrate), so they should be eaten within a day or two unless you choose to freeze them.

750 g boneless neck-end of pork, chopped finely with a cleaver or passed through the medium disk of a mincer •
250 g pork back fat, half of it minced finely or processed to a purée, the other half finely diced •
10 g salt • 2–3 g coarsely ground allspice, or 7 g dried crumbled summer savory •
4–5 ground black pepper • 2–3 g ground cumin • 10 g paprika •
1/2 small garlic clove, crushed • a little dry wine or beer, if needed •
about 2 metres sausage casing, soaked in acidulated tepid water for 30–40 minutes, then rinsed by running cold water through it

Mix everything together (except the alcohol and the casing), then knead thoroughly, adding a little wine or beer if the mixture is too stiff to go easily into the casing. Fry a spoonful of the mixture, taste and add more seasonings or flavourings if necessary. Then slide lengths of the wet casing on to the nozzle of the sausage-stuffing attachment of a mincer and make long coiled sausages—or form links by twisting the sausages at regular intervals alternately in opposite directions.

To cook the sausages, soak them in boiling water for 5 minutes (to soften the skins), then wipe dry and fry or cook over medium-hot embers or under the grill.

## POTTED MEAT

Yields about 700 g fried meat and crackling plus 350 g fat

*Kavurma* (Bosnian, Bulgarian, Serbo-Croat), from the Turkish *kavurma*, fried meat; *suzma* (Bosnian), *sazdurma* (Bulgarian), from Turkish *sızmak*, *sızdırmak*: 'to cause (the meat fat) to ooze out'

---

Although the names of this potted meat derive from Turkish, the recipe itself is a variation on the old Balkan meat conserves such as *babek* and *starets* (p. 43), which were packed into natural containers—an animal stomach bag (first stomach—paunch or rumen) or great gut—then briefly cooked, pressed and air dried.

The technique for short-term preservation of meat in pots or jars, as set forth here, is fairly common to the central and western parts of the Peninsula, though susceptible to many regional variations.

1 kg thick-end of belly pork, rind removed, fat diced small, meat cut into 2.5 cm cubes •
1 kg thin-end of belly pork, rind removed, fat diced small, meat cut into 2.5 cm cubes •
salt • 1 bay leaf • freshly ground black pepper •
1–2 allspice berries, crushed or ground

Weigh the cubed meat together with the diced fat and season with 10 g of salt to each kilogram of the mixture. Leave covered for 24 hours in a cool place. The salt will draw out moisture.

Next day, place the meat mixture in a heavy-based pan, add the spices, if you like them, put the lid on, and cook over a very gentle heat on top of the stove. When the pieces of pork have turned a nice brown colour, drain off the rendered fat into a basin and reserve.

Pack the cooked meat and crackling into heated jam jars, leaving about 2.5 cm of headspace. Use the reserved fat to top up the jars and provide a protective layer above the meat. Cool, then cover with jam-pot waxed paper disks to exclude air, and screw on the lids.

Store the meat in a dry cool place, or refrigerate; it will keep for a couple of weeks. After opening a jar, remove the top layer of fat and finish the contents within a day or two. Use it how you would fresh fried pork—in stews and casseroles.

# CHAPTER XII

# Poultry and Offal

### ROAST POULTRY

Before the onset of battery farming, roast chicken was esteemed, a Sunday dish unfailingly enjoyed. It still is in those households where barn-door fowl, usually raised on home-grown feed, roam around the yards and gardens. Ducks and geese do not take well to intensive methods; they still range free, their flesh much appreciated.

## ROAST PAPRIKA CHICKEN
Serves 4–5

*Zog pulë e pjekur* (Albanian); *pecheno pile* (Bulgarian, Macedonian); *friptură de pui de găină* (Romanian); *pečeno pile* (Serbo-Croat)—all meaning roast chicken

1–1.2 kg roasting chicken, oven ready, washed in cold water and dried thoroughly; giblets discarded • 25 g butter, at room temperature •
a little salt and freshly ground black pepper • vegetable oil • paprika

Mash the butter, salt and pepper together on a plate. Spread the butter mixture under the skin on either side of the breast. Coat the outside of the chicken with oil, sprinkle paprika all over and rub it in—to provide a really crisp, dark skin.

Lay the bird on its side on a rack in a roasting tin, and roast in a preheated 200°C/400°F/gas 6 oven for 30 minutes; turn and cook on the other side for another 30 minutes; finally roast breast upwards for a further 20–30 minutes, or until the meat is well done, the skin like crackling and dark chestnut-brown to the eye. Baste frequently with the pan drippings, especially towards the end of cooking.

Serve hot with buttered vegetables, rice or noodles, or cold with salad.

## STUFFED CHICKEN
Serves 4

*Pulastren i mbushur* (Albanian); *pulneno pile* (Bulgarian); *kotópoulo gemistó* (Greek); *polneto pile* (Macedonian); *punjeno pile* (Bosnian, Serbo-Croat); *piliç dolması* (Turkish)

1.5 kg fresh chicken, dressed weight, pieces of fat around the tail vent removed, washed in cold water and dried; giblets reserved • 50 g butter, at room temperature • 1/2 lemon

*Giblet stock*

neck, heart, gizzard (peeled), wing tips, legs cut off at the first joint and liver of the chicken • 2 carrots, peeled and halved • 1/4 celeriac, peeled (or 2 sticks of celery, cut up) • 1 parsnip, peeled and halved • 1/4 teaspoon salt • 1 teaspoon peppercorns

*Rice stuffing*

1 medium onion, chopped • 2 tablespoons sunflower oil • 25 g pine nuts, or chopped hazelnuts, blanched almonds or blanched and skinned walnuts • 100 g long-grain rice, washed and drained • 50 g mixed dried fruit, such as sultanas, seedless raisins, currants and/or soaked dried apricots, diced small • 1 teaspoon sugar • 1/8 teaspoon salt • 1/4 teaspoon dried crumbled oregano, or mint, or savory • 7 g butter • black pepper

For the stock, put the giblets (except the liver), the vegetables, salt and peppercorns in a saucepan, pour in 625 ml of water and bring to the boil. Simmer gently for 30 minutes, adding the liver towards the end. Strain the stock and reserve. Chop the heart and liver roughly. Discard the vegetables and spices.

For the stuffing, fry the onion in oil until soft and pale yellow, stir in the nuts and washed rice and continue frying for another minute or so. Add the chopped heart and liver, dried fruit, sugar, salt, herb and 150 ml of the stock. Simmer for no more than 7 minutes, just enough for the rice to absorb the liquid. Take off the heat and stir in the butter and a good grinding of black pepper. Taste for seasoning.

Place pieces of butter underneath the skin on each breast. Stuff the chicken, filling the cavity through its tail vent. Close the tail with string and a trussing needle, pushing the parson's nose into the vent. Squeeze the lemon juice over the chicken, rubbing it in with the palm of your hand, then place the bird in a roasting tin, on a rack just large enough to support it, breast up, and pour the rest of the stock in the tin. Roast in a preheated oven at 200°C/400°F/gas 6, without turning, for 1 3/4 hours, basting occasionally. By the end of this time, both the chicken and stuffing will be fully cooked, the flesh succulent, each rice grain separate, the skin crisp and well browned. Take the chicken out of the oven and remove the strings.

# ROAST DUCKLING WITH MORELLO CHERRY SAUCE
Serves 4

*Patka sus sos ot vishni* (Bulgarian); *patka sa umakom od višanja* (Serbo-Croat)

4 duckling joints, about 1.5 kg in total, skin on, excess neck skin and vent fat removed, washed and dried with a clean cloth • salt
*Sauce*
3 tablespoons brown sugar • 250 ml white wine •
400 g morello cherries, stalks removed and stoned • salt and pepper

Use a fork to prick the skin of the duckling joints all over. Rub in some salt and roast in an oven preheated to 180°C/350°F/gas 4 for about 45 minutes, if you like them slightly pink and moist, or 60-70 minutes until well cooked and crispy. Transfer to an oven dish with a lid and keep it hot.

Dispose of the excess fat from the roasting tin, add the sugar and wine to the caramelized juices over a medium heat and cook to dissolve while stirring and scraping up all the brown bits. Add the cherries, salt and pepper to taste, and cook for about a minute. Pour the sauce over the duck and serve immediately.

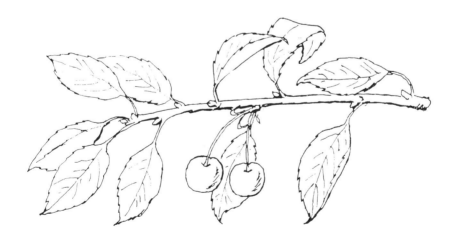

*Morello cherries*

# ROAST GOOSE WITH SAUERKRAUT
Serves 4

*Patë e pjekur me lakërarme* (Albanian); *pechena guska s kiselo zele* (Bulgarian); *pechena guska so kisela zelka* (Macedonian); *guska na podvarku* (Serbian)

This popular winter dish is also made with duck, chicken or older fowl, turkey or game birds. Before the North American turkey displaced the goose as the festive bird, goose with sauerkraut was traditional Christmas fare. A Serbian variation adds a little cooked rice and fried onion to the sauerkraut.

2.25-2.5 kg young goose, dressed weight, pieces of fat from around the vent removed • salt • 500–700 g (1 1/4–1 3/4 lb) shredded sauerkraut, home-made or bought in jars • 1 teaspoon paprika

Prick the goose all over with a fork, then rub the skin with a little salt. Truss the bird and place it on a rack set in an enamelled or porcelain roasting pan (the lactic acid in the sauerkraut that will be added might react chemically with a metal or earthenware container and give an unpleasant flavour to the dish).

Cook the goose in a preheated oven at 200°C/400°F/gas 6 for about 1 hour, pouring off the melted fat every 15–20 minutes into a jar (goose fat is beautifully flavoured and considered far superior to lard). Reduce heat to 160°C/325°F/gas 3 and cook for a further 2 hours (turning the bird over from time to time), until nearly all the fat has been shed, and the skin is crisp and richly browned.

While the goose is cooking, prepare the sauerkraut. Rinse it under cold running water, drain, add the paprika and simmer for about an hour, or until the sauerkraut is very tender, and nearly all the liquid has evaporated.

Half an hour before the end of cooking, remove bird and rack from the pan, skim the excess fat, add the sauerkraut and stir it round to mix with the juices and rich meaty deposits. Lay the goose over the sauerkraut and return to the oven to complete the cooking.

## CHICKEN STEW
Serves 3

*Jahni me mish zogu* (Albanian); *pileća jahnija* (Bosnian); *pileshka yahniya* (Bulgarian); *pileshka janija* (Macedonian); *tocană de pui* (Romanian); *pileća janija* (Serbian)

3 chicken pieces (breasts, thighs, or a mixture), skinned, halved and wiped dry •
25 g butter mixed with 2 tablespoons oil, or 40 g clarified butter • 350 g onions, sliced •
2 tablespoons tomato purée • 1 teaspoon paprika •
125 ml dry red wine, chicken stock or water (I prefer wine) • 1/2 teaspoon salt •
1/2 bay leaf plus 1 allspice berry, or 1/2 teaspoon dried marjoram or oregano •
1 1/2 tablespoons roasted flour (p. 340) • freshly ground black pepper • chopped parsley

Melt the fat in a large frying pan. Brown the chicken over a moderate heat, turning occasionally. Transfer to a stewpan.

Soften, but don't brown, the sliced onions by sweating them, with the lid on, in the same fat for 20–25 minutes. Stir in the tomato purée and paprika, cook for a further minute or so, then pour over the chicken in the stewpan and set on a gentle heat. Add the wine, salt, herb or spices and simmer for an hour, with a tight-fitting lid, until the meat comes away easily from the bone.

Sprinkle in the roasted flour, stirring continuously, then add a little stock or water, if necessary, and continue cooking for a few moments. Remove from the heat, season with pepper and finish with chopped parsley. Bread or mashed potatoes are the thing for this stew.

 

Who has a red beard but no comb?
[The turkey]

*Balkan riddle.*

## CHICKEN CHILLI
Serves 2

*Pile lyutika* (Bulgarian); *pile so luti piperki* (Macedonian)

1 young tender chicken (double poussin), weighing about 800 g, split lengthwise, or cut into 4–8 pieces, skinned and trimmed of any fat •
25 g butter and 1 tablespoon vegetable oil • 100 g onion, coarsely grated •
250 g ripe tomatoes, peeled and chopped • 1 tablespoon tomato purée •
125 ml chicken stock or water • 1/2 teaspoon salt •
2 large red peppers, grilled, skinned, seeded, diced small •
1 fresh chilli (or 2 or 3 for a fiery hot dish) grilled, skinned, seeded, pounded to a paste •
1 tablespoon roasted flour (p. 340)

Brown the chicken pieces lightly in the butter and oil. Remove with a slotted spoon to a saucepan. In the same fat briskly fry the onion, add the chopped tomatoes and tomato purée and reduce the juices by fast boiling. Stir in the stock or water and the salt, then pour over the chicken. Simmer for about half an hour, after which add the peppers and chilli. Continue to cook until the chicken is tender—another 10–15 minutes will suffice. Five minutes before the end of cooking, sprinkle on the flour and stir it in. Serve the chicken immediately, on hot plates. Fresh soft bread is the best mouth-cooling antidote.

## CHICKEN STEW WITH POTATOES
Serves 4

*Pile s kartofi* (Bulgarian); *pile so kompiri* (Macedonian); *pui cu cartofi* (Romanian); *pile sa krompirom* (Serbo-Croat); all meaning chicken with potatoes

A simple, homely dish, sometimes finished off (principally in Romania, Serbia and Croatia) with a little sour cream.

1.2 kg roasting chicken, cut up into serving pieces; or 4 chicken joints, about 1 kg in total
2 tablespoons sunflower oil or lard • 1 medium onion, finely chopped •
4 cloves garlic, chopped • 200 ml tomato juice • 1/2 teaspoon paprika • 1/2 teaspoon salt •
200 ml good chicken stock or water • 700 g peeled potatoes, cut into small pieces •
1 large green or yellow pepper, seeded, cut into small pieces; or 50 g frozen or freshly shelled, blanched peas • 3–5 tablespoons finely chopped parsley •
freshly ground black pepper

Roast the chicken in an oven set at 200°C/400°F/gas 6 for 20-25 minutes, or until half done. As soon as it is cool enough to handle, remove the skin.

While the chicken is roasting, fry the onion slowly until soft and golden in a heavy saucepan. Add the garlic and cook for half a minute only (no need to brown it). Stir in the tomato juice, paprika, salt and the stock or water. When the sauce comes to the boil drop in the partially cooked chicken joints, together with the potatoes and pepper pieces or peas. Simmer, covered, for about 45 minutes—at the end of this time the chicken should be very tender but not falling off the bone. Stir in the parsley and check for seasoning. Serve hot, sprinkled with black pepper.

# POACHED CHICKEN GARNISHED WITH TARHANA
Serves 4–5

*Pile s trahana* (Bulgarian); *tarhoniyás csirke* (Hungarian); *pile so tarana* (Macedonian); *pile s taranom* (Serbo-Croat); all meaning chicken with pasta shreds or pellets, from the Turkish *tarhana*, pasta shreds or pellets

Goose, duck, turkey or game birds can be served in the same way. When cooked, the pasta shreds have the consistency of a risotto.

About 1.5 kg chicken, cut into pieces •
salt • 300 g tarhana, fresh pasta shreds (p. 224) •
50 g unsalted butter or lard •
red paprika butter, prepared with 25 g butter or lard melted with 1 teaspoon paprika

Wash the chicken. Place it in a large saucepan. Season very sparingly with salt, and cover with water. Bring to the boil and cook at a bare simmer, shaking the pan from time to time, for 1–1 1/2 hours, until the chicken is very tender. Strain and reserve the stock. Remove the skin from the chicken, if you like. Arrange it on a large serving platter and keep it hot in a very low oven while you prepare the rest.

Fry the pasta shreds in the fat, in 2 batches, for about 8–9 minutes each, until they start to colour. Add them gradually to about 450 ml of boiling stock from the chicken and simmer, covered, for 9–10 minutes, until the pasta absorbs all the liquid and is tender.

Surround the chicken with a border of pasta, and dribble paprika butter over the pasta. Serve immediately.

# CIRCASSIAN CHICKEN
Serves 4 as a main course

*Cherkezko pile* (Bulgarian), *čerkes tauk* (Serbian), from the Turkish *çerkez tavuğu*, i.e. Circassian hen, presumably because Circassians were known to enjoy peppery-hot food

This chicken dish is often served cold—at room temperature rather than chilled—in which case the walnut mixture is diluted with about 75 ml stock only, and then poured, without cooking, over the chicken.

1–1.2 kg chicken pieces, skinned and trimmed of all fat • 50 g butter
*Court-bouillon*
2 carrots • 1 onion • zest of 1 lemon • 2 teaspoons black peppercorns • 1/4 teaspoon salt
*Walnut sauce*
100 g shelled walnuts • 1 garlic clove, chopped • 1/8 teaspoon salt •
50 g crustless, day-old bread, moistened in chicken stock and gently squeezed •
3 tablespoons walnut or sunflower oil • a large pinch (or more) of hot chilli powder
*To finish*
Red paprika oil, prepared with 3–4 tablespoons oil and 1 teaspoon sweet paprika and/or 1/4–1/2 teaspoon hot chilli powder

Put the carrots, onion, lemon zest and peppercorns with 250 ml water and bring to the boil. Drop in the chicken and poach, covered, for about an hour, adding the salt halfway through. Allow the chicken to cool in the stock, then remove. Strain and reserve the stock. Take the meat off the bones and cut in neat, bite-sized pieces.

You may prefer to blanch the walnuts in boiling water, in batches, then peel off their skins for a nearly white—instead of a pale grey—sauce. Pound or process the walnuts together with the chopped garlic, salt and bread. Add the oil and 125 ml of the stock from the chicken gradually, and season with chilli powder to taste. Transfer the mixture to a saucepan and simmer for a couple of minutes, stirring all the time, until the bottom of the pan can be seen, and the sauce is thick and creamy.

Shortly before serving, fry the chicken pieces in the butter until heated through and lightly browned. Arrange them, slightly heaped, on a large serving platter or on 4 heated dinner plates and cover with the hot sauce. Dribble over the paprika oil; or make indentations in the surface to form a simple pattern and pour the red oil into the indentations.

Serve immediately, with bread or boiled green beans and potatoes. In Turkey, the chicken would be surrounded with a border of cooked rice.

# FRIED CHICKEN
Serves 4

*Zog (pule) i fërguar* (Albanian); *purzheno pile* (Bulgarian); *kotópoulo tiganitó* (Greek); *prženo pile* (Macedonian, Serbo-Croat)

1–1.5 kg young chicken, dressed weight • about 100g plain flour • 1 teaspoon salt •
1/4 teaspoon freshly ground black pepper •
clarified butter, oil, lard or a mixture of fresh butter and oil—for shallow frying
*Marinade*
juice of 2 lemons or 5–6 tablespoons white wine vinegar • 4–5 tablespoons vegetable oil •
1 garlic clove, chopped • 1 teaspoon dried thyme, marjoram or oregano

Trim the wing tips and feet off the chicken and cut into small joints: the breasts in four pieces, the thighs in half, the drumsticks whole. The skin may be kept or discarded as you prefer.

Combine all the marinade ingredients in a deep bowl and turn the chicken pieces to coat them all over. Marinade at room temperature for 2 hours, or refrigerate for at least 4 hours or overnight. Remove the chicken from the marinade. Pat it dry. Discard the marinade. Mix the flour with the salt and pepper and roll each chicken piece in it, preferably about 1 hour before frying them.

Heat a shallow layer of fat in a frying pan over no more than moderate heat. Fry 5–6 pieces at a time to avoid crowding the pan, for about 13–15 minutes, turning on all sides. As they brown, transfer them to a roasting pan and bake them in a preheated oven at 150°C/300°F/gas 2 to complete the cooking to a degree of doneness that you prefer.


# OFFAL

Offal has always been widely consumed in the Balkans, though nowadays some people quail at it due to the high amounts of cholesterol (1000 milligrams in 100 grams of brains; 200–600 milligrams in 100 grams of sweetbreads, kidney, liver).

I have not included any recipes for brains in this collection, largely because they are difficult to obtain from modern butchers and the effort seemed therefore redundant, and because of their cholesterol content.

## 'MAIDEN'S BREASTS'
### Serves 4

*Djevojačke grudi* (Bosnian, meaning maiden's breasts); *drob sarma* (Bulgarian, Macedonian), *drob* (Romanian), *sarma od jagnjeće džigerice* (Serbian)—all meaning lamb's pluck wrapped up in caul

These popular packages are rather like British faggots, but made with lamb's pluck instead of pig's haslet. If lamb's caul is difficult to buy, use buttered foil.

300–400 g pluck of milk-fed lamb, comprising the liver, lights (lungs), heart, spleen and throat sweetbreads (thymus gland); or a combination of lamb's liver and heart sweetbreads (pancreas); or liver only; all purchased as fresh as possible •
300 g spring onions, white thinly sliced, green cut into 1 cm lengths and kept separate •
2 tablespoons vegetable oil • 6 garlic cloves, chopped •
150 g long-grain rice (thick grains, such as the easy-cook American rice, not the thin Basmati rice) • 2 tablespoons tomato purée •
1 teaspoon paprika • 1/2 teaspoon salt • 50 g butter •
1 heaped tablespoon each of chopped mint and parsley • freshly ground black pepper •
100 g lamb's caul, rinsed and soaked in cold water •
paprika and 25 g melted butter for topping

Soak the sweetbreads in cold water for at least an hour, then wash them well together with the rest of the pluck. Place the pluck in plenty of lightly salted simmering water and cook until tender, adding the sweetbreads and liver towards the end of the cooking. Strain the cooking liquid and reserve. Remove any membrane from the sweetbreads, then cut them into small pieces. Finally chop the lights and dice the liver to the size of a pea.

In a saucepan, soften the white parts of the spring onions in the oil, then add in sequence the chopped garlic, the rice, tomato purée, paprika and the green parts of the onions, stirring and cooking for a few moments after each addition. Pour in 350 ml of the reserved cooking liquid or hot water, add the salt, cover the pan and simmer for 20 minutes until the rice is tender and the cooking liquid absorbed—but check towards the end of the cooking time to make sure that the rice is not drying up. Remove from the heat and stir in the prepared pluck together with the butter, herbs and a fair grinding of black pepper. Taste for seasoning.

To shape the 'maiden's breasts', take the caul from the water and spread it out on a work surface. Cut it into 4 equal pieces with a pair of kitchen scissors. Place each piece of caul in a small bowl, mound a quarter of the rice mixture in it to form a dome and trim off any surplus caul before draping it over the mixture. Transfer the packages, with the caul's folded edges underneath, to a buttered baking dish and smear them all over with paprika and the melted butter.

Bake in a preheated oven at 180°C/350°F/gas 4 for 35 minutes, or until lightly browned. Serve hot, with a tablespoon of thick yoghurt on the side of each plate.

## WHITE PUDDING
(Liver sausage)

Makes 1 sausage, about 500 g in weight

*Eturnitsa* (Bulgarian from *etro*, a dialect word for liver, deriving from Old Slavonic); *džigernjača* (Serbo-Croat, from Turkish *karaciğer* 'liver'); *jetrnice* (Slovenian from the Old Slavonic *jetra*—liver)

---

This is a pork sausage that is prepared during the annual pig slaughtering in many parts of the Balkans, and as far west as the Czech republic and Slovakia, as well as Poland, where it goes by the name of *Jaternice* and *Jatrznica*, respectively.

The recipe itself admits certain variations. The Slovenes, for example, like to add parboiled rice to the sausage mixture; the Serbs—finely minced pig's lights (lungs) and skin, as well as fried minced onion.

200 g pig's liver, half of it minced, the other half diced or chopped •
200 g trimmings from the pig's head, chopped up with a cleaver or coarsely minced •
200 g pig's back fat, cut into tiny dice no bigger than match-heads • 1 1/2 teaspoons salt •
1 teaspoon freshly ground black pepper •
1/2 teaspoon ground coriander seeds; or dried crumbled savory or marjoram •
1/8 teaspoon ground cinnamon • 1/2 teaspoon ground cumin seeds •
2 allspice berries, crushed • 1 clove, crushed • 1 egg, lightly beaten •
1 pig's large intestine, washed, cleaned, turned inside out and washed again

Mix all the ingredients together. Stuff the intestine, tying the sausage at both ends with string. Pierce it here and there with a darning needle and place it on a greased rack, plate or trivet in a large saucepan (to prevent the sausage sticking to the bottom of the pan during cooking). Cover the sausage with water and keep it below the surface by placing an inverted plate on top. Bring quickly to the boil, then poach very gently for about an hour. Leave it to cool in the cooking liquid.

This sausage does not keep long; it should be used within a day or two.

# BLACK PUDDING IN THE BALKAN FASHION
(Blood sausage)
Makes about 800 g

*Kurmagjak* (Albanian); *kurvavitsa* (Bulgarian); *krvavitsa* (Macedonian); *caltaboș* or *cartaboș* (Romanian); *krvavica* (Serbo-Croat, Slovenian)

As with most regional recipes, there are many variations: some people add cooked pearl barley, rice or buckwheat; others—minced raw potatoes and even raw onion.

500 g pig's lights (lungs) and fatty trimmings from the neck, both parboiled, then diced minutely •
375 g pig's heart and kidneys (halved and cleaned) and pig's spleen and liver, all finely chopped with a cleaver •
125 g back pork fat, cut into tiny dice the size of a pea •
250 g fresh, coagulated pig's blood, chopped up • 25 g salt •
1/2 teaspoon each of coarsely ground black pepper and ground allspice •
pig's large intestines, turned inside out so that the fat is on their inner surface, well washed

Mix all the ingredients together well and fill the pig's intestines, tying and separating them at about 30 cm lengths. Prick the sausages all over with a needle. Lay them on a rack in a wide and shallow pan and submerge in hot water. Place a large plate over them and cover the pan tightly. Poach the black puddings for about 1 hour, pricking them from time to time to prevent them from bursting. Serve while still warm or at room temperature (but do not re-heat). Stored in a cold dry place, they will keep for about a week.

# A THICK STEW OF PORK LIGHTS
Serves 3–4

*Pljučna mešta* (Slovenian)

50 ml vegetable oil • 1 medium onion, finely chopped •
500 g pork lights (lungs), cooked in lightly salted water, trachea (the air-tube connecting a pair of lungs) removed, cooking liquid reserved •
25 g breadcrumbs • salt and freshly ground black pepper •
1–2 tablespoons finely chopped parsley • finely grated zest of 1 lemon •
1 tablespoon capers

Heat the oil in a heavy-based saucepan and fry the onion until just soft. Increase the heat, stir in the cooked lights, and keep stirring until they are heated through. Add the breadcrumbs and a little of the liquid saved from boiling the lights, but the consistency of the mixture must be thick. Season with salt and pepper to taste. Add the parsley, lemon zest and capers and cook for a further 4–5 minutes.

Serve hot, accompanied by plain boiled potatoes or rye bread.

# BAKED LAMB'S CHITTERLINGS
Serves 5 as a main course, 10 as accompaniment to drinks

*Pleneti chrevtsa na fourna* (Bulgarian); *pleteni tsrevtsa vo rerna* (Macedonian); *plentena crevca u pećnicu* (Serbian); all meaning plaited smaller intestines [baked] in the oven

1 kg cleaned and washed (preferably not bleached) lamb's chitterlings
(lamb's small intestine) •
a little stock or water • 2 teaspoons salt • freshly ground black pepper •
1 tablespoon finely chopped fresh mint or oregano • red paprika butter (p. 347)

Divide the chitterlings into 3–4 equal lengths. Tie them together at one end with a piece of string. Hang them from a peg and braid them neatly to make a long plait. Secure the other end. Lay the plait, ends tucked underneath, on a round and shallow, well greased, baking pan and coil into a spiral. Pour in a little stock or water, then sprinkle with salt, pepper, mint or oregano. Drizzle over the red paprika butter.

Bake in a preheated 160°C/325°F/gas 3 oven until tender—about an hour. Transfer the chitterlings to a warmed platter. Cut away the string. Serve hot, cut up into 2–3 cm pieces, with the pan juices poured over them.

# LAMB'S OFFAL ROASTED ON A SPIT
Serves 6–8 as a starter

*Koukourech* (Bulgarian), *kokorétsi* (Greek), *koukourek* (Macedonian), *cucureciu* (Aroumanian), *kokreç* (Turkish), from the Albanian *kukurec* or *kokorec* meaning lamb's viscera roasted on a spit, wrapped in caul and intestines; *šiš u košuljici* (Bosnian, literally, spit in a small shirt); *vitalac* (Croat, meaning something wound round something else)

---

The origin of this dish is Albanian, though it has spread throughout the Balkans. While the young lamb or kid is roasting, the offal would be cooked quickly and eaten to while away the waiting time. To make sure that everything cooks in the same time, all the offal is cut to about the size of a plum.

2 lamb's kidneys, surface membrane removed, cut in half lengthwise,
central white core snipped out •
1 lamb's spleen • 1 lamb's heart • the sweetbreads of the lamb •
1 lamb's lights • 1 lamb's liver, cleaned •
1 teaspoon each of salt and black pepper •
1 teaspoon dried crumbled savory or thyme •
1 lamb's caul •
about 2 metres lamb's small intestine, well washed inside and out •
150 g butter, melted

Sprinkle the cut offal meats with salt, pepper and savory or thyme and thread them alternately on to a spit. Wrap the caul closely round the meats and tie securely by winding the intestines round the caul. Brush the wrapped up spit all over with some of the melted butter and grill over hot coals, turning the spit slowly and continuously, and basting often with the rest of the butter, until well browned and cooked right through—about 30–45 minutes.

Pull the *kukurec* off the spit and serve it hot, sliced like a sausage, accompanied by salad and wine.

*Common thyme*

# CHAPTER XIII

# Game

The forests in the west are full of all kinds of game, but the villager would eat mainly peppers and vegetables, and sometimes a domestic fowl; the wild ones he would leave in peace...

The people in those parts consider hunting as an occupation of the idle... The farmer treats hunting with disdain, though the shepherd, the field-keeper and the herdsman, who work in the open country, hunt occasionally—because this does not get in the way of their job.

I. Basanovich (1891)

With the exception of Albania, Slovenia and Vojvodina, game has been comparatively unimportant in Balkan diet. Over the last fifty years, however, consumption has risen steadily, probably due to the creation of vast hunting reserves—such as the one on Mount Prenj in Hercegovina, and the Danube Delta Reserve in Bulgaria. The Romanian part of the Danube delta covers more than a million acres, and during the open season gun parties hunt the rich wild life in the marshes, forests and islands.

## BRAISED HAUNCH OF VENISON
Serves 4–6

*Zadoushena surna* (Bulgarian), *pirjana srna* (Serbo-Croat), *dušena srna* (Slovenian), all meaning braised roe-deer.

In this recipe it is the roe-deer (*Capreolus capreolus*) that is used rather than the larger red deer (*Cervus elaphus*).

1 haunch of venison • 100 g lardons • 50 g butter • 3–4 tablespoons vegetable oil • salt
*Marinade*
1 litre dry red wine • 1 small celeriac, peeled and diced • 1 small onion, finely sliced •
1 teaspoon black peppercorns • 2 carrots, finely sliced • 2 bay leaves •
2–3 sprigs parsley, thyme or celeriac leaves • 3 garlic cloves, diced small •
3 allspice berries

Combine all the marinade ingredients and marinate the venison for 1–2 days in a cold place, turning it a few times. Remove, wipe it dry and lard with the lardons.

Brown the meat on all sides in the hot butter mixed with the oil, then transfer to a heavy-based pan in which it will just about fit. Heat up the marinade with 1/2 teaspoon salt and pour it over the meat. Simmer, covered, until the meat is tender, about 2–2 1/2 hours. Remove from the pan and keep it warm in the oven while you strain and reduce the cooking liquid a little by fast boiling. Check the seasoning before pouring it over the carved meat for serving.

## VENISON MINCED STEAKS
Serves 5

*Gamsovi sesekljani zrezki* (Slovenian, meaning chamois minced steaks)

500 g minced or finely chopped venison •
50 g smoked pork fat or streaky bacon, diced small •
50 g crustless bread, soaked in water and squeezed dry •
3–4 button mushrooms, chopped and fried in lard or oil • 1 garlic clove, finely chopped •
1 small onion, finely chopped and fried in lard or oil • 1 egg, lightly beaten •
50 ml sour cream • 1/2 teaspoon each of salt and freshly ground black pepper •
1–2 tablespoons chopped parsley •
1/2 tablespoon each of chopped mint and marjoram • dry crumbs or flour for coating •
50 ml sour cream, a little vinegar and stock or slightly salted water for braising

Mix all the steak ingredients together well and shape into 5 flat oval patties. Dip them in breadcrumbs or flour and fry in hot vegetable oil on both sides until browned. Transfer them to a large, shallow saucepan, pour over the sour cream, a little vinegar and hot stock or salt water, cover and braise over a low heat for 5–10 minutes.

Serve in their own sauce with boiled potatoes, noodles or dumplings, and stewed cranberries if available.

## WILD BOAR WITH SAUERKRAUT
Serves 5–6

*Derr i egër me arme* (Albanian); *diva svinya s kiselo zele* (Bulgarian); *divlja svinja s kiselim kupusom* (Serbo-Croat)

The European wild boar (a sub-species of *Sus scrofa*) is a forest animal that feeds on roots and nuts. It inhabits the high mountain forest where it can roam freely. The thickly wooded and wild terrain south of the Gllava Pass in Albania is especially famous for its wild-boar hunting.

The flesh is extremely flavorous, and leaner than the domestic pig's. The meat of young wild pigs is a particular delicacy, while sausages have a lovely gamey flavour. They are prepared in exactly the same way as pork sausages (p. 185), but the meat must be well hung.

1.5 kg shredded sauerkraut, drained, the liquor reserved for marinating the meat •
1 kg wild-boar meat, well hung, cut into approximately 2.5 cm cubes and marinated in the sauerkraut liquor for 24 hours •
paprika • caraway seeds • 100 g lard, melted

In a large baking dish, arrange alternate layers of sauerkraut and drained meat pieces, starting and finishing with a sauerkraut layer, and sprinkling each layer with paprika, caraway seeds and lard. Pour any remaining lard on top. Bake in a preheated oven at 180°C/350°F/gas 4 for 2 1/2–3 hours, or until the meat is tender and most of the juices evaporated. Serve hot.

## SPIT-ROASTED FILLET OF WILD BOAR
Serves 5

*Shishqebap me mish derr i egër* (Albanian, meaning skewered meat of wild boar); *file ot diva svinya* (Bulgarian, 'fillet of wild swine')

1 kg wild-boar fillet, in one piece, marinated for a few hours in sunflower oil and sherry or similar wine • salt and freshly ground black pepper • a little melted butter

Drain the meat, but reserve the marinade. Season the meat lightly with salt and pepper. Thread it on to a long flat spit, wrap it in white paper, previously greased with melted butter, and secure the ends of the parcel with safety-pins.

Grill the meat, rotating it slowly over the ash-covered embers of a charcoal fire, for half an hour. Remove the paper and continue cooking, brushing the meat from time to time with the marinade, until done, about 1 hour in all. Remove from the spit and carve it thinly. Serve, if you wish, with fried potatoes and pickles.

## WILD-PIGLET CHOPS WITH JUNIPER BERRIES
Serves 4

*Divji prašič v brinovi polivki* (Slovenian)

4 thick loin chops of well-hung wild piglet • vegetable oil •
1 small onion, finely chopped • 1 tablespoon plain flour • pork stock or hot water •
salt • 1 large pinch sugar • 7 juniper berries, pounded to a paste •
1–2 whole cloves • 1 tablespoon wine vinegar

Fry the loin chops in hot oil until lightly browned; transfer them to a wide and shallow saucepan, laying them side by side.

In the same oil, fry the onion until golden, then stir in the flour. When it just turns colour, pour over a little hot stock or water before adding the onion mixture to the meat. Simmer very gently until the chops are barely tender, then stir in the remaining ingredients. Bring back to simmering point and cook for a further 10–15 minutes, or until the meat is ready. Serve hot with boiled potatoes.

# HARE, HUNTER'S STYLE
Serves 7–9

*Div zayak po lovdzhijski* (Bulgarian); *div zajak po lovechki* (Macedonian); *zec po lovački* (Serbo-Croat); *zajec po lovski* (Slovenian)

A whole leveret of brown hare (*Lepus europaeus*), gutted,
cut into 6 joints; or about 1.5 kg selected hare joints •
wine vinegar or natural yoghurt • plain white flour •
lard or oil or rendered back pork fat • 1 onion, finely chopped •
2–3 cloves garlic, chopped • 1–2 tablespoons tomato purée •
1 teaspoon paprika • 1/2 teaspoon salt •
1/2 teaspoon coarsely ground black pepper • 4 allspice berries, crushed • 1 bay leaf •
375 ml red wine • 500 ml good stock or canned consommé •
1 kg pickling onions, blanched, refreshed in cold water, drained and skinned

Place the hare joints in a glass bowl. Mix vinegar or yoghurt with an equal amount of cold water and pour over the meat to submerge. Cover the bowl and marinate in a refrigerator overnight or up to 24 hours.

About 3 or 4 hours before you plan to eat, remove the hare from the marinade. Discard the marinade. Pat the joints dry and toss them in flour. Brown them nicely in hot fat and transfer to a flame-proof casserole. Lower the heat and fry the chopped onion in the same fat until soft and golden, then stir in the garlic, tomato purée, paprika, salt, spices, wine and stock or consommé. Raise the temperature to boiling and pour the bubbling mixture over the hare. Bring the casserole to the boil, cover and cook in an oven preheated to 160°C/325°F/gas 3 for 2 hours.

When the time is up, brown the pickling onions in a little fat and add them to the casserole. Cook for a further 30–45 minutes until the hare is tender. Check the seasonings and discard the bay leaf. Serve with bread or mashed potatoes. Accompany, if you like, with a bottle of red wine—perhaps the same one you used for cooking.

## QUAIL GRILLED ON A RACK
Serves 4

*Putpudutsi pecheni* (Bulgarian); *prepelice pečene* (Serbo-Croat); both meaning quails baked [on a grill rack]

This recipe appeared for the first time in the 1894 edition of the Bulgarian cookery book *Family Treasure*. Grilling quail on a rack rather than spit-roasting is also common in some of the hunting areas of Vojvodina and Slovenia. Older quail can be kept in a cool place for up to 24 hours; young ones and farm-bred quail should be cooked on the day of shooting.

8 quail, drawn • salt and freshly ground pepper

Slice each quail lengthwise along the breastbone, leaving the two sides joined at the back. Spread the bird open and pound it gently with a meat bat to flatten it, at the same time working in some salt and pepper.

Arrange the prepared birds on a greased hot rack over glowing charcoal and grill them, turning once, until they are well done and nicely browned—about 10–15 minutes. Serve immediately.

## ROAST PARTRIDGE IN NESTS OF STRAW POTATOES
Serves 4

*Yarebitsa pechena na fourna* (Bulgarian); *jarebica pečena u pećnicu* (Serbo-Croat)

Young partridge have lighter-coloured legs than older specimens; their two large flight feathers are pointed, becoming rounded with age. Roast partridges are at their best when eaten slightly underdone.

2 plump, young partridge, hung for 3–4 days, then drawn, seasoned, trussed and barded with thin sheets of back pork fat •
250 ml wine • 4 hot slices fried bread •
hot, deep-fried straw potatoes

Roast the barded partridges in a preheated oven at 220°C/425°F/gas 7 for 20 minutes. Remove the bards and discard. Return the birds to the oven for a further 5 minutes or until their breasts are golden-brown. Halve the partridges, then place each half, cut side down, on a slice of fried bread. Spoon over the pan juices deglazed with the wine. Serve very hot, surrounding each portion with straw potatoes.


# ROAST PHEASANT
Serves 4

*Pechen fazan* (Bulgarian; Macedonian), *pečen fazan* (Serbo-Croat, Slovenian)

Pheasant, like turkey or chicken, is sometimes roasted on a bed of fried sauerkraut, which takes up the bird's flavour and juices exuded during cooking and becomes very tasty and aromatic.

1 brace young pheasants (that is, a cock and a hen), trussed and oven-ready •
2 thin slices of fresh pork back fat known as bards, large enough to cover the birds' breasts; or use streaky bacon rashers • 50 g butter • some plain flour

Rinse the pheasants under cold running water and wipe dry. Put half the butter inside each bird, then cover the birds' breasts with a bard (or bacon rashers) and secure in position with string. Place the pheasants in a roasting tin and roast in a preheated oven at 200°C/400°F/gas 6 for about 60 minutes, basting a few times with the pan juices. Remove the bards (or bacon) towards the end of the cooking, baste and dredge with flour, baste again and return the birds to the oven to allow the breast to brown.

For serving, either carve the pheasants into portions, arrange in the centre of a large serving dish and garnish with vegetables—for example, fried mushrooms and buttered green beans; or present them whole, with tail feathers placed at the tail end of each bird.

Accompany with gravy made from the skimmed juices left in the tin, deglazed with white wine.

# CHAPTER XIV

# Grains, Seeds, and Porridges

*Zhito* (Bulgarian, Russian), *žito* in Macedonian, Serbo-Croat and Slovenian, is a pan-Slavonic word meaning cereals: the grain of all cultivated grasses used for human food, or wheat. The word stems from the Old Slavonic *žita* meaning cereals or wheat, itself derived from *žit*, life—underlining the true significance of cereals, particularly of wheat, for all Slavic peoples.

## BOILED WHEAT
Makes 20 dessert portions or about 50 small offerings

*Grurë i zierë* (Albanian), *vareno zhito* (Bulgarian), *varena pshenitsa* (Macedonian)—all meaning boiled wheat; *žito* (Serbian, meaning wheat); *kolivo* (Bulgarian, Macedonian), *colivă* (Romanian), *koljivo* (Serbian), *koliva* (Turkish), from the medieval Greek *kóllivon*, boiled wheat, but which was originally a small coin which used to be distributed at memorial services, later replaced by wheat; modern Greek *kólliva*.

This flavourful mixture of wheat grains, sugar and nuts has gathered unto itself a host of ritual functions and meanings. It is possibly of pre-Christian Slavonic origin, but was adopted by the Eastern Orthodox Church and introduced into the cult of the dead. It is offered at funerals, memorial services and on All Souls' Day to churchgoers, in small spoonfuls on clean paper napkins. Small bowlfuls are afterwards sent to all the neighbours.

Boiled wheat is also made for the day of the patron saint of a family or a particular social unit. This ritual is known in Macedonia as *Služba*, Service, and in Serbia as *Slava*, Glorification. In Macedonia and Turkey, it is eaten to celebrate the appearance of a child's first tooth.

*Grains, Seeds, and Porridges*

Each Balkan country has its own formula of preparation, but essentially it is cooked wheat kernels, sugar, nuts (and sometimes seeds), and spices. The recipe below is one I have learnt, by precept and example, from my mother. It works with branless wheat, which in Bulgaria is sold in most groceries, supermarkets and ecclesiastical shops. Wheat with the bran skins still on remains chewy no matter how long it is cooked—as anyone who has eaten English frumenty will attest.

If you cannot find branless wheat, you can make your own. Wash and drain the required quantity of hard wheat grains. Spread it on a wet towel and leave for 3 hours. Put a spoonful or two into a deep wooden mortar and, using a wooden pestle (or the end of a rolling pin), pound the grains gently, without breaking them, for a few seconds. Now change the movement of the pestle, turning it round and round in a rotary motion, for another couple of seconds. Continue in this way, alternating the two kinds of motion; after a minute or two you will notice the skins of the grains coming off. Continue for another minute or so, then empty the mortar and start again with another spoonful or two of wheat grains. When all are processed, put them into a large pot and run tap water over them; the bran will rise to the surface and will be washed away. Drain the wheat, spread it on a clean tablecloth and leave it to dry out overnight. Next day, blow away any remaining bran skins. Now you have wheat with the coarse outer layers of bran removed, or *grouhana pshenitsa*, literally 'pounded wheat'. It is ready to be cooked or, if left to become completely dry, could be stored in a tight-lidded container in a cool place for up to six months.

500 g branless wheat • salt • juice of 1/2 lemon •
250 g plain white flour, roasted until pale golden (p. 340);
or 500 g salt-free rusks, finely ground and sieved •
500 g coarsely ground walnuts •
500 g finely ground vanilla sugar (p. 352), or icing sugar •
2 rounded teaspoons ground cinnamon •
1/2 teaspoon vanilla essence or 2 sachets vanilla sugar • grated zest of 2 lemons •
gold leaf or silver balls used for cake decoration

On the first day, wash and drain the wheat. Put it into a large, preferably new saucepan with a tight-fitting lid, or 'one that has not been used for the cooking of onion, garlic, fish, meat, fat or oil', says a note in my mother's old recipe notebook. Add cold water to cover 'two fingers above the grains', cover and leave overnight.

Early in the morning of the second day, without changing the water, heat the contents of the pan to boiling point, then let it simmer, with the lid still on, for 20 minutes. No need to stir. At the end of the cooking time, take a quick peep under the lid—most of the grains should have started opening up and some will be full-blown. Increase the heat slightly and then, without removing the lid, take the saucepan off the heat, wrap well with kitchen cloths and leave undisturbed for 24 hours.

On the third and final day, drain the wheat, reserving the liquid if you wish—it is traditionally used for making *Ashoure* (the next recipe). Rinse the grains with warm water and drain again. Now place a large sheet of plastic (formerly this was oilskin) on a table and put over it several layers of newspapers. Cover the newspapers with freshly ironed tea towels or a tablecloth. Spread the wheat thinly over the towels and leave it to dry for 12 hours.

Place it on a large, round, shallow tray, sprinkle lightly with salt to taste, then sprinkle it all over with lemon juice—a pastry brush comes in useful. Sieve about half the flour (or rusk crumbs) over the wheat, then shake the tray until every grain is coated with flour and stands separately. Add the walnuts, about 300 g of the sugar, the cinnamon, vanilla and lemon zest to the wheat, and mix thoroughly, using 2 large spoons, or a mixer or processor with the dough hook attached. If you have to leave the mixture standing for any length of time, cover it and keep it at room temperature.

Just before serving, or taking the wheat to church to be blessed, spread it out evenly on a large serving tray. In an ideal Balkan world, it should be an oval silver tray with side-handles. Sift the remainder of the flour (or crumbs) over the wheat, pressing it gently down, then sift the rest of the icing sugar evenly over the flour. Decorate the top with words or symbols, drawn with the handle of a spoon. If you wish, fill the indentations with silver balls or gold leaf strips.

*The Serbian version*
Besides being offered on the day of the patron saint, *žito* is also sold in most pastry shops throughout Serbia in individual glass bowls or goblets. I tasted it for the first time in the town of Kruševac: the boiled wheat was topped with whipped cream and garnished with a piece of candied lemon peel. It was quite delicious.

*Žito* is prepared in exactly the same way as in the master recipe, except that the wheat used is unprocessed whole wheat, with the bran layers on, so it needs to be cooked much longer, for at least 2 hours, or until soft enough to eat though still slightly chewy. The grains are then rinsed, patted dry and put through a mincer or coarsely ground in a food processor.

# BULGARIAN ROSE-SCENTED WHEAT DESSERT
Serves 4–5

*Hašure* (Bosnian), *ashoure* (Bulgarian), from the Turkish *aşure*, deriving from the Arabic name of a feast day on the 10th of Muharrem (the first month of the Muslim lunar year)

The Turkish sweet dish of this name, based on cereals and pulses, was distributed to the poor on the feast day mentioned above. The *Hašure* of Bosnia and Hercegovina, a festive dish resembling the Turkish original, is very variable and may consist of bulgur, barley, rice, maize, beans and lentils, prunes, figs, dates, currants and sultanas, fresh apples, pears, carob, oranges and cherries, almonds, hazelnuts and walnuts or, as they say in Bosnia, 'If not seventy, at least seven different kinds of fruits and grains should go into it'. To avoid overcooking the ingredients are cooked separately, then combined and poached a little longer to finish off and mingle the flavours. *Hašure* is usually served cold.

By contrast, the Bulgarian *ashoure* is a modest rose-scented dessert, usually a by-product of the boiled wheat described in the preceding recipe, because it often uses the cooking liquor of the wheat and a small quantity of the cooked kernels. It bears a strong resemblance to the old English dish called frumenty.

> 150 g cooked wheat grains–taken from making the previous recipe (or 50 g branless wheat, soaked overnight in 750 ml water and boiled until full-blown and very soft) •
> 500 ml strained hot liquid in which the wheat was cooked (if there is less, top up with hot water) • 2 tablespoons cornflour • 250 ml milk • 50 g sultanas • 100 g sugar •
> 25 g ground walnuts •
> 1/2 teaspoon concentrated rosewater, or a few drops vanilla essence
> *To finish*
> 15 g ground walnuts • ground cinnamon

Set aside 3 tablespoons of the cooked wheat, then press the remainder through a fine sieve, using a little of the hot liquid to help the starch of the grains pass through. Discard the residue.

Join in a pan the wheat starch, the rest of the hot liquid, the cornflour slaked with the milk, sultanas and sugar. Bring the mixture to boiling point. Cook over a fairly high heat for 2–3 minutes, stirring, until it achieves the consistency of pouring cream or custard. Remove from the heat and stir in the reserved grains and the walnuts, then the rosewater or vanilla. Ladle into individual bowls and garnish with ground walnuts and a sprinkling of cinnamon. Serve hot or at room temperature.

*Children's version*: Sweeten to taste the strained water in which the wheat was cooked, add a few tablespoons of the cooked kernels and serve warm sprinkled with ground walnuts. Much liked.

# A DISH OF POACHED CHICKEN OR TURKEY AND WHEAT

Serves 6 as a starter

*Keške* (Bosnian, Hercegovinian), *keshek* (Bulgarian), *keshchek* (Macedonian), *češkek* (Serbian), from the Turkish *keşkek*, ultimately from the Persian

This festive dish is borrowed from the Turkish kitchen. It is prepared during the winter when older hens and turkeys are slaughtered. The nineteenth-century Bulgarian folklorist Kouzman Shapkarev recorded how the dish was made in Ohrid in huge quantities for weddings. In the Central Rhodope mountains, *keshek* is sometimes cooked with rice instead of wheat.

> 500 g joints of older chicken, boiling fowl or turkey, skinned, excess fat removed •
> 125 g branless wheat (p. 209), soaked overnight in cold water and drained before cooking; or fine bulgur wheat (p. 44) • 100 ml hot milk • 50 g butter • salt and pepper •
> red paprika butter, prepared with 75 g butter and 1 teaspoon paprika

Poach the poultry joints in enough unseasoned water to cover for about 2 hours, until the flesh is practically falling off the bones. Lift them out with a draining spoon. Reserve the stock. When cool enough to handle, tear the flesh into tiny shreds, discarding the bones and any black bits, gristle or fat.

Return the stock to the heat, and when it comes back to the boil, add the wheat. Cover the pan and simmer for about 30 minutes (if using bulgur), or 45–50 minutes (if using branless wheat)—adding more hot water or milk if necessary, until the wheat is tender. Then stir in the meat, butter and salt and pepper to taste, and continue cooking, stirring and mashing continuously with a wooden spoon, for about 10 minutes or until the mixture is very thick. Spoon into earthenware bowls, pour over paprika butter and keep in a slow oven until ready to serve. *Keşkek* will keep well for 3 days in a refrigerator. Reheat over a fairly high heat in oil or butter, stirring until thoroughly heated through. Dress with paprika butter and serve hot.

## CRACKED WHEAT PILAFF
Serves 6–7

*Bollgur pilaf* (Albanian), *bungur-pilav* (Bosnian), *boulgour pilaf* (Bulgarian), *bulgur pilav* (Macedonian), from the Turkish *bulgur pilavı*, which stems from the Persian

In the Balkans, bulgur often substitutes for rice in pilaffs. Cracked wheat pilaff goes well with grilled or fried meat as an alternative to rice, noodles or potatoes.

1 large onion, finely chopped • 2 tablespoons oil • 200 g coarse bulgur wheat (p. 44) •
625 ml hot lamb or chicken stock • 1 tablespoon sultanas •
50 g pine nuts or blanched almonds, chopped • salt

Brown the onion in the oil. Stir in the wheat and fry for a minute, still stirring. Add the hot stock and sultanas, cover and bring to the boil. Simmer gently for about 25–30 minutes, adding a little more stock or hot water, if necessary, until the wheat is tender and all the liquid absorbed. Stir in the nuts and season with salt to taste. Serve hot in individual heated bowl or in one large serving bowl.

## BUCKWHEAT PORRIDGE
Serves 2

*Mlečna ajdova kaša* (Slovenian, meaning buckwheat porridge with milk, from the Old Slavonic *kaša* or *kašja*)

375 ml milk • 1 large pinch salt •
50 g buckwheat flour, milled from whole or husked grain •
4 teaspoons jam • pouring cream

Pour the milk into a wide and shallow heavy saucepan, add the salt and heat to boiling. Strew in the buckwheat flour, a little at a time, stirring as you do so. Continue cooking, stirring continuously over a low heat to prevent the mixture from sticking to the bottom of the pan, for 6–7 minutes, or until the porridge is smooth and a spoon drawn across the pan reveals the bottom clearly. Taste and season with extra salt if necessary. Pour the porridge into two small bowls and leave to cool. Serve as it is or topped with jam or cream.

## MILLET PORRIDGE
Serves 4–5

*Mlečna prosena kaša* (Slovenian, from Old Slavonic *kaša* or *kašja*)

Millet (*Panicum miliaceum*) is a neglected and almost forgotten cereal in most parts of Europe except as bird seed. It is still a time-honoured ingredient in the Slovenian kitchen. Millet porridge made with milk was served at weddings as a symbol of fertility; it tastes very much like rice pudding. The recipe below is from Gorenjska, in the extreme north west of Slovenia. It bears much similarity to the once popular Bulgarian *mlechna prosena kasha*. Millet can be bought at most health-food shops.

200 g millet • 1 litre milk • 1/2 teaspoon salt •
250 ml single cream, heated to just below boiling point • ground cinnamon • castor sugar

Put the millet into a bowl and pour boiling water over it. Strain it off through a fine sieve, but not through a colander or normal strainer as the tiny grains will pass through. Pour hot water again over the millet and leave overnight to soak. Without this preliminary soaking millet takes twice as long to cook.

Next day, strain the grain in the same way and transfer to a heavy saucepan. Add the milk and salt and bring to the boil. Cover and simmer over the lowest heat for 30 minutes, stirring frequently towards the end of the cooking time to prevent burning. The porridge is ready when the millet has absorbed all the milk and is very tender. Serve immediately in heated stoneware bowls. Pass round single cream, cinnamon and sugar.

## WHEATEN PORRIDGE WITH CHEESE
Serves 3–5 as a light main course

*Pshenichna kasha sus sirene* (Bulgarian), *kasha od pchenitsa so sirenje* (Macedonian), from the Old Slav *kaša* or *kašja*

A frugal dish quickly prepared with ingredients that are always to hand in the larder. It is sometimes transformed by incorporating pieces of boiled lamb, beef or chicken, fried mushrooms or cracklings and lard—in place of the butter or cheese. In Bulgaria, *kasha* is one of the principle vehicles for the harvest of wild mushrooms.

The *kasha* is cooked with a mushroom stock, and the mushrooms are fried and incorporated.

100 g unbleached white flour • 50 g butter; or 40 g butter plus 1 tablespoon oil •
1/4 teaspoon salt • 875 ml mixture half milk half water •
125 g feta cheese, or any other white cheese such as Lancashire, crumbled

Dry fry the flour in a heavy-based saucepan or deep frying pan for a minute or so until it begins to turn colour. Take the pan off the heat and stir in the fat and the salt. Allow the mixture to cool a little, then stir in the liquid gradually. Return to the heat and simmer for 2–3 minutes, stirring continuously. The consistency is correct when the porridge drops easily from a spoon without being shaken. Add the cheese and serve immediately.

Some people like to eat the porridge with bread.

There is a popular joke told about the people of the town of Gabrovo, well known for their thrift, if not parsimony. While playing *tabla* [backgammon] and talking over their coffee, friends asked a man from Gabrovo how he managed to become so much better off than he used to be.

'It's really quite simple,' he answered. 'But let me ask you first: when your womenfolk cook, let's say rice pilaff, how much rice do they use?'

'Well, how much? ... as much as is necessary.'

'Before pouring a cup of rice into the water, my wife removes a dozen grains or so and saves them for the next day. A dozen grains today, a dozen grains tomorrow ... '

# CORNMEAL PORRIDGE (POLENTA)
Serves 4–5 as a garnish, or 2–3 as a main dish

*Kaçamak* or *mëmëligë* (Albanian), *kachamak* or *mamaliga* (Bulgarian, Macedonian), *katsamáki* or *mamalíga* (Greek), *kačamak* or *mamaliga* (Serbian), from the Turkish *kaçamak* and the Romanian *mămăligă*, itself from the word *mamă*, which meant both mother and porridge for babies. The word for this dish in Macedonian is *bakrdan*, deriving from the Turkish *bakırdan*, from *bakır*, the copper pan in which the cornmeal is cooked. While the Bosnian and Croat word is *pura*, the Dalmatian Croats call it *palenta*, and the Slovenes *koruzna polenta*, from the Italian word

Patrick Leigh Fermor describes his visit to a Romanian shepherd in Transylvania during his trek across Europe in the thirties:

> There was nothing to drink but water, so we all had a swig out of the flask, sitting about the ledge on stools, and I ate *mamaliga* for the first time—polenta or frumenty, that is, made out of ground maize, the staple of country people in these parts; I had been warned against it, but perversely found it rather good.
> *Between the Woods and the Water*, 1986.

There used to be two major methods of cooking cornmeal. One was to pour the meal in a heap into enough simmering salted water to cover, then make a hole in the centre and leave it to cook for about an hour, after which the excess water was poured off and the cornmeal vigorously stirred until very stiff. The disadvantage of this method was that dry granules of uncooked cornmeal invariably remained inside the cooked heap. The other method was to strew the cornmeal into salted boiling water and cook it, stirring all the time, for half an hour to an hour.

Nowadays, the use of heavy-based non-stick saucepans eliminates the formation of uncooked bits of cornmeal and the need for long and laborious stirring.

100 g coarse yellow cornmeal • 1/4 teaspoon salt

Add the salt to 650 ml of water in a heavy non-stick pan. Bring to boiling point and strew in the cornmeal, evenly and gradually, so that the water remains on the boil and no lumps form. Remove from the heat and stir well. Return the pan to the heat, regulating it so the porridge hardly simmers, cover and leave to cook for 50–55 minutes. Then turn the heat up fairly high and stir continuously for about 5 minutes until the porridge is thick and a wooden spatula drawn across the base of the pan leaves a wide track that slowly closes up.

To serve, scoop out spoonfuls on to plates to form little cakes, wetting the spoon each time. Pour over a tomato or meat sauce or melted butter and sprinkle with grated cheese and/or cracklings. Alternatively, turn the porridge out into a wetted 18 cm round or square shallow dish and leave until cold. Cut into squares, rounds or wedges and fry in butter or oil, or toast under the grill. Serve hot in any of the ways already mentioned.

## POLENTA BAKED WITH CHEESE
Serves 4–6

*Kaçamak (mëmëligë) me djathë* (Albanian); *kachamak (mamaliga) sus sirene* (Bulgarian); *kačamak sa sirom* (Serbian); *mămăligă cu brînză* (Romanian); *peynirli kaçamak* (Turkish); *bakrdan so sirenje* (Macedonian); *koruzna polenta s sirom* (Slovenian)

This is an excellent modern method of making polenta: the cornmeal is briskly toasted in a dry frying pan prior to boiling which brings out its pleasant characteristic flavour. Substitute 400 g streaky bacon, crisply grilled and chopped, for the cheese for an alternative version.

125 g yellow cornmeal, coarsely ground • scant 1/4 teaspoon salt • 50 g unsalted butter • 300 g feta cheese, soaked for 1–2 hours, drained and crumbled; or the same quantity of Cheshire, Lancashire or white Stilton cheese, crumbled • 50 g hard kashkaval cheese or mature Cheddar, grated • tomato sauce, made with tomato purée (p. 345)

Put the cornmeal into a large saucepan and dry-fry it over a moderate heat, stirring all the time, for 3–4 minutes or until light beige. Off the heat, pour over 1 litre cold water and add salt. Return the pan and simmer for a few minutes until the cornmeal begins to splutter. Cover, reduce the heat and leave to cook for 25–30 minutes, stirring occasionally; then remove the lid and stir continuously for about 5 minutes, or until the polenta is very thick, and a wooden spatula starts to leave a wide track on the bottom. Off the heat, stir in the butter and the crumbled cheese. Check for seasoning. Turn it into a buttered ovenproof dish 20 cm in diameter. Bake on a top shelf of an oven preheated to 190°C/375°F/gas 5 for about 30 minutes, or until a pale skin forms on the surface. Leave to cool and set for at least an hour or overnight.

To serve, slice into wedges, sprinkle with the hard cheese and serve either at room temperature, or reheat in a moderate oven. Alternatively, grill it until the crust is crisp and golden brown. Serve on hot plates, with the tomato sauce.

## RICE WITH GARDEN PEAS
Serves 6–8 as a side dish

*Rizi-bizi* (Croat), from the Italian *risi e bisi*

The following recipe, popular along the Adriatic coast of Croatia, illustrates the depth of attachment of Dalmatians to Italian cooking.

50 g unsalted butter • 1 large onion, finely chopped • 200 g risotto rice •
about 700 ml hot meat, chicken or vegetable stock • scant 1/2 teaspoon salt, if necessary •
400 g tinned peas, drained weight, reheated, liquid discarded; or 440 g frozen peas;
or 300 g freshly shelled peas, pre-cooked in boiling unsalted water
with 1–2 teaspoons sugar, kept hot •
grated Parmesan, kashkaval or Cheddar cheese • freshly ground black pepper

Fry the onion in 25 g of the butter in a saucepan until slightly coloured. Add the rice and stir until it becomes translucent. Using a ladle, add the hot stock little by little. Season with salt only if necessary. After 25–30 minutes of simmering, the rice will be soft but still holding its shape, the dish moist but not soupy. Turn off the heat and stir in the hot drained peas, the rest of the butter and a generous quantity of grated cheese. Serve hot, sprinkled with a good grinding of black pepper.

> The pilaf, or buttered rice, the standing dish of Turkey ... is often brought in twice in the same dinner.
> John Cam Hobhouse (Lord Broughton), *Travels in Albania and Other Provinces of Turkey in 1809 & 1810*, new edition 1858.

## RICE PILAFF
Serves 2 or 3

*Pilaf* (Albanian, Bulgarian); *pilav* (Bosnian, Macedonian, Serbo-Croat, Turkish)
from the Persian

Pilaff is the dish of boiled rice or other grains (bulgur wheat or couscous) in which the cooked grains do not stick together but, as the Turks say, remain *tane, tane* (in separate grains). Apart from the plain buttered pilaff which is served with just a sprinkling of pepper, a great variety can be made using bits of cooked lamb, chicken, liver, fish, game birds, mincemeat, artichokes or fried aubergines or mushrooms.

25 g butter • 1 small onion, finely chopped •
10–15 g pine-nuts or sunflower seeds •
10 g blanched almonds, chopped • 100 g long-grained rice •
500 ml hot meat or vegetable stock, or water • 25 g sultanas •
salt and black pepper to taste

Melt the butter in a heavy saucepan and fry the onions until soft. Add the nuts and continue frying until golden brown. Stir in the rice and fry for a minute. Pour in the hot stock or water, add the sultanas and the salt, cover and cook over a low heat until the liquid is absorbed and the rice is tender.

Turn the pilaff out on to a wide, flat ovenproof dish and leave in a hot oven with the heat turned off for a few minutes to dry out. Grind pepper over the top, fluff the rice with two forks and serve immediately.

> The head dealt round wooden spoons, and gave us each a huge chunk of hot maize bread. The women set a large bowl of boiled lamb and *pillaf* on the table. Some one recounted that the former Padishah, Abdul Aziz, used to have twenty-four fowls stewed down daily to make the juice for his *pillaf* to be cooked in.
>
> M. Edith Durham, *High Albania*, 1909

# SWEET RICE PILAFF WITH CURRANTS AND SULTANAS
Serves 6–8 as a dessert or an accompaniment to chicken

*Kabuni* (Albanian); *kabuni-pilav* (Hercegovinian)

This pre-eminently Albanian dish is served either as a sweet dessert on its own, or as a sweet accompaniment to boiled chicken. *Kabuni-pilav* is also mentioned by the 18th-century Hercegovinian man of letters Bulbulija, and recorded as *kabun-iyye*, a Turkish medieval dish by Shirvani.

200 g round-grain (pudding) rice, washed and drained • 1/8 teaspoon salt • 50 g unsalted butter •
150 g small seedless raisins or sultanas, soaked in hot water or chicken stock for an hour, then drained •
50 g castor sugar or icing sugar—when served alongside chicken; or up to 100 g sugar when the pilaff is served as dessert • 1 teaspoon ground cinnamon

Put the rice in a pan with 450 ml cold water or chicken stock (which is just over twice the volume of the rice) and the salt. Bring to the boil, stir, cover, and simmer for 20 minutes, or until the rice is tender and the liquid absorbed. Off the heat, drop in the butter and toss the rice with two forks to separate the grains. Let cool.

When the rice is cold, arrange it in a large flat dish in alternate layers with the dried fruit, sprinkling each layer with the sugar mixed together with the cinnamon. Start with the rice and finish with a layer of dried fruit and a sprinkling of sugar.

# BALKAN RICE PUDDING
Serves 4–5

*Sutliash* (Albanian), *sutlyash* (Bulgarian), *sutlijaš* (Bosnian, Serbian), *sutlijash* (Macedonian), from the Turkish *sütlaç*; *rizógalo* (Greek)

In composition, *sütlaç* is similar to English rice pudding, but involves cooking the rice on top of the stove, sometimes first with water until the rice grains swell, and then with milk and sugar. It is served cold, sprinkled with cinnamon or, on occasions in Serbia, with sweetened raspberry or strawberry purée. In Turkey *sütlaç* is often flavoured with rosewater or mastic.

A Bulgarian tale has it that a widower's favourite dessert was rice pudding. When he remarried, no matter how much his new wife tried, she could not prepare it to his liking. One day, talking too long with a neighbour, she allowed the rice to stick to the bottom of the pan and burn. 'Now that's what I call a good sutlyash' exclaimed her husband, eating it with relish. What the new wife didn't know was that his last spouse, being rather careless, always burnt the pudding.

1 litre milk • 100 g round-grain (pudding) rice • 100 g sugar •<br>
a few drops of vanilla essence • ground cinnamon

Choose a heavy-based, wide and shallow saucepan. Put in the milk, rice and sugar. Bring quickly to the boil, stirring occasionally. Cover the pan and simmer over the lowest possible heat for 1 hour, or until the rice is tender and the dish is the consistency of double cream. Remove from the heat, stir in the vanilla, pour into individual bowls and let cool. Sprinkle with ground cinnamon and serve.

## SWEET SAFFRON RICE
Serves 4

Zerde (Bosnian, Macedonian), from the Turkish

During the last century, *zerde* was well-known. Gerov's Bulgarian dictionary of 1897 defines it as 'a boiled rice dish which the Turks serve to the poor at the mosques'. Nowadays, though, it has been largely forgotten in Bulgaria as everywhere else in the Balkans—except in Bosnia and Macedonia. In Turkey, saffron rice is invariably served at weddings.

50 g round-grain (pudding) rice • 100 g sugar •<br>
1/4 teaspoon saffron threads, soaked in 2 tablespoons boiling water for 8 hours or overnight •<br>
1/2 tablespoon cornflour, slaked with 1 tablespoon cold water •<br>
50 g blanched ground almonds mixed with 1/2 teaspoon ground coriander;<br>
or 50 g ground walnuts mixed with 1/4 teaspoon cinnamon

Cover the rice with 250 ml water and simmer over the lowest possible heat, covered with a tight-fitting lid, for 25 minutes or until the rice is very tender. Add the sugar, the strained liquid of the soaked saffron and the slaked cornflour. Continue cooking for a further 2–3 minutes or until you have a mixture about the consistency of batter. Ladle on to 4 small dessert plates, in a thin layer, and leave to cool. Cover the surface of the rice with flavoured almonds or walnuts and serve.

## TOASTED SEEDS

Salted toasted seeds are among the most popular snacks described by the Greek word *pasatempo* (from the Italian *passatempo*), to pass the time, and in Bulgaria as *zalugalki*, literally, 'to fool the appetite'.

Huskless varieties of pumpkin seeds and husked sunflower seeds are also occasionally roasted, but as they can be eaten as quickly as salted peanuts, almonds or popcorn they hardly qualify for passing the time. The cracking of each toasted seed between the front teeth to allow the kernel to fall into the mouth unbroken, and daintily discarding the husks (without spitting) is part of the fun of eating them.

# TOASTED PUMPKIN SEEDS

*Pecheni semki* (Bulgarian); *kolokithósporoi* (Greek); *pečene semenke* (Serbo-Croat)

Pumpkin seeds have their own delicate aroma which is heightened by toasting. They are a good source of unsaturated fatty acids and contain the active compound phytosterine which lowers the level of blood cholesterol.

In the autumn, each time a pumpkin is split open for cooking, the family will make more salted seeds. They are also sold in the streets in small paper cones or sachets. Sunflower seeds, with their husks still on, could be prepared in the same way as pumpkin seeds, though they would require briefer cooking.

Pumpkin seeds are coated with a mucous substance which cannot readily be dislodged by washing. To remove this, rinse them first, then dry them on a tray in a very low oven, until the mucous turns into a thin, brittle membrane which can be rubbed off easily between a tea towel. This done, rinse again and season with 1/2 teaspoon salt per each 100 g of seeds. Spread them out on the tray in a thin layer and roast them in a preheated oven at 190°C/375°F/gas 5 for about 20 minutes, checking every now and then to make sure they do not brown too much. They are ready when golden-brown on the surface but still pale within. Leave them to cool in the oven with the heat switched off and the door ajar. Stored in screw-top jars in a dry place they will keep for weeks.

# CHAPTER XV

# Pasta, Tarhana and Dumplings

Pasta is the family name for all the numerous shapes of paste prepared with durum or strong wheat flour. Its early history is still a matter of speculation. Although its modern development is so often ascribed to the Italians, its true origins are much further afield, in northern China, where wheat was grown and dough was steamed as early as 1200 BC. Besides plain noodles, the Chinese also knew of stuffed pasta—the forerunner of ravioli and tortellini. It seems likely that the innovation reached Constantinople by way of the trade routes across Central Asia.

The Turkic peoples were also familiar with pasta, perhaps acquired during long periods of contact with northern China. In Sir Gerard Clauson's pre-thirteenth century Turkish dictionary, there are many relevant entries: *ügre*, noodles, or broth containing noodles; *süt ügre*, milk and noodles; *tutma:ç,* some kind of farinaceous food, 'noodles, macaroni, vermicelli' and the like, 'a food well known to the Turks'.

The knowledge of making noodles could have come to some parts of the Balkans from Italy or Greece; or it may have been brought by Turkic tribes when they penetrated deep into the Peninsula in the seventh century AD, or even later—in the fifteenth century, after the conquest of the Balkans by the Ottoman Turks. Whatever their route and time of dispersal, noodles were a late development in the central rural regions, where they began to feature in country cooking as late as the turn of this century. Before that, the only type of pasta made in village households were the tiny pellets of *tarhana*—the saddle-bag staple of Turkic nomads, an ancient, yet still current kind of convenience food quickly and easily turned into a nourishing meal or substitute for bread.

Tarhana was first introduced into the Balkans by the Onogur (Unogundur) Turks when they established an independent state between the Danube and the Balkan Mountains in the seventh century AD; then re-introduced by the Ottoman Turks after the fall of Constantinople in 1453. It is known in all countries which once constituted the Ottoman Empire, in Iran, and in the Turkic-speaking republics of the former Soviet Union.

## TARHANA—GRATED PASTA SHREDS

Makes about 300 g fresh pasta shreds, or 225 g dried

*Trahana* (Albanian, Bulgarian), *trahana* or *tarhana* (Bosnian), *trahanás* (Greek); *tarhonya* (Hungarian), *tarana* (Macedonian, Serbo-Croat), from the Turkish *tarhana*; *ribana kaša* (Slovenian, meaning grated dough); *Geriebener Teig* (German, in Transylvania, also meaning grated dough)

In its simplest form, tarhana is prepared solely from flour and water; in more sophisticated versions it is mixed with milk, eggs, yoghurt or vegetable purées, and is occasionally soured by fermentation. This is the only known leavened pasta.

The dough is shaped into tiny shreds or pellets by grating, chopping, rubbing through a sieve or between the palms of the hands, before drying in the sun. It can be cooked like ordinary pasta, in plenty of boiling water, but the usual method is to simmer the shreds in soup, or in as much milk or water as they will absorb, so no nutrients are washed out.

2 medium eggs • 1/2 teaspoon salt • 200 g strong plain flour

In a bowl, whisk the eggs and salt together with a fork. Gradually add about 150 g of the flour to make a soft dough. Turn on to a work surface and knead with most of the remaining flour until very firm. Continue kneading, folding the dough over and pushing your thumbs into it to press it down, until all the flour has been used and the dough is very, very stiff but not crumbly. Knead a little longer to make it smooth, then form into a ball. You can grate the dough straightaway, but chilling in a freezer for about 2 hours makes the job easier.

For grating, cover the entire work surface with greaseproof paper. Grate the dough coarsely, moving the grater continuously over the paper so as to prevent the shreds from falling on top of each other and sticking together. The shreds may be cooked immediately or dried for future use.

The best way to dry them is to flour lightly one or two large roasting tins then carefully transfer the shreds to form a thin layer all over the tins. Dust again with flour and shake the tins to coat each piece. Use two forks to separate any shreds that have stuck together. Leave in a warm, dust-free place for a few days. A quicker method is to leave them in a cool oven (80°C/175°F/gas 'cool') for 2–3 hours until hard and completely dry. Shake them in a fine sieve to get rid of excess flour. Store in a jar or cotton bag hung in a dry larder. Like this they will keep for a year.

## TARHANA WITH CHEESE
Serves 6 as a side dish

*Trahana s kashkaval* (Bulgarian); *tarana so kashkaval* (Macedonian); *tarana sa kačkavaljem* (Serbo-Croat)

300 g fresh tarhana, as described above • 450 ml half milk, half water • 50 g unsalted butter • 50 g mature kashkaval cheese (or strong mature Cheddar) coarsely grated

Pour the mixture of milk and water into a saucepan. Add a knob of the butter and bring to the boil over a moderate heat. Use a spatula to sprinkle in the shreds gradually, so the liquid remains at boiling point. Lower the heat and simmer gently for 7–8 minutes; by the end of this time the shreds will have absorbed the liquid and will be tender but with a slightly resilient core.

Tip the cooked shreds into an ovenproof dish, spread them out and dot them with the remaining butter. Toss the mixture with a fork, check the seasoning and put the dish in a preheated oven at 100°C/200°F/gas 'low' for about 10 minutes to heat the dish through. Sprinkle with the grated cheese and serve directly on to heated plates.

## BROKEN BAKED PASTA
Makes about 250 g pasta

*Mlintsi* (Bulgarian), *mlinci* (Serbian, Slovenian), from Old Slavonic *mlin*, which is the word for a mill and something that is milled

This instant home-made pasta, the only one of its kind, needs no cooking, just soaking in hot salted water. According to the Slovenian cookery writer Andreja Grum, *mlinci* is the offspring of unleavened bread.

250 g strong white (preferably unbleached) flour • 1 egg •
100 ml water • a little extra flour for kneading and rolling

Make a well in the centre of the flour in a bowl. Crack the egg into the well and beat it lightly with a spoon. Draw in the flour gradually, adding about 100 ml water until a stiff dough is formed. A quicker method is to use the plastic blade in a food processor, first mixing the flour and egg, then adding the water gradually.

Knead the dough on a floured surface until smooth and elastic, then roll it out, beating it from time to time with the rolling pin until about 1.5 mm thick and about 45 cm in diameter. Allow to stand for an hour or two.

When the dough has dried a little, cut it into approximately 10 cm squares. Arrange the pieces on non-stick or very lightly greased baking sheets and cook them in a preheated oven at 150°C/300°F/gas 2 for 10–20 minutes, until they blister and take on a tinge of deep ochre-brown, and are dry. Leave to cool on the sheets, then break into small pieces and store in a cloth bag in a dry, airy place.

When you want to use the pasta, place the broken shards in a bowl and pour in sufficient hot salted water to cover by at least 2.5 cm. Leave to soak for 10–15 minutes, then drain and serve hot. They are in one respect a Balkan version of Yorkshire pudding, because they can be moistened with the fat poured off the joint before making gravy, then served with roast beef. Alternatively, mix with butter and ham or cheese, with honey, poppy seeds and cream, or with whatever takes your fancy, for an instant snack or meal. Pot noodles before their time.

## BAKED PASTA PUDDING
Serves 6

*Banitsa s mlintsi* (Bulgarian), *gibanica s mlincima* (Serbian), both meaning pie with broken baked pasta

---

*Semolina pudding*
500 ml milk (or milk and water) • 65 g sugar • 40 g semolina

125 g instant broken pasta as in recipe above, soaked for 15 minutes in hot, slightly salted water • 25 g melted butter • 2 stiffly beaten egg whites and 2 egg yolks • grated zest of 1/2 lemon • 1/2 teaspoon vanilla essence, or 1 sachet vanilla sugar • 25 g sultanas • 75 g feta cheese (or Lancashire or Cheshire), crumbled • vanilla-flavoured icing sugar for sprinkling

First prepare the semolina pudding. Bring the milk to near boiling point and sprinkle over the sugar mixed with the semolina. Simmer for 5 minutes, stirring occasionally, until the mixture thickens slightly. Remove from the heat.

Drain the soaked pasta well, and place it in a mixing bowl. Stir in the cooked semolina, about half of the melted butter, the egg yolk, lemon zest, vanilla, sultanas and the crumbled cheese, then fold in the beaten egg whites. Pour the mixture into a buttered 28 x 20 cm roasting tin and bake in a preheated oven at 180°C/350°F/ gas 4 for about 40 minutes, until set and golden brown. Brush the top with the remaining butter, sieve over a little vanilla sugar. Serve from the container, warm or cold, with pouring cream or on its own.


# ALBANIAN CANNELLONI, 'TUSCAN-STYLE'
Makes 6 rolls

*Kanelloni alla toskana* (Albanian)

*Meat filling*
1 small onion, finely chopped • 1 tablespoon vegetable oil •
1 tablespoon tomato purée • 1/2 teaspoon paprika • 1/4 teaspoon salt •
200 ml meat stock, or dry red wine, or water •
200 g minced beef, fried in its own fat, then drained of fat •
pancakes as described in the recipe on p. 254
*Topping*
1/2–3/4 quantity all-in-one cheese sauce (p. 342) •
grated nutmeg • finely grated cheese

In a covered saucepan, sweat the onion in the oil over a low heat until soft and pale golden. Stir in the tomato purée, paprika and salt, pour in the liquid and bring to the boil. Add the defatted meat and simmer for about 30 minutes, checking towards the end of the cooking time to make sure the meat mixture is not drying up.

Meanwhile, prepare the cheese sauce and flavour it with a little nutmeg, if you like. Prepare the pancakes; then cut a strip off the top and bottom of each pancake to give it a somewhat rectangular shape. Chop up the trimmings and stir them into the meat filling off the heat.

To shape the cannelloni, divide the meat filling into 6 and spoon a band along one lengthwise edge of each pancake. Roll them up and place close together in a greased 18 cm square baking dish or non-stick tin, flap side down. Pour over the cheese sauce and bake in a preheated oven at 180°C/350°F/gas 4 for about 20 minutes, or until browned. Serve immediately, sprinkled with grated cheese.

## BREAD DUMPLINGS
Makes 8–10 dumplings

*Knedli ot hlyab* (Bulgarian), *knedli od leb* (Macedonian), *knedle od hleba* (Serbian), from the German *Knödel*, dumpling); *okruglice od kruha* (Croat); *kruhovi cmoki* (Slovenian)

---

50 g salted butter, at room temperature •
125 g crustless white bread, soaked in a little milk, squeezed dry and mashed with a fork •
2 small eggs, well beaten • 125 g bread crumbs •
1 tablespoon parsley leaves, very finely chopped •
a little freshly ground black pepper • 50 g melted butter

Beat the butter until light and creamy with an electric hand-held beater or wooden spoon. Add in sequence the mashed bread, eggs, bread crumbs, parsley and pepper (but no salt) to make a soft paste. Refrigerate for at least 30 minutes, then take spoonfuls of the chilled paste and, with wet or oiled hands, mould balls the size of a small plum.

Half fill a large pan with stock or slightly salted water. When it comes to the boil, drop the dumplings into the liquid, cover and simmer gently for 20–25 minutes until cooked through. Transfer the dumplings to a hot dish and pour over the melted butter. Serve hot with a meat and vegetable stew instead of bread and butter.

## PLUM DUMPLINGS
Makes 16–18 dumplings

*Knedi sus slivi* (Bulgarian); *knedli so slivi* (Macedonian); *knedle sa šljivama* (Serbo-Croat); *češpljevi kneidli/cmoki* (Slovenian); from the German *Zwetschkenknödel*, plum dumplings

---

250 g floury potatoes, unpeeled • 25 g butter and 50 g butter to finish •
1 small egg • 125 g plain flour and a little extra for rolling out •
16–18 small, blue plums • 16–18 small lumps of sugar •
50 g dry bread crumbs • icing sugar • cinnamon

Boil the potatoes in their jackets and peel them while still hot. Put them in a bowl, add 25 g butter and mash thoroughly to make a homogenous mass that leaves the sides of the bowl. Leave to cool for 10 minutes, then blend in the egg. With a wooden spoon, stir in some of the flour, then turn the mixture out on to a work surface and knead in the remaining flour until you have a soft pliable dough. Cover with clingfilm and leave to relax in a cool place for 30 minutes.

Meanwhile, stone the plums without splitting the fruit in half; this is best done by easing the stone out with a small stick or skewer. Fill the stone cavity with a lump of sugar.

Divide the dough into 16–18 balls of equal size. On a lightly floured surface, roll each one into a thin round, brush the edges with water and wrap it round a plum to cover the fruit completely.

Bring a large saucepan of water to simmering point. Add 1/4 teaspoon of salt and lower the dumplings into the simmering liquid. Set the lid ajar over the pan and simmer steadily for 10–12 minutes depending on the size of the dumplings. After a minute or two of cooking, they will rise to the surface and, from time to time, will turn themselves over. When cooked, strain in a colander and rinse gently with cold water.

For the garnish, fry the breadcrumbs in 50 g butter until golden. Add the dumplings to the pan and roll them in the breadcrumbs. Keep cooking for a minute until they are encrusted with a golden-brown coating. Pile them on a hot plate, sprinkle with sugar and cinnamon and serve.

# CHAPTER XVI
# Breads, Pancakes and Fritters

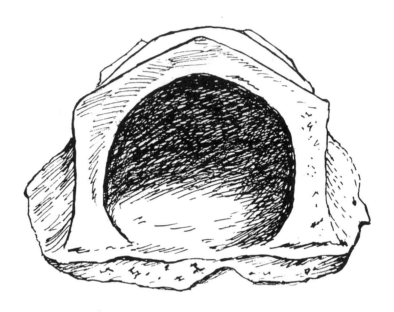

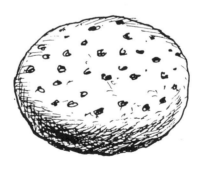

*A clay model made in approximately 4,300 BC of a bread oven, found in Stara Zagora, Bulgaria. It measures 5 cm wide by 6 cm deep. The top surface of the dome is decorated with impressions made with an acorn pressed into the wet clay. Also illustrated is another clay model, dating from approximately 5,100 BC, this time of a loaf of bread. The find was made from tell Bereket, near Stara Zagora. The holes appear to have been made with a stick, but imply the loaf was leavened.*

## Bread, Pancakes and Fritters

Bread is the staple of Balkan diet. It carries a load of spiritual meanings and is synonymous with food, livelihood, fertility and life itself. It is central to social and ceremonial life, symbolizing hospitality, when bread and salt is brought out as an act of courtesy to welcome important visitors, and fellowship—to refuse a proffered piece of bread may mean refusing a relationship.

Unleavened flat bread used to be baked in the embers of the hearth and was known as 'fresh' bread because it had to be eaten while still warm—becoming hard and unpalatable as it cooled. Another name is derived from the Latin *panis focacius* literally, hearth bread—compare the Italian *focaccia* and the French fougasse or *fouacé*. In Albanian, this was *pogaçe*, *pogacha* in Bulgarian and Macedonian, *pogacea* in Romanian and *pogača* in Serbo-Croat and Slovenian. The term was borrowed by Hungarians (*pogácsa*) and Turks (*poğaça* or *boğaça*). Later, the scope of the word was broadened to cover various kinds of loaves and pastries. As a ritual unleavened loaf of pre-Christian times, it has been associated with ancient pagan rites. After the conversion of the Slavs to Christianity, *pogachas* began to be made with leavened dough—but even today, because of pagan overtones, *pogachas* are never cut with a knife, nor taken to church to be blessed.

The oldest ritual leavened loaf which came into being soon after the Slavs embraced Christianity is shaped in a round, ring or like a cart and is called *kolach* in Bulgarian and Macedonian or *kolač* in Serbo-Croat and Slovenian, from the old Slavonic word for wheel, *kolò*. The term has been disseminated far beyond the Slavic languages; it has become *kulaç* or *kullaç* in Albanian, *kalács* in Hungarian, *colac* in Romanian and *kolaç* or *kolât* in Turkish. Again, the name has now been extended further to mean all types of breads, cakes and yeast cakes. Leavened bread, made from the finest flour, is used by the Orthodox Church for communion.

The term *pita* (from the Greek *píta* or *pítta*) means different things in the different countries. In Albania and Bulgaria, *pite* and *pita* respectively, refer not only to a flattish compact mass—such as a cake of wax, a round block of hard cheese, a honeycomb—but also to a round loaf or large flat bread or a bun. In Serbo-Croat and Macedonian *pita* is the word for a layered pie of fresh dough-sheets or sheets of puff pastry interleaved with a filling, a fresh-fruit cake, fruit tart or shortbread. In Istanbul *pide* can be a large bun, soft flat bread or even a pizza.

Besides native breads, a few have been imported, though generations of local cooks have altered them from their originals. There is the ring-shaped street bread called *gjevrek* (p. 47); *simit* (Albanian, Bosnian, Bulgarian and Macedonian, from the Turkish)—a baker's bun with unique taste and aroma, fermented by a spontaneous chick-pea leaven; *čurek* (Bosnian, from the Turkish *çörek*, from Arabic)—a largish bun, also prepared on a chick-pea leaven and shaped like the palm of a hand with four short fingers sticking out on either side. Before baking, the dough is sprinkled with *ćurekot* (from Turkish *çörekotu*)—seeds of the cultivated fennel flower *Nigella sativa*. A seventeenth-century Turkish traveller to Sarajevo, Evliya Çelebi (Čelebija), noted the hand-shaped bun was then known as *ručka-čurek* (hand-bun). And there are to be found, in town and country, the cake-like Christmas and Easter loaves of different origins, shapes and names of which the Balkan nations are justly proud.

1. Ring-shaped braided wedding loaf symbolizing the long hair of the bride which was cut as a sacrifice to a pagan god.
2. 'Infant' made for the festival of the Holy Innocents, which commemorates the slaughter of children by Herod.
3. Easter loaf named 'Doll' (Koukla). Sometimes a red Easter egg is inserted in the top part of the doll.
4. Plaited loaf for St George's Day. The meaning of the symbols is long forgotten and they are purely decorative.
5. Another Easter loaf, decorated with a curled swastika motif—in Sanskrit, the swastika stands for well-being.
6. Ritual loaf with seven bread rings on top, baked for the health of the cattle on the day of St Blasius, protector of livestock, named himself after the cattle god Volos of the ancient Slavs.

In the following recipes I have used mainly dried (granular) yeast which is more easily obtainable than fresh yeast, and which can withstand higher temperatures (up to 34°C/93°F) without producing a sour, over-fermented flavour. But if you wish, you could substitute fresh yeast for dried. In this case, however, double the quantity of fresh yeast, use tepid liquid instead of hand-hot, and prove the dough at lower temperatures—a warm kitchen (about 21°C/70°F) is the best place.

*The Holy Seal, moulded or carved out of wood or plastic used to stamp consecrated bread for Communion. The boxes running through the centre bear the Greek letters NIKA IC XC, meaning Christ Conquers. On the left, M is for the Virgin Mary; and the nine small triangles on the other side commemorate the nine ranks of the saints. I bought the seal in a church shop in Athens. In large towns and cities, consecrated bread is supplied commercially by a baker. In smaller towns it is baked by a pious, usually old, woman, who keeps the seal. Consecrated bread of the Eastern Orthodox Church is always leavened, in contrast to the unleavened of the Latin rite.*

## WHOLEMEAL BREAD
Makes 3 loaves of 700 g each

*Bukë e zezë* (Albanian); *cher hlyab* (Bulgarian); *crni kruh* (Bosnian, Croat); *mayro psomí* (Greek); *tsrn leb* (Macedonian); *pâine neagră* (Romanian); *crn hleb* (Serbian); *črn kruh* (Slovenian)—all meaning literally 'black bread'

The swing to wholemeal bread is recent and parallels that in the West. It began about thirty years ago with nutritionists emphasizing the importance of fibre, though Balkan diet has never really been too low in roughage. The scientists' recommendations were soon taken up by commercial bakers who produced wholemeal and Graham bread (named after Sylvester Graham, the nineteenth-century American food reformer) and more recently, by many keen home cooks.

This recipe distils all the Balkan versions I have come across, though quantities fit the standard British 'two-pound' loaf tin. The Balkan loaf is normally prepared from strong or medium-strength wholemeal flour, milled very finely, which—compared with soft flour—absorbs more water and makes a bigger loaf. The dough is given at least two rising periods, and is often made as an overnight dough raised with a sour, that is, a piece of dough reserved from a previous batch.

Wholemeal bread is never hurried: by tradition and because current research indicates that a longer fermentation, of three hours for instance, hydrolyzes about 60 per cent of the phytic acid present in wholemeal flour and so increases calcium absorption. To make a single loaf, reduce the ingredients proportionally, increasing slightly the proportionate amount of yeast.

20 g or 2 tablespoons dried yeast • 900 ml hand-hot water • 20 g or 1 tablespoon salt •
1.5 kg wholemeal strong flour (reserve 75 g for kneading and shaping) •
3 well greased loaf tins of 1.5 litre capacity

To reactivate the dried yeast, pour a little of the hand-hot water into a small bowl and sprinkle the yeast granules evenly all over. Dissolve the salt in the remaining water. Stand the yeast in a warm place for about 20 minutes until frothy.

Meanwhile, tip the flour into a large bowl. Stir in the salt water, and then the yeast to form a soft, slightly tacky dough. Turn it on to a floured surface and knead it with some of the reserved flour for about 4–5 minutes until smooth. Return the dough to the bowl, brush the surface with oil or butter and leave to rise at normal room temperature, away from draughts, for 2–3 hours or until doubled in volume. Then punch it down, turn it on to a floured surface and knead again for 2–3 minutes.

Divide into 3 portions, knead each briefly with a third of the remaining flour, shape into a loaf and drop into their tins. Brush the tops with oil or melted butter, and leave to rise for a second time in a warm place for about an hour.

While the dough is rising, heat the oven to 200°C/400°F/gas 6. As soon as the loaves have risen well above the rims of the tins, bake on the centre shelf of the oven for 40 minutes, or until the crust is pale brown and the loaves have slightly shrunk away from the sides of the tins. To test that they are cooked, tap each loaf on the under-side: it should sound hollow. Cool on a wire rack before slicing. Best eaten within 24 hours, but unsliced and well wrapped, the loaves will keep for a couple of days.

# RICE BREAD
Makes one round loaf

*Bukë me oriz* (Albanian); *hlyab s oriz* (Bulgarian); *hleb s pirinčom* (Serbian)

This is a soft white bread with excellent keeping qualities and flavour. A similar recipe for 'A Good and Inexpensive Bread' appeared in Petko Slavejkov's cookery book *Instructions for all Kinds of Dishes Prepared after the Manner of Istanbul* that was first published by the 'Macedonia' printing house in the Turkish capital in 1870. That recipe is made with 1 oka of rice boiled with 300 drams of water, 4 okas flour, a little salt and home-made leaven. An *oka* (from the Turkish *okka*) is an old unit of weight containing 400 drams, the equivalent of 1.282 kg. The dram, in Greek *drámi*, derives from the Greek coin *drahmí*. In Turkish, it was a *dirhem*.

50 g ground rice • 1/2 teaspoon salt • 300 g strong white flour •
7 g fresh yeast • 50 ml sunflower oil, or 50 g lard or butter, melted

Bring the ground rice to the boil in a pan with 275 ml water, stirring all the time; the rice will thicken almost immediately to a smooth paste of dropping consistency. Add the salt and leave to cool until lukewarm.

Transfer the rice to a mixing bowl. Stir in the flour, followed by the fresh yeast, dissolved in 1 tablespoon of tepid water, to form a very soft, sticky dough. Knead it, gradually working in most of the oil or fat, for about 5 minutes, occasionally lifting and slapping it down on the work surface. Return to the bowl, cover it lightly and leave in a warm kitchen to rise for about 1 hour, or until more than doubled in bulk. Knock down the dough on the work surface and knead briefly with the oil or fat that remains, using a spatula to scrape it off the table. Spread it in a well greased tin measuring approximately 23 cm in diameter. Smooth the surface of the dough with your fingers moistened with a little milk, and leave it for 45–50 minutes to rise again.

Bake the dough in a preheated oven at 200°C/400°F/gas 6 for 30 minutes until golden-brown on top and underneath. Turn it out and cool on a rack.

## BALKAN BAP LOAF
Makes 1 loaf of 23 cm diameter

*Pite* (Albanian); *pitka* (Bulgarian); *pita* (Romanian); *pide* (Turkish); from the Greek *píta* or *pítta*

My husband Tom and I got engaged in 1964, but then we had to wait six months for permission to get married, and then a further six months for permission to leave the country.

This year of anxious waiting proved to be very social—travelling round visiting friends and relatives, and joining in many happy get-togethers in the homes or the studios of fellow students from the Art Academy of Sofia.

At a friend's villa high in the Balkan Mountains, we were warmly welcomed by our hostess carrying a tray covered with an embroidered peasant cloth on which was placed a beautifully decorated bap loaf, *pitka*, with a small bowl of salt in the centre of the bread.

This was the ritual Slavic way of greeting guests with bread and salt (*hlyab i sol* in Bulgarian, *hleb s sol'yu* in Russian). Keeping to tradition, Tom and I each broke a piece and dipped it into the salt before eating it.

400 g strong white flour, preferably unbleached • 1/2 teaspoon salt • 2 teaspoons sugar •
50 g butter, melted and cooled to tepid (reserve 1–2 tablespoons for kneading) •
1 small egg • 20 g fresh yeast creamed with 100 ml tepid water •
about 100 ml tepid milk or thin plain yoghurt (or a mixture) •
a little warm milk to glaze • sesame seeds

Grease a 23 cm round baking tin, about 6 cm deep, and set to one side. Measure the flour in a mixing bowl and stir in the salt and sugar. Make a large well in the centre and add the egg, butter, yeast and milk or yoghurt. Mix to a soft, sticky dough that leaves the bowl clean. Knead it with the reserved butter for 4–5 minutes, slapping it down from time to time until smooth and elastic, then shape it into a ball and roll out to the size of your tin. Brush the top with milk, sprinkle thickly with sesame seeds and press them lightly into the dough.

Transfer to the greased baking tin and set to rise in a draught-free spot in a warm kitchen for 45–50 minutes or until the dough has almost trebled in volume.

Bake on the centre shelf of a preheated oven at 200°C/400°F/gas 6 for 20 minutes, until well browned on the surface and golden brown underneath. Cool on a rack, then wrap it in a clean cloth and overwrap in polythene to keep it soft. To serve, break the bread apart by hand.

## CHEESE BREAD
Makes 1 loaf of 30 cm diameter

*Toutmanik* (Bulgarian)

The alternative method of shaping this traditional Bulgarian loaf is to layer the dough rounds, instead of rolling them up, and interleave them with the filling and fat to form a stack. In the villages lard is often substituted for butter or oil.

Like the pizza of southern Italy, *toutmanik* is a by-product of breadmaking, though nowadays a richer milk dough is preferred because milk makes the crust thinner and softer.

1 tablespoon dried yeast • 1 large pinch sugar • 150 ml hand-hot water •
500 g strong white flour • 1 teaspoon salt • 2 tablespoons sugar • 200 ml hand-hot milk •
50 g butter, softened or melted, for kneading •
50 ml vegetable oil for greasing the baking pan and the dough sheets •
300 g *sirene* (feta) cheese or Cheshire cheese, crumbled; or *kashkaval* or Cheddar cheese, cut into 1–1.5 cm cubes •
4 eggs, lightly beaten (reserve 1–2 tablespoons for brushing the loaf)

Dissolve the yeast with a large pinch of sugar in the water. Leave in a warm place for about 20 minutes until frothy.

Put the flour into a mixing bowl. Stir in the salt, sugar, yeast and milk. Gather the mixture into a soft, sticky dough and knead it with the butter, scraping the dough off the work surface and slapping it down from time to time until all the butter is absorbed. Leave it to rise in a warm place for about 1 hour, until doubled.

While the dough is rising, mix the cheese with the beaten egg, remembering to reserve a little for glazing. Knock back the dough, knead it lightly and shape it into a thick sausage. Cut into 4 pieces. Roll each out into a thin round at least 30 cm in diameter. Brush liberally with oil. Apply the cheese filling to within 1 cm of the edges, then roll up firmly. Arrange the rolls in a tightly-wound spiral in a well oiled baking pan, 33 cm in diameter, starting from the centre, placing the rolls flap sides up. Pinch the ends of the rolls together to make a continuous spiral. Pour over the rest of the oil. Allow to prove in a warm place for 45–50 minutes. Bake the loaf as soon as it is puffy and spongy in an oven preheated to 180°C/350°F/gas 4 for 20 minutes. Remove from the oven, brush with the reserved egg and bake for a further 10 minutes, or until well browned and shining on top.

Leave to rest with a cover for 15 minutes, then uncover and allow to cool in the pan. Serve in wedges, like a cake.

## 'POUR-AND-BAKE' BATTER BREAD
Serves 4

*Touri-potpechi* (Macedonian, literally 'place and bake')

This is a unique Macedonian unleavened flat-bread made of many layers. The original utensil used for baking was the lid-oven or *vrshnik* described in Chapter III. Modern electric ovens in Balkan countries almost replicate the heat used in an oven like this because their heating elements are in the top and bottom and can be controlled independently. In a conventional western oven, where the heat comes from all sides, the problem is that the loaf tends to develop a hard bottom crust.

1 egg • 1/4 teaspoon salt • 250 g plain white flour • vegetable oil

To make the batter, beat the eggs with the salt in a bowl, then beat in, alternately, the flour and 450 ml water.

Generously oil a roasting tin measuring approximately 20 x 26 cm and pour in a thin layer of batter. Place in an oven preheated to 200°C/400°F/gas 6 for 15 minutes, or until the batter is set and spotted with brown here and there. Remove from the oven and brush the surface thoroughly with oil. Then pour a second thin layer of batter over the first and bake for another 10 minutes. Continue like this, pouring layers of batter, baking each one for 10 minutes, and brushing each baked layer with oil, until all the batter is used up. You should be able to make at least 5 thin layers. Then brush the final cooked layer with oil and bake for a further 5 minutes to complete the cooking. It takes about 1 hour from start to finish. Remove from the oven and leave the bread to cool in the tin.

Serve warm or at room temperature with butter and cheese, or olives, or frankfurters or fried sausages.

## RUSTIC LOAF
Makes 4 loaves

*Misërnike* (Albanian, meaning cornbread); *groushnik* (Bulgarian, meaning bread made from cornmeal and wheat flour); *koruzni kruh* (Slovenian, cornbread)

A soft, moist bread made with varying proportions of cornmeal to flour. The advantages of using part-cooked cornmeal is that the bread has no trace of grittiness and it keeps longer—for up to 3 days if well wrapped. It can be served spread with butter, or, like scones, with jam and cream.

200 ml milk • 600 ml water • 1 tablespoon salt •
350 g fine, yellow cornmeal, preferably stone-ground •
4 teaspoons dried yeast, or 25 g fresh yeast • 400–425 ml hand-hot water •
1 kg strong, white flour; reserve 75 g for kneading and shaping

Pour the milk and water into a saucepan, add the salt and bring to the boil. Pour in the cornmeal fairly slowly so that the water remains on the boil, stirring constantly—the mixture will thicken almost immediately. Stir over a low heat for 2–3 minutes until the mush is thick enough for a wooden spoon to stand upright in it. Cover the pan and leave to cool until just lukewarm.

Meanwhile, put the dried yeast into a small bowl and pour over 200 ml of the hand-hot water. Leave in a warm place for 15–20 minutes, or until the yeast is puffy. Alternatively, blend the fresh yeast with the same amount of tepid water and use immediately. Pour the yeast over the lukewarm cornmeal, breaking the mush into lumps with a spoon. Add in stages the remaining water alternately with the flour, working the mixture with your hand to make a medium-stiff dough. Knead the dough for about 5 minutes until smooth, then put it into the largest mixing bowl or saucepan you have, brush the top with oil or melted butter to prevent skinning, cover loosely and leave to rise in a warm place for 1 1/2–2 hours, until doubled in volume.

While the dough is proving, grease 4 x 1.25 litre loaf tins. Turn the risen dough out on to a floured surface and knead for a minute, using the reserved flour, then divide it into 4 equal portions. Shape each quarter into a small loaf and drop it into the prepared tin. Brush over with oil or melted butter. Put the tins in a warm place for about 1 hour, or until the dough has risen to the top of the tins.

Heat the oven to 220°C/425°F/gas 7. Bake the loaves for 45–50 minutes, or until they are golden brown on top, pale brown underneath and shrinking from the sides of the tin. Cool on a rack before slicing.

Two women of the household were kept all day and every day bread-making. The slap, slap as they whacked the heavy maize dough was ceaseless. It was kneaded in a great dug-out trough, beaten into a thin slab on a circular wooden shovel, and slipped on to the hot hearthstone, and baked under an iron cover, piled with hot wood-ash. Baked all unleavened and eaten hot and steaming.

Maize bread is eaten throughout the mountains—not because corn is lacking, but because the people infinitely prefer maize. They will even buy maize when it is double the price of corn. The maize is very coarsely ground, and the bread incredibly heavy. The people eat very large quanitites; it is their staple food. They are so used to its weight that they declare corn bread is no good—you never feel full.

M. Edith Durham, *High Albania*, 1909.

# CORNBREAD
Makes one loaf

*Prosenik* (Bulgarian); *proja* (Bosnian, Serbo-Croat), literally 'millet bread' because originally non-wheaten loaves were made chiefly from millet

In the not-too-distant past, cornbread was prepared daily by many Bulgarian and Serbian villagers, often without any eggs or milk, and eaten instead of wheaten bread. Now, this enriched version is served with white brine cheese and clotted cream, or sometimes with scrambled eggs as a beginning to a meal, or as a supper dish.

100 g coarse cornmeal • 1 large pinch salt • 1 small egg, lightly beaten •
15 g lard or butter, melted with 1 tablespoon sunflower oil (reserve a little for topping) •
400 ml milk • 1 teaspoon caraway seeds

Put the cornmeal into a mixing bowl. Using a wooden spoon or a hand-held electric beater, beat in the rest of the ingredients to make a thin pouring batter.

Generously grease a round baking pan measuring 21 cm across, and pour in the mixture. Bake in a preheated oven at 180°C/350°F/gas 4 for about 25 minutes or until just set. Pour over the reserved fat and bake for another 20 minutes, or until light-golden brown. Do not let it dry out or brown too much.

Serve warm or at room temperature.

*Bread, Pancakes and Fritters* 241

## CAKE-BREADS

*Kek me maja birre* (Albanian, meaning cake with yeast); *kozounak* (Bulgarian, from the Romanian) or *Velikdenski kozounak* (Easter bread); *kolednik* (Croat, Christmas bread); *tsouréki* (Greek, from Turkish *çörek*); *kozinjak* (Macedonian); *cozonac* (Romanian, from the Greek word *koudounáki*, a small bell, so called because of the shape of the loaf); *koulich* (Russian, from the Greek *koullíki*, itself from *koulloúra*, a round cake); *pinca* (Slovenian, from German *Pinza*), *Božič kolač* (Serbian, Christmas bread)

Yeast breads enriched with eggs, milk, butter and sugar take on cake-like qualities and texture. The vesicular, thread-like structure characteristic of many cake-breads, is achieved by working the dough with softened butter rather than with flour and by slapping the dough down hard on a work surface to strengthen the gluten. When baked, the crumb pulls apart into attractive, longish tufts.

In the past, enriched cake-breads were made in huge quantities for Christmas or Easter, using the finest strong flour available and only a very small amount of yeast. The dough was left to rise overnight, and on the next day it was given two more rising periods and a final proof in tins. This long preparation explains its exceptional keeping qualities (up to a week).

Nowadays few people care to bother with lengthy fermentation and kneading; besides, yeast-leavened cakes are manufactured products and can be bought at any time of the year.

*An aluminium* kuglov *(kugelhopf) mould, also made in copper, tinplate and earthenware. All moulds have a central tube almost level with the rim.*

## KUGLOF WITH DRIED FRUIT
Makes 1 tall, decorative loaf

*Kuglof* (or *kuglov*) *sa suvim groždjem* (Serbo-Croat, from Hungarian *kuglóf*, itself coming from German *Kugelhopf*)

The beauty and lightness of this spectacular confection depends almost entirely on the container in which it is baked. Use a deep, fluted metal *Kugelhopf* mould of 2 litres capacity. The presence of a funnel allows the heat to penetrate the centre of the loaf, so it cooks quickly without drying out. During baking, the tin is covered with a weighted metal sheet to prevent the dough from rising over the top.

*Kuglov* is most often made of a thick, yeasted batter which was once beaten with a wooden spoon or stretched between the hands to develop the gluten—either of which were tedious and unwieldy procedures. The electric mixer has taken all the work out of the hard beating and stretching, and saves time.

*Kuglov* normally needs only one rising, so is quicker to make than ordinary bread, and much less fat and sugar than cakes raised with baking powder, so less rich but just as tasty.

1 slightly rounded tablespoon dried yeast • 1/2 teaspoon sugar •
20 whole blanched almonds • 50 g unsalted butter • 50 g ground vanilla sugar •
2 small egg yolks • 1/4 teaspoon salt • finely grated zest of 1 lemon •
250 g strong white flour, preferably unbleached • 125 ml hand-hot milk •
100 g sultanas, currants or small seedless raisins, floured then sieved to shake out excess •
brandy or maraschino liqueur • vanilla-flavoured icing sugar

To prepare the starter, dissolve the sugar in 3 tablespoons of hand-hot water, sprinkle the yeast evenly all over and leave in a warm place for 20 minutes.

Meanwhile, prepare a *Kugelhopf* mould. Smear the inside heavily with butter, sprinkle with some flour, then tilt and shake the mould until well coated; tap to remove excess flour. Arrange the blanched almonds in a decorative pattern on the bottom. Butter also a small baking sheet or flat lid large enough to cover the top of the mould.

Cream the butter, sugar, egg yolks, lemon zest and salt together using a wooden spoon or in a mixer, then gradually beat in the flour, alternating with the milk and yeast to make a thick batter of stiff dropping consistency—that is, falling from a spoon when tapped on the rim of the container. Continue beating for a further minute or two, then fold in the dried fruit.

Spoon the batter into the mould—to just half fill it. Leave to rise in a warm place for about 2 hours, until it is within 1 mm of the rim of the mould. Place the buttered sheet or lid, greased side down, over the mould, and weigh it down with a kitchen weight or heavy pan. Bake in a preheated oven at 150°C/300°F/gas 2 for 1 hour, until dark golden-brown and just shrinking from the sides of the mould.

Leave in the tin for 10 minutes, then turn out on a rack over a plate to cool. You can fill a kitchen hypodermic syringe with alcohol and inject the loaf from all angles. To bring out the decorative markings, sieve a little sugar over the loaf.

## KUGLOF WITH WALNUTS
Makes 1 tall loaf

*Kuglof (kuglov) sa orasima* (Serbo-Croat)

1 tablespoon dried yeast • 1/4 teaspoon sugar • 1 medium egg • 35 g castor sugar •
1/4 teaspoon salt (but no salt if using salted butter) • grated zest of 1 large lemon •
1 sachet vanilla sugar • 250 g strong white flour •
about 4–5 tablespoons hand-hot milk (the stronger the flour, the more liquid it will absorb) •
1 tablespoon vegetable oil and 25 g butter, melted and slightly cooled, for kneading
*Walnut filling*
75 g ground walnuts • 50 g castor sugar • 1 teaspoon ground cinnamon •
1 medium egg white, stiffly beaten

To make the starter, heat 4 tablespoons water with 1/4 teaspoon sugar to hand-hot and pour it into a small bowl. Sprinkle the yeast evenly all over and leave in a warm place for 20 minutes, until the yeast is dissolved and frothy.

To make the dough, beat the eggs with 35 g sugar, salt (if using), lemon zest and vanilla sugar in a mixing bowl until thick and pale yellow. Gradually stir in the flour alternately with the yeast and enough milk to make a slack, sticky dough. Turn on to an unfloured surface and knead with the tablespoon of oil for about 5 minutes, until the dough is smooth and elastic. Return to the bowl and leave to rise in a warm place until trebled in volume—which will take about 2 1/2 hours.

Butter and flour a 2-litre *Kugelhopf* mould and a small baking sheet or flat lid as described in the previous recipe. Mix the walnuts, sugar and cinnamon, then fold in about half the beaten egg white to make a thick but spreadable paste.

Punch down the risen dough in the bowl, turn it out and knead it with the melted butter for 5 minutes, until the butter is incorporated and the dough is no longer greasy. Fill the dough by placing on a sheet of oiled, greaseproof paper and flattening it out to a 30 cm square. Spread the walnut filling to within 1 cm of the top edge of the dough. Wet the edge. Raise the side of the paper nearest to you and roll up the dough tightly. Transfer it to the prepared mould, using the paper as support, and wind it round the central funnel into a circle, seam-side down. Seal the joins of the dough. Press down firmly to even the surface.

Allow to rise a second time in a warm place for 1–1 1/2 hours, until almost to the top of the mould. Place the baking sheet (or lid) greased side down over the mould and weight it. Bake in the centre of a preheated oven at 150°C/300°F/gas 2 for 30–35 minutes, until lightly browned and just shrinking from the sides.

Leave the loaf in its tin for about ten minutes before turning it out on a wire rack placed over a plate. Sieve icing sugar over it. Leave to cool before slicing into wedges. This bread will keep well for a day or two in an air-tight container.

# CHOCOLATE RING
Makes 1 ring-shaped loaf

*Čokoladna potica* (Slovenian, literally, a chocolate roll)

This is an old Slovenian speciality, also known in Croatia, made originally with savoury fillings, and later with sweet—honey, sugar and walnuts, almonds, hazelnuts, poppy seeds or dried fruit. The apricot glaze is optional, but decorative, and keeps the loaf from drying out too quickly.

1 tablespoon milk, mixed with 2 tablespoons water, hand-hot • 1/4 teaspoon sugar •
1 tablespoon dried yeast • 25 g unsalted butter, at room temperature • 25 g caster sugar •
1 medium-sized egg • finely grated zest of 1 lemon • 1/8 teaspoon salt •
200 g unbleached strong white flour and a little extra for kneading • 50 ml hand-hot milk
*Chocolate filling*
25 g castor sugar • 1 medium egg, separated, the white stiffly beaten •
50 g milk chocolate, melted over a pan of hot (but not boiling) water, slightly cooled •
50 g coarsely ground walnuts, hazelnuts or blanched almonds
*Apricot glaze*
3 tablespoons apricot jam, sieved, then dissolved in 1 tablespoon boiling water

Dissolve 1/4 teaspoon sugar in the hand-hot liquid and sprinkle the yeast evenly all over. Leave in a warm place for 20 minutes until frothy and full of bubbles.

Beat the butter, sugar, egg yolk, lemon zest and salt in a mixing bowl until thick and yellow. Stir in the flour alternately with the yeast and milk to make a very soft, sticky dough. Turn out on to a very lightly floured surface and knead vigorously for a few minutes, using a little extra flour, until the dough is easy to stretch and free of lumps. For the first rise, return the dough to the bowl, cover loosely with plastic film and put it in a warm, draught-free place for 1 1/2 hours, until the dough has just about trebled in volume.

Butter thickly a 1-litre metal ring or savarin mould, dust the entire inner surface with flour, then tap off the surplus.

For the filling: beat the egg yolk and sugar together until light and pale yellow, then beat in the melted chocolate, add the nuts and gently fold in the egg white.

Turn the risen dough on to a lightly oiled work surface and knead it with oiled hands for a minute to disperse any air bubbles. Then put it on an oiled sheet of greaseproof paper and roll it out to a neat rectangle 50 cm long and 17 cm wide. Spread the filling evenly all over, leaving a margin of 2.5 cm along the top edge of the dough. With the help of the paper, roll the dough up tightly and place it in the mould, seam-side uppermost. Lightly press the roll into the mould to even the surface and seal the join on top by pinching the edges of the roll together.

Allow the dough to rise for a second time, in a warm place, for about an hour. When the dough has risen well above the top of the mould, put it in a preheated oven at 150°C/300°F/gas 2 and bake for 30 minutes, or until the top is brown, the base and sides a pale gold and the loaf has shrunk a little.

Leave the loaf in the tin for 10 minutes, then turn it out, rounded side up, on to a wire rack. While the loaf is cooling, boil the apricot glaze for 2 minutes until syrupy, then brush it over the entire surface of the bread. Another way of finishing is to sieve over some icing sugar.

> A passer-by saw a weeping child in the street.
> 'Why are you crying?' he asked.
> 'My mum gave me a lev to buy a chocolate and I lost it.'
> 'Don't cry. Here is another lev for you.'
> The child took the money and cried even harder.
> 'What's the matter now? Why are you still crying?'
> 'Because if I hadn't lost my lev I would have had now two levs to buy myself two chocolates.'

## PLAITED BREAD
Makes 1 large loaf

*Pleten kozounak* (Bulgarian); *tsouréki* (Greek); *pletenica* (Serbo-Croat); *pletenka* (Slovenian)

The shape of this bread has many interpretations: when it is baked for a wedding, it is a sign of the sacrifice of a young girl's hair; or it may be twisted to make an ear of wheat, and hence prosperity; or perhaps it will be merely a fancy loaf for the sake of it. It can be straight, or curl round in a hoop with the ends either open or closed, or at Easter it can be ornamented with red-dyed eggs.

50 ml milk, 1/4 teaspoon sugar, 1 tablespoon dried yeast for the starter •
75 g unsalted butter • 100 g sugar • 1/2 teaspoon salt • 3–4 tablespoons tepid milk •
500 g strong white flour • 4 small eggs, lightly beaten (reserve 1 tablespoon for glazing) •
2 sachets vanilla sugar, or 1 teaspoon vanilla essence •
grated zest of 1 large lemon, or 1/2 teaspoon pulverised mastic • 1 tablespoon rum •
25 g melted butter—for the second kneading •
15 g almonds, blanched and halved, or a little granulated sugar, for decoration

To make the starter, heat 50 ml milk with the sugar until hand-hot, then sprinkle in the yeast. Leave in a warm place for 15 minutes until the mixture froths up.

Melt the butter, sugar and salt together with 1 tablespoon of the milk over a low heat, then allow the mixture to cool to lukewarm.

Put the flour into a mixing bowl, stir in the butter mixture, the beaten eggs, vanilla, lemon zest or mastic, rum (if using), the yeast starter and enough of the remaining milk to make a soft, slightly sticky dough. Knead it for about 5 minutes in an electric mixer, or 7–8 minutes by hand, using a little extra flour, until the dough is smooth, pliable and rather stiff. Brush the top with oil and leave to rise in a warm place for up to 2 hours, until doubled in size.

Knock the dough back, and knead again, incorporating the extra 25 g of melted butter. Divide into 3 equal portions and shape each one rather like an oblong chunky sausage. Take one 'sausage' and holding one end, slap the other end down hard on the work surface; this elongates the dough and gives it the tufty texture so much admired in yeast-leavened cakes. Continue slapping the dough, from alternate ends, until it stretches to a strand 50 cm long. Now roll the strand back and forth under your palms just to even it out. Repeat the process with the other strands, then place them on a greased and floured baking sheet, next to each other and almost touching, and plait them loosely to make a loaf, starting at the centre and working towards yourself. Turn the baking sheet round and plait the rest. Tuck the ends under the loaf and brush its surface with oil to prevent a skin forming. Allow the dough to expand in a warm place to almost twice its size—which will take about 45 minutes. Glaze the top with the reserved egg and decorate with almonds or granulated sugar. Place the loaf in a preheated oven at 220°C/425°F/gas 7, on a shelf just below the centre, and immediately lower the temperature to 120°C/250°F/gas 1/2. Bake for about 30 minutes or until golden brown—avoiding overbrowning. Leave to cool on the baking sheet, then store in an air-tight bag. This loaf is best eaten within a couple of days.

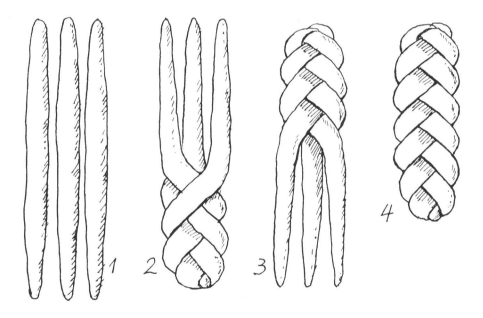

*Plaiting a three-stranded loaf. 1. Place three strands parallel to each other. 2. Starting from the centre, braid the strands and press them lightly together at the base. 3. Turn them through a half-circle so that the braided dough is away from you and plait the remaining strands. Tuck the ends neatly under. 4. Allow the dough to rise again.*

## WHOLEMEAL HONEY BREAD
Makes 1 tall decorative loaf

*Cher kozounak* (Bulgarian, meaning black cakebread)

This is a lovely variation on the ordinary white cakebread. Long rising accounts for its lighter and less compact texture than most wholemeal loaves. I call it Dee-Dee cake because I used to make it for my daughter Diana when she was a child.

1 teaspoon honey, 50 ml hand-hot water, 1 1/2 tablespoons dried yeast, •
375 g wholemeal flour (reserve 2–3 tablespoons for kneading) • 1 small egg •
100 g thick opaque honey • 1/8 teaspoon cooking salt • grated zest of 1 large lemon •
100 ml hand-hot milk • 50 ml sunflower oil for second kneading •
50 g walnuts, coarsely chopped • icing sugar, for dusting

Dissolve the honey in the water. Sprinkle in the yeast and, when dissolved, add 2 teaspoons of the flour and mix to a smooth batter. Leave in a warm place for about 20 minutes until the yeast sponge foams. Beat the egg lightly, and stir in the honey, salt, lemon zest and a little of the milk. Make a well in the centre of the flour and add this mixture, the yeast sponge and enough of the remaining milk to mix to a soft, sticky dough. Knead on a floured surface for about 10 minutes until moderately stiff and still slightly sticky. Return to the bowl, brush with oil and leave to rise in a warm place for about 2 hours, until trebled in size.

Knead again without any flour, adding small amounts of sunflower oil until it is used up. Allow a second rise in the bowl for about 2 hours, until trebled in volume. Meanwhile, oil a two-litre plain or fluted metal *Kugelhopf* mould. Sprinkle the mould with flour, then tip out the excess.

Knead the dough a third time to incorporate the walnuts, then shape into a round the diameter of your mould. Press two fingers and a thumb through the centre to make a hole, then press the dough down with your knuckles to spread it round the mould; it should fill it by a little less than half. Prove in a slightly warmer place than before. It will take about 1 hour for the dough to reach the rim.

Bake in the centre of an oven preheated to 180°C/350°F/gas 4 for about 35 minutes. It is ready when the top has risen above the rim and is well browned. Leave in the mould for a few minutes, then turn on to a rack and cool completely before cutting into wedges. Serve for tea with butter, clotted cream and honey, or on its own. Dust it with icing sugar: for the look of it and to enhance its sweetness. The bread is best on the day it is made.

## CHEESE ROLLS
Makes 16

*Milinki* (Bulgarian, meaning individual bread rolls as constituents of an entire *milina* loaf; from the Old Slavonic *mlin*, a mill)

This is an old Bulgarian bakers' speciality (which may have no filling at all), also made occasionally in the home. The topping is traditional and reserved exclusively for these rolls. The Bosnian *ćahija* (from Turkish *kâhi*, a three-cornered pastry puff) is similar, except the unfilled rolls are raised with a chick-pea leaven rather than with yeast.

1 egg, well beaten (reserve half for topping) • 1/4 teaspoon salt • 15 g fresh yeast • 150 ml tepid milk and water mixed • 250 g strong white flour • sunflower oil

*Filling*

25 g butter, melted with 1 tablespoon oil and cooled to tepid • 150 g feta cheese, washed, drained and crumbled; or 225 g Cheshire cheese, sprinkled lightly with salt and coarsely crumbled • 1 egg, lightly beaten

*Topping*

1/2 reserved beaten egg • large pinch salt • 1 1/2 tablespoons strong white flour • 15 g butter, melted and cooled to tepid

Blend half the egg with salt in a bowl. Dissolve the yeast in the milk and water and stir it in alternately with the flour to form a soft, sticky dough. Knead for 5 minutes on a floured surface until elastic and no longer sticky. Return to the bowl, sprinkle over some flour and leave at room temperature for 1 hour, until doubled.

Mix the filling ingredients together and set aside. Knock the risen dough back, knead it briefly, and divide into two. Roll into 30 x 25 cm rectangles, spread with an equal quantity of filling and roll up firmly. With a sharp knife, cut each roll into 8 pieces. Dip these into oil and arrange in a 23 cm round, ungreased baking tin in two concentric circles, cut side up—the outer circle made up of 10 pieces, the inner circle made up of 5 pieces, with the remaining piece in the centre. Leave to prove for about 45 minutes, or until well risen and touching each other.

Mix the topping ingredients together and spread on the pieces. Bake in a preheated oven at 180°C/350°F/gas 4 for 30 minutes. When done, the rolls should have merged together and be deeply golden on top and underneath. Separate them for serving after they have cooled in the tin for 15–20 minutes. They may be eaten warm, at room temperature, or reheated.

## CRESCENT ROLLS FILLED WITH WALNUTS
Makes 6

*Oifle me arra* (Albanian); *kifli s orehi* (Bulgarian); *kifle so orevi* (Macedonian); *chifli cu nuci* (Romanian); *kifle sa orasima* (Serbo-Croat); from German *Kipfeln*, crescent buns

It is thought that croissants—the Austrian *Kipfeln* or *Kipferln*, subsequently spreading to France—originated in Vienna at the time of the Turkish siege of the city in 1683. Their shape represented the Ottoman symbol, the crescent moon.

Besides walnuts, other good fillings are plum, quince or apricot marmalade, or ground poppy seeds or almonds mixed with milk and sugar.

2 teaspoons dried yeast, large pinch sugar, 100 ml hand-hot milk for the starter •
250 g strong white flour • 50 g vanilla-flavoured castor sugar or icing sugar •
1/4 teaspoon salt • grated lemon zest • 1 small egg, lightly beaten •
50 g melted butter or 50 ml sunflower oil
*Filling*
100 g ground walnuts • 50 g vanilla-flavoured castor sugar or icing sugar •
1 teaspoon ground cinnamon • 2 egg whites, lightly beaten
*Glaze*
2 egg yolks, lightly beaten with a few drops sunflower oil • granulated sugar

Sprinkle the dried yeast over the hand-hot milk to which a large pinch of sugar has been added. Leave in a warm place until frothy—about 20 minutes.

Stir the sugar, salt, lemon zest, egg and the yeast into the flour to form a rather stiff dough. Knead, without adding any extra flour, for about 5 minutes, gradually working in the melted butter or sunflower oil. Set to rise in a warm place for about 1 1/2 hours, until it doubles in volume. Knock it back, roll it out into a neat rectangle about 45 x 30 cm, and divide into 6 equal squares.

Mix the filling ingredients together. Spread one sixth on to each square of dough, leaving a narrow margin. Roll up firmly from corner to corner to make rolls with tapered ends. Lay the rolls on buttered baking sheets, well apart, with the loose corners underneath. Bend the ends of each roll slightly to form a crescent shape. Leave to prove in a warm place for 40—45 minutes. When the crescents are well risen and puffy, brush them with the beaten egg yolks and sprinkle with some sugar, if you like. Bake in an oven preheated to 150°C/300°F/gas 2 for about 20 minutes or until well browned on top. Cool on racks.

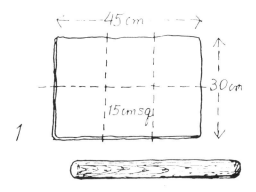

*Rolling up a crescent roll. 1. Divide the rolled dough into 6 equal squares. 2. Spread each square with the filling (leaving a narrow margin) and roll up from corner to corner under the fingers and palm of the hand in a forward, sweeping motion.*

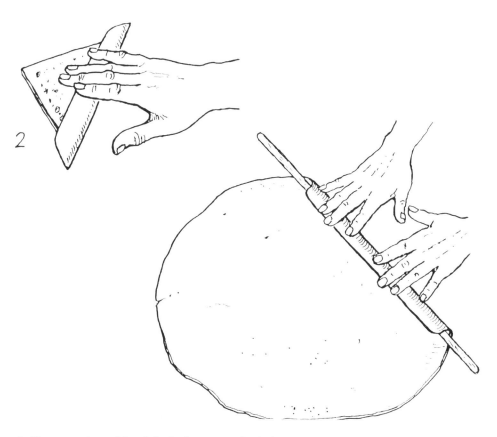

*Rolling out a sheet of dough for leaf pastry. Roll a little of the dough sheet forward and backward under the pressure of your fingers, starting at the centre and gradually moving your hands outwards as you roll. Repeat this several times until the whole sheet is rolled on to the pin.*

# SCALDED BREAD WITH MILK AND CHEESE
Serves 4

*Pëshesh me djathë* (Albanian); *popara sus sirene* (Bulgarian); *popara so sirenje* (Macedonian); *papara cu brînză* (Romanian); *popara sa sirom* (Serbo-Croat); *peynirli papara* (Balkan Turkish); the term *popara* is a Slavonic word meaning scalded bread.

> A gipsy, when asked what he would like to be given to eat, bread or cheese, answered artfully, '*Popara*.'
>
> *Balkan folk tale*

A tasty, well-balanced breakfast dish long established in the Balkans. Based on bread or rusks, it is sometimes made with hot water or tea instead of milk and, occasionally, from bread and hot walnut milk (p. 352) or diluted *tahan* (p. 55).

250–300 g crustless wholemeal or white bread, 2 days old, broken into bite-sized pieces (not too small) • 50 g unsalted butter • 150 g white brine cheese, such as feta, soaked in milk or water for 1 hour • 500–625 ml milk (different types of bread vary in the amount of liquid they absorb) • 2 tablespoons sugar • red paprika oil (p. 347) or melted butter

Divide the bread equally between 4 small oven-proof bowls. Dot the surface with knobs of butter and put the bowls in a preheated oven at 150°C/300°F/gas 2 for 15–20 minutes to warm through.

Pour the milk into a saucepan. Stir in the sugar and bring to the boil. Take the bowls out of the oven, stir in equal amounts of the cheese and pour in the milk. Cover each bowl with a plate and leave to stand for 1–2 minutes while the bread soaks up the milk. Serve the *popara* immediately with a teaspoon or two of paprika oil or plain melted butter sprinkled on top of each bowl.

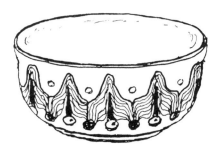

*An earthenware bowl from Troyan, Bulgaria, used to serve popara, kasha, soup or oshav.*

## RUSKS WITH POACHED EGGS
Serves 4

*Soulovar* (Bulgarian, Macedonian), from the Turkish *sulu*, watery, moist

200 g rusks, broken into bite-sized pieces • 4 eggs •
100 g sirene or feta cheese •
75–100 g red paprika butter, prepared with unsalted butter (p. 347)

Divide the rusks evenly among 4 individual ovenproof bowls and put them in a warm oven for 10–15 minutes to heat through. Meanwhile, poach the eggs as described on page 118 (but without adding vinegar to the water). When done, remove the bowls from the oven, stir in the cheese, pour in enough of the hot poaching liquid to moisten and swell the rusks, then place a poached egg in each bowl over the rusks and drizzle an equal quantity of the red paprika butter over each egg. Serve hot with a cup of tea for breakfast.

## PALACE BREAD
Serves 4

*Sarajski hlyab* (Bulgarian, from the Turkish *saray ekmeği*), also known in the north-eastern part of the country as *dzidzhi papo* which is childish language for something pretty to eat, deriving from the Turkish *cici*, toy, pretty, and the Bulgarian *papam*, I eat; *pohovane šnite sa vinom* (Croat, meaning egg-coated fried slices with wine) and *pohane vinske šnite* (Slovenian, egg-coated, fried wine slices), from the German *Schnitte*, slice

Close parallels of this sweet can be found in the *pain perdu* of France, the French Toast of America, and Britain's Poor Knights of Windsor.

4 large slices 2-day-old white bread, 1 cm thick, crusts removed •
2 eggs • 2 tablespoons milk or white wine • 50 g butter •
castor sugar and cinnamon, or apricot jam, or golden syrup heated with a little water, or orange-marmalade sauce (p. 351)

Beat the egg and milk (or wine) together. Heat the butter in a frying pan. Dip the bread slices on both sides in the egg mixture and fry them gently, in batches, until golden brown. Slip them on to individual plates and sprinkle with a little castor sugar and cinnamon, or serve them spread with a dollop of apricot jam, or with the golden syrup or orange sauce passed round separately in a sauceboat.

## BALKAN PANCAKES
Makes 6 thin pancakes

*Palachinki* (Bulgarian, Macedonian); *palačinke* (Serbo-Croat, from the Hungarian *palacsinta*, itself from the Latin *placenta*, which in turn comes from the Greek *pláka* for flat stone, slate, or slab); *clătite* (Romanian); *cvrtnjaki* (Slovenian)

75 g plain white flour • a large pinch of salt • 1 large egg •
150 ml milk and water in equal quantities

Put the flour and salt into a bowl. Make a well in the centre. Break the egg into the well and whisk it lightly, then gradually whisk in the liquid, drawing in the flour from the sides, until you have a smooth thin batter with the consistency of thin cream. Alternatively, put all the ingredients into a liquidizer, and blend for a few seconds. Leave the batter to rest for 30 minutes.

Brush a 20 cm frying pan with a little fat or wipe with a greased cloth and set over a medium heat. When very hot, pour in a small ladleful (the size of a small ice-cream scoop) of batter, tilting the pan to spread it as thinly as possible. When set and lightly browned underneath, after about 20–30 seconds, turn the pancake over to cook the other side. Repeat the process until the batter is used, stacking the cooked pancakes on top of each other.

Spread with a little jam, and roll up.

## YEASTED FRITTERS
Makes 13–14 fritters

*Petulla* (Albanian, from the Greek *pétalon*, petal—so called because the fritters are extremely thin); *mekitsi* (Bulgarian, from *mek*, soft—because their circumference is puffed up and soft)

Another joke on the parsimony of people from Gabrovo.
*At the fritter stall*:
    'Would you like me to sprinkle sugar on your fritters?' the vendor asked a man from Gabrovo.
    'Is it included in the price?'
    'Yes, it is.'
    Then please, wrap the sugar and I'll take it home to my wife.'

## Bread, Pancakes and Fritters

In Albania and Bulgaria, these fritters are appreciated as super-fast food rivalling the pizza in popularity. In Tirana they are sold right in the city centre, from a small work-shop called *Petulla te çastit* —'Instant Fritters'. Sometimes made from a plain dough without the egg enrichment, they are at their best when eaten piping hot from the fryer.

2 teaspoons dried yeast or 15 g fresh yeast, 1 large pinch sugar (only for dried yeast), 3 tablespoons water for the starter •
200 g strong white flour (reserve 25 g for kneading) • scant 1/2 teaspoon salt •
1 tablespoon sugar • 2 tablespoons warm milk • 1 small egg •
vanilla-flavoured icing sugar (p. 352) for dusting

To reactivate the dried yeast, dissolve the pinch of sugar in 3 tablespoons hand-hot water and sprinkle in the yeast. Allow to stand in a warm place until frothy (15–20 minutes). If using fresh yeast, simply blend it with 3 tablespoons lukewarm water and use immediately.

To make the dough, put the flour into a mixing bowl. Dissolve the salt and sugar in the milk and, using a table knife, stir this into the flour; then stir in the beaten egg and the yeast to form a very soft, sticky mass. Knead it on a work surface with the reserved flour for about 5 minutes, until you have a smooth, slightly tacky dough. With your fist, hammer the dough into a small round to fit the base of the bowl. Turn the dough in a scrap of oil in the bowl to prevent skinning. Let rise in a warm place. The dough will be ready to cook in about half an hour, when it has just about doubled in size.

Pour at least 1 cm oil into a small saucepan over a moderate heat. Tear a piece of dough, about 25 g in weight (the size of a large apricot) and, dipping your hands as often as necessary in a bowl of water, shape it first into a ball, then flatten it with your thumbs, working from the centre outwards, to stretch it into a round approximately 12 cm in diameter, paper thin inside and slightly thicker round the edges. Drop it into the hot oil and cook for about 1 minute on either side, or until the fritter is golden but not brown. Lift it out on to absorbent kitchen paper and pat it dry. Sieve a little sugar over the top and serve immediately while still warm. Repeat the process with the remainder of the dough.

# BALKAN JAM DOUGHNUTS
Makes 12 doughnuts

*Ponichki* (Bulgarian, from the Russian *ponchki*); *gogoașe* (Romanian); *krofne* or *krafne* (Serbo-Croat, from the German); *krofi* (Slovenian, from the German)

2 teaspoons dried yeast or 15 g fresh yeast, 1 large pinch sugar (for dried yeast only), 3 tablespoons water for the starter •
200 g strong white flour (reserve 25 g for kneading) • 25 g butter •
1/2 teaspoon salt • 40 g sugar • 2 tablespoons warm milk •
1 medium egg, beaten • 12 teaspoons thick jam for filling •
icing sugar for coating

Dissolve the dried yeast with a pinch of sugar in 3 tablespoons hand-hot water and set in a warm place for 20 minutes until frothy. Alternatively, cream the fresh yeast with 3 tablespoons tepid water.

Put the flour into a bowl and rub in the butter. Dissolve the salt and sugar in the warm milk and stir into the flour. Add the beaten egg and yeast and mix to a soft dough. Knead with the reserved flour on a work surface for about 5 minutes. Return to the bowl, brush the dough with a little oil and leave to rise in a warm place for about an hour, or until more than doubled in volume.

Turn on to a lightly oiled surface and knead again for a minute. Divide into 12 pieces, flatten into rounds and put a teaspoon of jam in every centre. Press the edges of each round with your fingers to thin them a little, then gather up over the jam and pinch together to seal the jam within.

Put the doughnuts on a lightly greased and floured baking sheet, smooth side up. Leave to prove in a warm place for a further 25 minutes until light and puffy.

Heat fat or oil in a deep-frying pan to 170°C/340°F. Fry the doughnuts, a few at a time, covering with a lid to allow them to puff up a little more, for 2–3 minutes, then turn them over and continue frying, this time uncovered, for another minute or two, until light golden-brown all over. Drain them of all excess fat, then roll in icing sugar. Serve the same day.

## BOSNIAN FRITTERS
Makes 25

*Bosanski pituljice* (Bosnian, from the Greek *pétalon*, a petal)

During the last century, *Posni pitoulitsi* or fast-day pancakes (fried in olive oil) were prepared in Macedonia on the Eve of St Jordan's Day (Epiphany), the 6th of January. The Bulgarian lexicographer Najden Gerov (1899) defined *Pitoulitsi* as 'Batter fried in walnut oil, sesame oil or butter'. Both kinds appear to have been made from plain batter—with or without eggs or milk.

200 g strong white flour (reserve 1 tablespoon for kneading) •
1/4 teaspoon salt • 1 tablespoon vegetable oil •
about 75 ml lukewarm milk •
25 g butter, melted over hot water and cooled to tepid •
vanilla-flavoured icing sugar for sprinkling

Sieve the flour with the salt into a bowl. Make a well in the centre and add the egg and oil, then stir in the milk to make a rather soft dough. Knead it well with some of the reserved flour, slapping the dough now and then on the kneading surface to develop the gluten. Return the dough to the bowl, sprinkle with the remaining flour and leave in a warm place to relax for 30 minutes.

When the time is up, divide into 8 pieces and roll them out into 15–17 cm rounds. Brush the rounds with the melted butter and place them one on top of the other. Leave the stack in a cool place to firm up the butter; then reverse the stack and roll it out into a thin circle. Draw up four opposite edges of the circle so that they meet at the centre and form a square. Fold this in half and, in the opposite direction, in half again. Roll it out into a neat 35 cm square. With a knife or pastry wheel, cut it into 25 small squares, or as many as required.

Fry the pieces in batches, in sufficient oil to cover the base of the pan to a depth of about 1 cm, until golden brown on both sides. Drain on absorbent kitchen paper, then sprinkle generously with vanilla sugar.

In Bosnia, these fritters are served with the afternoon coffee.

## LIGHT-AS-AIR SWEET FRITTERS
Makes about 50

*Mafishe* (Albanian), *mafiš* (Bosnian, Serbian), from the Turkish *mafiş*, meaning, finished, nothing left, from the Arabic *ma fihi säy*, 'there's nothing in it'—so named because the fritters melt almost instantly in the mouth.

Quickly prepared and even more quickly eaten, these sweet nothings have many local variations.

50 g plain white flour • large pinch baking powder • large pinch salt • 1 teaspoon icing sugar • 7–8 tablespoons lukewarm water • 1 egg white, stiffly beaten • icing sugar flavoured with a few drops of vanilla essence, for dusting

Sift the flour with the baking powder, salt and sugar into a bowl. Gradually stir in the water without beating too vigorously, then fold in the beaten egg white to make a smooth batter of thin, pouring consistency. Transfer to a small jug.

Heat about 1 cm oil in a frying pan until hot but not smoking. Pour 2–3 drops of batter for each fritter into the oil and fry over a fairly high heat, turning them once, until they puff up and turn crisp and golden brown on both sides. Drain them well on several changes of absorbent kitchen paper. Serve them immediately dusted with sugar.

## APPLE OR QUINCE FRITTERS
Serves 2–3

*Panirani yabulki ili dyuli* (Bulgarian); *jabuke ili dunje u šlafroku* (Serbo-Croat)

1 large dessert apple or 1 medium-sized ripe quince, peeled, cored and sliced into thin rings • icing sugar • 25 g plain flour • 2 large pinches baking powder • 1 large pinch salt • 50 ml white wine or cider • 1 large egg white, stiffly beaten

Sprinkle the fruit with icing sugar and set aside for approximately 2 hours. To make the batter, sift the flour with the baking powder and salt into a bowl. Pour in the wine and stir until smooth and creamy; fold in the beaten egg white.

Dip the fruit rings in the batter and deep-fry them in hot, but not smoking, oil until golden brown. Drain them on absorbent kitchen towels. Sprinkle with icing sugar, and serve warm or cold.

# CHAPTER XVII

# Leaf Pastry

Dough stretched or rolled into paper-thin resilient sheets is the basis of a vast number of sweet and savoury creations in Balkan cookery. These have no equivalent in the English vocabulary and may only loosely be called 'pies' for lack of a more suitable word. Pastry sheets like this rank among the world's most versatile materials. They can be placed one over the other to create layers, or rolled up into thin or thick, large or tiny, straight or coiled rolls. After that, they can be baked, fried or boiled like a pudding; or folded into intricate shapes with an infinity of fillings, from insubstantial to something heavy with meat, cheese, tarhana, bulgur or vegetables, all bearing different names according to language.

A leaf pastry dish marks the high point of almost every Balkan festival and season; it is equally at home at opulent as well as humbler tables. In the Balkans leaf pastry is both peasant and king.

Sold in the West as strudel pastry (from German *Strudelteig*), or as filo pastry (from the Greek *fýllo kroústas*, meaning leaf crusts or sheets), in Albania a sheet of dough is termed *petë* (from the Greek *pétalon*, flower petal). In the Bosnian dialect, it is *kora*, crust, or *jufka* (from the Turkish *yufka*, sheet of dough); in Bulgarian, Macedonian and Serbo-Croat—*kora* (crust) or *list* (leaf).

Leaf pastry was introduced into the Balkans by the Ottoman Turks after the fall of Constantinople in the fifteenth century, and into Hungary in the sixteenth— where it became known as *rétestészta*, strudel dough. In Austria *Strudelteig* is thought to have been acquired either directly from the Turks during the reign of Suleiman the Magnificent (1496–1566), when the Ottoman Empire stretched from Persia to the gates of Vienna, or to have been brought in by Hungarian and Serbian cooks.

The dough is made with very strong flour milled from hard wheat, which grows well in the Balkan climate and has the protein quality of Canadian wheat. The flour is stored at least for a month prior to use to allow the gluten to become tougher and more elastic, improving the dough's capacity to stretch. Normally prepared from flour, a little salt and water, if the flour does not contain enough gluten, the lack is partially redeemed by the addition of eggs plus an acid, such as vinegar, which strengthens the existing gluten and improves elasticity.

## LEAF PASTRY—MADE BY ROLLING

Makes 2 x 50 cm circular dough sheets

This basic recipe provides a small quantity—enough for 2–4 people—which is easier to make and handle. To roll the dough out into thin sheets you will need a long thin rolling pin or an ordinary wooden dowel about 2 cm in diameter, at least 70 cm long.

200 g strong white flour (reserve 2 tablespoons for kneading and rolling) •
1 tablespoon vegetable oil • 1/2 tablespoon white wine or cider vinegar • large pinch salt •
100 ml lukewarm water (the stronger the flour, the more water it will absorb) •
cornflour for rolling out

Sieve the flour into a mixing bowl. Make a well in the centre. Drop in the oil, vinegar and salt, and draw the flour from the sides to make a soft, sticky dough. Knead it with a little of the reserved flour for at least 10 minutes. Holding the dough at one end, slap it down hard on the kneading surface repeatedly, until smooth, elastic and no longer sticky. Form the dough into a flattened ball, put it in a lightly oiled bowl, then turn it over to oil the other side to prevent a skin from forming. Leave it, covered, to relax for at least 30 minutes in a warm place.

To roll out the dough, knead it again for a few minutes until bubbles appear, then divide it into 2 balls of equal size. Roll one ball out into a circle, about 30 cm in diameter, and sprinkle it lightly with some of the reserved flour. Now start gradually rolling the dough circle, a little at a time, around the pin; then roll it back and forth under your fingers with a steady pressure, starting at the centre of the rolled up dough and gradually sliding your hands outwards as you roll, so that the dough circle widens evenly and thinly (see illustration on p. 251). When you have wound the whole circle on to the pin, give it a quarter turn (90 degrees). Unroll the dough, spread it lightly with a little cornflour and repeat the rolling process. Do this several times until the dough becomes as thin as heavy-duty paper and about 50 cm in diameter. Cover it with a sheet of plastic or greaseproof paper. Roll out the second piece of dough in the same way, place it over the first and cover with more paper. Use the dough sheets immediately, or wrap in a freezer bag and store in the refrigerator for not more than 4 days, or in the freezer for up to 3 months.

# LEAF PASTRY—MADE BY STRETCHING
Makes about 325 g

Stretching dough by tossing it in the air is a special technique practiced by Balkan pastry cooks. The dough is first shaped into balls which are left to relax in a bath of warm melted butter or lard, then each ball is stretched into a thin circle by tossing it back and forth between the palms of the hands, then up and down, and then along the naked arm—after which the circle of dough is twirled round and round in the air, brought down and twirled again, until it becomes as thin as paper and almost transparent.

I have seen this done by a *banicharka*, a professional female pastry cook, whose job was to stretch dough several hours a day for making *banichki*—individual cheese pastries for sale in one of the many snack bars or takeaways of Sofia.

> 200 g strong white flour (reserve 2 tablespoons for kneading) • 1 egg •
> 2 tablespoons oil, melted butter or lard •
> 1/2 tablespoons white wine vinegar or cider vinegar • large pinch salt •
> 3–4 tablespoons lukewarm water • a little extra oil or melted butter for brushing

Prepare the dough exactly as described for the rolled dough sheets above, but adding an egg and enough lukewarm water to form a very soft, sticky dough. Work it in the bowl with your fingers until it leaves the sides of the bowl, then knead it vigorously on a floured surface for 15 minutes, slapping it down hard against the work surface from time to time to develop the gluten and ensure elasticity. Then brush the dough with oil or melted butter and leave covered with a warmed inverted bowl in a warm place (20°C/68°F) to relax for at least 30 minutes—the longer the better.

To stretch the dough, spread a clean tablecloth on a medium-sized table and sprinkle with flour. Warm an ordinary thick rolling pin. Roll out the rested dough in all directions, moving around the table, until it forms a 40 cm square or round. To prevent the dough from forming a skin or sticking to the pin, brush it with oil or melted butter when necessary. Flour your hands, then slide them palm-side down between the dough and the cloth and gently stretch the dough—working from the centre outwards, moving your hands apart and up and down repeatedly, and moving around the table to stretch the dough on all sides—until it turns into a large translucent sheet, its size governed by the quality of the flour used. Trim the thicker dough edges with a pair of kitchen scissors and discard; or knead them together, allow to relax, re-roll and stretch again.

# LEAF PASTRY—MADE FROM DOUGH STACKS
## Makes 2 x 40 cm circular sheets

*Djuzlema* (Bosnian), *giyozleme* (Bulgarian), from the Turkish *gözleme*, fritter or pancake

These are easier to prepare than plain or stretched sheets of dough since they do not need to be so super-thin. Each sheet is made by rolling out several buttered dough rounds together; when baked or fried, the heat separates the layers, puffing up the sheet and giving it a fairly flaky texture. The Albanians and Greeks have a similar pastry which they call simply 'home-made', and use it to prepare a small deep-fried turnovers—*byrekaqe* (Albanian) and *gkiousleméthes* (Greek). It is also well suited to pies with a top and bottom crust, cheese or meat rolls (made from half a dough sheet) and various fritters.

> 200 g strong white flour (reserve 2 tablespoons for kneading and rolling) •
> 1 tablespoon vegetable oil • 1/2 tablespoon white wine vinegar or cider vinegar •
> 1/8 teaspoon salt • about 100 ml lukewarm water (slightly more if flour is very strong) •
> 75 g butter, melted over hot water, then cooled to tepid

Prepare the dough as described for the rolled-out sheets of dough, above, then divide what you have made into 8 small balls. Using a thick rolling pin, roll each of these into a round about 17 cm in diameter. Coat 4 of the rounds thickly with melted butter and stack them one on top of the other. Leave on one side to allow the butter to firm up, then reverse the stack, so that the unbuttered base becomes the top. Press the top surface lightly with your fingers to join the rounds securely. Roll the stack out into one fine sheet of pastry, about 40 cm in diameter. Repeat the procedure with the 4 remaining rounds of dough. Leave the two sheets to dry out for about 10 minutes, then brush them with the rest of the butter and use immediately. It is also possible to interleave them with greaseproof paper and refrigerate for up to three days.

## MANY-PETALLED DOUGH SHEETS
Makes 2 x 40 cm circular sheets of dough

*Katmer kori* (Bulgarian, Macedonian), *katmer-kore* (Serbian), *katiméri* (Greek), from the Turkish *katmer*

The name derives from the Turkish word meaning double flower because the way each circle of dough is cut makes it looks rather like an open, many-petalled bloom. The 'petals' are folded one on top of the other, and the stack rolled out into one thin sheet. In baking, the nine layers separate and the dough rises—like puff pastry. Unlike puff pastry, though, it has a much lower fat content, part of which is unsaturated vegetable oil. *Katmer* is the national pastry of Macedonia.

100 ml lukewarm water • 1 tablespoon sunflower oil • 1 teaspoon wine or cider vinegar • 1/8 teaspoon salt • 200 g strong white flour • 50 g butter at room temperature, creamed

Measure the water, oil, vinegar and salt in a bowl and agitate with a spoon to form an emulsion. Add enough of the flour to mix to a dough—it should, at this point, be soft and slightly tacky. Turn the dough on to a floured surface and knead it vigorously with most of the remaining flour for 3–4 minutes, until it is smooth, elastic and free of stickiness.

Divide into 2 equal portions and, using the rest of the flour, knead each one into a ball. Flatten the balls with a rolling pin, then roll into rounds approximately 25 cm in diameter. Dot each one with an equal quantity of the butter and spread the blobs out gently. Now mark an imaginary inner circle, about halfway between the centre and the rim, then make 8 equally-spaced cuts from the inner circle to the edge of the dough to form equal sections or petals. As in the illustration overleaf, fold each opposing petal over the inner circle, one on top of the other, stretching the last one slightly so that it can cover the sides of the stack. Repeat this with the other round. Wrap the stacks separately in plastic film and refrigerate for an hour to allow the butter to firm.

At this point, work on a cool work surface brushed with oil. Roll each stack into a large, thin circle, brush with oil and stretch it over the backs of your hands until 40 cm in diameter and almost paper thin. Use immediately, or interleave the sheets with greaseproof paper and refrigerate for up to 3 days.

This pastry is used to make pies with top and bottom crusts, and thin rolls filled with meat or cheese. The Macedonians even prepare a kind of baklava with it. It is, however, unsuitable for multi-layered assemblages, because the weight of the dough sheets prevents the pastry from puffing up.

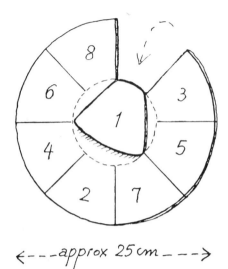

*Folding an eight-petalled dough-round. Mark in your mind's eye an inner circle midway between the centre and outer rim of the dough. Make 8 cuts outwards from that circle to the rim. Fold each opposite flap or petal over the inner circle, one on top of the other, stretching the last petal slightly to cover the sides of the stack.*

←---approx 25 cm---→

# CHEESE ROLLS MADE WITH A *KATMER* DOUGH
Makes 12 pieces

*Viti banichki s katmer kori* (Bulgarian, meaning little rolls with katmer dough sheets); *brza pita so katmer kori* (Macedonian, meaning quick pastry with katmer dough sheets)

These light and flaky little rolls, fragrant with butter, can accommodate a number of different fillings such as fried minced meat and onion, or stewed apples and sultanas,

2 round sheets of katmer dough as described in the preceeding recipe • a little vegetable oil • 125 g feta cheese, washed, drained and crumbled; or white Cheshire or Lancashire, crumbled and sprinkled with a little salt • 1 egg, lightly beaten • 1 egg yolk, creamed

Lay the dough sheets on an oiled surface and, using a sharp knife, cut each one in half. Combine the cheese with the egg. Spoon a quarter of the filling in a narrow strip along the cut edge of each sheet—almost from end to end. Fold the clear edges of dough over the ends of the filling. With your fingers, roll up to make 4 long thin rolls.

Arrange on a well buttered baking sheet, flap side down, spaced to allow for spreading. To make them shiny, brush them with egg yolk. Bake in a preheated oven at 200°C/400°F/gas 6 for 17 minutes, or until golden brown. Leave to cool on the sheet, then cut each roll into 3 pieces. Store, uncovered, in a dry larder or cupboard, for up to 3 days, or use immediately.

# FILO PASTRY CHEESE ROLLS
Makes 12–16 pieces

*Sirnica* (Bosnian, meaning cheese pastry); *viti banichki sus sirene* (Bulgarian, meaning little rolls with brine cheese)

200 g rectangular sheets of filo pastry •
50 g unsalted butter, melted; or 35 g unsalted butter melted with 1 tablespoon oil •
1 egg plus 1 egg white, beaten together with a fork •
2 tablespoons clotted cream or thick yoghurt •
125 g feta cheese, soaked for 1 hour, drained and coarsely crumbled; or Cheshire cheese, diced, then coarsely crumbled

Weigh the pastry sheets and cover them with a tea towel to keep them pliant. Mix the egg with the egg white, cream or yoghurt and cheese in a bowl with a spoon. Place a large piece of greaseproof paper, about the size of the pastry sheets, on a work surface and stack two sheets on it. Brush only the top sheet with a little of the melted butter, then spoon a thin band of the filling along the bottom long edge leaving about 2 cm clear at both ends. Fold over these ends to prevent the filling's moisture from escaping, and brush them with butter. Pick up the paper edge and roll the pastry tightly over the filling to make a long thin roll. Using the paper as support, transfer the roll on to a large buttered baking sheet, flap-side down. Brush all over with melted butter. Repeat with the rest of the sheets.

Bake the rolls in the centre of a preheated oven at 160°C/325°F/gas 3 for 17 minutes, or until pale brown. While still hot, cut into rolls 9 centimetres long. Serve warm or cold with tea, wine or beer.

*A box of Bulgarian commercial* kori *(filo)*—'Rolled out, FINE'.

*Leaf Pastry*

## PUMPKIN STRUDEL
Serves 6–8

*Slatka tikvara* (Bosnian); *vit tikvenik* (Bulgarian); *savijača od bundeve* (Serbo-Croat); and *byrek me kungull* (Albanian), *bundevara* (Serbian), when the pastry is layered, not rolled

300 g canned pumpkin, or freshly baked pumpkin pulp (p. 289), left to drain for 24 hours (if watery) then mashed or processed • 100 g sugar • grated zest of 1/2 lemon • 1/2 teaspoon ground cinnamon • 50 g ground walnuts • large pinch of mixed spice • 2 egg yolks • 4 egg whites, stiffly beaten • 200 g rectangular sheets of filo pastry • 50 g unsalted butter, melted; or 35 g unsalted butter melted with 1 tablespoon vegetable oil • vanilla-flavoured castor sugar (p. 352), or icing sugar for dusting

To make the filling, put the pumpkin pulp and the sugar into a large frying pan and cook briskly over a high heat, stirring all the time with a wooden spoon, until the purée thickens and the spoon leaves a wide clear track on the bottom of the pan. Allow to cool, stir in the aromatics, egg yolks and walnuts, and fold in the whites.

Make and bake the rolls in just the same way as in the preceeding recipe for cheese rolls. Once cooked, dust with sugar and leave to cool on the baking sheet.

There is another common filling using sweet pumpkins with low moisture content and firm flesh: *Cucurbita maxima*, the winter (turban) squash or *Cucurbita moschata*, the cushaw (fiddle-back) squash. To make this, grate finely a 500 g peeled piece of sweet pumpkin and fry over a moderate heat in 50 g unsalted butter until soft. Stir in 50 g sugar and 100 ml milk and continue cooking, stirring most of the time, until very thick. Leave until cold, then add the same flavourings, walnuts and eggs as before.

## PUFF PASTRY STRUDEL
Makes 8 pieces

*Strudel me brumë milfej* (Albanian); *Strudel (milföy)* (Turkish); both from the French *millefeuille*; *shtroudel ot hilyadolistno testo* (Bulgarian, literally 'strudel with thousand-leaved dough'); *štrudla (savijača) od lisnatog testa* (Serbo-Croat, meaning strudel of leaf dough), all from the German *Blätterteigstrudel* or *Butterteigstrudel*

250 g puff pastry, just thawed if frozen •
250 g peeled and cored sweet apples, half of them coarsely grated, half diced small •
25 g castor sugar • 25 g sultanas • 25 g finely ground rusks •
1/4 teaspoon ground cinnamon or mixed spice • vanilla-flavoured icing sugar for dusting

Roll the puff pastry on a lightly floured surface into a thin rectangle, 30 x 50 cm, and trim to shape any uneven edges. Cut it into two long strips.

Mix the filling together and divide into two portions. Place a band of half the filling lengthwise down the centre of each strip, almost from end to end. Brush the long edges of the pastry with a little water, fold over the filling and press down gently along the join to seal. Pinch the ends

Arrange the rolls spaced well apart on a buttered baking sheet. If necessary, curve them to fit. Make several diagonal cuts in the top of each roll to allow steam to escape during baking. Place them in the upper half of a preheated oven at 200°C/400°F/gas 6 and immediately reduce the heat to 180°C/350°F/gas 4. Bake for 25 minutes, or until pale brown and crisp. Allow to cool in the tin, then cut each roll into four pieces and dust with sugar. They are at their best when just prepared; if kept till the next day, the pastry will begin to soften.

Cherry strudel may be made by substituting 275 g sweet stoned cherries for the apples, and a little cherry liqueur or vanilla flavouring for the spice; omit the sultanas.

## LAYERED PASTRY WITH COURGETTES
Serves 4

*Lyaskovska banitsa s tikvichki* (Bulgarian)

This pastry is a speciality of the town of Lyaskovets in northern Bulgaria.

> 350 g courgettes, unpeeled, diced small • 1 egg plus 1 egg yolk, lightly beaten •
> 15 g onion, very finely chopped • scant 1/4 teaspoon salt •
> a good grinding of black pepper •
> 1 bunch fresh dill, finely chopped (or 10–15 dried dill seeds, crushed in a mortar) •
> 50 g butter melted with 1 tablespoon oil (reserve a little for brushing the top of the pastry) •
> 200 g filo pastry sheets (if frozen, allow to thaw in their wrapper)

Combine all the ingredients save the pastry in a bowl and mix well. Grease a roasting tin measuring 28 x 20 cm. Lay the pastry sheets in the tin, gathering each one into wavy folds (to give height and lightness to the dish), and scattering 2–3 tablespoons of the filling over each sheet. Brush the top sheet with the reserved butter and bake in the centre of a preheated oven at 160°C/325°F/gas 3 for about 30 minutes, or until well browned on top and underneath. Serve warm or cold with yoghurt.

*Leaf Pastry*

## LAYERED PASTRY WITH CHEESE
Serves 6

*Lakror me djathë* (Albanian); *banitsa sus sirene* (Bulgarian); *tyrópitta* (Greek); *pita so sirenje* (Macedonian); *plăcintă cu brînză* (Romanian); *pita sa sirom* (Serbo-Croat, but called *gibanica sa sirom* when the pastry sheets are baked before use); *gibanica s sirom* (Slovenian); *peynirli börek* (Turkish)

This dish is eaten on both festive and everyday occasions. It is also served on the stroke of midnight on New Year's Eve with a silver coin concealed between layers of pastry signifying good luck and prosperity through the year for the finder (in Albania and Greece), or a coin plus cornel buds wrapped individually in little slips of paper foretelling the finder's good fortune (in Bulgaria).

300 g filo pastry sheets (if frozen allow to thaw in their wrapper) •
65 g unsalted butter (or 40 g unsalted butter melted with 2 tablespoons oil) •
3 eggs, separated, the whites stiffly beaten •
4 tablespoons thick plain yoghurt, double cream or sour cream •
200 g feta cheese, soaked in water for half an hour, drained and coarsely crumbled with a fork; or 250 g Cheshire or white Stilton cheese, crumbled and seasoned sparingly with salt

Keep the pastry covered with a cloth to prevent the sheets from drying. Just melt the butter and keep it warm. Blend the egg yolks with the cream or yoghurt, then stir in the cheese and fold in the stiffly beaten egg whites.

Grease a roasting tin 28 x 20 x 5 cm deep, or a circular baking tin 25 x 5 cm deep, with some of the melted butter, and line the bottom with two pastry sheets lightly brushed with butter, buttered side up. If the sheets are torn or too small, patch them with a piece from another. Scatter over 2–3 tablespoons of the filling, then continue layering buttered sheets, gathering each into light folds before you trim off any excess— to introduce height and air—and scattering the filling after every second or third sheet, until it is used. Place the last two buttered sheets flat on top, cut the stack with a sharp knife into 6 wedges or rectangles, and pour over any remaining butter.

Place the tin just above the centre of a preheated oven at 200°C/400°F/gas 6 and immediately lower the temperature to 180°C/350°F/gas 4. Bake for 20 minutes, then reduce the heat to 150°C/300°F/gas 2 and cook on a lower shelf for a further 25 minutes. At the end of this time, the crust should be deep golden brown, the base underneath pale brown; if not, bake a little longer. When cooked, leave to cool a little, then cut into portions. Serve warm or cold with tea.

This dish may be prepared ahead of time and rewarmed in the oven.

# LAYERED PASTRY WITH MINCED MEAT

Serves 6–9 as a starter, 4 as a main course

*Byrek me mish i grirë* (Albanian); *burek s mlevenim mesom* (Serbian, from the Turkish *börek*, leaf pastry); *banitsa s mlyano meso* (Bulgarian); *pita so meleno meso* (Macedonian); *plăcintă cu carne tocată* (Romanian); *kıymalı yufka böreği* (Turkish)

250 g minced beef, lamb or pork • 15 g butter (or lard or 1 tablespoon oil) •
250 g leeks, white parts only, chopped; or 1 medium-sized onion, finely chopped •
1/2 teaspoon paprika • 1/8 teaspoon salt •
1/2 teaspoon chopped mint leaves; or a large pinch of dried mint •
freshly ground black pepper • 1 egg white, lightly beaten •
250 g filo pastry sheets •
vegetable oil for brushing • 1 egg yolk for glazing

Brown the minced meat in a dry frying pan. Drain off all the fat and discard. Transfer the meat to a saucepan, add a little water (1–2 tablespoons), then the butter, leeks or onion and paprika and simmer gently until the meat is tender and all the liquid evaporated—about 20 minutes. Off the heat, stir in the salt, mint and pepper to taste. Leave to cool, then add the beaten egg white.

Butter a 28 x 20 cm roasting tin. Trim each sheet of filo so that it is about 5 cm longer or wider than the tin. Brush each sheet with oil and lay in the pan, lightly rumpled, scattering every second sheet with filling before laying the next one on top of it, and using any trimmings to form an extra layer. Finish with two dough sheets, folded to the size of the tin, just brushed with oil. To make the pastry shiny, brush the top sheet with egg yolk blended with 1 tablespoon water.

Bake the pastry in the centre of a preheated oven at 160°C/325°F/gas 3 for 40 minutes, or until deep golden brown on top. Transfer to a cooling rack and cover with a baking sheet for 5–10 minutes to soften the crust, then serve accompanied by boiled green vegetables and mashed potatoes.

# PASTRY AMULETS FILLED WITH CHEESE
Makes 18–20 pastries

*Byreçka* (Albanian), *burekčići* or *buredžici na hamajliju* (Bosnian, literally—'little pastries shaped like amulets'), from Turkish *muska böreği*, amulet pastries, so called because each pastry looks like a small cloth or leather amulet bag worn round the neck of a Turkish child or adult, containing a protective charm against the 'Evil Eye'; *pirozhki sus sirene* (Bulgarian), from the Russian *pirozhki*; *tiropittákia* (Greek, meaning small cheese pastries)

These light and crisp Turkish pastries are popular in many parts of the Balkans as party or tea-time delicacies. Besides cheese, they come with other fillings such as minced meat with onion, chopped ham with hard-boiled eggs, sweetened chestnut purée, nuts mixed with egg white and sugar, or pumpkin marmalade.

1 small egg, beaten • 125 g feta cheese, soaked in water for about 1 hour, then crumbled; or same amount of white Stilton or Lancashire, crumbled • 200 g rectangular sheets of filo pastry • 50 g unsalted butter melted with 1 tablespoon of vegetable oil

Fold the beaten egg into the crumbled cheese. Cut the stack of pastry sheets lengthwise into strips about 8–9 cm wide and 45 cm long. Brush the whole length

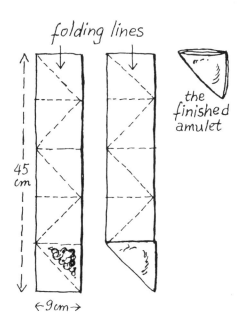

of each strip with the melted butter and place 1 teaspoonful of the filling in one corner. Fold the bottom corner over the filling to form a triangle, then fold the triangle over again at a right angle. Continue folding at right angles until you reach the end of the strip (see illustration).

Place the pastries (with the loose end tucked) on 2 buttered baking sheets, and brush the top surface of each one with the remaining butter.

Bake in the middle of a preheated oven at 180°C/350°F/gas 4 for 10–12 minutes, until puffy and pale golden brown. These pastries are best eaten on the same day—hot or cold, while still crisp and flaky.

# CHAPTER XVIII

# Biscuits, Cakes and Pastries

Cakes and biscuits were never an integral part of Balkan cookery. They have only been absorbed into the diet as the region has become more open to influences from western Europe. This is shown in the words used for the foods themselves. Some derive either from the French *biscuit* or the old French *biscoit* (itself from the Latin *biscoctus*, twice baked), or from the English word *cake*. These include *biskotë* (Albanian), *biskvita* (Bulgarian), *mpiskóto* (Greek), *biskvit* (Macedonian), *biskvit* or *keks* (Croat), *biskvit* or *kolačić* (Serbian), *keks* (Slovenian), and the Romanian *bişcot(ă)*.

The other popular (and older) Balkan term for biscuits is *gurabije* or *gurabie* (Albanian), *kourabiya* or *korabe* (Bulgarian), *gurabija* (Bosnian, Macedonian, Serbian), *kourampiés* (Greek), and *corabea* (Romanian), from the Turkish *kurabiye* or *gurabiye*, ultimately derived from Arabic.

These words cover an incalculable number of regional variations, of which I have included a few of the most typical and traditional.

## SPONGE FINGER BISCUITS
Makes 13–15

*Biskota savajar* (Albanian); *bishkoti* (Bulgarian); *piškote* (Serbo-Croat); from the Romanian *bişcot(ă)*

1 large egg, separated • 50 g castor sugar • 1/2 teaspoon vanilla flavouring •
75 g plain white flour • 1/2 teaspoon baking powder •
vanilla-flavoured icing sugar for dusting (p. 352)

Beat the egg white until thick. Add about a third of the sugar and continue beating until it stands up in stiff glossy peaks. Beat the egg yolk with the remaining sugar and the vanilla until pale yellow and frothy. Sift the flour with the baking powder and fold it into the egg yolk mixture alternately with the egg white.

Spoon the mixture into a piping bag fitted with a 9 mm plain nozzle. Pipe about 10 cm long strips, spaced well apart, on to a greased baking sheet dusted with flour. Bake in the middle of a preheated oven at 160°C/325°F/gas 3 for 18–19 minutes, until firm to touch and coloured with a hint of beige. Cool on a wire rack. Store in an air-tight tin.

## OLD-FASHIONED SODA BISCUITS IN THE MODERN WAY
Makes 26–30

*Gurabije me kos* (Albanian), *kourabii s kiselo mlyako* (Bulgarian), *gurabii so kiselo mleko* (Macedonian), *gurabije s kiselim mlekom* (Serbian), all meaning biscuits with thick yoghurt

2 eggs • 125 g castor sugar • 125 ml sunflower oil • 125 ml thick-set yoghurt •
a few drops real vanilla essence or 1/4 teaspoon vanilla flavouring •
finely grated zest of 1 lemon • 1/2 teaspoon bicarbonate of soda •
500 g white unbleached flour • vanilla-flavoured icing sugar for dusting (p. 352)

Put the eggs, sugar, oil, yoghurt, flavourings and bicarbonate into a mixer bowl. Using the beater, mix on maximum speed under the mixture is light and creamy. Add the flour and mix to a soft dough on minimum speed, switching off as soon as it is incorporated.

Spoon on to 2 greased baking sheets in 26–30 piles, allowing plenty of room for spreading. Mould each one into a ball and flatten slightly with the palm of your hand or the back of a fork. Bake in the centre of a preheated oven at 180°C/350°F/gas 4 for 26 minutes, or until the biscuits colour lightly all over. Swap the sheets from top to bottom halfway through cooking. The cracked tops are a characteristic feature. While still warm, put them in a box or plastic bag with vanilla sugar and a sliced vanilla pod and shake to coat with the sugar. Close the box or bag when the biscuits are completely cold and store in a dry place for two days at most.

In Serbia, these are usually made with good quality lard instead of oil.

## WHITE SHORTBREAD BISCUITS
Makes 20

*Gurabije me gjalpë* (Albanian, 'butter biscuits'), *beli kourabii* (Bulgarian, 'white biscuits')

When we celebrated the marriage of a classmate of mine in the small mountain town of Elena in Bulgaria, three shining new metal buckets were filled to the very top with these biscuits white with icing sugar. In village households, they are sometimes prepared with home-made lard instead of butter.

100 g butter at room temperature • 25 g vanilla-flavoured castor sugar (p. 352) •
grated zest of 1 lemon, or a few drops vanilla flavouring • 150 g plain flour •
icing sugar for dredging • 1/2 split vanilla pod

Beat the butter until light and creamy. Add sugar and the flavouring and continue beating until the mixture is almost white. Stir in the flour and knead into a smooth malleable dough without using any liquid. Divide into 20 pieces and form into balls. Arrange them, a little apart, on a large ungreased baking sheet. Refrigerate for at least 30 minutes. Bake in a slow oven preheated to 120°C/225°F/gas 1/4 for 35–40 minutes. The point is to cook the biscuits without allowing them to colour, so keep an eye on them, especially towards the end of the cooking time. While still hot, roll in icing sugar to coat them evenly, then leave to cool on a wire rack. Store in an air-tight tin with extra icing sugar plus a vanilla pod.

## WALNUT MACAROONS
Makes 7–8

*Amareta me arra* (Albanian), *amareti od oraha* (Croat), from the Italian *amaretti*; *orehovki* (Bulgarian, 'walnut macaroons'); *macroni od oraha* (Croat, from the French *macarons*); *puslice od oraha* (Serbian, meaning walnut kisses)

Before the days of non-stick utensils, waxed baking paper and rice paper, macaroons were baked on trays coated with beeswax: the trays were heated, then rubbed with a piece of beeswax held at one end with cloth to protect the hand. The recipe here is the classic formula for soft, melt-in-the-mouth, yet not too sweet, walnut macaroons.

75 g shelled walnuts • 25 g granulated sugar • 2 egg whites (small or medium eggs) •
25 g icing sugar • 1/4 teaspoon ground cinnamon

Grind the walnuts and granulated sugar together in a food processor or rotary nut mill. In a mixing bowl, whisk the egg whites until stiff, then beat in the icing sugar gradually. Continue beating until the egg whites stand in firm, glossy peaks. With a metal spoon, fold the walnuts into the egg whites—gently but thoroughly.

Pipe the mixture into small rounds, using a plain nozzle, or place heaped spoonfuls at intervals on to a non-stick baking sheet or one lined with waxed paper. Swirl a palette knife on the surface of each round, lifting it quickly to form peaks. Bake just below the middle of a preheated oven at 160°C/325°F/gas 3 for 25 minutes, or until the macaroons are crisp on the surface but still slightly moist in the centre, and their edges are tinged brown. When done, carefully lift from the baking sheet and transfer to a rack to cool. Serve or store for a few days in a tightly closed container. Should they become a bit too soft, they can be crispened at 150°C/300°F/gas 2 for about 5 minutes.

### SYRUP-BASED BISCUITS

This group of biscuits divides into two sorts: those made with honey and quite light in colour, and those made with pekmez (p. 52) and chestnut-coloured. Both are reminiscent of the British gingerbread men or 'husband's' biscuits, but contain no ginger. Although once prepared without fat, eggs or a raising agent and quite hard, they are now made lighter by the addition of bicarbonate of soda, a little fat and sometimes eggs. In all syrup-based recipes, honey and pekmez are interchangeable. If you cannot find pekmez in your local delicatessen or healthfood store, use malt extract which is similar in taste.

## CHRISTMAS BISCUITS

Makes about 50–55 biscuits if cut with an 8.5 cm cutter in the shape of a Christmas tree

*Koledni biskvit ili medenki* (Bulgarian, meaning Christmas biscuits or honey biscuits); *medenjaci* (Serbo-Croat), *medeni kruhki* (Slovenian), both meaning honey biscuits

These biscuits should be prepared four to five weeks ahead of time to allow them to soften and all the flavours to develop.

250 g honey • 250 g icing sugar •
250 g walnuts or blanched almonds, finely ground then pounded to a paste •
1 teaspoon ground cinnamon • 1/4 teaspoon ground cloves •
about 1/4 nutmeg, freshly grated • finely grated zest of 1 lemon • pinch of salt •
300 g plain white flour • 1 teaspoon bicarbonate of soda

In a saucepan, cream the honey with the sugar, then add the walnuts or almonds, spices, lemon zest and salt. Bring the mixture to the boil, stirring all the time, and cook for a few seconds. Remove from the heat and allow to cool a little.

Sieve the flour with the bicarbonate of soda and stir it in to make a rather stiff, sticky dough. Knead it lightly with a little extra flour until smooth but still sticky. Wrap it in plastic film or polythene and leave at room temperature for 24 hours.

Next day, roll the dough out on a lightly floured surface to 5 mm in thickness and cut out with biscuit cutters as many Christmas shapes as you can. Make a small hole at the top of each biscuit with the point of a small knife. Arrange on greased and floured baking sheets, spacing well apart to allow for expansion. Bake in a preheated oven at 150°C/300°F/gas 2 until they faintly turn colour, about 10 minutes at the most. Cool on racks. Store in tightly closed tins for a month to let them soften.

Afterwards, decorate with piped icing and tiny silver balls. Insert a length of transparent nylon through the hole of each biscuit and hang it on the Christmas tree.

## GRAPE BISUITS

Makes about 40 biscuits if you use a 4 cm star-shaped cutter
(but you can give them any shape you like)

*Mustakoulki* (Bulgarian, meaning biscuits made with grape juice)

25 g unsalted butter • 1 tablespoon vegetable oil • 50 g soft brown sugar •
25 g pekmez (p. 52) or malt extract • 1 teaspoon ground cinnamon •
1 large pinch ground cloves • a little freshly grated nutmeg •
2 small eggs • 1/2 teaspoon bicarbonate of soda •
100 g blanched almonds, finely ground then pounded to a paste •
125 g plain white flour, and a little extra for kneading and rolling
*Icing*
85–90 g icing sugar • 1 tablespoon hot milk

Place the butter, oil, sugar, malt extract or pekmez and spices in a saucepan. Bring to the boil, stirring well to blend together. Leave to cool a little, then beat in the eggs and bicarbonate of soda, and stir in the almonds and the flour. Gather the dough into a ball and knead it lightly until smooth. Wrap in clingfilm and refrigerate or freeze for 20 minutes to firm up.

Roll the dough on a floured surface to a thickness of about 5 mm and cut out stars with a biscuit cutter or a sharp knife and template. Arrange on a greased baking sheet and bake in a preheated oven at 160°C/325°F/gas 3 for 13–15 minutes until firm to the touch.

Meanwhile, make the icing. Beat the sugar with the hot milk to a smooth, thick yet runny consistency. Spread or pipe on to the biscuits. Return them to the oven, leaving the door open, until the icing is sufficiently dried.

# PEPPER BISCUITS
Makes about 40 biscuits if cut with a round wavy cutter 5 cm in diameter

*Paprnici* (Bosnian); *paprenjaci* (Serbo-Croat); *mali kruhki* (Slovenian)

In Bosnia pepper biscuits were baked for various Islamic religious festivals. In Slovenia, they were often made with rye flour instead of wheat, cut into heart shapes or a person's initials and given as love tokens—because the fusion of honey and pepper was reckoned to have aphrodisiac qualities. Earlier recipes contained less fat than they do today, and the raising agent was not bicarbonate of soda, but bread leaven or hartshorn.

150 g unsalted butter • 75 g sugar • 2 tablespoons honey • 2 egg yolks • pinch of salt •
1 teaspoon ground cinnamon • 3 cloves, finely crushed •
1 teaspoon freshly ground black pepper • grated zest of 1 lemon • 150 g ground walnuts •
250 g plain flour, and a little extra for kneading and rolling •
1/2 teaspoon bicarbonate of soda

Cream the butter, sugar and honey together with a wooden spoon until a light fluffy mass. Beat in the yolks, followed by salt, cinnamon, cloves, pepper and lemon zest, then stir in the walnuts and the flour, sieved with the bicarbonate of soda, to make a soft pliable dough.

Turn on to a lightly floured work surface, knead briefly until smooth and roll to a thickness of 5 mm. Cut out rounds or a variety of shapes (hearts, stars, crescents, animals, initials) with biscuit cutters. Arrange on greased baking sheets, allowing room for the biscuits to spread and, if you wish, put a peppercorn on the top of each one as decoration.

Bake in a preheated oven at 160°C/320°F/gas 3 for 10–15 minutes or until lightly coloured. Remove carefully (they are fragile) to cooling racks. Brush them with warmed honey for an appetizing glaze, or decorate them with icing (p. 275).

# LEMON-FLAVOURED PLAIN CAKE
Makes one 19 x 10 cm loaf

*Kek ordiner* (Albanian), *obiknoven keks* (Bulgarian), both meaning ordinary cake; *biskvit obični s maslacem* (Serbo-Croat, meaning ordinary cake with butter)

My mother was a pianist, one of the first graduates of the first Bulgarian conservatoire established in Sofia at the beginning of this century. Concert pianist before her marriage, she gave up her career to become a piano teacher, mother and wife.

Although the everyday cooking was done by my two grandmothers who lived with us, mother always found time to cook the sweet course from one of her recipes diligently recorded in her many cookery notebooks. When imported lemons appeared in the shops (lemons do not grow in Bulgaria), she used to make us her favourite lemon cake which was baked in a loaf tin almost half a metre long. This is the recipe.

125 g butter or margarine, or equal quantities of each • 125 g castor sugar • finely grated zest of 1 lemon • 3 large eggs • 200 g plain white flour • 2 teaspoons baking powder

Beat the butter or margarine with sugar and lemon zest to a light fluffy cream, then beat in the eggs, one at a time. Sift the flour with the baking powder and fold it into the creamed mixture to form a thick batter of stiff dropping consistency. Spoon into a greased 21 x 11 cm loaf tin lined with greased greaseproof paper. Smooth it level. Bake in the centre of a preheated oven at 180°C/350°F/gas 4 for an hour, until the top is well browned. Leave to cool in the tin for 5 minutes, then turn on to a wire rack. The cake is best served on the same day it is made.

## *KUGLOV* WITH SUNFLOWER OIL
Makes 1 x 18 cm round cake

*Kek me vaj luledielli* (Albanian, meaning cake with sunflower oil); *kuglov* (or *kuglof*) *sa praškom za pecivo* (Serbo-Croat), from the German *Backpulverkugelhopf* (in Austria *gugelhupf*) meaning moulded cake with baking powder—so called to differentiate it from one raised with yeast

This light, lemon-flavoured cake baked in a kugelhopf mould is as pleasing to the eye as to the palate. It is rather like the famous Austrian *Backpulvergugelhupf*, and I have seen similar confections in good pastry-shops in Durres and Istanbul where they were just called *kek* in both Albanian and Turkish.

2 eggs • 200 g castor sugar • 125 ml sunflower oil • finely grated zest of 1 lemon • 200 g plain white flour • 1 teaspoon baking powder • 5 tablespoons milk • vanilla-flavoured icing sugar for dusting (p. 352)

Beat the eggs with an electric hand beater, mixer or rotary whisk until light and pale yellow, then add the sugar, oil and lemon zest, beating after each addition. On minimum speed, fold in the flour and the baking powder alternately with the milk to make a thickish mixture of pouring consistency.

Pour the mixture into a buttered and flour-dusted 2-litre kugelhopf mould. Bake on a shelf just below the centre of a preheated oven at 150°C/300°F/gas 2 for 1 hour, or until the cake is browned on top and slightly shrinking from the sides of the mould.

Leave to cool in the mould for 10 minutes, then turn it out on a wire rack set over a plate. Sieve over enough vanilla sugar to accentuate the decorative markings of the cake. Slice for serving when completely cold. Stored in an airtight container, it will keep for 2–3 days.

## WALNUT LOAF
### Serves 8

*Kek me arra* (Albanian); *orehov keks* (Bulgarian); *cevizli kek* (Turkish); *kolach so orevi* (Macedonian); *prăjitură cu nici* (Romanian); *kolač sa orasima* (Serbo-Croat); *orehov kolač* (Slovenian)

'How can a man die who has a walnut tree in his garden?' goes an old country saying. The walnut tree has been cultivated in the Balkans since Thracian times. Eating walnuts was not only pleasurable but, so the thought went, kept a person in glowing health—the probable explanation of the popularity of anything containing walnuts. Fragrant, cold-pressed walnut oil, sweet in after-taste, that people sometimes make for themselves from their own walnuts, is often used in place of butter to enhance the flavour of the cake.

50 g salted butter, at room temperature • 3 tablespoons walnut or sunflower oil •
100 g castor or icing sugar • 2 eggs, separated, yolks lightly beaten, whites stiffly beaten •
1/2 teaspoon ground cinnamon or vanilla flavouring • 200 g plain flour •
2 teaspoons baking powder • 6–7 tablespoons milk •
75 g walnuts, coarsely chopped, dusted with flour then sieved to remove excess flour •
50 g sultanas, floured and sieved in the same way

Put the butter, oil, sugar, egg yolks and cinnamon or vanilla into a mixing bowl and beat together with an electric hand beater for 2–3 minutes, until the mixture is thick, light and fluffy.

Sift the flour with the baking powder twice, then fold it in alternately with the milk and the beaten egg whites to make a mixture of stiff dropping consistency—that is, it should fall from a spoon when gently shaken over the bowl. Carefully stir in the walnuts and sultanas.

Turn the mixture into a loaf tin, measuring approximately 21 x 11 x 5 cm, greased and lined with greaseproof paper (also greased), and smooth it level. Bake in the centre of a preheated oven at 160°C/325°F/gas 3 for 1 hour, or until risen, well browned on top and firm to the touch.

Leave in the tin for 5–10 minutes. Turn on to a rack, remove the paper and allow to cool. It can be kept for a few days well wrapped in a polythene bag, and will only gain in flavour.

## FRESH FRUIT CAKE
Serves 4

*Kek me fruta* (Albanian); *plodova pita* (Bulgarian); *voćni kolač* (Serbo-Croat)

This combination of cake with fresh, seasonal fruit is one of the most loved Balkan sweets. For a lighter texture, the cake is usually made with sunflower oil rather than butter.

1 egg • 75 g vanilla sugar • 3 tablespoons sunflower oil •
100 g plain flour, sieved twice with 1 slightly rounded teaspoon baking powder •
1 1/2 tablespoons milk •
8–9 ripe apricots, halved and stoned;
or 200 g cherries, stoned weight;
or 200 g apples, peeled and cored weight, sliced into wedges •
vanilla-flavoured icing sugar (p. 352) for dusting

Beat the egg, first on its own, then with the sugar, until thick and pale yellow, then fold in the oil, lightly but thoroughly, followed by the flour, twice sifted with the baking powder. Stir in the milk to make a mixture of dropping consistency.

Turn into a buttered cake tin measuring about 25 x 19 x 4 cm, lined with buttered greaseproof paper. Arrange the fruits decoratively on top (if using apricots—hollow-side up) without touching each other to allow some room for expansion.

Bake in a preheated oven at 180°C/350°F/gas 4 for about 30 minutes, or until the cake rises among the fruits and is golden brown. Leave to cool in the tin, then turn it out, remove the paper and sieve a little icing sugar over the top. Serve warm or cold with pouring cream.

## BISHOP'S BREAD
Makes 1 tall fancy loaf about 18 cm diameter

*Vladishki hlyab* (Bulgarian); *biskupski kruh* (Croat); *valdičin hleb* (Serbian); from the German *Bischofsbrot*

Unlike the plain fatless sponge below, bishop's bread stores well (4–5 days) wrapped closely in plastic film or polythene. The dried fruits account for the keeping qualities.

100 g shelled walnuts, coarsely chopped • 75 g sultanas •
75 g dates, stones removed, chopped finely • grated zest of 1 lemon •
1/2 teaspoon ground cinnamon • 200 g plain flour • 1 teaspoon baking powder •
3 size 1 eggs, separated • 200 g castor sugar

Mix the nuts and fruits with the lemon zest and cinnamon. Sieve over them the flour mixed with the baking powder and rub it in with your fingertips to keep them from sticking together. In another bowl, beat the egg whites until very stiff. In a third bowl, beat the egg yolks with the sugar until light and pale yellow.

Fold the egg yolk mixture into the fruit and flour mixture alternately with the egg whites. Then spoon into a greased and floured 2-litre fluted kugelhopf mould with a central funnel. Bake in a preheated oven at 150°C/300°F/gas 2 for 1 hour, until well risen and dark on top. Leave to cool in the tin for 10 minutes, then turn on to a wire rack and leave to cool completely. Serve sliced very thinly.

## FATLESS SPONGE CAKE
Serves 4

*Pandispanjë* (Albanian); *patišpanja* (Bosnian); *pandishpan* (Bulgarian); *pantespáni* (Greek); *pandişpan* (Romanian); *patišpanj* (Serbo-Croat); *pandispanya* (Turkish); from the French *pain d'Espagne*

A light fatless sponge is the most difficult of all cakes to prepare, demanding of time, skill and care. A well-whisked mix of eggs and sugar should produce a light, well risen cake without baking powder, but you can make sure of it by adding a teaspoonful to the flour.

3 medium eggs, preferably one day old, separated •
1 tablespoon vanilla-flavoured sugar, or 1 sachet vanilla sugar • 75 g castor sugar •
1/2 teaspoon vanilla flavouring • grated zest of 1/2 lemon •
65 g plain white flour • 1 teaspoon baking powder

Whisk the egg whites until they form stiff peaks, then whisk in the vanilla sugar and set aside. Beat the castor sugar gradually into the egg yolks and continue beating until the mixture thickens, doubles in volume and turns pale yellow, light and creamy—this should take 5 minutes using an electric beater, or at least 15 minutes with a wire whisk—then beat in the flavourings. Sieve the flour with the baking powder (if used), and fold into the egg yolk mixture alternately with the egg whites. Pour into a buttered and floured 20 cm cake tin, or two or three 17.5 cm sandwich tins.

Bake in the middle of a preheated oven at 180°C/350°F/gas 4 for 30–35 minutes for a deep cake, about 10–15 minutes for shallow layers, until it has puffed and browned well, and has shrunk from the sides of the tin. Remove from the oven and stand the tin upside down on a wire rack. When quite cold and set, remove from the tin and sprinkle with icing sugar; or fill with jam and whipped cream, or vanilla ice cream and dust the top with sugar.

## PASTRY

Proper English shortcrust pastry is little known in the Balkans, especially in rural areas. Pie, flan and tartlet recipes based on English shortcrust, often re-rendered or mistranslated from French or English, appear only incidentally in cookbooks and women's magazines. However, a continental type of sweet pastry, usually flavoured with lemon zest, rum or vanilla, is quite popular in central and western parts where it is known as *linzer* (after the Austrian town of Linz on the Danube). Apart from an egg yolk or two, and sometimes a little oil, no other form of liquid is used in the dough, so a pastry case is less likely to shrink when baked blind.

My first acquaintance with shortcrust pastry was in a thriving vegetarian restaurant in the centre of Sofia where a mixed-fruit tart, made with brown flour and fragrant with cherries, plums and fruits of all kinds, was a daily special. This restaurant disappeared when all private enterprises were closed down. It was aptly named Yasna Polyana, meaning 'Clear Glade' after Tolstoy's family estate Yasnaya Polyana, where Tolstoy wrote *War and Peace* and *Anna Karenina*, and spent the later years of his life close to nature, working with his hands and abstaining from wine, meat and white bread. His writings exerted influence on the Slavonic Balkan intelligentsia of the turn of the century as well as shaping Russia's intellectual life. The tart was culinary offspring of his ideology.

# LOVE LETTERS
Makes 4

*Ljubavna pisma* (Serbian)

Love letters, shaped in a delicate *linzer* pastry and flavoured with rum and lemon, come to us from Vojvodina, displaying the strong Central European influence exerted on the cookery of this northern province of Serbia.

*Filling*
25 g biscuit crumbs or salt-free rusk crumbs • 1 tablespoon rum •
25 g coarsely ground walnuts • grated zest of 1 lemon • 25 g icing sugar •
1 medium egg white, lightly beaten

*Pastry*
100 g plain white flour • 1/4 teaspoon baking powder • pinch of salt •
1 tablespoon ground vanilla sugar, or icing sugar • 25 g unsalted butter, in small pieces •
1 1/2 tablespoons vegetable oil • 1 medium egg yolk •
vanilla-flavoured icing sugar for dredging

For the filling, moisten the crumbs with the rum, then work in all the remaining ingredients to make a stiff, pliable paste.

To make the pastry, sieve the flour (less 1 tablespoon reserved for rolling out), baking powder, salt and sugar into a bowl and mash in the butter, oil and egg yolk with a fork. Blend together with 1 tablespoon water to make a smooth, soft dough.

To shape the 'letters', sprinkle the work surface with the reserved flour and roll the dough to a neat 22 cm square. Cut this into 4 equal-sized squares. Put a quarter of the filling, moulded into a small rectangle, diagonally across the centre of each square. Moisten the edges, then fold the four corners to the centre on top of the filling and make an envelope. Press the envelopes lightly to flatten and seal them.

Arrange on a buttered baking sheet and bake in a preheated oven at 180°C/350°F/gas 4 for about 20 minutes. When just beginning to colour lightly, remove from the oven and dredge liberally with sugar. Cool on a rack.

## CARAWAY STRAWS
Makes about 40

*Biskota stapë me kripë* (Albanian), *soleni pruchki* (Bulgarian), *slani štapići* (Serbo-Croat), all meaning salty sticks

These light, melt-in-the-mouth savouries are ideal for afternoon tea; if they are to be served with wine, sprinkle coarse salt crystals as well as the caraway over the straws before baking.

*Yeast starter*
15 g fresh yeast • 50 ml milk, heated to tepid with a pinch of sugar •
1 tablespoon of the sieved flour

*Dough*
250 g strong white flour (reserve 2 tablespoons for kneading) • 1/2 teaspoon salt •
1 tablespoon icing sugar •
125 g unsalted butter at room temperature; or 65 g unsalted butter and 4 tablespoons vegetable oil •
1 small egg for glazing • caraway seeds for sprinkling

Cream the yeast with the milk and stir in a tablespoon of the sieved flour. Leave the mixture to stand for about 20 minutes until risen and frothy.

Sieve the flour with the salt and sugar into a bowl. Add the butter, cut into small pieces, and sprinkle on the oil, if used. Rub the flour and fats together with your fingertips until thoroughly amalgamated, then stir in the yeast to make a soft, sticky dough. Turn it out on a work surface and knead it with the reserved flour for 8–10 minutes until smooth and no longer sticky. Rest for 15–20 minutes for the dough to relax.

To shape the straws, roll out and trim the edges of the dough to a neat rectangle 1 cm thick and 20 cm wide. Cut it lengthwise into 2 strips each 10 cm wide, and then across into 1–1.5 cm wide strips or straws. Brush them with the beaten egg and sprinkle with caraway seeds. Arrange in even rows on well oiled baking sheets with a space of 1–1.5 cm between each straw. Leave to prove in a warm place for 30 minutes, or until risen and puffy.

Bake on the middle and lower shelves of a preheated oven at 200°C/400°F/gas 6 for 8–10 minutes until golden brown—but watch them as they can easily burn. Cool and store in a lidded plastic box.

## CHEESE TURNOVERS
Makes 34–36

*Sirenki* (Bulgarian)

Many of the older inhabitants of the town of Russe remember these yeast-raised pastries as the speciality of *Baj* (a courteous form of address to a middle-aged man) Dencho—a very unusual pastry-chef who had his shop on the main street. I say unusual, because Baj Dencho was also a talented sculptor. Every winter, when the pavement tables were brought in, he would erect in their place—to the delight of all passers-by—huge snow sculptures depicting various well-known artists, politicians and historical personalities. This recipe is dedicated to his memory.

2 teaspoons dried yeast • 2 tablespoons milk • 1/2 teaspoon sugar •
250 g strong white flour (reserve 2 tablespoons for kneading) • 1/2 teaspoon salt •
1 tablespoon vanilla-flavoured icing sugar (p. 352) • 125 g unsalted butter • 1 small egg
*Filling*
1 egg, lightly beaten • 100 g sirene (feta) cheese, mashed coarsely with a fork •
1 small egg, lightly beaten, for glaze

Heat the milk with the sugar to hand-hot. Sprinkle in the yeast and leave in a warm place for 20 minutes until frothy. Sift the flour with the salt and vanilla sugar into a bowl, rub in the butter, then beat in the egg and stir in the yeast mixture to make a soft, sticky dough. Turn it out and knead with the reserved flour for about 5 minutes until smooth, still soft but no longer sticky. Leave in a warm place for about 1 1/2 hours, until doubled. Oil 2 baking sheets and keep them on one side. Make the filling by blending the beaten egg with the cheese and set aside as well.

Knock back the risen dough, knead it for a minute, then roll it out to a thickness of 3 mm. Using a plain round pastry cutter 7 cm across, cut as many circles as you can. Distribute the filling evenly among the dough rounds, placing about half a teaspoon on one half of each round and leaving a small margin round the edges. Fold the other half over the top and press lightly to seal the filling.

Brush the turnovers with the beaten egg. Arrange them on the baking sheets, allowing some room for spreading, and leave to rise in a warm place, for about 25 minutes, until light and puffy. Bake just above and below the centre of a preheated oven at 140°C/285°F/gas 1 for about 17 minutes, or until golden brown; the glaze will give them a beautiful glossy finish. Cool on a rack. They will keep for 2–3 days, stored uncovered in a dry cupboard or larder.

# CHAPTER XIX

# Fruit Desserts, Creams and Ice-creams

> I have another memory of the market at Zara [Zadar]! It was my second visit to the capital of Dalmatia in the last days of May, and there was even more colour in the scene, for it was cherry time. Such cherries in such profusion I had never seen before, and perhaps, unless some good fairy brings me back to Zara in the merry month of May, shall never see again. Picturesquely shaped baskets of very large proportions were everywhere heaped with the lovely fruit—whitehearts, blackhearts, glowing in the sun! Vegetables, eggs, and home-made olive oil, accustomed objects of the market, were swamped by the mass of colour and faded into insignificance. It was a cherry market—a symphony in crimson!
>
> Maude M Holbach (1908)

At cherry-time, market stalls are still piled high with all kinds, sweet, semisweet and sour. Strawberries are also super-abundant, and later on come apricots, mulberries and figs—white and green and brown and deep purple with velvety red-tinged flesh. Still later, with autumn, arrive pears and apples, huge melons and water melons and big downy quinces with their exquisite aroma and golden-hued flesh which turns rose-red when slowly cooked.

In the Balkans fruit is plentiful, cheap and much loved. In season, it is preferred to any cake or pastry, arranged at table in the most attractive way possible or simply in clear glass bowls embedded in ice.

The recipes here are light, comparatively low in calories—since they contain little or no fat—and trouble-free. They can all be enjoyed as the perfect end to a summer meal.

## COMPOTE

*Komposto* (Albanian), *kompósta* (Greek), from the Turkish *komposto*, from the Italian *composta*, stewed fruit, itself from the Latin *compositus*; *kompot* (Bulgarian, Serbo-Croat), *compot* (Romanian), from the French *compote*, also from the Latin *compositus*.

This describes a light summer dessert of a single fresh fruit, or a macédoine of complementary fruits, poached and served in a generous amount of light syrup. The word *hošaf* in the Bosnian dialect, like the Turkish *hoşaf*, is a compote of fresh or dried fruit in a thin syrup, while the Albanian *oshaf* and the Bulgarian *oshav* or *oshaf* are customarily made with dried fruits or a combination of dried and fresh. Compote may be flavoured with vanilla, clove, cinnamon or lemon zest; is served well chilled, often with ice in it, and sometimes laced with plum or cherry brandy, liqueur or sweet wine.

# CHAMPAGNE COMPOTE IN A WATERMELON
Serves 10–12

*Pulnena dinya* (Bulgarian); *polneta lubenitsa* (Macedonian); *punjena lubenica* (Serbo-Croat); *karpuz dolması* (Turkish); all meaning stuffed watermelon

An elegant centrepiece for a party.

1 large watermelon • 1 small aromatic melon, flesh scooped out with a vegetable baller • 3–4 ripe peaches, peeled and diced • 200 g icing sugar • 3–4 tablespoons rum or Cognac • chilled champagne or sparkling wine

From the stem end of the watermelon, cut a large slice in a zig-zag pattern to make a lid. Cut out the flesh and clean out the inside with a spoon.

Remove the seeds from the flesh and cut into bite-sized cubes. Return them to the shell. Add the sweet melon balls, the peaches and the sugar. Pour over the rum or Cognac, cover with the lid and chill.

Shortly before presentation, bed the watermelon in a bowl of crushed ice. Discard the lid. Pour in the chilled champagne or sparkling wine to come almost to the rim of the shell and serve.

# MORELLO CHERRY COMPOTE
Serves 4–6

*Komposto me vishnja* (Albanian); *kompot ot vishni* (Bulgarian); *kompot od višanja* (Serbo-Croat); *hošaf od višanja* (Bosnian, from the Turkish, ultimately from Persian)

A favourite. Stoned sweet cherries, peeled fresh figs, peach, plum and apricot halves, peeled and quartered sweet apples, pears and quinces can be cooked in the same manner, but will need less sugar (about 100 g sugar or honey per 600 g prepared fruit).

In Bosnia, morello cherry compote is thickened slightly with cornflour. It was recorded by the seventeenth-century Turkish traveller Evliya Çelebi (Čelebija), who noted that the people of Sarajevo stored snow and ice covered with straw in their cellars, and used it in the presentation of this compote.

600 g morello cherries, stalks removed, stoned • 150 g sugar • a little maraschino liqueur

Place the sugar in a fairly large saucepan with 1 litre water. Dissolve over gentle heat. Put in the cherries, cover and poach until tender. Cool, add the liqueur, if you like, and chill. Serve with crushed ice, perhaps with ratafia biscuits.

# POACHED QUINCES FILLED WITH CREAM
Serves 6

*Vareni dyuli* (Bulgarian), *kuvane dunje* (Serbo-Croat)—both meaning boiled quinces; *ayva tatlısı* (Turkish, meaning quince sweet)

Quinces and cream is the most delicious combination—unsurpassed even by strawberries and cream.

6 small quinces (about 1 kg), down rubbed off •
300 g sugar • 250 ml double cream, chilled

Choose a saucepan that will hold the quinces upright. Put in the sugar, pour in 300 ml water and stir briefly. Wash and wipe the quinces but do not peel. Slice off the stalk end and remove the hard cores with the seeds. Drop the parings and the seeds into the pan with the sugar and put in the prepared quinces.

Bring the contents very, very slowly to the boil, then simmer gently with the lid on for 45 minutes, or until the quinces are soft but not disintegrating. Halfway through the cooking time, turn them over. Lift them into glass bowls, removing any clinging seed or parings. Leave to cool.

Boil the pan juices until syrupy and sticky. Strain, then pour a little syrup into and around each fruit and refrigerate—the syrup will turn to salmon pink jelly. Serve with double cream poured (or piped) in the cavity left by the cores.

# GLAZED APPLES WITH CLOTTED CREAM AND NUTS
Serves 4

*Tufahije* (Bosnian, from the Arabic)

The Bosnian version of this dish is traditional, though the recipe originally came from Baghdad. It appeared for the first time in Turkish in an early cookery manuscript by Shirvani as *Tuffâhiyye*, a somewhat different confection made of apples, sugar and flour.

4 medium dessert apples, about 500 g • 75 g sugar •
1/2 stick cinnamon • 5 cloves • 50 g ground walnuts •
100 g fresh clotted cream (*kajmak*) or 125 ml double cream, stiffly whipped

Put the sugar and 250 ml water in a saucepan that holds the apples comfortably. Heat gently, stirring from time to time, until the sugar dissolves. Bring to the boil and cook the syrup rapidly for 1 minute. Remove from the heat.

Core the apples, hollow out the flesh somewhat to make room for the filling, then peel them thinly. Lower into the hot syrup, cover the pan and simmer for 8–10 minutes, until they are tender but still holding their shape. Shake the pan occasionally to help the apples turn over and cook evenly. Lift them out and stand upright on a plate. Leave to cool. Remove the spices. Reduce the syrup by fast boiling, uncovered, to about 75 ml, then cool.

To make the filling, mix the walnuts with 2 tablespoons of the syrup and 2 tablespoons of the cream and stuff into the apple cavities, dividing any remaining filling between 4 small bowls or ramekins before standing an apple in each bowl. Spoon the remaining syrup over the apples to glaze them and top them with the remainder of the cream. Decorate with glacé cherries and serve chilled.

*Fruit Desserts, Creams and Ice-creams*

# BAKED PUMPKIN
Serves 15–20

*Kungull i pjekur* (Albanian); *pečena tikva* or *pečena bundeva* (Bosnian, Serbo-Croat); *pechena tikva* (Bulgarian, Macedonian); *fırında kabak* (Turkish)

Come late autumn, stalls start mushrooming in many Balkan towns displaying large trays of baked pumpkin halves the size of bicycle wheels. Slices of pumpkin are wrapped in paper and eaten, just as they are, in the streets.

These pumpkins are a special cultivar of *Cucurbita maxima*, the American winter (turban) squash, also known as sugar pumpkin, introduced by the Turks into the Balkans in the sixteenth century, then locally developed. The thin near-white rind houses firm orange flesh containing up to 9 per cent sugars and much less water than the common *Cucurbita pepo* pumpkin, so it is very suitable for roasting.

If you are baking a common pumpkin, for instance the Hundredweight variety, allow a cooking time of about 4 hours at 190°C/375°F/gas 5, occasionally ladling out the juices as they collect in the halves. It is ready when it stops exuding juice and is nicely burnt around the edges. An 8 kg common pumpkin will yield about 3.5 kg of baked pulp.

1 large whole sugar-pumpkin, weighing about 8 kg • thin honey or pekmez • 250 g ground walnuts • 1/2 teaspoon ground cinnamon

Scrub the pumpkin under running water with a stiff brush, removing all traces of earth from the rind. Wipe dry, trim off most of the stalk, then cut in half lengthwise to give two large basin-shaped shells. Scoop out the seeds and, if you wish, reserve them to make toasted pumpkin seeds (p. 222). Scrape away some of the fibrous matter from the inner surfaces, then place each half cut side up on a large baking tray. Bake near the top of a preheated oven at 200°C/400°F/gas 6 for about 2 hours. Sugar-pumpkins do not produce juices during baking. They are ready when the cut surfaces are burnt due to the caramelization of the sugars in their composition.

Slice the baked pumpkin into large chunks without removing the rind. Serve with lots of honey or pekmez to spoon over each portion. Pass the walnuts (mixed with cinnamon if you like that) separately in a bowl, for sprinkling on top.

# BAKED PUMPKIN PURÉE
Serves 6

*Pure me kungull në furrë* (Albanian); *tikveno pyure na fourna* (Bulgarian); *pire od tikve u pečnicu* (Serbo-Croat)

---

375 g thick, canned or freshly baked and drained pulp of the common pumpkin, *Cucurbita pepo* •
2 eggs, separated, whites stiffly beaten • 50 g castor sugar •
grated zest of 1 lemon • 50 g ground almonds or walnuts • 25 g sultanas •
1/2 teaspoon ground cinnamon (if using walnuts)

Put the pulp into a mixing bowl. In a bowl apart, beat the egg yolks with the sugar and lemon zest until light and pale, then fold into the pumpkin pulp. Stir in the nuts and sultanas (and cinnamon, if using walnuts), and fold in the egg whites.

Pour into a greased and floured baking dish 19 cm in diameter, and bake in a preheated oven at 180°C/350°F/gas 4 for about 35–40 minutes, until set and a deep golden brown on top. Leave to cool in the oven with the door open and the heat switched off. Serve warm or cold, with cream or sprinkled with icing sugar.

There is a variation called *nakip ot purzhena kestenka* (Bulgarian), and *koh od pržene bundeve* (Serbo-Croat, from the German *kochen*, to cook) which is made with the sugar-pumpkin (*Cucurbita maxima*). If this variety is available, coarsely grate or process in several batches a 600 g peeled piece of the pumpkin, fry it gently in some butter until soft and thick, and use this in place of the canned or baked pumpkin.

There is a folk-character called Hitur Peter (Crafty Peter) in Bulgaria, to whom any number of jokes and witticisms are attributed. His Turkish counterpart is Nasreddin Hoca. Here is one about pumpkin.

> Hitur Peter started selling baked pumpkin in front of the main entrance to the National Bank in Sofia. Soon he succeeded in making a tidy sum of money. Towards the end of the season an acquaintance asked him for a small loan.
>
> 'Look here, my friend,' Hitur Peter said. 'When I opened this stall, the bank and I made a contract not to engage in competition. The bank pledged not to sell any pumpkin, and I—not to lend any money.'

# BAKED WALNUT AND POTATO PUDDING
Serves 8

*Kartofen nakip s orehi* (Bulgarian); *koh od krompira i oraha* (Serbo-Croat); from the German *kochen*, to cook

Walnuts and cinnamon are best for this but you can use finely ground blanched almonds and a little almond vanilla flavouring instead.

500 g baked potatoes, peeled and mashed (about 700 g raw mealy potatoes) •
4 eggs, separated • 150 g castor sugar • large pinch salt •
150 g ground walnuts • finely grated zest of 2 lemons • 1/2 teaspoon cinnamon •
25 g sultanas, soaked in brandy • icing sugar for dusting

Beat the egg whites to stiff peaks. Beat in 25 g of the sugar to give them added stiffness. Put all the remaining ingredients except the sultanas and icing sugar in another large bowl and beat briskly with a wooden spoon or an electric mixer until smooth. Fold in the sultanas and the beaten egg whites.

Turn into a buttered and floured 22.5 cm round tin about 5 cm deep, and bake in a preheated oven at 180°C/350°F/gas 4 for 45 minutes, until well browned on the surface. Remove and sieve over icing sugar. Leave to cool in the tin for 5–10 minutes before cutting into wedges. Serve warm or cold, with pouring cream or on its own.

# BAKED STUFFED NECTARINES
Serves 4

*Pulneni glatkokori praskovi* (Bulgarian); *punjene breskve, glatke kore* (Serbo-Croat)

4 large firm nectarines (or peaches, the down rubbed off), halved and stoned •
25 g blanched almonds, pounded or finely ground • 50 g semi-sweet biscuits, crushed •
25 g ground vanilla sugar • 50 g orange rinds preserved in syrup, drained weight, chopped; or candied orange peel, chopped not too small • 7 tablespoons red dessert wine
(such as the Dalmatian red *prošek*) • 1 tablespoon castor sugar

Widen the cavities of the nectarines by scooping out a little flesh with a teaspoon. Put the flesh with the rest of the ingredients except the castor sugar into a small bowl and mix lightly together, with approximately 3 tablespoons of the red dessert wine to form a loose paste.

Butter a shallow ovenproof dish just large enough to contain the nectarines in a single layer, arranging them cut-side up. Heap the stuffing into the hollow of each half, pour round 4 tablespoons of wine and sprinkle over the castor sugar. Bake in a preheated oven at 200° C/400° F/gas 6, on a shelf above the centre, for about 15 minutes, or until set and pale brown. Serve well chilled, the baking juices poured over, with cream or ice-cream.

## BAKED SWEET PLUMS
Serves 4–6

*Pecheni slivi* (Bulgarian); *šljive pečene u pećnici* (Serbo-Croat)

The Balkans are famous for their plums, and a special variety of large, exceptionally sweet, dark-blue plums with a whitish bloom on their skins are grown for drying, cooking and preserving. If you are using this variety, add 2–3 tablespoons of vinegar to offset the sweetness of the fruit and sugar.

1 kg ripe, sweet plums, stones left in,
or pushed out with a small stick without splitting the fruit •
150 g sugar • 1 stick of cinnamon

Put the fruit and sugar in a buttered baking dish large enough to hold them in a thin layer and leave them to macerate for 24 hours. Next day, add cinnamon and 100 ml water. Bake in a slow oven heated to 120°C/250°F/gas 1/2 for about 2 hours, turning the fruit over at intervals, until most of the juices have evaporated and the plums are wrinkled. Remove from the heat. Discard the cinnamon. Refrigerate. This is an excellent dessert, served on its own or with whipped or pouring cream. Stored in small jam jars, the plums will keep for a week or two.

# QUINCE SALAMI

*Salam ot dyuli* (Bulgarian); *salama od dunja* (Macedonian, Serbo-Croat)

1 kg large ripe quinces, cut into wedges without peeling or coring •
750 g sugar • strained juice of 1 lemon •
150 g mixed crystallized fruits such as apricots, pears, cherries or plums, diced if large •
250 g walnuts, roughly chopped • granulated sugar for coating

Boil the quinces with a little water until soft and mushy, then purée while hot. Discard the skins and seeds. Transfer the purée to a preserving pan, add the sugar and lemon juice, and cook over a moderate heat, stirring continuously, until the sugar dissolves and the purée thickens and leaves the sides of the pan. Remove from the heat and stir in the fruits and nuts.

Turn on to a work surface and shape it into a thick sausage or salami as soon as it is cool enough to handle. Roll it in granulated sugar and leave to cool completely. Serve thinly sliced into rounds.

For quince Turkish delight, cook the quince purée as above, but omit the crystallized fruits. Pour the purée over greased grease-proof paper set in a tin 2.5–3 cm deep. When cold, slice into cubes and dust with icing sugar. Store in a plastic or wooden box, the layers separated with more icing sugar.

# LEMONS AND CREAM
Serves 1

*Limona me ajkë* (Albanian); *limoni sus smetana* (Bulgarian)

5–6 slices of preserved lemon (p. 331), diced or left whole, plus some of their syrup •
1 tablespoon brandy • 25 ml double cream, stiffly whipped

Place the lemon slices together with a tablespoonful of their syrup in a small glass bowl. Pour over the brandy, if you like it alcoholic, and top up with whipped cream. Finish by drizzling a little more syrup over the whole.

## BAKED BATTER PUDDING WITH APPLES
Serves 3–4

*Nakip* (Bulgarian); *zljevenka* (Serbo-Croat); *zlivanka* (Slovenian)

This is a lovely, moist pudding which could be made with any fruit: stoned white cherries, morello cherries, halved plums, apricots or sliced pears, or stoned prunes soaked in some liqueur or brandy.

25 g butter • 400 g dessert apples, peeled, cored and sliced into thin wedges •
50 g sugar • 100 g plain flour • pinch of salt • 2 eggs •
250 ml milk and water in equal quantities •
1–2 tablespoons Cognac, vanilla liqueur or Calvados •
vanilla-flavoured icing sugar (p. 352)

Melt the butter in a shallow earthenware, porcelain or cast iron baking dish approximately 23 cm in diameter. (Do not use a tin because the edges of the pudding tend to get too brown.) Tilt the dish to coat the sides with butter, then add the apple and sugar and mix together.

Put the flour, salt, eggs, milk and water into a liquidizer or food processor and blend for a few seconds until smooth and bubbly; alternatively, whisk the mixture thoroughly until smooth. Pour over the fruit and leave to stand while the oven is heating to 180°C/350°F/gas 4. Bake on the centre shelf for 1 hour, or until set and golden brown. Sprinkle on top with the liquor and/ or icing sugar before cutting into portions. Serve warm, with single cream or on its own.

If you are planning to cook this in advance, bake for 50 minutes instead of 1 hour, then re-heat at the same temperature for 10–15 minutes.

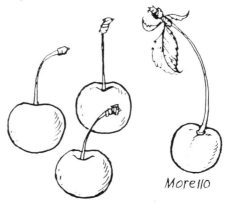

*Sweet and acid (Morello) cherries*

# BLANCMANGE, BALKAN STYLE
Serves 4

*Muhalebi* (Albanian); *malebi* (Bulgarian); *muhalebija* (Bosnian); from the Turkish *muhallebi* or *mahallebi*, from the Arabic original

This sweet, featured in medieval Islamic manuscripts, has come to the Balkans through the Turks. First made with rice starch or pounded rice flour, today all too often with cornflour or a mixture of fine rice flour and cornflour, it might be approximated to the eighteenth-century English blancmange—milk, rice flour and almonds perfumed with rose-water.

In Bulgaria, individual portions of *malebi* are normally prepared without sugar, then turned out like small castle puddings and laced liberally with a fragrant, red sauce. In Bosnia *muhalebija* contains sugar and is served without a sauce, but sprinkled with ground cloves and cinnamon.

4 tablespoons rose-water • 40 g cornflour •
500 g semi-skimmed milk (or 3 parts ordinary milk to 1 of water)

First of all, moisten 4 cups or bowls of 250 ml capacity with the rose-water. Slake the cornflour with a little of the milk to a smooth, thin cream. Warm the rest of the milk and pour it into the slaked cornflour. Return to the heat and, stirring continuously, bring to boiling point. Still stirring, simmer for 1–1 1/2 minutes until the mixture is a thick pouring consistency, then pour equal quantities into the prepared cups or bowls.

The cups are then filled with an equal amount of red fruit sauce for which you will find recipes on pages 350 and 351. Make the one you prefer, and pour it over hot. Cool, then refrigerate to set. Turn them out into individual glass bowls and let them regain room temperature before serving.

*Blueberries*

# CORNFLOUR JELLY (WITHOUT GELATINE)
Serves 5–6

*Medena paluza* (Bosnian, meaning cornflour jelly made with honey), from the Turkish *paluze*, cornflour jelly, originally from the Persian

There are two main versions of *paluza* in Bosnia. Both are based on cornflour. One is prepared with fresh or dried stewed fruit, the other—described here—is made with honey and appears to be the authentic Turkish version. *Paluze* appeared for the first time in the oldest printed Turkish cookery book, *Refuge of Cooks* by Mehmed Kâmil (Istanbul, 1844), and then in Turab Efendi's *Turkish Cookery Book* written in English and published in London in 1864. Turabi Efendi advises that the cooked jelly be flavoured with 'essence of rose or orange flower', 'poured into a mould previously oiled with almond oil', and 'ornamented on top with some skinned pistachios or almonds'. It is best made in a heavy non-stick saucepan, otherwise it will need lengthy cooking over a very low heat, and constant stirring to avoid sticking and burning.

150 g honey • 50 g cornflour • rose water for rinsing the bowls • ground walnuts

Pour 1 litre of water into a non-stick heavy saucepan and add the honey. Bring to the boil, without skimming, then stir in the cornflour slaked with 100 ml cold water. Cook the mixture over no more than medium heat for about an hour, stirring from time to time until the mixture starts thickening. From then on you must stir constantly to prevent burning. The jelly is ready when it achieves the consistency of thick honey. Pour it immediately into small bowls each moistened with 2 teaspoons of rose-water. Allow to cool, then refrigerate. Unmould the jellies on to individual dessert plates and sprinkle lightly with ground walnuts.

*Medlar*

# APPLE CREAM
Serves 5

*Kisel ot yabulki* (Bulgarian), *kiselj od jabuka* (Serbian), from the Russian *kiselj*, fruit cream; *višnjab* (Bosnian), from the Persian *vişne*, cherry and *ab*, juice or water

The fresh, concentrated flavour of this dessert is good reason for its popularity in Bulgaria and Serbia. Other fruits, such as cherries, morello cherries, bilberries, apricots, peaches and soft fruits are all used.

500 g sweet dessert apples (or cooking apples, if you prefer the cream with a more piquant sweet-sour taste), unpeeled, each apple cut into 16 wedges and cored • 75 g cornflour or potato flour • 100 g sugar

First squeeze all the juice from the cut-up apples—the best and most hygienic way of doing this is to use an electric juice extractor. Cover and refrigerate the juice until needed.

Now put the apple residue into an enamelled saucepan, pour over 1 litre of water and bring the mixture to the boil. Simmer, uncovered, over a moderate heat, for 10 minutes, stirring from time to time. Strain the liquor through a fine nylon sieve and leave to cool a little; discard the debris.

Mix the cornflour or potato flour with the sugar in a saucepan. Add the apple liquor gradually, then bring to the boiling point; the mixture will thicken almost immediately. Cook over a moderate heat for one minute, stirring continuously. Remove from the heat and stir in the chilled raw apple juice.

Pour the cream into glasses or glass bowls and refrigerate for at least 5 hours to firm. Serve as they are, or decorate with a little whipped double cream.

## GRAPE PUDDING
Serves 5–6

*Krem me pekmez* (Albanian); *petmezena kasha* (Bulgarian); *moustaleuriá* (Greek)

This is a traditional dessert prepared at grape harvest. If pekmez syrup is unobtainable, reduce by boiling 1 litre unsweetened red or white grape juice to about 750 ml, and use it in place of the diluted syrup.

75 g cornflour • 50 g granulated or dark brown sugar • 250 g pekmez syrup (p. 52) • ground walnuts, toasted sesame seeds or chopped blanched almonds • ground cinnamon

Slake the cornflour, sugar and a little water in a bowl. In a saucepan, dilute the pekmez syrup with a scant 500 ml water, bring to the boil and add the cornflour mixture. Simmer briskly, stirring, until the pudding thickens. Leave to cool a little, then pour into individual bowls or glasses. When cold, it can be finished with a sprinkling of nuts and cinnamon or with toasted sesame seeds.

## QUINCE CREAMS WITH COGNAC
Serves 4–6

*Krem ot dyuli v chashi* (Bulgarian), *krem od dunji vo chashi* (Macedonian), *krem od dunja u čašama* (Serbo-Croat), all meaning quince cream in glasses

500 g quinces, peeled, cored and sliced • 50 g granulated sugar • 1/2 teaspoon grated lemon zest • 1 tablespoon Cognac • 100 ml double cream, whipped with 2 tablespoons icing sugar • glacéed fruits, or fruits preserved in syrup (pp. 325-330), drained

Put the quinces into an enamelled saucepan with 1–2 tablespoons water, the sugar and lemon zest. Cover and cook gently until tender and all the liquid has evaporated. Sieve or process to a purée. Sprinkle with Cognac and fold in the whipped cream. Spoon into stemmed glasses with a wide bowl. Decorate with glacéed or syruped fruits, serve sponge fingers.

## CHOCOLATE CREAM
Serves 4–5

*Krem me çokollatë* (Albanian), *shokoladen krem* (Bulgarian), *krem so chololada* (Macedonian), *crem od čokolade* (Serbo-Croat)

250 g good plain chocolate (reserve 1–2 squares for grating) •
3 tablespoons Cognac or coffee liqueur •
250 ml double cream, stiffly whipped (reserve 4 tablespoons for decoration)

Break the chocolate into pieces and melt it with the alcohol in a small bowl over boiling water. Remove from the heat and leave to stand until cool before folding in the whipped cream. Then pour into stemmed wine glasses and leave to set. Serve chilled, with a final touch of the cream you reserved and grated chocolate.

## ALBANIAN TRIFLE CREAMS
Serves 4

*Zupa* (Albanian), from the Italian *zuppa inglese*, 'English soup'

There are perhaps as many variations of *zupa* in Albania as there are of trifle in Great Britain, but this one is, I think, the nicest.

50 g sponge finger biscuits (or left-over fatless sponge cake) coarsely crumbled •
1 tablespoon milk • 2 tablespoons Cognac •
white confectioner's custard as in the recipe on p. 354 flavoured with a few drops of vanilla essence • confectioner's custard as in the recipe on p. 353 •
75 g plain chocolate, broken into squares • 50 g unsalted butter, at room temperature •
50 g icing sugar • 25 g chopped green pistachio nuts or walnuts

Moisten the crumbled sponge fingers with milk and Cognac and divide half of this between 4 stemmed wine glasses. Prepare the white confectioner's custard in the quantity given in the recipe on p. 354. While still hot, divide between the glasses. When set, spoon over the rest of the sponge mixture. Prepare the confectioner's custard. Remove the pan from the heat and immediately add the chocolate. Stir until the chocolate melts. Top the glasses with the chocolate mixture, leave to cool, then refrigerate.

Beat the butter soft. Add icing sugar to make butter cream. Add a swirl to each trifle and scatter the pistachios or walnuts. Chill for at least 4 hours before serving.

## LEMON JELLY
Makes 500 ml

*Zhile limonash* (Albanian); *limonovo zhele* (Bulgarian); *žele od limuna* (Serbo-Croat); from the French *gelée*

---

25 g sultanas • 15 g powdered gelatine • 150 g sugar •
thinly pared zest of 2 medium lemons, cut into wide strips, and the strained juice •
essential oil of lemon or lemon flavouring •
a few drops yellow food colouring such as annatto or turmeric extract (optional)

Rinse the sultanas clean with hot water then soak them in cold water for an hour or so and drain. Simmer the lemon zest in 375 ml water for 5 minutes, then strain and discard the zest. Dissolve the gelatine and the sugar in the strained hot liquid, stirring over a low heat until clear and syrupy. Do not allow to boil. Remove from the heat and add the lemon juice, sultanas, and the flavouring (and colouring, if you wish). Add more water to make up the total quantity to 500 ml. Pour into a 500 ml fancy mould or shallow tray rinsed with cold water. Cover and leave overnight in the refrigerator to set firmly. To serve, dip the mould up to the rim in hot water. Invert on to a wetted serving dish and give a sharp shake. If using a tray instead of a mould, turn the jelly out in the same way and chop it up. Serve in glasses with thin cream and tiny, cherry-sized meringues.

## RASPBERRY JELLY
Serves 4

*Zhile me manaferra të buta* (Albanian); *malinovo zhele* (Bulgarian); *žele od malina* (Serbo-Croat)

---

200 g raspberries • 150 g sugar • 15 g powdered gelatine • 1 tablespoon lemon juice

Simmer the raspberries with 125 ml water and the sugar until soft—about 1 minute. Force through a fine nylon sieve to remove the seeds, then re-heat. Dissolve the gelatine in the very hot raspberry purée, stir in the lemon juice and top up with cold water to 500 ml. Tip into 4 glasses, cover and place in a refrigerator or a cool place to set. This goes well with vanilla ice-cream.

## RASPBERRY SORBET
Serves 6

*Malinov sladoled* (Bulgarian); *sladoled so malini* (Macedonian); *sladoled od malina* (Serbo-Croat)

200 g sugar • 400 g raspberries (thawed, if frozen) • 2 tablespoons orange juice

Make the syrup by dissolving the sugar in 100 ml water over a low heat, then boil rapidly for 1 minute. Set aside to cool. Mash, then force the raspberries through a fine nylon sieve to remove the seeds. Add the orange juice and the cold syrup to the fruit. Pour into a freezer-proof tray and freeze for about 1 1/2 hours or until slushy. Remove from the freezer and beat the sorbet with an electric rotary beater to break down the ice crystals. Repeat the process 3 or 4 times during the freezing process. About 20 minutes before serving, transfer the sorbet to the refrigerator to soften slightly.

Fresh strawberries or mulberries may be substituted for the raspberries; their flavour is also enhanced by orange juice.

## YOGHURT ICE-CREAM
Serves 4–5

*Sladoled ot kiselo mlyako* (Bulgarian); *sladoled od kiselog mleka* (Serbian)

Yoghurt ice was prepared in my father's house long before it became popular in the United States—first by the traditional churning method, and later in the freezing compartment of the refrigerator. I make it now in the freezer, either with fresh fruit or with partially thawed fruit purée made by forcing soft fruit through a seive, discarding the seeds and mixing the pulp with sugar as specified in this recipe.

The basic preparation works admirably with every kind of soft fruit. Loganberries produce a crimson cream, blackberries a deep purple one, strawberries, rose pink. Bilberries, raspberries, mulberries and red, white or black currants are other possibilities.

Yoghurt ices have a smooth texture; the crystals are extremely fine, almost imperceptible—which is not the case with ordinary home-made water ices. Much less rich than ice-cream made with cream, they are quick and easy to prepare, need no whisking during freezing or the use of fast-freeze, and are truly delicious.

200 g hulled strawberries or raspberries, passed through a fine nylon sieve and chilled •
150 g icing sugar, or better, finely ground granulated sugar •
200 g thick strained yoghurt, preferably home-made and not too sour (or pasteurized Greek strained yoghurt, or low-fat, set Bio yoghurt), chilled

Put the ingredients in a mixing bowl and beat with an electric or rotary beater until well blended. Pour into a plastic freezer box, cover and freeze for 2 1/2 to 3 hours, or until just frozen and still pliable. Form into half-balls with an ice-cream scoop and refreeze. To serve, put the scoops in champagne glasses or stemmed glasses with a wide bowl. Leave to stand for 10 minutes at room temperature, or about 40 minutes in the refrigerator.

## WHITE ICE-CREAM
### Serves 4–6

*Akullore me ajkë* (Albanian), *kaymaklı dondurma* (Turkish), both meaning ice-cream made with cream; *semtanov sladoled* (Bulgarian, Slovenian), *sladoled od pavlaka* (Macedonian), *sladoled od pavlake* (Serbo-Croat), all three literally meaning sweet ice made with cream

As the names indicate, this is ice-cream made from frozen, sweetened cream. It is considered by many to be the finest of all ice-creams, the 'real thing'.

250 ml double cream, well chilled • 85–90 g icing sugar, sieved •
1/4 teaspoon vanilla extract (or 3 sachets vanilla sugar, or 1 teaspoon vanilla flavouring),
or use 2 tablespoons cherry brandy or maraschino liqueur (though Albanian and Dalmatian maraschino liqueurs will change the colour of the ice-cream to greyish pink)

Put the double cream, sugar and chosen flavouring into a chilled bowl and whip the mixture (with a chilled whisk) until it thickens and forms soft peaks. Pour into a suitable container, cover and freeze for about 3 hours or until just firm, then serve in spoonfuls or scoops. You can also freeze the mixture in individual waxed-paper trifle cases or paper baking cases.

# SALEP ICE-CREAM
Serves 6

*Akullore me salep* (Albanian); *sladoled sus salep* (Bulgarian); *salepli dondurma* (Turkish)

Salep ice-cream is made without egg yolks or cream so it contains little cholesterol. Because of its bland unassertive flavour, it can accommodate various flavourings such as powdered mastic, ground ginger, rosewater or cherry brandy. Or you can just pour an aniseed-flavoured spirit or liqueur over each portion.

1 teaspoon ground salep • 100 g sugar • 500 ml full-cream milk

Turn your freezer to 'fast freeze' or the refrigerator to its coldest setting an hour before starting to make the ice-cream. Blend the salep, sugar and 5 tablespoons of the cold milk together in a bowl. Bring the remainder of the milk almost to the boil and pour over the salep mixture. Return to the pan and simmer, uncovered, for 15–20 minutes, stirring frequently with a wooden spatula, until the mixture thickens to a consistency slightly thinner than that of single cream. Allow to cool, then pour into a lidded plastic box, leaving at least 5 cm headspace, and freeze until firm, whisking with a rotary or electric beater 4–5 times during freezing to break down any ice crystals.

To serve, dip the box in hot water, unmould the ice-cream and cut it into six portions. One of the red fruit dessert sauces described on pages 350–351 would be an excellent accompaniment.

# CHAPTER XX

# Syruped Sweets and Sweetmeats

Luscious, flour-based compositions drenched with gleaming syrup are part of the Balkan Ottoman legacy. Then, there were no cakes, no fancy gâteaux, no petits fours nor chocolate confections of any kind in the majority of pastry-shops. What they had to offer were principally *baklava*, *kadaif*, *revani* and other syruped pastries, as well as confectionary *halva*.

It was also the custom then to present many of these delicacies at certain social and domestic celebrations. Over the years, however, the recipes departed considerably from their Turkish prototypes, modified by generations of home cooks who began to substitute a lighter fruit syrup, a wine-based syrup or even milk for the heavier Turkish original. Sometimes, Balkan housewives dispensed with syrup altogether, for example in the Dry Baklava, a little-known variation on perhaps the world's most celebrated syruped pastry, baklava.

## BAKLAVA
Makes a 20 x 20 cm square

*Bakllava* (Albanian); *baklava* (Bosnian, Bulgarian, Macedonian, Serbo-Croat); *mpaklavás* (Greek); *baclava* (Romanian); from the Turkish *baklava*

In its simplest form, baklava is constructed by stacking buttered sheets of leaf-pastry or filo (sometimes as many as eighty) interleaved with nuts. The stack is then cut into triangular, rhomboidal or diamond-shaped pieces. More complex shapes are accomplished by rolling a sheet of dough around a filling of nuts, cooked pumpkin or confectioner's custard, then coiling the roll into a large spiral or several individual ones. Once baked, baklava is impregnated with a honey or sugar syrup.

500 g sugar • thinly pared zest of 1 lemon • a good squeeze of lemon juice •
1/2 teaspoon vanilla flavouring • 400 g filo pastry sheets •
150 g unsalted butter or 125 g salted clarified butter, or 100 g butter and 50 ml vegetable oil • 200 g coarsely ground walnuts, blanched almonds or pistachio nuts •
finely grated zest of 1 lemon

## Syruped Sweets and Sweetmeats

Make the syrup by bringing the sugar, pared lemon zest, a squeeze of lemon juice and 500 ml cold water slowly to the boil. Simmer without stirring for 5 minutes, until the mixture reaches 104°C/220°F and begins to look syrupy. Cool, add the vanilla flavouring then refrigerate. (If the chilled syrup seems rather thick, dilute it with a little hot water so that later it can easily penetrate the cooked pastry.)

Melt the butter (or butter and oil) in a small pan and keep warm. Cut the stack of dough sheets into a square to fit a 20 cm buttered baking dish. (Remember that tinplate may react chemically with the lemon juice in the syrup.) Reserve the trimmings to intersperse, well buttered, between the layers. Mix the nuts with grated lemon zest.

Place the dough sheets, two at a time, in the baking dish, brushing each one with melted butter before laying over the next. Sprinkle some of the walnut mixture over every second sheet. Finish off with 2–3 buttered sheets on top. Pour over any remaining butter, then refrigerate for 30 minutes to firm the butter. With a sharp knife, cut the assemblage into diamond shapes, rhomboids or triangles. Bake in a preheated oven at 180°C/350°F/gas 4 for about 40 minutes, then increase the heat to 200°C/400°F/gas 6 and bake for a further 10 minutes, or until the pastry is lightly browned. Remove from the heat and immediately pour the cold syrup over the hot baklava. Cover and leave for 24 hours to absorb the syrup.

The next day, if there is any unabsorbed syrup in the dish, drain it and let it thicken slightly over a moderate heat. Pour it over the baklava to glaze the top. Baklava will keep well for up to a week if tightly covered and stored in a cool larder.

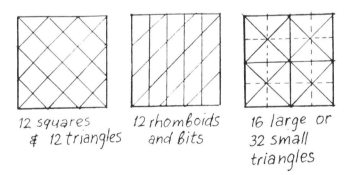

*Three traditional ways to slice baklava. The rhomboid is the most typical shape.*

## BAKLAVA IN SNAIL SHAPES
Makes 14–15 sensibly small pieces

*Pita na ružice* (Bosnian, Serbo-Croat, meaning pastry shaped like little roses); *baklava na ohlyuvi* (Bulgarian, meaning more prosaically, baklava in snail shapes)

My husband Tom and I had these most delicious spirals topped with white vanilla ice cream at the Loksantra restaurant in Athens. The confection was called *Hanoúm pagotó*, 'Turkish-Lady's ice cream'. This recipe is a variation on the basic baklava.

200 g sugar • a squeeze of lemon juice •
200 g rectangular filo pastry sheets (if frozen, thaw in their wrapper) •
75 g coarsely ground walnuts • 1/2 teaspoon ground cinnamon •
100 g unsalted butter, melted

Bring the sugar, lemon juice and 200 ml water to the boil and cook over a moderate heat for 3–4 minutes until a thin syrup forms. Cool, then refrigerate.

Lay the stack of pastry sheets on a work surface. Cover the top sheet with the walnuts, sprinkle with cinnamon and roll the whole stack into a tight roll. Cut into 3.5 cm pieces. Arrange them, cut side up (so the spiral pattern can be seen) and touching each other, in an ungreased enamelled baking dish 15 cm across. Tuck in between the whorls any loose walnut that may have dropped from the spirals, then spoon the melted butter over each spiral and all around. Bake in the centre of a preheated oven at 160°C/325°F/gas 3 for about 20–25 minutes, or until golden. Remove, then pour over the chilled syrup. Cover the dish. Serve next day with coffee or ice cream.


Another joke against the thrifty inhabitants of Gabrovo:

A man called Pencho visits his friend for Christmas.
   'Pencho, did you get my last letter?'
   'Which letter? You don't mean the one in which you asked me to bring you a tray of baklava?'
   'That's the one.'
   'I got no such letter,' answered Pencho, who needless to say was from the town of Gabrovo.

## DRY BAKLAVA
Makes one round of 22 cm

*Suva baklava* (Macedonian)

This recipe was gathered a few summers ago in the beautiful old town of Ohrid in Macedonia. It is made with *katmer* pastry—the most characteristic pastry in Macedonia, but also well known in other parts of the Peninsula.

*Katmer pastry*
150 ml lukewarm water • 1 1/2 teaspoons sunflower oil •
2 teaspoons wine or cider vinegar • large pinch salt • 300 g strong white flour •
75 g butter at room temperature, creamed • a little extra oil
*Filling*
200 g ground walnuts
(or a mixture of toasted sesame seeds, ground unskinned almonds and walnuts) •
200 g icing sugar • grated zest of 1 large lemon •
1 sachet vanilla sugar (or a few drops vanilla extract) • 1/2 teaspoon ground cinnamon •
1 large egg white, stiffly beaten

Butter generously a baking tin, about 22 cm in diameter and 4–5 cm deep. Prepare 3 *katmer* pastry rounds the same size as the baking tin, using the quantities above and following the method given on page 263.

Mix the nuts with the sugar and flavourings, and fold in the beaten egg white. Place one round of pastry in the tin and sprinkle with oil. Add half the filling in blobs and spread it out gently right up to the edges. Cover with a second round, sprinkle again with oil and cover with the rest of the filling. Lay the third round on top, brush it generously with oil and refrigerate the assemblage for 2 hours, or until required.

Preheat the oven to 200°C/425°F/gas 7 with a shelf in the centre. Cut the chilled pastry into diamond-shaped pieces about 4 cm wide, place in the oven and immediately lower the temperature to 180°C/350°F/gas 4. Bake for 50 minutes to 1 hour until the pastry is light golden brown on top, and crisp and golden underneath. While still warm, cut once again to separate the pieces.

Keep for at least 24 hours in the tin (at room temperature) before serving to allow time for the pastry to set and all the flavours to develop. It is as delicious as baklava made with syrup.

# TRIGONAS—TRIANGULAR SYRUP TURNOVERS
### Makes 8

*Trigona me petë byreku* (Albanian), *trigouni s kori za banitsa* (Bulgarian), both meaning trigonas with leaf pastry, from the Greek *trígona*, triangular syrup pastry

Regional variations on *trigona* use almonds, puréed chestnuts or confectioner's custard as a filling, or even omit the filling altogether. Some Albanian pâtisseries make the pastries dry and serve the syrup in a small jug.

100 g coarsely ground walnuts • 50 g castor sugar •
1 teaspoon mixed spice or ground cinnamon • grated zest of 1 lemon • 1 egg yolk •
a syrup of 200 g sugar, 1 teaspoon lemon juice, 150 ml water •
16 rectangular sheets of filo pastry, about 300 g, trimmed to 23 cm squares •
4 tablespoons sunflower oil for brushing

Prepare the filling by combining the walnuts with the sugar, spice and lemon zest. Divide into 8 equal portions. For the glaze, blend the egg yolk with a few drops of water. Make a clear syrup by bringing the sugar, lemon juice and 150 ml water slowly to the boil, then simmer for 2–3 minutes. Pour into a wide, shallow glass or enamel container and leave to stand until just tepid.

Brush two pastry squares with oil and lay them, oiled side up, one on top of the other. Place a portion of the filling on one quarter of the square. Fold the four corners to meet in the centre, one of the corners covering the filling completely. Brush the top with oil. Fold in half to form a triangle and brush again. Halve again to make a smaller triangle. Brush a third time. Repeat with the rest of the squares.

Arrange the turnovers on a well-greased baking sheet. Paint their tops with egg yolk glaze. Bake in a preheated oven at 150°C/300°F/gas 2 for 16–17 minutes until golden brown. Place them while still warm in the syrup, basting them to make them shiny. Leave to stand in a cool place for a few hours—but do not refrigerate. In the syrup, they will keep for 3-4 days in a cool larder.

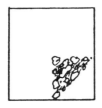 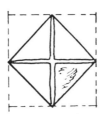 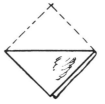 

the finished trigona

## SEMOLINA CAKE STEEPED IN SYRUP

*Revani* (Albanian); *rahvanija* (Bosnian); *revane* (Bulgarian); *revaní* (Greek); *ravanija* (Macedonian); from the Turkish *revani*

This is a celebrated Turkish dish which is, broadly speaking, little more than a cake or fatless sponge cake soaked, like a savarin, in syrup. Over the years, Balkan domestic cooks have happily adapted the original to suit their own tastes, adding coffee, wine or aniseed-flavoured spirits to the syrup, reducing the quantity of sugar; or even eliminating the sugar syrup altogether—replacing it with diluted honey or unsweetened milk. Ground walnuts, or walnuts and chocolate, are often included in the cake mixture, particularly in the fatless version. The Bosnian 'Sweetheart' cake which follows is just one example of the breed.

## BOSNIAN SWEETHEART CAKE
Serves 9

*Bosanski sevdidžan* (Bosnian, meaning sweetheart, love of my soul, from the Turkish *sevda*, love, and *can*, soul, life)

85 g sugar • 1 tablespoon lemon juice • 1/2 teaspoon vanilla flavouring
*Cake*
100 g unsalted butter, softened • 75 g castor sugar • finely grated zest of 1 lemon
2 medium eggs • 75 g fine semolina • 75 g plain white flour •
2 teaspoons baking powder • 4 tablespoons milk or 5 tablespoons single cream

Bring the sugar, 200 ml water and the lemon juice to the boil over a low heat, then boil for half a minute. Leave it to cool then add the vanilla.

Beat the softened butter until light and pale, add the sugar and lemon zest and continue beating until the mixture is even lighter and almost white. Add the eggs, one at a time, beating well after each addition. Fold in the semolina and the flour (previously sieved with the baking powder) alternately with the milk or cream to make a rather stiff batter which just drops from a spoon. Turn into a buttered and floured 18 cm square cake tin, smooth the top and bake in the middle of a preheated oven at 180°C/350°F/gas 4 for 55 minutes until browned.

Remove from the oven and pour the cold syrup over the hot cake. Return to the oven, the heat switched off, and leave for at least 1 hour until cold, to allow the semolina grains to swell. Serve on its own, or with whipped cream and candied fruits.

# CAKE SOAKED IN FRAGRANT MILK
Serves 12

*Revani me qumësht* (Albanian); *mlechno revane* (Bulgarian); *ravanija so mleko* (Macedonian); all meaning *revani* with milk

800 ml milk • 5 cm piece vanilla pod, split, or 1/2 teaspoon pure vanilla extract •
4 eggs • 200 g castor sugar • 250 g strong white flour •
1 teaspoon baking powder • whipped double cream

Heat the milk with the vanilla pod to boiling point. Cover and put aside to infuse until cold; remove the pod, refrigerate the milk. Alternatively, flavour the same amount of cold milk with the vanilla extract, cover and refrigerate.

Beat the eggs, tip in the sugar and beat until pale, thick and frothy. Using a metal spoon, fold in the flour (sieved previously with the baking powder) as lightly—but thoroughly—as possible. Turn into a greased and floured roasting pan, preferably of stainless steel, measuring 28 x 20 cm. Level off, and bake in a preheated oven at 180°C/350°F/gas 4 for 35–40 minutes, or until the cake is golden brown. Remove from the oven, and immediately pour over the chilled, flavoured milk—you will hear a hissing sound as the cold milk makes contact with the hot pan. Cool, then slice into 12 rectangles. Serve plain, or decorate each portion with whipped cream.

# KADAIF
Serves 12–16

*Kadaif* (Albanian, Bosnian, Bulgarian, Macedonian, Serbo-Croat); *kandaífi* or *kataífi* (Greek); *cadaif* (Romanian); from the Turkish *kadayıf*, from the Arabic

The dough for this extraordinary confection could be termed 'spun' because it is drawn into long threads as thin as button cotton. Its full Turkish name, *tel kadayıf* (*tel* meaning wire, thread, or single hair) is used to differentiate it from *ekmek kadayıf*, which is a fairly large, disc-shaped kind of rusk, and from *yassı kadayıf*, which is similar to *ekmek kadayıf* but smaller.

In the Balkans, *tel kadayıf* has been prepared in small workshops and at home by pouring a flour and water paste through a special saucepan with a few holes (each hole being approximately 2 mm in diameter) in the base on to a shallow, circular, tinned copper tray lightly coated with beeswax or butter, set well above glowing charcoal. The threads of dough were allowed to dry, rather than cook, on the tray before they were put away. Nowadays, however, spun dough is an industrial product. It can be bought from Greek or Turkish shops in London, for instance in Goodge Street or Green Lanes.

The confection itself is usually baked (with or without a filling) on a large circular tray. Small oblong rolls of *kadaif* filled with nuts are the sort mostly served in restaurants and pastry-shops in the Balkans.

> 400 g *kadaif* dough • 175 g butter, melted and cooled until just warm • 600 g sugar •
> 1/2 tablespoon lemon juice • 1 vanilla pod, split in half lengthways •
> almond flavouring or real almond extract (if using almonds) •
> 200 g coarsely ground walnuts, green pistachios or blanched almonds
> lightly toasted under the grill or in the oven •
> 500 ml double cream, stiffly whipped

Have ready two ungreased baking pans, each measuring 27 cm in diameter, preferably of stainless steel, ovenproof glass or enamelled iron.

Divide the *kadaif* dough equally between the pans and pour on equal quantities of the warm butter. Using a couple of forks, toss the *kadaif* as if it were a salad, until each strand glistens with fat. Put the pans in a preheated oven at 200°C/400°F/gas 6 and immediately reduce the setting to 160°C/325°F/gas 3. Bake for 30-40 minutes, or until the dough turns a delicate shade of beige on top. Allow to cool, uncovered.

Meanwhile, make the syrup: pour 600 ml water in a pan with the sugar, add the lemon juice and the vanilla pod and bring slowly to the boil. Cook over a moderate heat for 4–5 minutes, then leave to cool until lukewarm. Remove the vanilla pod, add the almond flavouring or extract and pour the syrup immediately over the *kadaif* in the pans. Leave in a cool place until you are ready to serve.

To assemble, sprinkle the nuts over the *kadaif* in one of the pans and toss them lightly into the top layer. Spoon half the whipped cream over the walnuts. Using two forks, put the contents of the second pan over the cream gingerly and delicately, so as to attain height and airiness. Top with the remaining cream. Cut into squares before serving.

# CHOUX FRITTERS WITH A LIGHT SYRUP
Makes 13–15

*Tullumba* (Albanian); *tulumbe* (Bosnian, Serbian); *touloumbi* (Bulgarian); *tulumbi* (Macedonian); from the Turkish *tulumba tatlısı*, 'pump sweet', on account of the dough being pumped or forced through a pastry syringe.

These fritters, piped through a star-shaped or serrated nozzle into plump, finger-length cylinders, look rather like the ridged stalk of a pumpkin—hence their alternative Bulgarian name: *tikveni druzhki*, pumpkin stalks. They may be found in most Balkan pâtisseries, where they are served accompanied by a glass of water.

*Choux pastry*
40 g butter, cut into pieces • 65 g strong white flour, sieved •
2 medium-sized eggs •
1/2 teaspoon vanilla flavouring

*Syrup*
100 g sugar • a few drops lemon juice •
vanilla flavouring or rum

Bring the butter and 100 ml water slowly to the boil. Draw aside. Immediately, tip in all the flour and beat rapidly with a wooden spoon until the mixture comes away from the sides of the pan. Allow to cool. Then beat in the eggs one at a time, together with the vanilla. Do not overbeat.

Dissolve the sugar in 100 ml water and add the lemon juice before simmering for 1 minute to make a light syrup. Cool to room temperature, then add the vanilla or rum.

Pipe the choux paste in small batches, in strips about the length of your finger, directly into a deep pan of cold oil, cutting off each length with a knife dipped in the oil. Use a 2 cm star-shaped or serrated nozzle—the latter is preferable since it will give deeper ridges. Put the pan on the heat, and gradually increase the temperature of the oil to medium high.

When the fritters have risen and are crisp and golden on all sides (this should take 8–10 minutes), drain them then drop them into the cold syrup. Turn the fritters over several times to absorb the syrup, then lift them out. Repeat with the remainder of the paste, always starting the frying with cooled oil. Serve at room temperature with a glass of water.

## SYRUPED BISCUITS

*Tatlije* (Bosnian, Serbian), *tatlii* (Macedonian), from the Turkish *tatlı*, meaning confection, sweet

In Bosnia-Hercegovina, Serbia and Macedonia, this is the generic name for a fairly large, round biscuit made of rich butter (or butter and lard) dough that does not spread during baking. Some are plain, others moulded around a walnut filling, but all are bathed in scented syrup once they are baked. In Bosnia they are sometimes called *smokvice* or figs, each having a tiny pastry stalk pushed into the centre to simulate a dried fig. Another name is *hurmašice* or dates (from the Turkish *hurma*, originally from the Persian), when they are given an oval shape.

The Serbs make a different kind, the so called *Carigradske tatlije*, literally 'King's Town sweets'—King's Town being the old Balkan name for Istanbul. The main ingredient of these is semolina cooked in milk and sugar until thick and used in place of flour. The sweets are rather like the famous Turkish *Kadıngöbeği*, or Turkish lady's navel: plump, round biscuits with a small dimple in the centre.

# ALBANIAN WALNUT BISCUITS
Makes 10 biscuits

*Sheqerpare* (Albanian, meaning syruped biscuits with walnuts), from the Turkish *şekerpare*, literally 'sugar pieces'

50 g unsalted butter • 1/2 small egg • 1 tablespoon icing sugar • pinch of salt •
100 g plain white flour • 25 g coarsely chopped walnuts •
1/2 teaspoon ground cinnamon • 100 g sugar •
1 tablespoon orange-flower water or a few drops of vanilla flavouring

Cream the butter, egg, icing sugar and salt together and stir in the flour. Knead to a stiff, smooth dough which leaves the bowl clean. Divide into 10 pieces; shape each one into a small ball, then flatten to a thin round. Mix the walnuts with the cinnamon and put a little of the mixture into the centre of each round. Bring two sides over to form a seam across the filling and pinch together, then roll into an oval shape—rather like a chunky sausage.

Arrange on a lightly greased baking tray. Bake in a preheated oven at 150°C/ 300°F/gas 2 for 20 minutes until they just start to colour. Cool on a wire rack.

To make the syrup, dissolve the sugar in 75 ml water over a low heat, then boil rapidly for 1 minute. Cool until tepid, add the orange-flower water or vanilla flavouring.

Soak the biscuits in the syrup for 1 hour, turning them from time to time. Place them on a serving dish and discard or store the syrup which remains.

## HALVA

*Hallvë* (Albanian); *halva* (Bosnian, Bulgarian, Romanian); *halvás* (Greek); *alva* (Macedonian; Serbo-Croat); from the Turkish *helva*, from the Arabic

Halva is the name of both the household sweetmeat and the commercial sugar confection common to all countries in the Balkans. When made at home, halva can be based on wheat flour, cornmeal, cornflour, rice starch or ground rice, semolina, and even soya grits, with varying proportions of butter, sugar, milk or water. It is generally prepared by frying or roasting the meal, then adding the sugar in the form of a milk- or water-based syrup. The fried or roasted nuts are frequently incorporated after the cooking to keep them crisp. If it is cooked with more liquid than usual, halva moulds well while still hot. So it is often cast in sculptured wooden (nowadays plastic) moulds in lots of designs and shapes.

## HALVA MADE WITH FLOUR
### Serves 6

*Hallvë me miell* (Albanian); *halva s brašnom* (Bosnian); *halva s brashno* (Bulgarian); *alva so brashno* (Macedonian); *alva s brašnom* (Serbian); from the Turkish *un helvası* (flour halva), or *gaziler helvası* (halva of the Islamic warriors for the faith). *Halvás me anthóneron* (Greek), 'halva with rosewater', is also made with flour but is perfumed with rosewater, and contains pistachios or pine nuts instead of walnuts

This is the oldest of all types of home-made halva sweetmeats, and is brought out on many special occasions.

150 g flour, preferably unbleached, or 150 g roasted flour, pale coloured (p. 340) •
150 g slightly salted butter, cut into small pieces •
150 g granulated sugar • grated zest of 1 lemon •
75 g shelled walnuts, coarsely chopped • 400 ml milk • cinnamon

Put the flour into a large, thick-based frying pan and dry-fry it over a medium heat, stirring almost constantly, until it just starts to colour. If you are using pre-baked flour, stir it around until just heated through. Add the butter and allow to melt, then, using a wooden spatula, stir the butter and flour together for a few seconds until the mixture is crumbly and a rich golden-ochre. Remove the pan from the heat and stir in the sugar, walnuts, lemon zest and milk.

Bring the mixture to the boil over a low heat, stirring continuously—it will quickly thicken and leave the bottom of the pan. Cover, switch off the heat and leave to stand for a few minutes. Crumble the halva mixture with a fork and serve warm or at room temperature, sprinkled with cinnamon.

## SEMOLINA HALVA
Serves 4

*Hallvë me jermik* (Albanian); *irmek halva* (Bosnian); *gris halva* (Bulgarian); *halvás simigdalénios* (Greek); *griz alva* (Macedonian); *alva od griza* (Serbian); from the Turkish *irmik helvası*

Semolina halva was served to me in the nicest possible way in the Zafer Restaurant in Konya in Turkey—topped with a piece of honeycomb, and a big blob of cream.

50 g almonds, blanched, skinned and thoroughly dried •
75 g unsalted butter •
100 g semolina •
125 g sugar

Slice each almond lengthwise into 4–5 pieces, then cut these across into tiny dice so that, when fried, the almonds can brown at the same time as the semolina.

Heat the butter in a lidded, deep frying pan which can go into a warm oven and stir in the almonds and semolina. Cook over a very low heat, stirring from time to time, for about 25–30 minutes, until tinged a light golden brown.

Meanwhile combine the sugar with 150 ml water. Bring to the boil, stirring until the sugar has dissolved. Pour the hot syrup over the semolina mixture and immediately cover with the lid. Transfer to an oven heated to 100°C/200°F/gas Low and leave for about an hour to allow the semolina grains to swell; then crumble the halva mixture lightly with a fork and serve cold, or hot on heated dessert plates.

# SOUL FOOD
Serves 4–5

*Džanećija* (Bosnian, Hercegovinian)

The name of this ancient sweet is derived from the Turkish *can*, a word of Arabic provenance meaning soul. In Bosnia-Hercegovina *džanećija* has come to mean heavenly sweet, a dish for the soul. But perhaps even more interesting than the name is the method of caramelizing sugar in butter—a little known technique which binds together the flavours of each ingredient.

100 g rice flour (or very finely ground rice) • 50 g slightly salted butter •
75 g sugar • 25 g ground walnuts •
4–5 teaspoons icing sugar, sieved •
1/2 teaspoon ground cinnamon •
grated zest of 1 lemon •
125 ml chilled double cream and 2 tablespoons icing sugar for topping

In a small bowl, blend the rice flour to a thin paste with 50 ml water, and set aside. Melt the butter in a heavy-based saucepan over moderate heat. Add the sugar and cook, stirring constantly with a wooden spatula, for 4–5 minutes, until the butter separates and the sugar turns a rich golden-brown caramel. Off the heat, add 450 ml water. Return the pan to the stove and heat the mixture for a few moments to dissolve the caramel (which hardens in contact with the cold water). Then stir up the rice flour paste and pour it into the caramel sauce, stirring as you do so. Cook over a low heat for 10–15 minutes, or until the mixture turns into a thick, smooth mass which comes away from the bottom of the pan when stirred. Remove from the heat and allow to cool a little. Rinse 4–5 small glass bowls with warm water and divide the sweet equally among the bowls.

Mix the walnuts, icing sugar, cinnamon and lemon zest together and scatter over each bowl of soul food. Shortly before serving, whip the cream and 2 tablespoons icing sugar until stiff and decorate.

# CHAPTER XXI

# Preserves

Preserving fruit, meat, fish and vegetables is an important industry in the Balkans. Yet, despite year-round availability in jars and tins, vast quantities of food for winter storage are still prepared in the majority of Balkan households by long-established, traditional methods. Preservation of fresh produce traces its origins to times when herbs, wild fruits and vegetables were dried during the summer months for use in the lean seasons. Around the fourth century BC, Thracian tribes were certainly pickling vine shoots in brine, as well as salting and smoking beef and mutton for their own consumption and for export. The preserves that I describe follow recipes that have been proved over generations. For the most part they are, for me, better than the manufactured alternatives.

## SAUERKRAUT

*Lakërarme* or *arme* (Albanian); *kiseli kupus* (Bosnian, Croat); *kiselo zele* (Bulgarian); *láhanon toursí* (Greek); *kisela zelka* (Macedonian); *varză acră* (Romanian); *kiseo kupus* (Serbian); *kislo zelje* (Slovenian); all meaning sour cabbage. *Lakër turshi* (Albanian), from the Turkish *lahana turşusu*, means pickled cabbage

Sauerkraut is cabbage that has been subjected to spontaneous lactic-acid fermentation. Enzymes in bacteria found on most vegetables convert lactose (milk sugar—contained in the juice of white cabbage) into lactic acid—a natural preservative.

Sauerkraut has a long history in the Balkans. The Thracians (who had extensive vineyards) prepared a forerunner of sauerkraut by putting young vine shoots in a jar over a layer of barley, covering them with a cloth bag containing wood ashes, filling the jar with brine and leaving it to ferment spontaneously. Later on 'soured cabbage' is mentioned in medieval Bulgarian monastery records. Today sauerkraut is part of the staple winter diet, and one of the chief sources of vitamin C. Although often made at home, whole heads of sauerkraut are also sold from the barrel at the greengrocer's shop.

## WHOLE-LEAF SAUERKRAUT
Makes 1 barrel

The commonest method of preparation is to ferment whole cabbages in brine in wooden barrels. This is customarily done at the beginning of winter—the cool temperatures induce a slow lactic-acid fermentation resulting in firm, crisp sauerkraut to stay in good condition till early spring. The best cabbage is the winter white because it is higher in sugar. It must be freshly picked; cabbage with yellowish, soft leaves, which has been stored for a long time, is unsuitable. Each region, even each household, has its own additions to the basic recipe. Sliced quinces give cabbage and liquor an amber colour; a few pieces of beetroot or red cabbage lend a delicate shade of pink. Horseradish adds flavour and acts as a natural preservative. A handful or two of cracked dried grains of maize turns the liquor into a pleasant bubbly drink—a great cure for hangovers.

This recipe is for serious sauerkraut makers. Before embarking on it, perhaps the novice should experiment with smaller quantities such as those in the recipe for shredded sauerkraut below.

> 100 kg freshly picked, firm, white cabbage, each weighing between 1 and 2 kg (or enough cabbage to fill just over three-quarters of your barrel) •
> salt, any kind, provided it contains no additives that might affect fermentation •
> 500 g of either horseradish, quince or beetroot pieces, cracked dried maize grains, a string of hot chilli peppers or a combination of any of these additions

You will need an oak or beech barrel, with a tap, that holds approximately 200 litres. It should be scrubbed meticulously clean, then rinsed and scalded with boiling water. You will also need a double square of scalded muslin to fit inside the barrel's rim, 2 boiled laths or 1 scrubbed and scalded oak or beech board cut to fit snugly inside the rim, and a heavy non-porous stone, sterilized in boiling water for 15 minutes. In a place with a constant winter temperature, such as a cellar, raise the barrel from the ground to make space underneath the tap to draw off the liquid.

Trim the stalks flush to the base and remove any damaged outer leaves. Use a small paring knife to make a cross cut about 4–5 cm deep through the centre of the core to allow the brine to penetrate.

Pack the cabbage compactly into the barrel, cores facing upwards, filling any gaps with cabbage halves or quarters. Between each layer, distribute some of the flavourings or colourings listed above. Fill the barrel just over three-quarters.

Prepare a brine by boiling water with 5 per cent salt; filter or strain the solution through a cloth (especially if your water is hard) and allow to cool until tepid. Cover the cabbage with the brine and then with the muslin. Criss-cross the laths (or lay the board) on the muslin. Fold the muslin's corners over the wood and weigh it down with the stone to keep the cabbage immersed. Pour more brine into the barrel to cover this moveable top and the stone, then put on the barrel's own lid and throw over a clean cloth to exclude any dust. Leave to ferment.

After a week (or when bubbles appear), remove the stone, board and muslin and scald them with boiling water. Drain off the brine into a clean container and pour it back over the cabbage. Replace the muslin, board and stone. This is done 2–3 times a week during the first few weeks of fermentation, later once a week, until the cabbage liquor clears and the cabbage turns sour. If any scum should appear, skim it from the top of the brine, wipe any scum off the inside of the rim with a clean cloth and top up with extra brine made with 2 per cent salt to maintain the original level.

The sauerkraut is ready to eat when fermentation has ceased (bubbles have stopped rising) and both cabbage and its liquor are pleasantly sour to the taste. Whenever sauerkraut is taken from the barrel, the muslin, board and stone should be washed in hot water and replaced.

## SHREDDED SAUERKRAUT

Makes 1 x 3.25 litre jar

This is made in smaller quantities in large glass jars. It can be plain, or flavoured with sliced lemons or apples, peppercorns, bay, juniper, caraway, or dill.

3 kg freshly picked, tight, white cabbage • 75 g rock or sea salt (with no additives)

You will need a preserving jar that holds 3.25 litres, or indeed any other kind of jar provided it has a plastic-lined, acid-resistant lid. In addition, equip yourself with two well scrubbed beech laths (or any other untreated hardwood laths) just large enough to fit inside the neck of the jar and a pebble or river stone about the size of an apple, sterilized in boiling water for 15 minutes.

Remove the central core from the cabbage and trim off any damaged outer leaves. Wash the cabbage well, reserve one or two whole leaves, then shred the remainder finely. Place on a large tray, sprinkle with the salt and mix thoroughly. Leave to stand for 30–40 minutes.

Pack the cabbage firmly into the jar, pressing each layer down well with a wooden mallet until juice appears on the surface. Fill the jar to the neck, then fit the reserved whole leaves on top and criss cross the beach laths over them to prevent any loose cabbage shreds from rising to the surface of the brine that will form from the salt and juices. Lay the stone on the laths to hold them down. Put the lid on and leave at warm room temperature of 20°–23°C (68°–73°F) for 10 days. If any scum should rise, spoon it off. After this, move the jar to a cool and dry place where the temperature is 10°–12°C (50°–54°F). The fermentation should be complete within the next 10–15 days.

Store the sauerkraut, covered with the lid, in a cold shed or cellar where the temperature is 4°–6°C (39°–42°F), or refrigerate. If you prepare it in the late autumn, it will keep until the end of January.

## PICKLED CORNELIAN CHERRIES
Makes 4 x 750 ml jars

*Drenki nalozheni v otset* (Bulgarian), *Drenjina u sirćetu* (Serbo-Croat)

These are served as an accompaniment, usually to pork and game dishes.

2 kg ripe cornelian cherries (p. 46), unstoned •
4 tablespoons salt • 4 tablespoons sugar •
100 ml cider vinegar •
2 large pears, peeled, cored and quartered

Wash the cherries and distribute them equally among 4 x 750 ml preserving jars. Add to each jar a tablespoon of salt, a tablespoon of sugar, 25 ml vinegar and 2 pear slices, top up with cold water and screw on the caps. Shake the jars a few times to help dissolve the salt and sugar, then store in a cool dark place. After 30 days they will be ready to eat.

# PICKLED GRAPES

*Grozdenitsa* (Bulgarian); *üzüm turşusu* (Turkish)

At vintage time in September, grapes are often preserved by natural fermentation in condensed grape juice. The addition of mustard slows down and weakens the fermentation process so that it does not turn into wine.

white dessert grapes in bunches with loosely-packed firm berries, washed in water acidulated with vinegar, then rinsed, drained and left to dry • white grape juice • calcium carbonate (if using freshly-squeezed juice) • black mustard seeds (*Sinapis nigra*), coarsely crushed

This is an approximate recipe. It will all depend on how many grapes you are going to pickle, and how large a container you use. Choose a glass jar or earthenware crock large enough to accommodate the grape bunches comfortably. The first thing to do is to calculate how much liquid you are going to need. The simplest way is to put the grapes in the crock, then pour grape juice over them to fill the crock completely. Drain this off into a saucepan and add to it an equal quantity of fresh juice so that you are now dealing with double the original amount. This needs to be reduced and condensed by boiling. Firstly, add the calcium carbonate to freshly squeezed juice at a rate of 5 g to each litre of juice. (Shop-bought grape juice needs no calcium carbonate since it has already been clarified and deacidified). Boil the mixture for 5 minutes, then strain it through muslin. Return the juice to the heat and reduce it by rapid boiling by almost half. Leave to cool.

Provide yourself with two flat muslin bags—each roughly the same diameter as the crock or jar—and fill them with crushed mustard seeds. Arrange the grape bunches in the container in layers, placing one of the muslin bags between the layers, the other on top of the grapes. Pour the condensed grape juice over to cover. Place a scrubbed board on top to keep the fruit and mustard submerged. Cover the container with cloth or greaseproof paper and tie with string. ·

Store the grapes for 35–40 days; they are ready to eat when the juice has become pleasantly sharp and tart. This pickle will keep until the next grape harvest.

## MIXED PICKLE
Makes one 3-litre jar

*Turshi e përzjerë* (Albanian, 'mixed pickle'); *šarena turšija* (Bosnian), *sharena tourshiya* (Bulgarian), *sharena turshija* (Macedonian), literally 'many-coloured pickle', from the Turkish *karısık turşu*, 'mixed pickle'

There are many pickles based on all sorts of individual vegetables such as peppers, chilli peppers, pickling onions, or green-garlic heads, but this recipe is for a mixture, which is the most widely enjoyed.

500 g peeled carrots, sliced into rounds •
300 g cauliflower florets • 250 g tiny courgettes, topped and tailed •
200 g green tomatoes which have just begun to change colour and are near yellow •
250 g small stuffing peppers or thin long salad peppers, the stalk-end sliced off, deseeded •
25 g piece of celariac, chopped • 25 g horseradish, thinly sliced •
25 g garlic cloves, peeled and halved • 50 g celeriac tops or celery leaves •
25 allspice berries • 1 tablespoon black peppercorns •
10 bay leaves • 2 teaspoons dill seeds •
75 g salt • 100 ml wine vinegar

Choose a large glass jar which holds about 3 litres and sterilize with boiling water. Fill the jar with the vegetables, distributing the celeriac, horseradish and other flavourings evenly amongst them. Leave a 1 cm space between the vegetables and the neck of the jar. Place a boiled wooden board that fits inside the neck of the jar and weigh it down with a pebble about the size of an apple (also boiled for a few minutes) to keep everything immersed.

Make the liquor by boiling the salt and vinegar with 1.5 litres of water for 2–3 minutes. Leave to stand for 10 minutes, then pour it over the vegetables. Ensure that the liquid comes just above the weighted board; add more hot water if necessary. Cover with a loosened lid and keep for a week in a warm kitchen until the juice has cleared. Tighten the lid and store in a cool, dark place. The pickle will be ready to eat in 2–3 weeks.

# GRAPE JUICE AND WALNUT SAUSAGE
Makes 1 sausage

*Suxhuk* (Albanian), *balsoudzhouk* (Bulgarian), *soutzoúki* (Greek), *sudžuk* (Serbo-Croat), from the Turkish *sucuk*, sausage, and *balsucuğu*, honey sausage

At vintage time, every household with a dessert vineyard and a walnut tree converts the autumn surplus into preserves and sweets, among them this unique and sugarless 'sausage'. The base is sweet grape must. The clear juice is poured off the sediment, then deacidified with calcium carbonate (100 g per 20 litres of juice). Once strained, it is boiled to concentrate the natural grape sugars. *Soutzoúki* is made commercially in Greece, but sometimes they use sugar syrup instead of grape must. This is never so nutritious or flavoursome as one that has been properly made at home.

In Albania, Serbia and Croatia this is rarely, if ever, sausage shaped. The cooked mass is mixed with walnuts, poured into a large pan and cut into squares when cold.

2 litres clear grape juice •
250 g cornflour and a little extra for coating •
200 g freshly-shelled walnut halves

Slake the cornflour with a little of the grape juice. Pour the remaining juice into a saucepan and boil it over a medium heat to reduce by half. While the juice is bubbling, thread a needle with a strong button thread, tying a cocktail stick at the knot end. Thread the walnut halves, one by one, through the centre. Tie another cocktail stick over the last walnut to hold the string together, then loop the end of the remaining thread.

Dilute the cornflour mixture with a few spoonfuls of the boiling juice, then pour the mixture back into the pan. Cook for a minute or two over a very low heat, stirring continuously with a wooden spatula, until a thick, viscous paste. Remove the pan from the heat and immerse the string of walnuts in the hot paste, holding it by the looped end. Lift the walnuts out and hang them to dry in a warm place or in the sun. When the coating is no longer sticky, dip the walnuts again into the boiling paste, then let them dry once more. Repeat this procedure as many times as you wish, or until the sausage is 3–3.5 cm in diameter. The thicker the sausage, the tastier it is. After the final coating, leave to dry completely, then roll it in cornflour. Wrap it closely in greaseproof paper and hang it in a dry airy place; it will keep for several months.

## SPOONSWEETS

On the day of the saint after whom a person is named, a constant stream of people—relatives, friends, casual acquaintances and even complete strangers—flows in and out of the house of the person whose name-day is celebrated. They come to offer their good wishes, bringing as a present an apple, or orange or lemon if they are in season. The visitors are welcomed warmly and served *sladko* [spoonsweet] in small glasses or crystal saucers, a glass of plum brandy and Turkish coffee.

Kouzman A. Shapkarev, 1891

Come summer, all kinds of fruit, flowers and vegetables are preserved in syrup—to be offered to visitors as spoonsweets, with a glass of water, coffee and perhaps, liqueur or brandy. Spoonsweets are also used in the kitchen in cakes and pastries—instead of candied fruit; and at the table as an instant topping for creams, ice cream and blancmanges. Here are a few of the most popular, tried and tested by generations of cooks, all passed down by the women of my family.

*Threaded orange rinds.*

# ORANGE RINDS PRESERVED IN SYRUP
### Makes about 2 x 500 g jars

*Gliko me lëkurë portokalli* (Albanian), from the Greek *glykó portokáli*; *sladko ot portokalovi kori* (Bulgarian), *slatko so kora od portokali* (Macedonian), *sladko od pomorandžinih kora* (Serbo-Croat), *portakal kabuğu reçeli* (Turkish), all meaning sweet of orange rind

1 kg or 5 medium thin-skinned oranges •
750 g sugar •
juice of 1 lemon, strained •
3–4 tablespoons Cointreau, plus a little extra for dipping

Grate a little of the zest off the oranges to remove some of its bitterness and any chemical sprays or wax coating. Score the rind of each fruit with a knife into 8 segments, then carefully peel them off. Reserve the flesh for another recipe.

Make two necklaces as illustrated opposite. Roll the segments tightly and use a large needle to thread them, one by one, on to a piece of thick white cotton (not synthetic thread). Pack them close to prevent unrolling and tie the ends of the thread to make a necklace once you have strung half the segments. Repeat with the remaining peel. Put the necklaces into a large pan, cover with at least 2 litres of water and simmer for about 1 hour with the lid on, until the rinds are soft but not disintegrating. Drain well and discard the liquid.

To cook the preserve, make a syrup by putting the sugar, lemon juice and 375 ml water into a preserving pan. Heat gently, stirring, until the sugar dissolves. Drop in the necklaces and bring to the boil. Cook over a fairly high heat, without stirring, for about 25 minutes to 114°C/238°F on a sugar thermometer. At this temperature drops of the hot syrup hold their shape softly in a glass of cold water but dissolve when given a few stirs, and the cooled syrup is as thick as honey. Remove from the heat, cool, cover and leave to stand for at least 24 hours.

The next day, warm 2 x 500 g screw-top jam jars and their lids in an oven at 100°C/200°F/gas Low until needed. Re-boil the preserve to 114°C/238°F, allow to cool for 30 minutes, then carefully pull out the cotton threads. Stir in the Cointreau. Ladle the orange rolls into the jars and pour in the syrup up to the rims. When completely cold, cover with waxed paper discs which have been dipped in a little Cointreau, then screw on the lids. Store in a dry, dark place. Let stand at least a week before using. These are eaten singly, in a glass or crystal saucer, with a little of the syrup.

## GREEN-WALNUT PRESERVE
Makes about 2 x 500 g jars

*Gliko me arra të papjekura* (Albanian, meaning spoonsweet with unripened walnuts from the Greek *glykó*, fruits or vegetables preserved in syrup); *sladko ot orehcheta* (Bulgarian) and *slatko od oraščića* (Serbo-Croat)—both meaning spoonsweet of small, i.e. young, walnuts; *karydáki frésko glykó* (Greek, 'spoonsweet with fresh walnuts'), *slatko od zeleni orevi* (Macedonian, meaning spoonsweet of green walnuts)

A spectacular preserve of glistening, whole, jet-black walnuts soaked in syrup. Green walnuts for preserving are gathered when they are fully grown but not quite ripe: about the end of May in the Balkans, and early July in the southern half of England. At this stage, a walnut looks like a large green plum, and the shell under its fleshy outer casing is still soft enough to be pierced with a needle.

Wear rubber gloves to avoid getting long-lasting stains on the fingers.

250 g, or about 45–50 unripe walnuts • 500 g sugar •
rind of 1 thin-skinned orange, quartered, cut into strips about 4 cm long and 3–4 mm wide; or 45–50 thick slivers of blanched almonds, 3–4 mm wide •
juice of 1/2 lemon

Peel the walnuts thinly, prick all over with a large needle, then slice a little piece from the tops and bottoms. Use a skewer to make a hole approximately 3–4 mm wide right through each nut: it will later house a strip of rind or a sliver of almond.

To remove the bitterness, soak in cold water for a whole week, changing the water every 12 hours until it remains clear. Then, starting with fresh water, simmer the walnuts in 2 changes of water, until soft. An alternative method is to cover the walnuts with cold water, bring slowly to the boil and cook for a minute or two. Drain, and repeat the process seven times, or until the water remains clear and the fruits are tender. Drain well, then insert an almond sliver or a strip of rind into each walnut so that the rind sticks out at both ends.

Make a syrup by dissolving the sugar in 250 ml water over a low heat and bringing to the boil. Add the drained, stuffed walnuts and simmer until the syrup thickens slightly. Cover the pan with a wet cloth and leave to stand overnight.

Next day, add the lemon juice and cook over a higher heat until the syrup thickens or reaches 113°C (235°F) on a sugar thermometer. Cover as before and leave again until the following day.

On the third day, sterilize the jars and their lids in a slow oven. Reheat the walnuts and pour into the hot jars until they are full to the brim. When cold, screw on the lids and store in a dark dry place.

*Green walnuts*

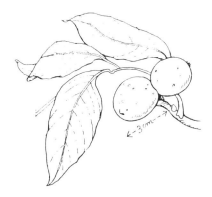

# MORELLO CHERRIES PRESERVED IN SYRUP
Makes about 1.5 kg

*Gliko me vishnja* (Albanian, from the Greek *glykó*); *recelj od višanja* (Bosnian, from the Turkish *reçel*); *sladko ot vishni* (Bulgarian), *výssino glykó* (Greek), *slatko od višanja* (Serbo-Croat), *vişne reçeli* (Turkish), from the Old Slavonic *viš'nja*, morello cherry

As well as a spoonsweet, this makes a lovely sherbet mixed with ice cubes and water, or stir it into low-fat plain yoghurt for a dessert. Although morello cherries have sufficient organic acid of their own (1.5–1.8 per cent), adding lemon juice or half a teaspoon of citric acid ensures the preserve will not crystallize, even when stored over a long period (up to two years).

For best results, stone and cook the fruit as soon as possible after picking.

500 g fully ripe, dark red, stoned morello cherries
(stoned weight, including any juice released during stoning) •
1 kg sugar • juice of 1/2 lemon

Put the sugar, 250 ml water and the juice released by the fruit during stoning into the preserving pan. Heat gently until the sugar has dissolved. Increase the heat, and when the syrup comes to the boil, add the cherries and cook for about 20 minutes, skimming as necessary.

Leave overnight in the syrup. Next day, add the lemon juice and boil until the syrup thickens and reaches 112°C/234°F on a sugar thermometer. Alternatively, test a little on a cold saucer; if the drops do not spread, the preserve is ready. Ladle into hot jars. Seal when cold.

## ROSE PETAL PRESERVE
Makes about 800 g

*Gliko me trëndafila* (Albanian, from the Greek *glykó* and *triantáfyllo*, rose); *djulbešećer* (Bosnian, from the Turkish *gülbeşeker*, conserve of roses); *sladko ot rozi* (Bulgarian); *triantáfyllo glykó* (Greek); *slatko od ruža* (Macedonian, Serbo-Croat); *dulceață de trandafir* (Romanian, from the Greek *triantáfyllo*, rose); *gül reçeli* (Turkish)

An all-Balkan favourite—as far north as Wallachia in Romania. It has mildly laxative properties, so is used sparingly, whether as a spoonsweet or in cooking.

> Here are a few of the most suitable roses for preserving:
> *Rosa damascena* var *trigintipetala*. Damask rose: the red rose of south-eastern Europe and Turkey that provides attar of roses. The Damask rose is used in the majority of Balkan rose-petal preserves.
>
> *Rosa damascena oleifera* var *alba*. White damask rose, which yields an inferior essence for extraction. Used as surrounding hedges for the Damask rose fields in the Valley of Roses in Bulgaria. It makes a greyish-looking, though highly aromatic, rose-petal preserve.
>
> *Rosa gallica officinalis*. Red rose of Lancaster, apothecary's rose or rose of Provins. The preserved petals long retain their fragrance.
>
> *Rosa gallica officinalis* var *conditorum*. A deep magenta-crimson variety of the apothecary's rose, at one time used in Hungary for the manufacture of attar of roses and for preserving.
>
> *Rosa alba semiplena*. White rose of York. An ancient descendant of *Rosa gallica*, with intensely fragrant white blooms.

In Balkan regions where these specific roses are unavailable, some add rose water or a drop of attar of roses to preserves made with other garden varieties—so long as they have not been budded or grafted but grown on their own roots.

The preserve is considered properly prepared when the petals do not squeak under the tooth but, squeak or no squeak, it is lovely spread thinly on griddle cakes and scones.

This passage from the book *Zelenite Prishultsi* ('The Green Newcomers') by K. Starchev and T. Trifonov illustrates the importance to Turkey of the Bulgarian town of Kazanluk as a producer of attar of roses—the 'liquid gold'. It is said that it takes more than 100,000 roses to produce just 25 grams of attar.

> In May 1850, all the inhabitants of Kazanluk in the Valley of Roses, together with their children who were dressed in white and carrying bunches of roses, gathered on the main road to the east of the town to meet Sultan Abdul Medzhit. All the rose bushes edging the road were left unplucked to frame the Sultan's way with their blooms.
>
> When the Sultan appeared, the children surrounded the carriage on both sides, waving their roses, while the grown-ups poured rose-water on the road in front of the Sultan all the way to the outskirts of Kazanluk. In the town itself, they sprinkled attar of roses on the streets as they walked in front of the carriage, until the Sultan reached the *konak* [government house]. There, at the entrance of the building, one schoolboy greeted the Sultan with a solemn stanza recited in Turkish.
>
> Next day, the army physicians who accompanied the Sultan immunized the children and the welcoming crowd against small-pox. The Sultan himself gave each child four *besliks* [five-piastre silver coin].

100 g prepared scented petals, freshly picked from roses which have not been sprayed with insecticides, fungicides or other chemicals •
600 g castor, granulated or golden granulated sugar •
juice of 1 lemon, or 1 teaspoon citric acid dissolved in 1 tablespoon warm water

Snip or pinch off the white tougher base and any damaged part of the petals and tear them into pieces. Rinse under running cold water. Drain in a colander, squeezing out the excess water with your hands. Place the petals in a wide enamelled saucepan and add 300 ml water. Bring to boiling point, mashing the petals with a potato masher, then simmer over a low heat for 5–10 minutes, continuing to mash, until the petals are tender. Remove from the heat, add the sugar and stir carefully— without splashing the sides of the pan with with sugar—until the sugar is dissolved. Add the lemon juice or citric acid solution, bring back slowly to the boil, then boil rapidly for 5–10 minutes, without stirring or skimming, to 110°C/230°F, or until a little syrup dropped into a glass of cold water falls to the bottom without dispersing but dissolves at once when stirred. Remove from the heat and pot into hot jars. Close as usual when cold.

# ACACIA FLOWERS PRESERVED IN SYRUP

*Sladko ot byala akatsia—salkum* (Bulgarian, from the Turkish *salkım*); *dulceaţă de salkîm* (Romanian); *slatko od belog bagrema* (Serbo-Croat)

The white aromatic pea-flowers produced in long pendulous racemes on the false acacia or locust tree, *Robinia pseudoacacia*, are especially attractive to bees—and children—who like to suck the sweet nectar tucked away at the base of the blooms. The flowers are gathered in early summer, when not quite fully open, and prepared in the same way as rose petals in syrup.

# QUINCE JAM
Makes about 1.5 kg

*Recelj od dunja* (Bosnian, from the Turkish *reçel*), *kydóni glykó* (Greek), *slatko od dunja* (Macedonian), *ayva reçeli* (Turkish), all meaning quince preserve; *sladko ot sturgani dyuli* (Bulgarian), *slatko od struganih dunja* (Serbo-Croat), preserve of grated quinces

A very traditional, very easy jam.

1 kg large, very ripe quinces •
1 kg sugar •
1 teaspoon citric acid or juice or 1 lemon

Rub the quinces with a cloth to remove the down. Wash them well and wipe dry.

Bring the sugar, citric acid or lemon juice and 500 ml water to the boil over a gentle heat. Then raise the temperature and cook the mixture, without stirring, to 105°C/221°F, or until syrupy. Remove the pan from the heat.

The quinces may be thinly peeled or unpeeled. Cut them into julienne strips the size of matchsticks or pine needles, dropping the strips immediately into the hot syrup to avoid discoloration. An alternative method is to grate all of the quinces (except the cores) directly into the pan of syrup using a coarse grater. Return the pan to the heat and cook over the lowest possible heat (so that the jam will acquire a deep orangey-pink colour) to 105°C/221°F, or until a teaspoon of the syrup sets on a cold saucer.

Stir in the froth from the surface of the jam (this is almost pure pectin), ladle into hot jam jars, then cool and close up in the usual way.

## LEMONS PRESERVED IN SUGAR
Makes 2 kg uncooked preserve

*Zapazvane na limoni sus zahar* (Bulgarian), *čuvanje limuna u šećeru* (Serbo-Croat)

These are delicious in lemon tea. Diced small, they can be added to cake and pudding mixtures instead of crystallized fruits. A little of their syrup, mixed with ice and water, makes a cool, refreshing drink; and the flavour of many creams and jellies is greatly enhanced by a little of the syrup.

1 kg lemons • 1 kg castor sugar •
a few coriander seeds, or cloves and pieces of cinnamon

Wash the lemons in warm, soapy water, rinse them well and wipe dry. Lightly grate the zest and discard. Slice the lemons into rounds 5 mm thick. Remove the pips. Pack the fruit slices and sugar in alternate layers in small jam jars with screw-on caps. Start with the sugar and finish with a thick layer of sugar to come to the rim of the jars. Pack firmly, filling any gaps with spices of your choice and halved or quartered lemon slices to eliminate air pockets. Screw the lids on tightly and leave the jars in a cool, dark larder. During the first few days, shake the jars occasionally to help the sugar to dissolve. Let the lemons macerate in their own syrup for at least a month before use. They will keep for up to a year.

## PUMPKIN MARMALADE OR BUTTER
Yields just over 2 x 400 ml jars

*Marmalad ot tikva* (Bulgarian), *marmelada od tikve* (Serbian), from the Portuguese *marmelada*

During winter months this conserve is mixed with ground roast almonds or crushed walnuts, sprinkled with cinnamon and served as a dessert. It can also be used as a filling for small pastries like the amulets described on page 270.

1 kg canned pumpkin, or pumpkin pulp obtained by baking about 2.2 kg common pumpkin, *Cucurbita pepo*, or about 1.5 kg sweet pumpkin with a firm flesh such as *Cucurbita maxima* or *Cucurbita moschata* • 750 g granulated sugar

Scrape the flesh off the baked pumpkin (p. 289); discard the skin. Put the pulp in a fine colander set over a bowl, cover, and leave overnight to drain.

Next day, add the pulp to the sugar into a preserving pan and stir over a low heat until the sugar is dissolved. Cook over a fairly high heat, stirring with a wooden spatula all the time, until the mixture takes on a deep orange-brown tinge and the spatula leaves a clean path at the bottom of the pan—about 20 minutes. Fill hot jars to the very top with the hot conserve. Leave in a 100°C/200°F/gas Low oven for about 2 hours, or until a thin skin forms on the surface. Screw the lids on when completely cold. This will keep for a year in a dark, dry larder.

## PLUM MARMALADE OR BUTTER
Makes about 6 x 400 ml jars

*Marmelatë kumbullash* (Albanian); *marmalad ot slivi* (Bulgarian); *marmalad od slivi* (Macedonian), *marmaladă de prune* or *magiun* (Romanian); *marmelada od šljiva* (Serbo-Croat); *erik marmelatı* (Turkish); from the Portuguese *marmelada*, a quince preserve—from the *marmelo*, a quince

When Balkan varieties of the large deep-blue plums with richly sweet flesh are used, plum butter (or marmalade) can be made without any sugar at all—long, slow boiling concentrates the fruit's natural sugars to provide a sweet conserve with magnificent taste and flavour.

2 kg ripe, blue-skinned cooking plums or damsons, unstoned, stalks removed • granulated sugar

Place 6 x 400 g jam jars and their lids in an oven set at 100°C/200°F/gas Low until ready to fill.

Put the plums and 125 ml water in a preserving pan, cover, and simmer over a low heat until the fruit is practically disintegrating. Rub through a coarse plastic sieve. Discard the stones and skins. Weigh the pulp. Add an equal amount of sugar. Once you have completed this stage, you can leave the fruit until the next day if that helps your routine

Stir over a low heat until the sugar dissolves, then raise the heat and boil, without skimming but stirring almost constantly, until the mixture thickens and reaches 108°C/227°F. At this temperature, the paste will erupt and spit, and a blob will set on a chilled saucer and could be lifted off in one piece.

Ladle the hot conserve into heated jars. When cool, screw on the lids and label. This will keep for at least a year.

# CHAPTER XXII

# Non-alcoholic Drinks

> In the early years of the ninth century AD, Kroum, the legislator Khan, came to the throne. ... Under him, the first Bulgarian Code of Laws was established; it was based on custom. In the brief, probably legendary, data on it, which has come down to us, severe sanctions against stealing, slander and begging were provided, and even an order that all vines should be uprooted as a measure against drunkenness.
>
> N. Todorov, *A Short History of Bulgaria*, 1977.

Balkan people select their drinking water carefully, and value highest the pure mineral water freely available from communal spa-fountains found in town squares all across the Peninsula. In Sofia, lots of people fill bottles and demi-johns from the fountains in front of the central, Turkish-style, municipal baths—the water itself being jocularly known as 'pensioner's apéritif', since the task of fetching water for the family is most often down to grandfather.

Freshly-squeezed fruit juices, iced diluted yoghurt drinks, herbal and lemon China tea, *boza*, syrups of all kinds and the ubiquitous Schweppes and Cola are also enjoyed—particularly on a hot summer's day—as well as cups of strong black coffee sipped in outdoor cafés.

## TURKISH COFFEE
### To serve 1 person

*Kafe e zezë* (Albanian), *kafés maýros* (Greek), both meaning black coffee; *Bosanska turska kahva* (Bosnian, 'Bosnian Turkish coffee'); *Toursko kafe* (Bulgarian, 'Turkish coffee'); *Srpska kafa* (Serbian, 'Serbian coffee'); from the Turkish *kahve*, coffee, stemming from the Arabic

---

One of the pervading bits of folklore about coffee says that you will get as many kisses as there are bubbles on top of your cup. Another one deals with fortune-reading: for this, after you have drunk your coffee, you invert a saucer over the cup, swirl cup and saucer around together, then turn them over (still together) and leave to stand for a few minutes to allow the sediment to dry out and form pictures.

To make an authentic cup of Turkish coffee with a crown of froth, you will need an individual Turkish-coffee pot (pp. 41,42) holding approximately 75 ml liquid below the neck and a proper Turkish-coffee cup without a handle (pp. 34,35), of 85–90 ml capacity. You will also need freshly medium-roasted coffee beans—of any variety that you like, though I prefer the blend of Mocha and Mysore to the other kinds: it is strong, but never too harsh.

To make more coffee, use a larger pot (or several individual pots) and multiply the ingredients as necessary.

It seems that the majority of Turks prefer their coffee straight and bitter, with no sugar, so it is customary to serve coffee accompanied by something sweet—a biscuit, a piece of cake or Turkish delight, a tiny saucer with fruit preserved in syrup. Some Balkan people, such as the Serbs, also like to offer a small glass of plum brandy.

1 tablespoon (approx 5 g) medium-roast coffee, freshly ground as fine as talcum powder •
2 teaspoons castor sugar for a sweet coffee; or 1 teaspoon for a medium-sweet; or none at all—for strong coffee with some kick in it •
pinch of salt ( supposed to bring out the flavour)

Put the coffee, the sugar and salt, and 50 ml of good drinking water into an individual Turkish-coffee pot—the mixture should come just to the neck. Bring very slowly to the boil, stirring once. Now, if you are making the coffee in front of a guest, allow the coffee to froth up to the top and pour the froth into a small Turkish coffee-cup. Repeat the process once or twice, then pour the rest of the coffee into the cup, add a few drops of water or rosewater to settle the grounds and serve the coffee immediately while still very hot. Serving lukewarm coffee to a visitor causes real offence because it means that he or she is unwelcome.

If you are making coffee in the kitchen, when the coffee froths up to the top, remove from the heat and allow it to subside. Repeat this process once or twice. Then put the coffee pot on a tray accompanied by an empty cup and a glass of fruit juice or cold water and bring to the table. Pour out the coffee carefully so that the froth rises to the top of the cup, while a good deal of the sediment remains in the pot. The coffee is drunk hot, in small sips, avoiding any grounds which settle.

There are variations to the black coffee described here. It can be served with cream—called *kapuciner* in Serbo-Croat, from the Italian *capuccino*—if you float a layer of sweetened whipped cream on the top of the coffee; or half an egg yolk can be whipped up with a little icing sugar and rum and poured over the top in the same fashion as the cream; or you can make a pot of mocha coffee by using equal quantities of coffee and cocoa.

## Non-Alcoholic Drinks

One autumn in 1988, on our way to the Black Sea, my husband Tom and I stopped in Razgrad, the principle town of the Ludogorie district (previously Deliorman) in north-eastern Bulgaria. This region was, and to a certain extent still is, densely populated by Turks—descendants of the families who stayed behind in 1878 after the Ottomans withdrew to their present borders.

While sipping thimblefuls of thick, scalding black coffee in the town's square, we were joined by two middle-aged, stockily built Turks who, after asking permission to sit at our table, engaged us in lively conversation. In answer to my question as to how they prepared Turkish coffee, one of them replied in fluent Turkish which, in translation, sounded something like, 'Before making coffee, repeat to yourself the incantation, "Freshly roasted, freshly ground, freshly made but never boiled." '

I have followed this advice for making good coffee ever since.

*Pitchers for fetching water from the village well or fountain, or for storing water.*

*1. A 17th-century Turkish water-cooler,* su testi, *found in Hungary (National History Museum, Budapest). A water-cooler is an unglazed clay vessel filled with drinking water and hung up in the shade. Water seeps through the pores of the pot and evaporates, so keeping the liquid cool inside.*
*2. Contemporary village water carrier, known as* bardak *in Bosnia,* stomna *in Bulgaria, and* barde *in Macedonia. Glazed and decorated on the outside, it has a drinking nipple on the handle.*
*3. Unglazed water cooler of 1802, found in the attic of a church in the centre of Sofia. (National History Museum, Sofia.)*

## ICED COFFEE
### To serve 1 person

*Ajskafe* (Bulgarian), *Viner ajskafe* (Serbo-Croat, meaning Viennese iced coffee): from the German *Eiskaffee*

150 ml freshly-made strong black coffee
(or 1 teaspoon instant coffee dissolved in 150 ml hot water) •
1 tablespoon icing sugar • 1 tablespoon crushed ice •
2 large scoops (or 85–90 g) vanilla ice cream • 50 ml double cream •
1 teaspoon icing sugar

Dissolve the tablespoon of sugar in the hot coffee. Allow to cool, then refrigerate. In a tall glass of approximately 300 ml capacity, put the ice cream over the crushed ice and pour over the chilled coffee. Do not stir. Whip the cream (with or without the teaspoon of sugar) until it stands in soft peaks and float it on top of the coffee. Serve with 2 straws and a long spoon. Perfect, when lazing in a deck chair in the garden on a hot summer day.

## HOT COCOA DRINK
### To serve 1 person

*Goreshto kakao s voda* (Bulgarian, meaning hot cocoa with water); *napitak od kakaa sa vodom* (Serbo-Croat, meaning a drink of cocoa with water)

This cocoa is made in the same way as Turkish coffee, but the result is slightly thicker.

10 g cocoa powder •
2 teaspoons sugar • 15 ml double cream

Pour 125 ml water into a small saucepan or Turkish coffee pot. Bring to the boil and remove from the heat. Mix the cocoa and sugar to a smooth paste in a small bowl with a little of the hot water. Trickle this into the remaining hot water and stir briskly. Return to the fire. Allow the cocoa to froth up to the rim of the container and remove from the heat. Serve immediately in a cup slightly larger than that used for Turkish coffee. Top with cream, if you wish.

## APPLE NECTAR
Makes about 1.8 litres

*Nektar ot yabulki* (Bulgarian); *nectar de mere* (Romanian)

Morello cherries, apricots, peaches and many other fruits can be prepared in exactly the same way.

1 kg peeled and cored cooking apples, cut into segments •
3 cloves • 400 g sugar •
the strained juice of 1 lemon

Choose 250 ml screw-top bottles and put them, together with their tops, a soup ladle and a plate on a baking tray in an oven heated to 120°C/250°F/gas 1/2 for 30 minutes or until ready to fill. Sterilize a large kitchen funnel by boiling it for 10–15 minutes. Keep it in the water until needed.

Put apples and cloves with 300 ml water in an enamelled pan and simmer over a very low heat for 30 minutes. Discard the cloves. Purée the pulp in a food processor or liquidizer, or push it through a nylon sieve. Return to the pan.

In another pan, prepare a syrup by dissolving the sugar in 1 litre water over a low heat, then boiling briskly for two minutes. Pour the syrup and the lemon juice into the purée, mixing well. Return to the heat and cook gently for 10 minutes.

To fill the bottles, transfer the hot plate from the oven to the top of the stove close to the pan. Put the bottles, one at a time onto the plate. Set the funnel in the bottle neck, then ladle the bubbling nectar through the funnel, filling the bottle up to the top. Work quickly so the nectar is bottled at boiling temperature. Immediately screw down the lid and leave to cool. Repeat with the remaining bottles.

Serve well chilled in small glasses, with biscuits or a slice of cake. Shake the bottle first. The nectar will keep in a cool dark place for about 4 months.

## LEMON TEA
To serve 1 person

*Rouski chaj* (Bulgarian, 'Russian tea'); *čaj s limunom* (Serbo-Croat, 'tea with lemon')

1 heaped teaspoon black Russian tea (grown in the Caucasus) •
lemon juice •
sugar •
1 lemon slice

Heat a small teapot. Add the tea leaves and pour 250 ml boiling water over them. Leave to infuse for 3–4 minutes, covered. Pour into a cup or heatproof glass and add lemon juice and sugar to taste. Float a slice of lemon on top. Serve hot or ice cold.


## LIME-BLOSSOM TISANE
To serve 1 person

*Çaj me lule bliri* (Albanian); *lipov chaj* (Bulgarian); *čaj od lipe* (Serbo-Croat)

Lime-blossom tea is made by treating dried blossoms exactly as you would tea leaves. It is a popular winter drink, especially in the countryside. The blossoms are picked from three main species growing throughout Europe (including the Balkans and the British Isles): the small-leaved lime, *Tilia cordata* (syn *parvifolia*), the large-leaved lime, *T platyphyllos*, and the silver lime, *T argentea* (syn *tomentosa*). The parts used are either the flower bunches (the cymes), or the flower bunches together with the attached leaf (bract). They are picked in July before nut-like fruits about the size of a pea are formed.

1 rounded tablespoon dried lime blossom •
sugar or honey

Rinse a teapot with hot water, drop in the lime blossom and pour on 250 ml freshly boiled water. Allow to brew for 3–4 minutes covered with a tea cosy. Strain into a warmed cup. Stir in sugar or honey to taste.

## CAMOMILE TISANE

*Chaj ot lajkouchka* (Bulgarian); *čaj od kamilice* (Serbo-Croat)

This is prepared in exactly the same way as lime-blossom tisane except that a smaller amount of dried camomile flowers (about 1 rounded teaspoon) is used.

## YOGHURT DRINK
Serves 6–8

*Dhallë* (Albanian); *ajran* (Bosnian, Bulgarian, Macedonian), from the Turkish *ayran*, yoghurt diluted with cold water and snow or ice

500 ml full fat, strained or thick-set yoghurt (sheep's or cow's milk); or 1 litre low-fat plain yoghurt •
1 litre cold water, soda water or naturally carbonated mineral water •
a little salt (optional) • crushed ice

Put the yoghurt in a bowl and whisk it with a wire whisk or an electric beater until creamy. Add salt and pour in the water gradually, beating all the time. Alternatively, mix all the ingredients (except the ice) together in a blender or food processor until frothy. Serve immediately in tall, chilled glasses with plenty of ice.

## HOT SALEP DRINK
Serves 3-4

*Salep* (Albanian, Bosnian, Bulgarian, Macedonian), from the Turkish *salep*, from Arabic

The Balkans experience hot, dry summers, but winters can be long and severe. It is then that hot drinks like salep come into their own.

1 teaspoon ground salep • 500 ml milk •
3 tablespoons granulated sugar or ground candy-sugar crystals
(adding 1 tablespoon less or more to suit your taste) •
ground ginger

Add the cold milk gradually to the sdalep in a saucepan, stirring as you pour. Bring to the boil, add the sugar and simmer for about 10 minutes, stirring from time to time, until syrupy. Serve hot, in small cups, with a little ground ginger sprinkled over the top.

# CHAPTER XXIII

# Sauces and Standard Preparations

## ROASTED FLOUR

This is a good standby for the larder, much appreciated by people who do less frying and use less fat. Roasted flour has many uses in the kitchen: for thickening all kinds of stews and braises, for making sauces and gravy, and for preparing halva and kolivo.

Spread some plain white flour, preferably unbleached, in a roasting tin in an even layer about 5 mm thick, and place in a preheated oven at 230°C/450°F/gas 8. Bake for 20–25 minutes, or until it develops its own unmistakable aroma and is ivory in colour with a hint of beige; or cook for 30–35 minutes for a darker shade—approaching the colour of a brown egg shell. There is no need to stir the flour during baking. Cool, then sift on to a sheet of greaseproof to remove any lumps and, with the help of the paper, tip it into dry jam jars. Covered, it will keep for a few months in a dry cupboard or larder.

## ROUX

*Zaprshka* (Macedonian), *zaprška* (Serbo-Croat), *prežganje* (Slovenian) all meaning something fried; *purzheno brashno* (Bulgarian, meaning fried flour)

The old dishes of Bosnia, Hercegovina and Dalmatia never relied on this combination of fat and flour cooked together. However, it was often found in other Balkan countries, though it is used less and less today.

To blend the roux smoothly with the liquid, the fat in this recipe weighs slightly more than the flour.

25 g butter, lard or margarine • 2 tablespoons flour

Choose a heavy-based saucepan. Melt the fat in the pan, blend in the flour, and cook gently, stirring all the time, for 3–4 minutes or until the flour slowly turns a pale golden colour. Leave to cool, then whisk in a little cooking liquid from a pan containing hot soup, stew or braise. Add more liquid, in small quantities, until the mixture is quite thin; then stir this slowly back into the pan from which the liquid was taken and simmer for a further 20 minutes.

# FLOUR-BOUND SAUCE

*Salcë me miell* (Albanian), *brashnen sos* (Bulgarian), *sos od brashno* (Macedonian), *umak sa brašnom* (Serbo-Croat), *močnata umaka* (Slovenian)

You can first fry the flour in butter, but for health reasons, nowadays, Balkan people do much less frying and prefer the non-fry, simmering method set out below.

50 g roasted flour, or plain flour dry-fried (without fat)
until lightly coloured and allowed to cool •
about 500 ml cold water, meat stock or vegetable stock made with
2 carrots and 1 each of parsnip, celeriac and onion •
50 g butter, or 50 ml vegetable oil (or a mixture) • 1/4 teaspoon salt

Put the flour into a thick-based saucepan. Add the cold liquid little by little, stirring well after each addition, then put in the fat and salt and bring to the boil stirring. Reduce to a simmer and cook for a minute or two, stirring continuously, until the mixture turns to a smooth, not too thick sauce. Taste for seasoning.

*Variations*

*Garlic and vinegar sauce*: add 1–2 garlic cloves pounded in a mortar with a pinch of salt plus vinegar to taste. Reheat for a few minutes and serve.

*Herbed sauce:* stir in a finely chopped bunch of dill or parsley, or a handful of chopped chives. Reheat but do not boil.

*Sour cream sauce*: allow the sauce to cool a little, then stir in 3–4 tablespoons of sour cream or double cream and a little lemon juice. Let the sauce warm through, but do not reboil.

## WHITE SAUCE

*Salcë e bardë* (Albanian); *byal sos-beshamel* (Bulgarian); *aspri sáltsa-mpesamél* (Greek); *beli umak-bešamel* (Serbo-Croat)

This is a Balkan version of the French sauce béchamel. For a smooth sauce, free of lumps, leave the roux to cool completely before combining it with the cold milk.

50 g butter or lard, or a mixture of oil and butter •
50 g plain flour • 500 ml milk •
1/4 teaspoon salt • freshly grated nutmeg •
freshly ground black pepper

First make a pale roux: melt the fat in a pan, then blend in the flour. Cook gently for a minute or so until the flour just barely turns colour. Leave the roux to cool completely, then gradually add the cold milk, stirring vigorously with a wooden spatula, and salt. Place the pan on the heat and bring to the boil, stirring continuously; the sauce will thicken almost immediately. Stir in black pepper and grated nutmeg for extra flavour.

*Variations*

*All-in-one white sauce*: This sauce is used as a topping for moussaka, cannelloni and dishes which are given a gratin finish. To make it, put all the above quantities of butter, flour and 600 ml milk together in a saucepan over a moderate heat and stir or whisk for a few minutes until the sauce thickens. Season to taste.

*All-in-one cheese sauce*: switch off the heat under the cooked white sauce and stir in 75–100 g grated hard cheese such as kashkaval or Cheddar or crumbled semi-hard cheese such as feta, Lancashire or Cheshire.

*Yellow bechamel sauce*: Beat 2 egg yolks with a little cold milk or cream, then gradually mix in spoonfuls of the hot, not boiling, white sauce into the egg mixture. Beat this into the remaining sauce. Heat again gently, but do not let the sauce boil or it may curdle.

# BALKAN SAUCE FRICASSÉE

*Sos frikase* (Bulgarian); *umak od limuna i žumanaca–frikaso* (Serbo-Croat)

2 egg yolks • 2 slightly rounded tablespoons flour • 2 tablespoons lemon juice •
500 ml cold meat, chicken or vegetable stock, potato water or water •
1/2 teaspoon salt • freshly ground black pepper •
15 g butter, or 2–3 tablespoons sour cream • 1 tablespoon chopped parsley

Blend the egg yolks with the flour and lemon juice. Gradually thin the mixture with stock or water. Season with salt and pepper to taste and simmer, stirring all the time, for 3–4 minutes, until slightly thickened. Remove from the heat and stir in the butter or cream and the parsley.

Use with poached chicken, lamb or beef, or poached fish and shellfish.

# TOMATO SAUCE

# WITH FRESH TOMATOES AND ONION

The sauce is most commonly used with fried minced meats, fried vegetables or pasta.

1 medium onion, peeled and chopped •
2 tablespoons vegetable oil
(or strained oil left from the frying of the meats or vegetables which the sauce accompanies) •
4 teaspoons sugar •
1 kg ripe tomatoes, cut up and cooked in their own juices until soft, then passed through a sieve to remove the skins and seeds •
1–2 tablespoons tomato purée • 1/2 teaspoon salt •
1/4 teaspoon each of ground cumin and black pepper • 25–50 g unsalted butter

Gently sweat the onion in oil in a covered saucepan until soft. When it starts to colour, stir in the sugar and keep stirring until the onion is golden; then add the strained tomatoes, tomato purée, salt, cumin and black pepper. Simmer until the sauce thickens slightly—about 10–15 minutes—and use as necessary.

# TOMATO SAUCE

## WITH FRESH TOMATOES AND GARLIC

*Salcë domatesh* (Albanian); *domaten sos* (Bulgarian); *sáltsa tomátes* (Greek); *sos od domati* (Macedonian); *umak od paradajza* (Serbian); *umak od rajčica* (Croat); *domatesli salça* (Turkish)

This thick, concentrated tomato sauce is enjoyed poured hot or cold over cooked meats, poultry, fish, pasta or fried vegetables. Canned tomatoes can be used instead of fresh, but then you may have to sieve the sauce to remove skins and seeds.

1 kg large, very ripe tomatoes, peeled, quartered, gently squeezed to remove the seeds, then chopped •
1/2 teaspoon paprika • 1/2 teaspoon salt •
1 teaspoon sugar • 1 bay leaf • 1/4 teaspoon chilli powder •
1/4 teaspoon dried herbs such as basil, marjoram or thyme—or a mixture •
1 tablespoon vegetable oil •
3 or more garlic cloves, pounded to paste with a pinch of salt •
50–100 ml olive oil or sunflower oil; or 50–100 g butter •
freshly ground black pepper • 1 tablespoon chopped parsley

Put the tomatoes, paprika, salt, sugar, bay leaf, the chilli powder and herbs, and the oil together in a heavy enamelled or non-stick pan, cover, and cook over a fairly high heat for about 1 hour. Then reduce to low and simmer for a further one to one and a half hours, stirring now and then, until the tomatoes have reduced to a thick, dark-red pulp. Discard the bay leaf, then either blend to a purée in a food processor or press through a sieve.

Add the garlic, olive oil or butter, black pepper and chopped parsley, and return the sauce to the boil. It is now ready to serve, but is just as tasty when reheated next day; or you can ladle it into a jar, allow to cool, pour olive oil over the surface and cover. In a cool place, it will keep for at least a week.

## TOMATO SAUCE WITH TOMATO PURÉE

1 tablespoon vegetable oil • 1 tablespoon flour •
1 tablespoon tomato purée • 1 teaspoon paprika •
125 ml meat or vegetable stock, or water •
3 tablespoons dry red wine • 1 1/2 teaspoons wine vinegar •
1/2 bay leaf • 5–6 allspice berries •
1 pinch each of ground cloves and cinnamon; or a good pinch of mixed herbs •
a liberal grinding of black pepper • salt •
1–2 teaspoons sugar •
1 clove of garlic, crushed • crushed chillies

Heat the oil in a frying pan, stir in the flour and cook briskly until it barely turns colour; stir in the rest of the sauce ingredients (except the chillies) in sequence, then simmer the mixture for a minute, stirring all the time. Remove from the heat and discard the bay leaf and allspice berries. Keep hot, or reheat before serving. At table, pass round crushed chillies separately.

## QUICK TOMATO SAUCE

This thin tomato sauce usually accompanies roasted, peeled, then fried salad peppers, fried aubergine slices or *kyufteta*.

2 tablespoons vegetable oil (or oil left from the frying of *kyufteta* or vegetables which will be finished off with this sauce) •
4–5 garlic cloves, peeled and pounded to a cream with a pinch of salt •
350 g tinned peeled tomatoes, drained weight, passed through a sieve, seeds discarded •
1/4 teaspoon salt

Lightly fry the garlic in the oil, then pour in the tomatoes and add the salt. Bring the mixture to the boil and cook for no longer than a minute if you want to retain the fresh taste of the sauce, or 10–15 minutes for something thicker.

# WALNUT AND GARLIC SAUCE

*Tarator* (Albanian, Bulgarian, Macedonian, Serbian), from Turkish *tarator*, from the Persian; *teretur* (Bosnian), from Turkish dialect *teretor*; *skorthaliá* (Greek)

To save time, this sauce can be prepared in an electric food processor by grinding the nuts with the sliced garlic and the salt, then adding the bread, oil, vinegar or lemon juice and stock or water, but the result is not as smooth as when the mixture is thoroughly pounded in the old-fashioned way with a pestle and mortar.

25 g cloves of garlic, peeled • 1/4 teaspoon salt •
100 g shelled walnuts
(or pine nuts, blanched almonds, lightly toasted skinned hazelnuts or cashew nuts) •
50 g crustless, day-old bread, moistened and gently squeezed
to press out excess stock or water •
3 tablespoons walnut oil (or sunflower or olive oil, if using nuts other than walnuts) •
1 tablespoon white wine vinegar or lemon juice •
about 75 ml meat or chicken stock or water

Pound the garlic with the salt in a mortar. Add the nuts in batches and pound to a velvety smooth paste. Work in the bread with the pestle, then, using a wooden spoon, beat in the oil gradually and stir in the vinegar plus sufficient stock or water to make a mixture which flops easily from the lifted spoon. Check for seasoning.

Serve with fried meat, seafood or vegetables.

*Variations*

*Walnut and yoghurt sauce*: stir in last of all, 375 g plain drained yoghurt.

*Bread and garlic sauce*: omit the nuts; use 150 g bread, 4 tablespoons of olive oil and enough cold liquid to obtain the consistency of thick cream.

# YOGHURT AND GARLIC SAUCE

*Kos me hudhra* (Albanian); *kiselo mlyako s chesun* (Bulgarian); *kiselo mleko so luk* (Macedonian); *iaurt cu usturoi* (Romanian); *kiselo mleko s belim lukom* (Serbian); *sarımsaklı yoğurt* (Turkish)

In the Balkans, the combination of yoghurt and raw garlic is credited with health-giving qualities. The sauce is usually spooned over stewed, baked or fried vegetables, or placed under fried or poached eggs.

1–2 garlic cloves, skinned • salt • 250 g thick-set, plain yoghurt

Pound the garlic with a pinch of salt in a mortar, then blend in the yoghurt gradually. Adjust the seasoning. Use immediately, or cover and refrigerate.

# RED PAPRIKA BUTTER

100 g butter (salted or unsalted) • 1 tablespoon paprika

Heat the butter and paprika together in a small bowl placed over boiling water. As soon as the butter has melted and become a brilliant salmon pink, pour it through a tea strainer lined with gauze into a small screw-top jar. It will keep for a month in the refrigerator. It can be reheated whenever its use is called for, but it is best not allowed to bubble so that it can retain its nutritional value.

For immediate consumption, this butter needs no straining. Just pour off the clear, red liquid without disturbing the sediment.

# RED PAPRIKA OIL

100 ml sunflower oil or olive oil • 2 teaspoons paprika

Put the oil and paprika together into a small saucepan or a Turkish coffee pot and heat very gently until the oil turns a bright cherry-red. Remove from the heat and allow the paprika to settle, then carefully pour off the clear oil into a small screw-top bottle fitted with a one-hole dropper (a soy sauce bottle serves the purpose). Store in a cool dark place.

## ORANGE-COLOURED CARROT BUTTER

100 g carrot, scraped and finely grated • 100 g butter, preferably unsalted

Gently fry the carrot in the butter for 2–3 minutes until soft. Strain through a fine strainer applying pressure with the back of a spoon to extract as much butter as possible. Discard the residue.

This butter is used as a garnish sprinkled hot over any meat and vegetable soup. Store in a refrigerator; reheat before using.

## GARLIC VINEGAR

*Bedava sirke baldan tatlıdır.*
Free vinegar is sweeter than honey.

Turkish saying.

5–6 cloves of garlic, peeled, cut into strips the size of pine needles • wine or cider vinegar

Put the garlic into a 250 ml screw-topped bottle with a one-eye stopper and fill with vinegar, leaving about 1 cm of space at the top. Close the bottle securely, shake daily for a week, use after 15 days. Garlic vinegar has a short storage life and is best used within a few weeks; after this time there is a gradual loss of piquancy.

Herbal, spiced or fruit-flavoured vinegars can be made in the same way.

# SMALL ENRICHMENT SAUCE FOR SOUPS, STEWS AND BRAISES

*Zapruzhka* (Bulgarian), *zaprshka* (Macedonian), *prežganje* (Slovenian), *zapřška u luku* (Serbo-Croat), all meaning something fried with onion

In some parts of the Balkans, housewives add roasted flour to their soups or stews towards the end of the cooking—instead of frying plain flour together with the onion. A number of recipes also require the addition of tomato purée or peeled chopped tomatoes, normally after frying of the flour.

1–2 tablespoons sunflower oil, or 15–25 g lard, butter, clarified butter or margarine •
50 g onion, very finely chopped • 1 tablespoon plain white flour •
1/4–1/2 teaspoon paprika • 150 ml tepid stock, water or cooking liquid

Fry the onion slowly and evenly, with or without a lid, until completely soft and golden—this may take half an hour or even a little longer. Stir in the flour and continue frying until it turns pale yellow. Off the heat, add the paprika (it burns easily), and the cooking liquid, stock or water, and cook for a further minute until the mixture forms a thin, smooth sauce. Pour this into the soup, stew or braise and simmer for 20 minutes more.

# EGG-AND-LEMON FINISHING SAUCE
Makes about 435 ml

*Ndërtim me vezë dhe limon* (Albanian); *zastrojka s jajtsa i limon* (Bulgarian); *sáltsa aýgolémono* (Greek); *zachin so jajtsa i limon* (Macedonian); *začin s limunom i jajima* (Serbo-Croat); *limon yumurta terbiyesi*(Turkish), 'finishing sauce with egg and lemon'; *začin sa žumancetom i limunom* (Bosnian, 'finishing sauce with egg yolks and lemon')

Finishing sauces, much used in Balkan cooking, are based on eggs, cream, yoghurt, flour, nuts or garlic, and used to bind, thicken, flavour or acidify soups and the cooking juices of meat or vegetable dishes, but this is the one most often encountered. It can be prepared with or without flour. The advantage of adding a little flour to the egg and lemon mixture is that the sauce does not curdle when simmered carefully.

> 2 egg yolks • 2 slightly rounded tablespoons plain flour
> 2 tablespoons strained lemon juice •
> salt and freshly-ground white pepper

Blend the egg yolks in a bowl with the flour and the strained lemon juice. Gradually stir in hot cooking liquid from a stew, braise or soup. You will need about 500 ml liquid for a sauce (more for a soup); if that much is not available from the dish you are cooking, make up the quantity with stock or water. Pour this back into the cooking pan and simmer for 5–6 minutes, stirring or whisking, until slightly thickened. Season with salt and white pepper, if necessary.

# BRILLIANT-RED SOFT FRUIT SAUCE (UNCOOKED)

Symbolic of health, happiness and the joy of living, red sauces are traditionally served with milk puddings and blancmanges as well as being brilliant with ice creams. This is the best since it gets its perfume and colour from the fruit, not from synthetic flavourings and dyes.

> 200 g ripe, over-ripe or squashed strawberries, raspberries or blackberries •
> about 100 g ground vanilla sugar, or the same amount of honey, melted

Force the fruit through a fine nylon or stainless-steel sieve to make a purée; discard the seeds. Blend with the ground sugar, adding less or more to suit your taste. Alternatively, mix with the warm, melted honey and allow to cool. Pour the sauce into a jug for serving and serve at any temperature.

## CRIMSON MORELLO CHERRY SAUCE

Red cherry jam or redcurrant jelly can be used to similar effect.

200 g morello-cherry preserve (p.327) •
1–2 tablespoons cherry brandy or maraschino

Put the preserve with 4 tablespoons water in a small saucepan. Bring to the boiling point and cook for 2 minutes, stirring all the time. Remove from the heat and stir in the cherry brandy or liqueur, if desired.

This sauce can be used strained or with the fruit in it.

## ROSE-WATER SAUCE

100–125 g honey •
1–2 tablespoons triple-distilled rose water
or, if you have it, 1 drop attar of roses or 2–3 tablespoons rose petal preserve (p. 329) •
cochineal grains or red food colouring

Melt the honey in a small saucepan. Remove from the heat. Stir in the rose-water or attar or rose-petal preserve and enough cochineal or red food colouring to make a bright red sauce. No need to strain. Serve hot or ice cold.

## ORANGE-MARMALADE SAUCE

4–5 tablespoons orange marmalade •
1 tablespoon triple-distilled orange-blossom water, or 2 tablespoons Cointreau

Mix the marmalade with a dash of water—just enough to make it runny. Add the orange-flower water or Cointreau. Serve with the peel in the sauce, or strained, hot or cold.

## WALNUT MILK
Makes about 300 ml

Walnut milk is pale golden-ochre in colour; if you require a pure white nut milk, use either blanched almonds or freshly-gathered shelled and peeled walnuts. (When fresh, walnuts are easy to peel). Nut milk was, and still is, in demand at Lent or on other fasting days as substitute for cow's milk. Because of its delicate scent and flavour, it is also used on ordinary, non-fast days as the basis of ice cream, blancmange, custard, sweet and savory sauces, sherbets and elixirs.

100 g shelled walnuts

Grind the walnuts finely in a food processor. Pour in 375 ml cold water and process until the mixture is well blended and capped with a white froth. Pour the mixture into a saucepan and bring very slowly to near boiling point.

Meanwhile, line a colander set over a bowl with a scalded square of cotton or poplin. Pour the walnut liquid into the colander and leave to drain for 20–30 minutes. When most of the liquid has dripped through, gather up the four corners of the cloth together to form a bag; then twist and squeeze the bag to wring out any remaining liquid. Discard the pulp or use it in a sauce.

To sterilize the walnut milk for use, pour it back into the pan and bring just to the boil. Use immediately, or refrigerate for up to a week, or freeze.

## VANILLA SUGAR

400 g castor or icing sugar • 2–3 vanilla pods, split lengthways in half

Put the sugar into an airtight jar and bury the vanilla pieces in the sugar. Put the lid on securely. The sugar will be ready to use in about a week. Store in a cool, dry place. It can be kept for a long time. You can use the same vanilla pieces several times.

To turn vanilla-scented castor sugar into icing sugar, simply grind it, with or without a small piece of vanilla pod, in a coffee or spice mill.

# CONFECTIONER'S CUSTARD or CRÈME PÂTISSIÈRE

This cream can be flavoured in dozens of different ways, with rum and melted chocolate, maraschino, Cointreau, Pernod, citrus zest, rose-water, ground almonds, praline or—as here—with a vanilla pod. If preferred, the pod could be replaced with a few drops of real vanilla extract, vanilla liqueur or 10–15 drops vanilla flavouring stirred into the cooked cream.

200 ml milk •
5 cm piece vanilla pod, split lengthwise •
2 egg yolks •
50 g castor sugar •
2 tablespoons plain flour

Pour the milk into a small saucepan, add the vanilla pod and bring to just under boiling point. Cover, and leave to infuse for about 10 minutes.

Meanwhile, put the egg yolks and sugar into a bowl and beat together until pale and creamy. Sieve over the flour and beat it in. Add the warm milk and beat for a second or two until you have a thin, foamy batter. Pour this back into the saucepan (with the vanilla pod in it) and bring to the boil, stirring constantly. Cook over a very low heat, stirring from time to time, until the cream thickens—this will take about 5 minutes.

Use immediately, or transfer to a small bowl and cover the surface with a circle of buttered greaseproof paper to prevent skin forming. The cream may be kept refrigerated for about a week. Before use, remove the vanilla pod and reheat (if necessary), adding a little milk.

# WHITE CONFECTIONER'S CUSTARD

This is the Balkan alternative to the West European confectioner's custard. It is used to fill eclairs, cream horns, cakes and leaf pastries.

> 25 g cornflour (or fine rice starch) •
> 75 g sugar •
> 200 ml milk •
> a few drops vanilla flavouring, concentrated rose- or orange-flower water, a little rum or grated lemon zest to taste

Blend the cornflour and sugar with enough of the milk to make a thin smooth paste. Heat the remaining milk, and when it comes to near boiling point, stir in the cornflour paste. Cook over a low heat for a few seconds until the mixture thickens. Remove from the heat and stir in the chosen flavouring. Use as required.

There are two variations:

*White confectioner's custard with ground rice* is a cream that sets rather firm. To make it, mix 15 g cornflour and 50 g sugar with a little of 200 ml milk and set aside. In a rinsed-out non-stick or enamelled pan, mix 15 g ground rice with the rest of the milk and simmer gently for 5 minutes, stirring from time to time. Then pour in the cornflour mixture and cook, stirring, for a few more moments, until quite thick.

*White confectioner's custard with butter* is made by preparing the ground-rice version which is left to cool, though stirred from time to time. Meanwhile, beat 100 g unsalted butter until light and fluffy, then beat in the cooled confectioner's custard, a little at a time, to form a soft, smooth mass. Flavour as you wish with alcohol, coffee extract or vanilla.

# Bibliography

Names of authors or book titles marked with an asterisk are mentioned in the text.

## Cookery Books

Atanasova, A., (compiler), *Morski izkousheniya* [Sea Temptations], Lada, Sofia, 1994. A small book containing seafood recipes, mainly traditional, but a few—like soup from sauerkraut liquor with caviar—quite unusual.

Bakos, E., *Mehlspeisen aus Österreich* [Flour-based confections from Austria], Ueberreuter, Vienna 1975. A splendid collection of authentic recipes, my favourite book on Austrian pâtisserie.

Cakebread, S., *Sugar and Chocolate Confectionery*, Oxford U.P. 1975.

Cane, K.M., *Përgatitja e ëmbëlsirave* [Preparation of confections], publishing house '8th November', Tirana 1982. Recipes based mainly on foreign pâtisserie: savoury leaf-pastries (pies), creams and ice creams, fruit preserves and sweets [*bonbonet*]. One of the very few Albanian cookery books published in Albania. [A number have been published in America].

Cholcheva, P., *Yastiya s meso* [Meat dishes], Fama, Sofia 1994. The author is one of the most liked and respected Bulgarian cookery writers. She has dedicated 60 years of her life writing about food—as a journalist and author of numerous cookery books. This is her latest work.

Countess Morphy, *Recipes of all Nations*, Selfridge, London, n.d.

Davidson, A., *Mediterranean Seafood*, Penguin Books, Harmondsworth, revised edition 1981; first published in 1972. A valuable handbook of seafood species, with over 200 recipes from the Mediterranean and Black Sea.

*Delev, A., *Semejno sukrovishte* [Family Treasure], Sofia 1894. A domestic manual. The 'Cookery Book' section includes the most important traditional and ritual dishes of the previous century. There is also a list of the names of all subscribers to the book.

Georgiev, H., et al, *Shornik retsepti za koulinarni izdeliya v predpriyatiyata za obshtestveno hranene* [Collection of recipes designed for catering establishments], Naouka i Izkoustvo, Sofia, 1956. A reference book for professionals issued by the Ministry of Interior Commerce.

Georgieva R., *Gotvarska kniga* [Cookery book], Sofia, n.d. Old Bulgarian recipes. The absence of sunflower oil dates this prior to 1920, when its manufacture began.

*Grum, A., *Slovenske narodne jedi* [Slovenian national dishes], Založba Centralnega Zavoda za Napredek Gospodinjstva, Ljubljana 1978. An outstanding work divided into two parts, dishes common to the whole of Slovenia, and regional cuisines.

Halıcı, N., *Nevin Halıcı's Turkish Cookbook*, A Jill Norman Book, Dorling Kindersley, London 1989. The classic cuisine of Istanbul, and also recipes from all over Anatolia.

*Halıcı, N., *Türk Mutfağı* [Turkish cuisine], Güven Matbaasi, Ankara 1985. Recipes are presented with impeccable precision.

Hanneman, L.J., *Pâtisserie*, Heinemann, London, 4th edition 1979. The standard trade manual.

*I.K.B. and Sp T.K., *Prakticheska gotvarska kniga i vegetariyanska kuhnya* [Practical cookery book and vegetarian cuisine], I.K. Bozhinov, Sofia 1908. My acquisition of this book has a small history. It was given as a present to Alan Davidson in Sofia when he was researching Bulgarian fish species for the revised edition of his *Mediterranean Seafood*. Alan kindly sent me a photocopy of the book because 'it was part of my heritage'.

Ivanova, K., *Frizer* [Freezer], Gea, Vratsa. N.d., but after 1994.

Karaneshev, T. Dimitrov, A., and Semerdzhiev, A., *Sbornik retsepti za sladkarski proizvedeniya* [Collection of recipes for flour-based confections], Sofia 1969. Written by three professional pastry cooks, a manual for the trade.

Kut, A.T., *Açıklamalı yemek kitapları bibliyografyası* [Bibliography of Turkish printed cookery books, 1844-1933], Feryal Basimevi, Ankara 1985.

*Kut, G., 'On the additions by Shirvani' [15th century?] to his translation of a cookery-book [13th century]' in *First International Food Congress*, Ministry of Culture and Tourism, Ankara 1986.

*Lakišić, A., *Bosanski Kuhar* [Bosnian cookbook], Svjetlost, Sarajevo 1979. Traditional cookery in Bosnia and Herzegovina. An exceptional mixture of old Ottoman and Slavic recipes. Some of the Turkish dishes, now forgotten even in Anatolia, have been preserved intact in Bosnia and Herzegovina. Of great interest are the old restaurant menus, utensils and dishes served at Bosnian feasts and picnics.

Lang, G. *The Cuisine of Hungary*, Penguin Books, Harmondsworth 1980.

Macnicol, F. *Hungarian Cookery*, Penguin Books, Harmondsworth 1978.

Marjanović-Radica D., *Dalmatinska kuhinja* [Dalmatian cookery], Mladost, eighth edition, Zagreb 1982.

Mark, T., *Greek Islands Cookery*, Batsford, London 1978.

Marković, S.P. [editor], *Veliki Narodni Kuvar* [Great National Cuisine], Narodna knjiga, Belgrade, 20th revised edition 1979. Over 700 pages of tested recipes, mostly from the Serbian kitchen. A capital work.

Merdzhanov, K., *Rodopski yastiya* [Rhodope dishes], Zemizdat, Sofia 1992. Frugal recipes gathered from the Smolyan district.

Michev, B., Najdenov, A., Chortanova, S., and Malinov, T., *Divite plodove, hrana i lechebno sredstvo* [The wild fruits—food and medicine], Zemizdat, Sofia 1973. A detailed description, plus recipes, of all wild and feral fruit trees in Bulgaria.

Paradeisi, X., *Sígxroni 'ellinikí mageirikí* [Contemporary Greek cookery], Athens 1976, fourth edition, first published in 1971.

Peeva T. and Popova E., *Rukovodstvo po gotvarstvo* [Cookery handbook, subheaded: prepared for the agricultural and domestic schools and for the Bulgarian housewife], Izgrev, Pleven 1934. Exclusively national dishes.

Penchev, Dr. V., 'Boza' [Millet drink], in *Zdrave* [Health], a monthly publication of the Central Committee of the Bulgarian Red Cross, No.8, Sofia 1979.

Petrov, Dr. L., Dzhelepov, Dr. N., Jordanov, Dr. E., and Ouzounova, S., *Bulgarska natsionalna kuhnya* [Bulgarian national cuisine], Zemizdat, Sofia, 1978. Each dish bears the name of the town or village from which it was collected.

Ramazani, N. *Persian cooking*, U.P. of Virginia, Charlottesville, 1982. First published in 1932.

Sagrak, M and Boško, T., *Hrvatska kuharica* [Croatian cookbook], Stvarnost, Zagreb 1976.

*Shirvani, Muhammed bin Mahmud, *Tabh-i Et'ime* [Instruction in cookery]. This was the first Turkish cookery manuscript, probably translated in the 15th century, from the 13th century Arabic *Kitâbü't-tabîn* [The book of cookery]. At the end of his translation Shirvani added in his own handwriting 77 recipes.

*Slavejkov, P.R., *Gotvarska kniga ili nastavleniya za vsyakakvi gostbi spored kakto gi pravyat v Tsarigrad i razni domashni spravki* [Cookbook, or instructions for all kinds of dishes prepared after the manner of Istanbul, and other household references]. First edition, printing house 'Macedonia', Istanbul 1870. The greater part of this book is a literal translation from the first printed Turkish cookbook *Melceüt-Tabbâhîn*.. Slavejkov himself was a prolific writer, poet, novelist and journalist, as well as connoisseur of good food and accomplished cook. It was said that nobody could surpass the taste of young lamb he roasted whole in a pit.

Stan, A., *The Romanian cookbook*, Citadel Press, New York 1963. A useful book of recipes written by a lady with a sense of humour.

Stefanova, E.A., *Rukovodstvo po gotvarstvo* [A cookery handbook], published by Chipev Bookshop, Sofia 1903. A compenium of native Bulgarian and wider European recipes..

Stoyanova R., Cherkezova M., *Kakvo da prigotvim ot testo?* [What could we prepare from dough?], Mateks, Sofia 1993. Recipes for leaf-pastries, breads, biscuits, and cakes.

Şavkay, T., *Fırın yemekleri* [Baked dishes], Borcam, Istanbul 1986. Unlike English casseroles, all these dishes are baked uncovered.

*Tako sa Kuhale naše bake* [Our grandmothers cooked like this], Nakladni Zavod Znanje, Zagreb 1982. This comprises two old books: Ivan Birling's *Nova z-kup szlošena Zagrebechka szokachka kniga* [Newly compiled Zagreb cookbook], 'in six parts, containing instructions for the preparation of 554 dishes', Ferencz Rudolf, Zagreb 1813; and the 1873 edition of *Nova Zagrebačka Kuharica* [New Zagreb cookbook] subheaded 'practical handbook for stewing, baking and preserving'; compiled by Maria Kumičič.

Totovič, V. *Vojvodijanski Kuvar* [Vojvodina cookbook], fourth edition, Cirpanov, Novi Sad 1982. A useful collection of recipes with a strong central European flavour.

Tselementes, N., *Greek Cookery*, D.C.Divry Inc., New York 1977, first published in 1950. The former cook to the Greek Royal Palace, an authority on Greek cooking.

Tsolova, M., Stoilova, V. and Ekimova, S. *Izpolzouvane na zelenchoutsite i plodovete v domakinstovoto* [The use of vegetables and fruits in the household], Zemizdat, Sofia 1978.

*Turabi Efendi, *Turkish Cookery Book*, W.M. Watts, London 1864. This is the English translation of the first printed Turkish cookery book *Melceü't Tabbâhîn*. The first Turkish cookery book printed in the English language.

Vizvari, M., *Treasure Trove of Hungarian Cookery*, fourth edition, Corvina, Kiado 1981. The author was a well-known Hungarian actress and hostess (born 1879). Her recipes are a joy to read and follow.

*Wilson, C.A., 'The Saracen connection: Arab cuisine and the Mediaeval West', *Petits Propos Culinaires* 7, 1981.

Yordanov, Dr E. and Chortanova, S., *Lovno-ribarska kouhnya* [Game and fish cookery], Zemizdat, Sofia 1976. A catalogue of species, and recipes

## History and Archaeology

Alexander, J., *Yugoslavia before the Roman conquest*, Thames and Hudson, London 1972.

Beshevliev, V., *Purvobulgari, Istoria* [The first Bulgarians, History], Izdatelstvo na Otechestveniya Front, Sofia, 1984.

Clissold, S., [editor], *A Short History of Yugoslavia*, Cambridge U.P., 1966.

Dimitrov, D.P., *Land of Ancient Civilisations*, Foreign Languages Press, Sofia 1961.

Glenny, M.,*The Rebirth of History, Eastern Europe in the Age of Democracy*, Penguin, Harmondsworth 1993.

Hutchinson, R.W., *Prehistoric Crete*, Penguin, Harmondsworth 1965.

Kaneva-Johnson M., 'The Eneolithic bread oven and loaf of bread', *Petits Propos Culinaires* 9, 1981.

Koka, A., *Kultura Ilire parahistorike në Shgipëri* [The Illyrian prehistoric culture in Albania], Albanian Academy of Sciences, Archaeology Instituyte, Tirana 1985.

Kosev, D. (editor-in-chief])*et al, Istorya na Bulgaria*, vol I, Bulgarian Academy of Sciences Publishing House, Sofia 1979.

Leaf, A., MD, 'Every day is a gift when you are over 100', *National Geographic*, vol 143, January 1973.

Pamlényi, E., (editor), *A History of Hungary*, Corvina Press, Budapest 1973.

Renfrew, C., 'Ancient Bulgaria's golden treasures', *National Geographic*, vol 158, July 1980.

Roussev, S., 'Mediaeval trade', in *Sofia News*, 23 July 1980.

Srejović, D and Babović, L., *Umetnost Lepenskog Vira* [The art of Lepenski Vir], Izdavački zavod Jugoslavia, Belgrade 1983.

*Todorov, N., *A Short History of Bulgaria*, Sofia Press 1977.

Todorova, Dr H., 'Vest ot Kameno-mednata epoha' [Tidings from the neolithic-chalcolithic age), in *Zhenata Dnes* [Today's Woman], published by the committee of the Bulgarian women's movement, No. 1, Sofia 1981.

Trayanov, P., 'Tajnata na Azmashkata mogila' [The secret of the Azmak tell], in *Kosmos*, a monthly magazine, no.10, Sofia 1964.

Vulchev, J., 'Drevniyat Bulgarski kalendar' [The ancient Bulgarian calendar], in *Zhenata Dnes* [Today's woman], no.12, Sofia 1992.

Wilson, C.A., *Food and Drink in Britain*, Constable, London 1973.

## Ethnography, Travel and Linguistics

Arnaoudov, Prof M. (editor), *Bulgarski poslovitsi i gatanki*, [Bulgarian proverbs and riddles], Hemous, Sofia *c* 1936.

*Basanovich, I., *Materiali za sanitarnata etnografia na Bulgariya Lomski okrug* [Materials on the sanitary ethnography of Bulgaria, district of Lom], in *Sbornik narodni oumotvoreniya* [A State Collection of Folklore] started in 1889 by I.D. Shishmanov, vol V, Sofia 1891.

*Celebija, Evlija, *Putopis* [Travel notes], vol 1 and 2, Svjetlost, Sarajevo, 1957. A translation into Serbo-Croat of the Turkish original.

*Clauson, Sir Gerard, *An Etymological Dictionary of pre-thirteenth Century Turkish*, Oxford U.P., 1972.

*Durham, M.E., *Through the Lands of the Serb*, Edward Arnold, London 1904.
*Durham, M.E., *High Albania*, Edward Arnold, London 1909.
*Fermor, Patrick Leigh, *Between the Woods and the Water*, John Murray, London 1986.
*Gardiner, L., *Curtain Calls, Travels in Albania, Romania and Bulgaria*, 2nd ed., Readers Union, Newton Abbot 1977.
Georgiev, V.I., *Bulgarska etimologiya i onomastika* [Bulgarian etymology and onomastics], vol.10, published by the Bulgarian Academy of Sciences, Sofia 1960.
*Gerov, N., *Rechnik na Bulgarskij yazik* [Dictionary of the Bulgarian language], vol. 1-5 published by Suglasije, Plovdiv 1895-1904; vol. 6, Plovdiv 1908.
*Ginchev, T., *Gancho Koserkata*, first published in the periodical *Trud*, Turnovo 1889. Ginchev was one of the builders of the Bulgarian literary language, a novelist, ethnographer and folklorist, depicting country life in great detail.
*Ginchev, T., *Povesti* [Novels]: *Zhenitba* [Wedding], first published in *Trud*, Turnovo 1891; and *Zinalata stena* [The Gaping Chasm], first published in *Trud* in 1887.
*Hall, D.J., *Romanian Furrow*, Methuen, London 1933.
*Holbach, M.M., *Dalmatia, the land where East meets West*, John Lane, The Bodley Head, London 1908. An enthusiastic account of the beauty of the Adriatic coast, and the visits to Montenegro and Hercegovina.
Hysa, I. D-R., *Fjalor Shquip-Anglisht*, Albanian-English dictionary, Rilinda, Prishtine 1988.
Jordanova, L., *Narodno prilozhno izkoustvo*[People's applied arts], Narodna Prosveta, Sofia 1974.
*Karavelov, L., *Bulgare ot staro vreme* [Bulgarians of former times], first published in Russian in Moscow 1867, then in Bulgarian in Bucharest, printing house Svoboda, 1872.
Kiselincheva, M. (translator), *Balkanite prez pogleda na dve anglijski puteshestvenichki ot XVIII vek* [The Balkans through the eyes of two English lady-travellers in the 18th century], Otechestven Front, Sofia 1979. This book includes translations of the letters of Lady Mary Wortley Montagu (vol. I, 1708-1720), and Elizabeth Lady Craven (1789).
Kovács, L.K.,' Prerabotkata na ovcheto mlyako u Transilvanskite Madzhari v Roumunia' [The processing of sheep's milk by the Transylvanian Magyars in Rumania], in *Izvestiya na Etnografskiya Institut i Mouzej* [Proceedings of the Ethnographic Institute and Museum], vol.VI, Bulgarian Academy of Sciences Publishing House, Sofia 1963.
Petrović, P.Ž., 'O problemu krsnoga imena' [About the problem of the lineal family name] in *Izvestiya na Etnografskiya Institut i Mouzei* [Proceedings of the Ethnographic Institute and Museum], vol. VI, Bulgarian Academy of Sciences Publishing House, Sofia 1963.
Shapkarev, K.A. *Sbornik ot Bulgarski Narodni Oumotvoreniya* [Collection of Bulgarian national folklore], first published in Sofia 1891. The author was a self-taught folklorist, born in Ohrid in 1834. He collected his source material from Macedonia and western Bulgaria.
*Sitwell, S., *Roumanian Journey*, Oxford U.P. 1992, first published Batsford, London 1938.
**The Complete Letters of Lady Mary Wortley Montagu*, vol.I, 1708-1720, ed. R. Halsband, Oxford U.P. 1965.
*Vakarelski, H., *Etnografiya na Bulgaria* [Bulgarian Ethnography], Naouka i Izkoustvo, Sofia 1974. An extensive work gathered in the course of several decades.

*Vazov, I., *Pod igoto* [Under the yoke], first published in Odessa 1888, then in the periodical *Sbornik za narodni oumotvoreniya, naouka i knizhnina* [Collection of folklore, science and literature], Ministry of Public Education, Sofia 1889. The book depicts the family and public life of the common people, their patriotism and struggle for liberation.

## General Works on Nutrition and Natural History

Aykroyd, W.R. and Doughty, J., *Wheat in human nutrition* (FAO Nutritional Studies No.23), Food and Agriculture Organisation of the United Nations, Rome 1971.

*Basioli, J., *Sportski ribolov na Jadranu* [Sport fishing in the Adriatic], third edition, Nakladni Zavod Znanje, Zagreb 1981.

Daskalov, Academician H., *et al*, *Zelenchoukoproizvodstvo* [Vegetable-growing], Zemizdat, Sofia 1985. Written for agronomists, technicians and students, this is my vade-mecum on vegetable growing.

Eekhof-Stork, N., *The World Atlas of Cheese*, Paddington Press, New York and London 1977.

Gruncharov, Dr V., 'V mesetsite s boukvata R' [In the months with the letter R], in *Zhenata dnes* [Today's Woman], No.1, Sofia 1993.

Katrandzhiev, Dr K., *Bulgarskoto kiselo mlyako* [Bulgarian yoghurt], Bulgarian Academy of Sciences Publishing House, Sofia 1962.

Kinkov, B., 'Dulgoletnitsite ot Smolyansko' [The long-lived people of Smolyan district] in *Rodolyubie*, No.12, Committee for Bulgarians abroad, Sofia 1986.

Mitchel, Rynbergen, Anderson and Dibble, *Nutrition in health and disease*, J.B. Lippincott Company, Philadelphia, 16th edition 1976.

Muus B.J., and Dahlstrøm, P., *Collins Guide to the Freshwater fish of Britain and Europe*, Collins, London 1978.

Pechev, K., *et al*, *Bezalkoholnite pitieta i napitkite vuv vruzka s hraneneto* [Non-alcoholic and alcoholic drinks in nutrition], Zemisdat, Sofia 1961.

*Pejchev, Prof P. and Penev, Prof P., *Lechebni i hranitelni svojstva na mlyakoto i mlechnite produkti* [Therapeutic and nutritive values of milk and dairy products], Hristo G. Danov, Plovdiv 1977.

Popović, Prof Dr M., *Povrtarstvo* [Vegetable growing], Nolit, Belgrade 1981.

*Starchev, K. and Trifonov, T., *Zelenite prishultsi* [The Green Newcomers], Zemizdat, Sofia 1977. Non-native decorative shrubs, trees, fruit trees, herbs and spices in Bulgaria.

# INDEXES

# Index of the Recipes by Country
(Including some names in their original languages)

## ALBANIA

Aubergine caviar, 65
Aubergines stuffed with onion and garlic, 96

Baklava, 304
Beef, boiled, 161; kebabs baked in paper parcels, 162
Biscuits, old-fashioned soda, 272; shortbread, white, 272; sponge fingers, 271; syruped, 313; walnut, 313; walnut macaroons, 273
Black olive stew, 68
Blancmange, 295
Bowl kebab, 177
Bread, rice, 235; rustic, 239; scalded with milk and cheese, 252; wholemeal, 233

Cake, fatless, 280; fresh fruit, 279; lemon-flavoured, 276; semolina, soaked in syrup, 309; soaked in milk, 310; walnut, 278
Cake-bread, 241
Canneloni, Tuscan style, Albanian, 227
Caraway straws, 283
Cheese slices, fried, 116
Chicken, fried, 195; roast paprika, 187; stew, 191; stuffed, 188; with wheat, 212
Chocolate cream, 299
Coffee, Turkish, 333
Compote, 286; morello cherry, 287
Cornmeal porridge, 216
Courgettes, baked, 106; fried, 109
Crescent rolls filled with walnuts, 250

Elbasan casserole, 159

Fish, baked with onions, 139; fried hake in batter, 135; parcels, 134
Fritters, choux, with a light syrup, 312; light-as-air, sweet, 258; yeasted, 254

Fruit butter: plum, 332

Grape pudding, 298
Green bean stew, 90; with lamb, 164
Green-walnut preserve, 326
Goose, roast, with sauerkraut, 190

Halva, 314; flour, 314; semolina, 315

Ice cream, salep, 303; white, 302
Imam bayildi, 96

Jelly, lemon, 300; raspberry, 300

Kabuni, 220
Kadaif, 310
Kapama, 163
Kos, 122
Kukurec, 200
Kuglov with sunflower oil, 277
Kyufteta, grilled, 152; fried, 153; in tomato sauce, 154; in onion sauce, 155

Lamb, and yoghurt casserole, 159; stew with green beans, 164; with parsley, 160; with peas, 163; with spinach, 164; with spring onions, 163
Lamb's offal roasted on a spit, 200
Lemons and cream, 293

Mafishe, 258
Marmalade (see Fruit butters)
Morello cherries preserved in syrup, 325
Muhalebi, 295

Nettle purée, 89

Offal, lamb's, roasted on a spit, 200
Orange rinds preserved in syrup, 325
Oysters, grilled, 144

Pasta, grated, 224
Pastry, amulets filled with cheese, 270; layered with cheese, 268; layered with minced meat, 269
Peppers, stuffed with rice, 100; with meat, 182
Petulla, 254
Pickle, mixed, 322
Pilaff, rice, 218; sweet, with currants and sultanas, 220; cracked wheat, 213
Polenta, 216; baked with cheese, 217
Potato cakes, 112
Pudding, black, 198; grape, 298
Pumpkin, baked, 289; purée, baked, 290

Rice, bread, 235; pudding, 220; and potato casserole, 94; (see also Pilaff)
Rose-petal preserve, 328

Salad, cos-lettuce, 70; cucumber and yoghurt, 68; grilled pepper, 70; mixed summer, 72
Salep drink, hot, 339
Sauce, egg-and-lemon finishing, 349; flour-bound, 341; fresh tomato and garlic, 344; walnut and garlic, 346; white, 342; yoghurt and garlic, 347
Sauerkraut, 317
Sausage, blood, 198; grape juice and walnut, 323
Sausages, charcoal-grilled skinless, 151; pork, 185
Shish-Kebab, 148
Spinach, cakes, 111; purée with fried eggs, 88
Soup, fish, 82; meatball, 81; pork knuckle, 80; sour lamb, 75; tomato, 85; tripe, 78; vegetable, 83
Stew, black olive, 68; chicken, 191; green bean, 90; (see also Lamb)
Strudel, puff pastry, 266; pumpkin, 266
Sucking pig, roast, 146

Sutliash, 220

Tarator, 346
Tarhana, 224
Tisane, lime-blossom, 338
Tomatoes with rice, 91
Trifle creams, Albanian, 299
Trigonas, 308

Veal escalopes, plain, 157; Viennese style, 158
Vegetable casserole, 104; with meat, 181
Vine-leaf rolls with rice, 98; and meat, 168

Walnuts, salted, 64

Wheat, boiled, 208; cracked, in pilaff, 213
Wild boar fillet, spit roasted, 204; with sauerkraut, 203

Yoghurt, 122

Zupa, 299

# BOSNIA

Apple cream, 297
Apples, glazed with clotted cream and nuts, 288
Aubergine caviar, 65
Aubergines stuffed with onion and garlic, 96

Baklava, 304; in snail shapes, 306
Beef, steaks, grilled, 152; stew with rice, leeks and potatoes, 168
Biscuits, pepper, 276
Blancmange, 295
Bosnian pot with meat and vegetables, 173; Bosnian fondue, 114
Bread, cornbread, 240; wholemeal, 233
Buranija, 92

Cake, fatless, 280; semolina, syruped, 309; sweetheart, 309
Caviar, aubergine, 65
Cheese rolls with filo pastry, 265
Chicken, poached with wheat, 212; stew, 191; stuffed; 188
Coffee, Turkish, 333
Compote, morello cherry, 287
Cornbread, 240
Cornmeal porridge, 216

Fish grilled over embers, 132
Fritters, Bosnian, 257; choux, with a light syrup, 312; light-as-air, sweet, 258

Halva, 314; flour, 314; semolina, 315
Hashure, 211
Hercegovinian pot with meat and vegetables, 174

Imam bajildi, 96

Jam, quince, 330
Jelly, cornflour (without gelatine), 296

Kadaif, 310
Kapama, 163
Kavurma, 188
Kebab, sweet, 176
Kyufteta fried, 153; grilled, 152; in onion sauce, 155; in tomato sauce, 154

Lamb, stew with green beans, 164; with parsley, 160; potatoes, 165; spinach, 164; spring onions, 163
Lamb's offal roasted on a spit, 200

'Maiden's breasts', 196
Morello cherries preserved in syrup, 327
Moussaka, aubergine, 178; with potatoes, 180

Papazjanija, 166
Pasta, grated, 224
Pastry, amulets filled with cheese, 270; leaf pastry - made from dough stacks, 262
Pickle, mixed, 322
Pilaff, cracked wheat, 213; rice, 218; sweet rice, 220
Pirjan, 94; with meat, 168
Pituljice, 257
Polenta, 216
Potted meat, 186
Priest's stew, 166

Proja, 240

Rice pudding, 220; sweet saffron, 221 (see also Pilaff)
Rose petal preserve, 328

Salad, cos-lettuce, 70; winter black-radish, 69
Salep drink, hot, 339
Sauce, egg-and-lemon finishing, 349; walnut and garlic, 346
Sauerkraut, 317
Sausages, charcoal grilled skinless, 151
Shish kebab, 148
Soul food, 316
Soup, iced cucumber, 87; meatball, 81; sour lamb, 75; tomato, 85; tripe, 78; vegetable, 83
Stew (see Beef, Chicken, Lamb, Priest's)
Strudel, pumpkin, 266
Suzma, 186

Tarhana, 224
Tufahije, 288

Vegetable casserole, 104; with meat, 181
Vine-leaf rolls with rice, 98; with meat, 168

Wheat, cracked, in Pilaff, 213; with poached chicken or turkey, 213

Yoghurt, 122; strained, 123; drink, 339

Zerde, 221

# BULGARIA

Acacia flowers preserved in syrup, 330
Apple, cream, 297; nectar, 332
Ashoure, 211
Aubergine caviar, 65; moussaka, 178
Aubergines stuffed with onions and garlic, 96

Baklava, 304; in snail shapes, 306
Banitsa, with cheese, 268; courgettes, 267; minced meat, 269; mlintsi, 226
Beef, boiled, 161; kebabs in paper parcels, 162; pot roasted, 172; stew with prunes, 167
Biscuits, Christmas, 274; grape, 275; old-fashioned soda, 272; shortbread, white, 272; sponge fingers, 271; walnut macaroons, 273
Black-olive purée, 95; stew, 68
Blancmange, 295
Bowl kebab, 177
Bread, cheese, 237; cornbread, 240; dumplings, 228; palace, 253; plaited, 246; rice, 235; rustic (with cornmeal), 239; scalded, with milk and cheese, 252; wholemeal, 233; wholemeal with honey, 248;
Broccoli, baked with eggs and cheese, 96
Buraniya, 92

Cabbage-leaf rolls with meat and rice, 170
Cake, bishop's, 280; fatless, 280; fresh fruit, 279; lemon-flavoured, 276; semolina, soaked in syrup, 309; soaked in milk, 310; walnut, 278
Cake-bread, 241
Caraway straws, 283
Carp stuffed with walnuts, 136
Caviar, aubergine, 65; semolina, 64
Celeriac stuffed like artichokes, 101
Cheese, grilled in paper parcels, 116; melted, 112; slices fried, 116

Cheese rolls, with yeast, 249; with katmer dough, 264; with filo pastry, 265
Chicken, Circassian, 194; chilli, 192; fried, 195; poached, garnished with tarhana, 193; or turkey, with wheat, 212; roast paprika, 187; stew, 191; stew with potatoes, 192
Choban gyuvech, 95
Chocolate cream, 299
Cocoa drink, hot, 336
Coffee, Turkish, 333; iced, 336
Compote, 286; Champagne, in a watermelon, 286; morello cherry, 287
Courgettes, baked, 106; fried, 109; with rice, 93
Cornmeal porridge, 216
Crescent rolls filled with walnuts, 250

Doughnuts, jam, 256
Duckling, roast, with morello cherry sauce, 189
Dumplings, bread, 228; plum, 228
Dzidzi papo, 253

Eggs, baked with cheese, 119; mish-mash, 118; poached with rusks, 252; poached with yoghurt, 118; scrambled with peppers and tomatoes, 118

Fish, baked in a dough jacket, 137; casseroled, 138; fried hake in batter, 135; fried whitebait, 133; grilled over embers, 133; parcels, 134; stuffed with walnuts, 136
Fritters, apple or quince, 258; choux, with a light syrup, 312; raised with yeast, 254
Fruit butters: plum, 332; pumpkin, 331

Goose, roast, with sauerkraut, 190
Grape pudding, 298
Green bean stew, 90
Green-walnut preserve, 326
Guerilla kebab, 162

Halva, 314; flour, 314; semolina, 315
Hare, hunter's style, 205

Ice cream, raspberry sorbet, 301; salep, 303; white, 302; yoghurt, 301
Imam bayaldu, 96

Jam, quince, 330
Jelly, raspberry, 300; lemon, 300

Kapama, with spring onions and garlic, 163
Katmer, 263
Kavurma, 186
Kebab, baked in paper parcels, 162; bowl, 177; guerilla, 172; shepherd's, 175; shish, 148; meatball shish kebab, 149
Kolivo, 208
Koukourech, 200
Kozounak, 241
Kyufteta, in egg-and-lemon sauce, 156; in onion sauce, 155; in tomato sauce, 154; baked in yoghurt custard, 154; fried, 153; grilled, 152

Lamb, mixed grill, 150; stew with green beans, 164; with spinach, 164; with peas, 163; with potatoes, 165; with spring onions, 163; whole roast - for St George's Day, 147
Lamb chitterlings, baked, 199; offal, roasted on a spit, 200
Leeks in white wine, 90
Lemons, preserved in sugar, 331; and cream, 293

'Maiden's Breasts', 196
Malebi, 295
Marmalade (see Fruit butters)
Mechka (bear), 117
Mish-mash, 118
Milinki, 249
Mlintsi, 225; banitsa with, 226
Morello cherries preserved in syrup, 327
Moussaka, aubergine, 178; with potatoes, 180
Mussels, stuffed, 142

# Index

Nakip, 294
Nectar, apple, 337
Nectarines, stuffed, baked, 291
Nettle, purée, 89; soup, 86

Orange rinds preserved in syrup, 325

Pancakes, 254; stuffed with mushrooms, 107; stuffed with vegetables, 106
Partridge, roast in nests of straw potatoes, 206
Pasta, broken baked, 225; grated, 224; pudding, 226
Pastry, amulets filled with cheese, 270; layered with cheese, 268; with courgettes, 267; with minced meat, 269; leaf pastry made from dough stacks, 262; many-petalled dough sheets, 263
Pepper relish, 66
Peppers, fried with tomato sauce, 110; fried, stuffed with cheese, 110; grilled in salad, 170; stuffed with meat, 182; stuffed with rice, 100
Pheasant, roast, 207
Pickle, mixed, 322
Pickled cornelian cherries, 320; grapes, 321
Pig, suckling, roast, 146
Pilaff, cracked wheat, 213; rice, 218; sweet, with currants and sultanas, 220
Piryan, 94
Plakiya, 138
Plums, sweet, baked, 292
Polenta, 216; baked with cheese, 217
Pinchki, 256
Popara, 252
Pork, and rice casserole, of the Slavs, 160; with sauerkraut, 172; knuckle soup, 80
Potato cakes, 112
Potted meat, 186
Priest's stew, 166
Pudding, baked walnut and potato, 291; baked batter, with apples, 294; baked pasta, 226; black, 198; grape, 298; rice,

220; white, 197
Pumpkin, baked, 289; purée, baked, 290
Pumpkin seeds, toasted, 222

Quail grilled on a rack, 206
Quince, creams with Cognac, 298; jam, 330; salami, 293
Quinces, poached, filled with cream, 287; stuffed with beef or veal, 184; Turkish delight, 293

Revane, 309, 310
Ribnik, 137
Rice, bread, 235; and potato casserole, 91; pudding, 220 (see also Pilaff)
Rose-petal preserve, 328
Roux, 340
Rusks with poached eggs, 252

Salad, cos-lettuce, 70; cucumber, 68; dried-fish, 731; grilled pepper, 70; mixed summer, 72; sauerkraut, 72; winter black-radish, 69
Salep drink, hot, 339
Sarmi, 168, 170
Sauce, egg-and-lemon finishing, 349; flour-bound, 341; fresh tomato and garlic, 344; fricassee, 343; small enrichment, 349; walnut and garlic, 346; white, 342; yoghurt and garlic, 347
Sauerkraut, 317; rolls with meat and rice, 170; salad, 72 (see also Soup)
Sausage, blood, 198; grape juice and walnut, 323; liver, 197
Sausages, pork, 185; skinless, charcoal-grilled, 151
Sazdurma, 186
Schnitzel, Universal, 157
Shepherd's casserole, 95
Shish kebab, 148
Sindirme, 115
Soup, bean, monastery, 84; cucumber, iced, 87; fish, 82; gardener's, 83; meatball, 81; nettle, with walnuts or cheese, 86; pork knuckle, 80;

sauerkraut, cold, 70; sauerkraut, with pork, 76; sour lamb, 75; sour, of lambs' tongues, 76; tomato, 85; tripe, 78; vegetable, 83
Spinach, purée with fried eggs, 88; cakes, 111
Stew, black olive, 68; green bean, 90; priest's, 166 (see also Beef, Chicken, Lamb)
Strudel, pumpkin, 266; with puff pastry, 266
Sutlyash, 220

Tarama, 67
Tarator, 87, 346
Tarhana, 224; with cheese, 225
Tea, lemon, 338
Tisane, camomile, 339; lime-blossom, 338
Tomato casserole, Thracian, 108
Tomatoes with rice, 91
Toutmanik, 237
Touloumbi, 312
Trigouni, 308
Turnovers, cheese, 284

Veal escalopes, plain, 157; Viennese style, 158
Vegetables, braised, 102; casserole, 104; casserole with meat, 181
Venison, braised haunch of, 202
Vine-leaf rolls with rice, 98; with meat and rice, 168

Walnuts, salted, 64
Wheat, boiled, 208; dessert, rose-scented, 211; dish of poached chicken or turkey, 212 (see also Pilaff)
Wheaten porridge with cheese, 214
White cabbage, baked, 103
Wild boar fillet, spit-roasted, 204; with sauerkraut, 203

Yoghurt, 122; strained, 123; drink, 339

Zapekanka, 95
Zapruzhka, 349

# CROATIA

Acacia flowers preserved in syrup, 330
Aubergine caviar, 65

Baklava, 304; in snail shapes, 306
Beef, boiled, 161; kebabs baked in paper parcels, 162; stew with prunes, 167
Biscuits, Christmas, 274; pepper, 276; sponge finger, 271; walnut macaroons, 273
Black-olive purée, 95
Bread, cornbread, 240; dumplings, 228; palace, 253; plaited, 246; scalded, with milk and cheese, 252; wholemeal, 233
Broccoli baked with eggs and cheese, 96
Brodet, 140

Cake, Bishop's, 280; fatless, 280; fresh fruit, 279; lemon-flavoured, 276; walnut, 278
Cake-bread, 241
Caraway straws, 183
Caviar, aubergine, 65
Celeriac stuffed like artichokes, 101
Cheese, Liptaur, home-made, 117; slices, fried, 116
Chicken, fried, 195; poached, garnished with tarhana, 193; roast paprika, 187; stew with potatoes, 192; stuffed, 188
Cocoa, drink, hot, 336
Coffee, iced, 336
Compote, 286; Champagne in a water melon, 286; morello cherry, 287
Cornmeal porridge, 216
Courgettes, baked, 106; fried, 109; with rice, 93
Crescent rolls filled with walnuts, 250

Doughnuts, jam, 256
Duckling, roast, with morello cherry sauce, 189
Dumplings, bread, 228; plum, 228

Eggs, baked with cheese, 119; poached, with yoghurt, 118; scrambled with minced meat, 119

Fish, grilled over embers, 132; fried, whitebait, 133; parcels, 134; stew, 140
Fritters, apple or quince, 258
Fruit butter: plum, 332

Green bean stew, 90
Green-walnut preserve, 326

Hare, hunter's style, 205

Ice cream, raspberry sorbet, 301; white, 302

Jam, quince, 330
Jelly, lemon, 300; raspberry, 300

Kadaif, 310
Kavurma, 186
Koh of broccoli, 96; walnut and potato, 291
Kolednik, 241
Kuglof, with dried fruit, 242; with sunflower oil, 277; with walnuts, 243
Kyufteta fried, 153; grilled, 152

Lamb, mixed grill, 150; sour soup, 75; stew with spinach, 164; with green beans, 164
Lamb's offal roasted on a spit, 200
Leeks cooked in white wine, 90
Lemons preserved in sugar, 331

Marmalade (see Fruit butters)
Morello cherries preserved in syrup, 327
Moussaka, aubergine, 178
Mussels, in white wine, Dalmatian style, 142; stewed fan mussels, 141; stuffed, 142

Nectarines, stuffed, baked, 291
Nettle purée, 89

Orange rinds preserved in syrup, 325
Oysters, grilled, 144

Pancakes, 254; stuffed with vegetables, 106
Partridge, roast, in nests of straw potatoes, 206
Pasta, grated, 224
Pastry, layered with cheese, 268

Peppers stuffed with cheese, fried, 110; stuffed with meat and rice, 182
Pheasant, roast, 207
Pickled cornelian cherries, 320
Pilaff rice, 218
Pork with sauerkraut, 172; with white cabbage, 171
Potted meat, 186
Pudding, baked batter with apples, 294; baked walnut and potato, 291; black, 198; white, 197
Pumpkin, baked, 289; purée baked, 290
Pumpkin seeds, toasted, 222

Quail grilled on a rack, 206
Quince, creams with Cognac, 298; jam, 330; salami, 293; Turkish delight, 293
Quinces, poached, filled with cream, 287

Rice, with garden peas, 218; pilaff, 218; risotto, 143
Rizi-bizi, 218
Rose-petal preserve, 328
Roux, 340

Salad, cos-lettuce, 70; cucumber and yoghurt, 68; grilled pepper, 70; sauerkraut, 70; winter black-radish, 69
Sauce, egg-and-lemon finishing, 349; flour-bound, 341; fresh tomato and garlic, 344; fricassee, 343; small enrichment, 349
Sauerkraut, 317
Sasage, blood, 198; grape juice and walnut, 323; liver, 197
Sausages, skinless, charcoal grilled, 151
Scampi risotto, 143
Schnitzel, Universal, 157
Shish kebab, 148; meatball shish kebab, 149
Soup, fish, 82; meatball, 81; pork knuckle, 80; sour lamb, 75; sauerkraut, with pork, 76; tomato, 85; vegetable, 83
Spinach purée with fried eggs, 88
Stew, green bean, 90; (see also Beef, Chicken, Fish, Lamb)

Strudel, pumpkin, 266; with puff pastry, 266
Sucking pig, roast, 146
Tarama, 67
Tarhana, 224; with cheese, 225
Tea, lemon, 338
Tisane, lime-blossom, 338; camomile, 339
Tomatoes with rice, 91
Veal escalopes, plain, 157; Viennese style, 158
Vegetable casserole, 104; with meat, 181; macedoine to serve with roast beef, 102
Vegetables mixed, braised, 102
Vine-leaf rolls with meat and rice, 168
Venison haunch, braised, 202
Walnuts, salted, 64
White cabbage, baked, 103
Wild boar with sauerkraut, 203
Yoghurt, 122

## GREECE

Aubergine, caviar, 75; moussaka, 178; stuffed with onion and garlic, 96
Baklava, 304
Bread, plaited, 246; wholemeal, 233
Bowl kebab, 177
Cake, fatless, 280; semolina, syruped, 309
Cake-bread, 241
Caviar, aubergine, 65
Cheese slices, fried, 116
Chicken, fried, 195; stuffed, 188
Coffee, Turkish, 333
Compote, 286
Cornmeal porridge, 216
Courgettes, fried, 109
Fish, casserole, 138; fried in batter, 135; grilled, 132; stew, 140
Grape pudding, 298
Green-walnut preserve, 326
Halva, 314; flour, 314; semolina, 315
Imam Baildi, 96
Jam, quince, 330
Kadaif, 310

Kapama, 163
Kolliva, 208
Kyufteta, with egg-and-lemon sauce, 156; fried, 153; grilled, 152
Lamb stew with spring onions, 163
Lamb's offal roasted on a spit, 200
Morello cherries preserved in syrup, 327
Moussaka, aubergine, 178; with potatoes, 180
Mpourani, 92
Orange rinds preserved in syrup, 325
Pasatempo, 222
Pasta, grated, 224
Pastry, amulets filled with cheese, 270; layered with cheese, 268; many-petalled, sheets, 263
Peppers stuffed with meat, 182
Priest's stew, 166
Pudding, rice, 220; grape, 298
Pumpkin seeds, toasted, 222
Rice pudding, 220
Rose-petal preserve, 328
Salad, cos-lettuce, 70; cucumber and yoghurt, 68; dried fish, 73; mixed summer, 72
Sauce, egg-and-lemon finishing, 349; fresh tomato and garlic, 344; walnut and garlic, 346; white, 342
Sauerkraut, 317
Sausage, grape juice and walnut, 323
Sausages, pork, 185
Shish kebab, 148
Skorthalia, 346
Soup, cucumber, iced, 87; fish, 82; meatball, 81; pork knuckle, 80; tomato, 85
Stew, fish, 140; lamb, 163; priest's, 166
Stifado, 166

Taramosalata, 67
Tomatoes with rice, 91
Trahana, 224
Trigonas, 308

Vegetable casserole, 104
Vine-leaf rolls with rice, 98; with meat and rice, 168

Wheat, boiled, 208

Yoghurt, 122

## MACEDONIA

Aubergine caviar, 65
Aubergines stuffed with onion and garlic, 96

Baked beans, Macedonian, 105
Baklava, 304; dry (without syrup), 307
Beef, boiled, 161; steaks, grilled, 152; stew with prunes, 167
Biscuits, old-fashioned, soda, 272; syruped, 313

Bread, dumplings, 228; 'pour-and-bake' batter, 238; scalded, with milk and cheese, 252; wholemeal, 233
Cabbage-leaf rolls with meat and rice, 170
Cake, semolina, soaked in syrup, 309; soaked in milk, 310; walnut, 278
Cake-bread, 241

Caviar, aubergine, 65; semolina, 64
Cheese rolls made with katmer dough, 264
Chicken chilli, 192; fried, 195; poached, garnished with tarhana, 193; roast paprika, 187; stew, 191; stew with potatoes, 192; stuffed, 188
Chocolate cream, 299
Compote, Champagne, in a

watermelon, 286
Cornmeal porridge, 216
Crescent rolls filled with walnuts, 250
Courgettes, baked, 106; fried, 109; with rice, 93

Dumplings, bread, 228; plum, 228

Eggs, poached, with yoghurt, 118; with rusks, 253; fried with spinach, 88
Escalopes, plain, veal, 157

Fish, baked in a dough jacket, 137; baked with onions, 139; carp stuffed with walnuts, 136; casserole, 138; fried whitebait, 133; grilled over embers, 132; parcels, 134
Fritters, choux, with a light syrup, 312
Fruit butter: plum, 332

Goose, roast, with sauerkraut, 190
Green-walnut preserve, 326

Halva, 314; flour, 314; semolina, 315
Hare, hunter's style, 205

Ice cream, raspberry sorbet, 301; white, 302
Imam bajildi, 96

Jam, quince, 330

Kadaif, 310
Kulbastija, 152
Kyufteta, fried, 153; grilled, 152
Lamb, stew with green beans, 164; with parsley (shketo), 160; with peas, 163; with spinach, 164; with spring onion, 163
Lamb's chitterlings, baked, 199; offal roasted on a spit, 200

Marmalade (see Fruit butters)
Moussaka, aubergine, 178; with potatoes, 180

Nettle purée, 89

Orange rinds preserved in syrup, 325

Pancakes, 254
Pasta, grated, 224
Pastry, layered with cheese, 268; many-petalled, 263; with minced meat, 269
Peppers, fried with tomato sauce, 110; stuffed with cheese, fried, 110; stuffed with rice, 100; stuffed with meat, 182
Pheasant, roast, 207
Pickle, mixed, 322
Pilaff, cracked wheat, 213; rice, 218
Polenta, 216; baked with cheese, 217
Pork, with sauerkraut, 172; sausages, 185
Potato, cakes, 112; casserole, 94
Priest's stew, 166
Pudding, black, 198
Pumpkin, baked, 289

Quince, creams with Cognac, 298; jam, 330; salami, 293; Turkish delight, 293
Quinces stuffed with beef or veal, 184

Rice, pilaff, 218; pudding, 220; sweet saffron, 221
Rose-petal preserve, 328
Roux, 340
Rusks with poached eggs, 253

Salad, cos-lettuce, 70; cucumber and yoghurt, 68; grilled pepper, 70; grilled pepper and tomato, 71; sauerkraut, 72
Salep drink, hot, 339
Sauce, egg-and-lemon finishing, 349; flour-bound, 341; fresh tomato and garlic, 344; small enrichment, 349; walnut and garlic, 346; yoghurt and garlic, 347
Sauerkraut, 317; with pork, 172; rolls with meat and rice, 170
Sausage, blood, 198
Sausages, pork 185
Schnitzels, Universal, 157
Shepherd's casserole, 95
Shish kebab, 148; meatball shish kebab, 149
Soup, cucumber, iced, 87; fish, 82; meatball, 81; nettle, with walnuts or cheese, 86; pork knuckle, 80; sour lamb, 75; sour, of lambs' tongues, 76; tomato, 85; tripe, 78; vegetable, 83
Spinach purée with fried eggs, 88
Stew, priest's, 166 (see also Beef, Chicken, Lamb)

Tarhana, 224; with cheese, 225
Tomatoes with rice, 91

Veal escalopes, plain, 157
Vegetable casserole, 104; with meat, 181
Vegetables, mixed, braised, 102
Vine-leaf rolls with rice, 98; with meat and rice, 168

Wheat, boiled, 208, with poached chicken or turkey, 212; cracked, in pilaff, 213
Wheaten porridge with cheese, 214

Yoghurt, 122; drink, 339; strained, 123

# ROMANIA

Acacia flowers preserved in syrup, 330

Baklava, 304
Beef, boiled, 161
Biscuits, sponge finger, 271
Bread, scalded, with milk and cheese, 252; wholemeal, 233

Cake, fatless, 280; walnut, 278
Cake-bread, 241
Celeriac stuffed like artichokes, 101
Chicken, roast paprika, 187; stew, 191; stew with potatoes, 192
Compote, 286
Cornmeal porridge, 216
Cozonac, 241

Crescent rolls filled with walnuts, 250

Doughnuts, jam, 256

Fish casserole, 138
Fruit butter: plum, 332

Halva, 314

Kadaif, 310

Kyufteta, fried, 153; grilled, 152; in tomato sauce, 154
Lamb's offal roasted on a spit, 200
'Maiden's Breasts', 196
Marmalade (see Fruit butters)
Mechka (Urs), 117

Nectar, apple, 337

Pancakes, 254
Pastry, layered with cheese, 268; layered with minced meat, 269
Polenta, 216; baked with cheese, 217

Pork, with sauerkraut, 172; sausages, 185
Priest's stew, 166
Pudding, black, 198

Rose-petal preserve, 328
Salad, cos-lettuce, 70; grilled pepper, 70
Sauce, yoghurt and garlic, 347
Sauerkraut, 317; rolls with meat and rice, 170
Sausages, blood, 198; pork, 185; skinless, charcoal grilled, 151
Shish kebab, 148

Soup, fish, 82; meatball, 81; sauerkraut with pork, 76; sour lamb, 75; tripe, 78
Spinach cakes, 111
Stew, priest's, 166 (see also Chicken)
Stufat, 166

Veal escalopes, plain, 157
Vegetable casserole, 104; with meat, 181
Vine-leaf rolls with meat and rice, 168

Wheat, boiled, 208

## SLOVENIA

Alleluia, 91

Beef, boiled, 161
Biscuits, Christmas, 274; pepper, 276
Bread, dumplings, 228; palace, 253; plaited, 246; rustic (with cornmeal), 239; wholemeal, 233
Brodet, 140
Buckwheat porridge, 213

Cake, walnut, 278
Cake-bread, 241
Cheese, melted, with bacon, 114
Chocolate ring, 244
Cornmeal porridge, 216

Doughnuts, jam, 256
Dumplings, bread, 228; plum, 228

Fish, grilled over embers, 132; stew, 140
Friko, 114

Gibanica, 268

Hare, hunter's style, 205

Ice cream, white, 302

Krofi, 256

Millet porridge, 214

Pancakes, 254,
Pasta, grated, 224; broken, 225
Pastry layered with cheese, 268
Pheasant, roast, 207
Pinca, 241
Polenta, 216; baked with cheese, 217
Pork, with white cabbage, 171; lights, stew, 199
Pudding, baked batter, with apples, 294; black, 198; white, 197

Roux, 340
Salad, cos-lettuce, 70; cucumber

and yoghurt, 68; mixed summer, 72; sauerkraut, 72; winter black-radish, 69
Sauce, flour-bound, 341; small enrichment, 349
Sausage, blood, 198; liver, 197
Sauerkraut, 317; salad, 72
Sirchek, 117
Soup, fish, 82; tripe, 78
Stew (see Fish, Pork)
Sucking pig, roast, 146

Tarhana, 224

Venison, braised haunch of, 202; minced steaks, 202

Wild-piglet chops with juniper berries, 204

Yoghurt, 122

Zlivanka, 294

## TURKEY

Aubergine caviar, 65
Aubergines stuffed with onion and garlic, 96

Baklava, 304
Beef, boiled, 161; kebabs baked in paper parcels, 162; steaks, grilled, 152; stew with prunes, 167
Blancmange, 295
Borani, 92
Bowl kebab, 177
Bread, scalded, with milk and cheese, 252

Cabbage-leaf rolls with meat and rice, 170
Cake, fatless, 280; semolina, syruped, 309; walnut, 278
Caviar, aubergine, 65
Chicken, Circassian, 194; stuffed, 188; cooked with wheat, 212
Coffee, Turkish, 333
Compote, 286; in a watermelon, 286
Cornflour jelly without gelatine, 296

Courgettes, fried, 109
Cornmeal porridge, 216
Cracked wheat pilaff, 213

Eggs, poached with yoghurt, 118; scrambled with minced meat, 119

Fish, casserole, 138; grilled over embers, 132 (see also Salad)
Fritters, choux, with a light syrup, 312
Fruit butter: plum, 332

Halva (Helva), 314; flour, 314; semolina, 315
Ice cream, salep, 303; white, 302
Imam bayildi, 96

Jam, quince, 330

Kabuniyye, 220
Kachamak, 216
Kadaif, 310
Kapama, 163
Kofte, fried, 153; grilled, 152; in egg-and-lemon sauce, 156; in onion sauce, 154
Kulbasti, 152

Lamb stew with spring onions, 163
Lamb's offal roasted on a spit, 200

Marmalade (see Fruit butter)
Morello cherries preserved in syrup, 325
Muhallebi, 295
Mussels, stuffed, 142

Orange rinds preserved in syrup, 325

Paluze, 296
Pasta, grated, 224
Pastry, amulets filled with cheese, 270; layered with cheese, 268; layered with minced meat, 269
Peppers, stuffed with meat, 182
Pickle, mixed, 322
Pickled grapes, 321
Pilaff, cracked wheat, 213; rice, 218
Polenta baked with cheese, 217
Potato cakes, 112
Priest's stew, 166
Pumpkin, baked, 289

Quince jam, 330
Quinces, poached, filled with cream, 287; stuffed with beef or veal, 184

Revani, 309
Rice pilaff, 218; pudding, 220; sweet saffron, 221
Rose-petal preserve, 328

Salad, cos-lettuce, 70; cucumber and yoghurt, 68; dried fish, 73; grilled pepper, 70; mixed summer, 72; winter black-radish, 69
Salep drink, hot, 339
Sauce, egg-and-lemon finishing, 349; fresh tomato and garlic, 344; walnut and garlic, 346; yoghurt and garlic, 347
Sausage, grape juice and walnut, 323
Sausages, skinless, grilled, 151
Sauerkraut, 317
Shish kebab, 148
Soup, calf's or sheep's head and trotters, 80; fish, 82; meatball, 81; tomato, 85; tripe, 78
Stews (see Beef, Lamb, Priest's)
Strudel with puff pastry, 266

Tarama, 67
Tarator, 346
Tarhana, 224
Tas kebab, 177

Vegetable casserole, 104; with meat, 181
Vine-leaf rolls with rice, 98; with meat and rice, 168

Wheat, boiled, 208; cracked, 213; with poached chicken or turkey, 212

Yoghurt, 122; drink, 339; strained, 123

Zerde, 221

## YUGOSLAVIA (SERBIA, MONTENEGRO, KOSOVO & VOJVODINA)

Acacia flowers preserved in syrup, 330
Apple cream, 297
Aubergine caviar, 75; moussaka, 178
Aubergines stuffed with onion and garlic, 96

Baklava, 304; in snail shapes, 306
Beef, boiled, 161; kebabs baked in paper parcels, 162; pot roast, 172; steaks, grilled, 152; stew with prunes, 167
Biscuits, Christmas, 274; old-fashioned, soda, 272; pepper, 276; sponge finger, 271; syruped, 313; walnut macaroons, 273
Black-olive purée, 95
Bowl kebab, 177
Bread, dumplings, 228; plaited, 246; rice, 235; scalded with milk and cheese, 252; wholemeal, 233
Broccoli, baked with eggs and cheese, 96

Cabbage-leaf rolls with meat and rice, 170
Cake, bishop's, 280; fatless, 280; fresh fruit, 279; lemon-flavoured, 276; walnut, 278
Caraway straws, 283
Caviar, aubergine, 76
Cheese, grilled in paper parcels, 116; slices, fried, 116
Chocolate cream, 299
Chicken, Circassian, 194; fried, 195; roast paprika, 187; stew, 191; stew with potatoes, 192; garnished with Tarhana, 193; cooked with wheat, 212; stuffed, 188
Chitterlings of lamb, baked, 199
Cocoa drink, hot, 336
Coffee, iced, 336; Turkish, 333
Compote, 286; Champagne, in a watermelon, 286; morello cherry, 287
Cornbread, 240
Cornmeal porridge, 216
Courgettes, baked, 106; fried, 109; with rice, 93
Crescent rolls filled with walnuts, 250

Doughnuts, jam, 256
Duckling, roast, with morello cherry sauce, 189
Dumplings, bread, 228; plum, 228

Eggs, baked with cheese, 119; fried with spinach, 88; poached with yoghurt, 118; scrambled with mincemeat, 119

Fish, fried hake in batter, 135; fried

# Index

whitebait, 133; grilled over embers, 132; grilled trout with clotted cream, 133; parcels, 134; stuffed carp with walnuts, 136
Fritters, apple or quince, 258; choux, with a light syrup, 312; light-as-air, sweet, 258
Fruit butter: plum, 332

Gibanica, 268; with broken pasta, 266 (see also Pastry, layered)
Goose, roast with sauerkraut, 190
Green-walnut preserve, 326
Guerilla kebab, 162

Halva, 314; flour, 314; semolina, 315
Hare, hunter's style, 205

Ice cream, raspberry sorbet, 301; white, 302; yoghurt, 301
Imam bayildi, 96

Jam, quince, 330
Jelly, lemon, 300; raspberry, 300

Kadaif, 310
Kapama, 163
Kavurma, 186
Koh, 291
Krofne, 256
Kuglof, with dried fruit, 242; with sunflower oil, 277; with walnuts, 243
Kyufteta, baked in yoghurt custard, 154; fried, 153; grilled, 152; in onion sauce, 155; in tomato sauce, 154

Lamb, mixed grill, 150; shepherd's kebab, 175; stew with green beans, 164; peas, 163; potatoes, 165; spinach, 164; spring onions, 163 (see also Soup)
Liptauer, home-made, 117
Love letters, 282
Lemons preserved in syrup, 331

'Maiden's Breasts', 196
Marmalade (see Fruit butters)
Mlinci, 225
Morello cherries preserved in syrup, 327
Moussaka, aubergine, 178; with potatoes, 180

Nectarines, stuffed, baked, 291

Nettle purée, 89
Orange rinds preserved in syrup, 325
Pancakes, 254; stuffed with vegetables, 106
Partridge, roast, in nests of straw potatoes, 206
Pasta, baked pudding, 226; broken, baked, 225; with cheese, 225; grated, 224
Pastry, layered with cheese, 268; layered with minced meat, 269; many-petalled sheets, 263
Pepper relish, 66
Peppers, fried, with tomato sauce, 110; stuffed with cheese, 110; stuffed with meat, 182; stuffed with rice, 100
Pheasant, roast, 207
Pickled cornelian cherries, 320
Pilaff, rice, 218
Pirjan, 94
Plums, sweet, baked, 292
Polenta, 216; baked with cheese, 217
Pork, with cabbage, 171; with sauerkraut, 172
Potato cakes, 112
Potted meat, 186
Pudding, baked batter with apples, 294; baked pasta, 226; baked walnut and potato, 291; black, 198; rice, 220; white, 197
Pumpkin, baked, 289; purée baked, 290
Pumpkin seeds, toasted, 222

Quail grilled on a rack, 206
Quince creams with Cognac, 298; jam, 330; salami, 293; Turkish delight, 293
Quinces, poached, filled with cream, 287

Rice, bread, 235; pilaff, 218; pudding, 220
Risotto, 143
Rose-petal preserve, 328
Roux, 340

Salad, cos-lettuce, 70; cucumber and yoghurt, 68; grilled pepper, 70; mixed summer, 72; sauerkraut, 72

Sauce, egg-and-lemon finishing, 349; flour-bound, 341; fresh tomato and garlic, 344; fricassee, 343; small enrichment, 349; walnut and garlic, 346; white, 342; yoghurt and garlic, 347
Sauerkraut, 317; rolls with meat and rice, 168; with roast goose, 190 (see also Soup, Wild boar)
Sausage, blood, 198; grape juice and walnut, 323; liver, 197
Sausages, skinless, charcoal grilled, 151
Scampi risotto, 143
Schnitzels, Universal, 157
Shepherd's kebab, 175
Shish kebab, 148; meatball shish kebab, 149
Spinach purée with fried eggs, 88
Soup, fish, 82; meatball, 81; pork knuckle, 80; sauerkraut, cold, 79; sauerkraut with pork, 76; sour lamb, 75; sour, of lamb's tongues, 76; tomato, 85; tripe, 78
Stew, green bean, 90 (see also Beef, Chicken, Lamb)
Strudel, pumpkin, 266; with puff pastry, 266
Sucking pig, roast, 146

Tarama, 67
Tarhana, 224
Tea, lemon, 338
Tisane, camomile, 339; lime-blossom, 338
Tomatoes with rice, 91

Veal escalopes, plain, 157; Viennese style, 158
Venison, braised haunch of, 202
Vegetable, casserole, 104; with meat, 181; macedoine to serve with roast beef, 102
Vegetables, mixed, braised, 102
Vine-leaf rolls with meat and rice, 168

Walnuts, salted, 64
Wheat, boiled, 208; with poached chicken or turkey, 212
White cabbage, baked, 103
Wild boar with sauerkraut, 203

Yoghurt, 122

# General Index

(The lists of foreign names that follow the English recipe titles have not been indexed, but most foreign names that occur in the text itself are included.)

Acacia flowers preserved in syrup, 330
*Acipenser güldenstädti*, 125; *ruthenus*, 125, 130; *stellatus*, 125; *sturio*, 125
Adriatic hotel, near Durres, Albania, 159
Adriatic Sea, 124-7, 129
Aegean Sea, 127, 131
Albania, 10-11, 72, 201
Albanian lamb and yoghurt casserole, 159; lamb stew with parsley, 160; trifle creams, 299; walnut biscuits, 313-14
*Alburnus alburnus*, 125
All Souls' Day, 208
All-in-one cheese sauce, 342
All-in-one white sauce, 342
Alleluia, 91
*Amberliya rakiya*, 14
America, 7-8
Amulets, pastry, with cheese, 270
*Anancamptis pyramidalis*, 55
Anchovies, 138
*Anguilla anguilla*, 127
*Antipastë*, 11
Apple, cream, 297; fritters, 258; nectar, 337
Apples, baked batter pudding with, 294; glazed, with clotted cream and nuts, 288
Arda, river, 124
Artichokes, celeriac stuffed like, 101
Ashoure, 211-12
Asp, 124
*Aspius Aspius*, 124
*Astacus*, 126
Athens, Greece, 306
Attar of roses, 7, 328-9
Aubergine, 7; and walnut caviar, 65; caviar, 65; moussaka, 178-9; stuffed with onion and garlic, *Imam Bayildi*, 96-7; fried, 109
*Auflauf*, 17
Avicenna, 12
*Aÿgotáraho(n)*, 124, 127
Ayran, 120

*Babek*, 43, 186
*Bábsajt*, 18
*Backpulvergugelhupf*, 277
Bacon, Slovenian melted cheese with, 114

*Baj Ganyu*, 132
Baked batter pudding with apples, 294
Baked beans, Macedonian, 40, 105
Baked broccoli, eggs and cheese, 96
Baked courgettes, 106
Baked eggs and cheese, 119
Baked fish with onions, 139
Baked lamb's chitterlings, 199
Baked pasta pudding, 226-7
Baked pumpkin, 289
Baked pumpkin purée, 290
Baked stuffed nectarines, 291-2
Baked sweet plums, 292
Baked walnut and potato pudding, 291
Baked white cabbage, 103
Baklava, 304-5; dry, 307; in snail shapes, 306
Balkan Mountains, 1
*Balmoush*, 113
*Banichki*, 261
Bap loaf, 236
*Barbus meridionalis petenyi*, 130
Barley, naked, 3
*Basan*, 34
Basanovich, I, 201
*Baščaršijski sahan*, 22
Basioli, Josip, 128
Batter, bread, 238; pudding, baked, with apples, 294
Bean, soup, monastery, 84-5; stew, green, 90
Beans, green, lamb stew with, 164-5; haricot, baked with cabbage, 103; Macedonian baked, 105
Béchamel, 342; yellow, 342
Beef, air-dried (*pasturma*), 62; boiled, 161; kebabs baked in paper parcels, 162; pot-roasted silverside, 172-3; quinces stuffed with, 184; roast, vegetable macédoine to serve with, 102; shish kebab of, 148-9; skinless sausages, 151; steaks, 152; stew with prunes, 167; stew with rice, leeks and potatoes, 168
Belgrade, 18, 66
Beluga, 138
Beluga caviar, 60
Beluga sturgeon, 124-5
Berat, Albania, 159
Bereket, Bulgaria, 3
Berlin Root, 52
*Between the Woods and the Water*, 216

*Binto*, 125
*Biryan*, 94, 168
Biscuits, 271-84; Albanian walnut, 313-14; Christmas, 274-5; grape, 275; pepper, 276; soda, 272; sponge finger, 271; syruped, 313-14; white shortbread, 272-3
Bishop's bread, 280
Black olive purée, 95; stew, 68
Black pudding, 198
Black radish salad, winter, 69-70
Black Sea, 124-9, 131
Blancmange, 295
Bleak, 125
Blood sausage, 63, 198
Blueberries, 295
Boar, wild, see Wild boar,
*Bogrács*, 30
Boiled beef, 161
Boiled wheat, 208-10
Bonito, 132, 140
*Book of the Duchess, The*, 16
*Borani*, 91-2
*Borș*, 17
*Bosanski šiš*, 22
Bosnia, 276
Bosnia-Hercegovina, 21-2
Bosnian fondue, 114; fritters, 257; pot with vegetables, 173-4; 'sweetheart' cake, 309
*Boulgour*, 27-8; see also *Bulgur*
*Boutaraga*, 124
Bowl kebab, 177
*Boza*, 45, 48
Braised haunch of venison, 202
Braises, enrichment sauce for, 349
Brandy, 14, 54; plum, 19, 22
*Brano loudouvano mlyako*, 29
Bratwurst, 17
Brawn, 60, 80
Bread, 230-58; ancient, 3-4; and garlic sauce, 346; and salt, 236; batter, 238; bishop's, 280; cheese, 237; dumplings, 228; palace, 253; plaited, 246-7; rice, 235; scalded, with milk and cheese, 252; wholemeal, 233-4; wholemeal honey, 248
Bread ovens, 3-4, 33
Brill, 135
*Brînză de Burduf*, 20
Broccoli with eggs and cheese, baked, 96
*Brodet*, 125-8, 130-1, 140
Broken baked pasta, 225-6
Brown hare, 205
Brown trout, 131
Buckwheat, 25, 45; porridge, 213
Buffalo butter, 121

*Bulbulija*, 220
Bulgar-Turks, 5- 6, 17, 113
*Bulgari ot Staro Vreme*, 59
Bulgaria, 12-14
Bulgarian melted cheese, 115
Bulgarian rose-scented wheat dessert, 211-12
*Bulgur*, 44, 213; see also *Boulgour*
Bushaq of Shiraz, 165
Butter, 120-3; carrot, 348; plum, 332; pumpkin, 331-2; red paprika, 347
*Byal Muzh*, 113
*Byrekaque*, 262

Cabbage, 8; baked white, 103; baked with haricot beans, 103; white, pork pot with, 171
Cabbage-leaf rolls with meat and rice, 170
*Cacik*, 63, 69
*Cahija*, 249
Cake, Bosnian 'sweetheart', 309; fresh fruit, 279; lemon-flavoured plain, 276-7; semolina, 309; soaked in fragrant milk, 310
Cake-breads, 241-8
Cakes, 271-84; potato, 112; spinach and potato, 112
Calcium carbonate, 52, 321
*Căldare*, 38
Camomile tisane, 339
Canapés, 60
*Cannelloni*, 227
*Capreolus capreolus*, 202
*Capsicum annuum*, 8; see also Pepper, sweet,
Caraway straws, 283
*Carigradske tatlije*, 313
Carob, 45
Carp, 125, 130, 134; stuffed with walnuts, 136
Carrot butter, 348
*Cașcaval*, 16
Casserole, Albanian lamb and yoghurt, 159; fish, 138; mixed vegetable, 104; pork and rice, 160-1; rice and potato, 94; shepherd's, 95; Thracian tomato, 108
Casseroles, 35, 40
Cauldrons, 30, 38
Caviar, 60, 125; aubergine, 65; aubergine and walnut, 65; false, 60; semolina, 64
Çelebi, Evliya, 32, 232
Celeriac stuffed like artichokes, 101
Celts, 5
*Cervus elaphus*, 202
*Ćevapčići*, 18
*Chalcalburnus chalcoides*, 125
Champagne compote in a watermelon, 286
Chaucer, Geoffrey, 16
Cheese, 113-19; as part of meze, 60; baked broccoli, eggs and, 96; bread, 237; fried peppers stuffed with,

110; grilled in paper parcels, 116; in Albania, 11; in Montenegro, 20; in Romania, 15; in Smolyan, 28; in Yugoslavia, 18; layered pastry with, 268; nettle soup with walnuts or, 86; pastry amulets filled with, 270; polenta baked with, 217; rolls, 249; rolls made with filo pastry, 265; rolls made with katmer dough, 264; sauce, 106-7; sauce, all-in-one, 342; scalded bread with milk and, 252; slices, fried, 116; tarhana with, 225; turnovers, 284; wheaten porridge with, 214-15; see also specific types
Cherries, cornelian, 46; cornelian, pickled, 320; morello, 294; morello, compote of, 287; morello, preserved in syrup, 327; morello, sauce, 351
Chick-pea, 7; leaven, 231; *neblebi*, 51-2
Chicken, Circassian, 194; chilli, 192; fried, 195; poached with pasta shreds, 193; poached with wheat, 212; roast paprika, 187; stew, 191; stew with potatoes, 192-3; stuffed, 188; wheat with chicken and turkey, 61
Chilli, 8, 9
Chios, 51
*Chiroz*, 61, 73, 126
Chitterlings, lamb's, 199
*Chiviya*, 125
Chocolate cream, 299; ring, 244-5
*Chondrostoma nasus*, 129
*Chorba*, 19, 74; Bismark, 79
Choux fritters with a light syrup, 312
Christmas biscuits, 274-5
*Ciorbă*, 16
Circassian chicken, 194
Clauson, Sir Gerard, 223
*Clibanus*, 34
Clotted cream, 50, 121; and strawberries, 60; glazed apples and nuts with, 288; grilled trout with, 133
Cockles, 143
Cocoa drink, 336
Cod, 126, 138
Coffee, cups, 34; iced, 336; mills, 41-2; pot, 37, 41-2; Turkish, 333-5
Cognac, quince creams with, 298
Cold sauerkraut soup, 79
*Complete Letters of Lady Mary Wortley Montagu*, 26
Compote, 286-7; Champagne in a watermelon, 286; morello cherry, 287
Confectioner's custard, 353; white, 354
*Cookbook, or Instructions for all Kinds of Dishes*, 25
Corfu, 140
Cornbread, 239-40
Cornelian cherry, 46; pickled, 320
Cornflour jelly, 296
Cornmeal porridge (polenta), 216-17
Cos lettuce salad, 70

Courgettes, baked, 106; fried, 109; layered pastry with, 267; with rice, 93
*Cozonac*, 15
Crab, warty, 126
Cracked wheat pilaff, 213
Cracklings, 60, 91
Crayfish, 126, 143
Cream, 120-3; apple, 297; chocolate, 299; lemons and, 293; poached quinces filled with, 287-8; quince, 298; see also Clotted cream
Creams, 285-303; Albanian trifle, 299
Crème pâtissière, 353
Crescent rolls filled with walnuts, 250; rolling out, 251
Crete, 3
Crni Drim, river, 127
Croatia, 22-3
Croissants, 250
Cucumber and yoghurt, 63; salad, 68-9
Cucumber soup, iced, 87
*Cucurbita, maxima*, 7, 289; *moschata*, 7; *pepo*, 7, 289; see also Pumpkin,
*Cuisine of Hungary, The*, 22
*Curekot*, 232
*Curtain Calls*, 15, 16-17
Cushaw squash, 54
*Cyprinus carpio*, 125, 130, 134

Daire restaurant, Sarajevo, 32
Dalmatia, 22-3, 218
Damask rose, 7, 328
Danube, river, 124, 125, 130-1
Danube bleak, 125
Danube Delta Reserve, 201
Date-shell, 143
*Ded*, 24
Dencho, Baj, 284
Dentex, 126, 140
Divan, 165
*Djathë Kaçkavall*, 10
*Djathë Kasher*, 10
*Djevrek*, 47
Dobrogea, Romania, 16
*Dolalma*, 21-2
*Döner kebab*, 32
Doughnuts, jam, 256
Drava, river, 125
Dried fish salad, 73
Drinks, 333-9
Dry baklava, 307
Dublin Bay prawn, 127
Dubrovnik, Croatia, 135

Duckling, roast, with morello cherry sauce, 189
Dumplings, 223-9; bread, 228; plum, 228-9
Durham, M. Edith, 11, 19, 21, 93, 145, 219, 240
Durres, Albania, 159, 177
*Džanećija*, 316

Easter, see breads
Eel, 127, 140
Egg-and-lemon finishing sauce, 82, 349; meatballs with, 156
Eggs, 113-19; baked broccoli, cheese and, 96; poached, with rusks, 253; spinach purée with fried, 88-9
Einkorn, 3
Elbasan, Albania, 159
Elbasan casserole, 159
Enrichment sauce, 349
Epiphany, 257
*Eriphia spinifrons*, 126
Escalopes, veal, 157-8; Viennese style, 158
*Esox lucius*, 129, 141

Faggots, 197
*Family Treasure*, 206
Fan mussels, stewed, 141
Fatless sponge cake, 281-2
Fennel, 232
Feta cheese, 47
Filberts, 7
Filo pastry, see Leaf pastry,
Finishing sauce, egg-and-lemon, 349
Fish, 124-44; baked in a dough jacket, 137; baked with onions, 139; casserole, 138; grilled over embers, 132; in Bulgaria, 12; parcels, 134; salad of dried, 73; soup, 30, 82; stew, 140; see also specific species
Flat breads, 231
Flounder, 127, 135, 140
Flour, roasted, 340
Flour-bound sauce, 341
Focaccia, 231
Fondue, Bosnian, 114
*Foufoú*, 32
Fragrant milk, cake soaked in, 310
French toast, 253
Fresh fruit cake, 279
Fricassée sauce, 343
Fried cheese slices, 116
Fried chicken, 195
Fried courgettes, 109
Fried hake in batter, 135
Fried peppers stuffed with cheese, 110
Fried peppers with tomato sauce, 110-11
Fried whitebait, 133
Fritters, 230-58; apple or quince, 258; Bosnian, 257; choux, with a light syrup, 312; light-as-air sweet, 258; yeasted, 254-5
Fruit cake, fresh, 279
Fruit desserts, 285-303
Fruit, soft, sauce, 350

Gabrovo, Bulgaria, 215, 254, 306
*Gadus morhua*, 126
*Gălutși*, 17
Game, 201-7
*Gancho Koserkata*, 30, 66
Gardiner, Leslie, 15, 16-17
Garlic, and tomato sauce, 153; and vinegar sauce, 341; aubergine stuffed with onion and, 96-7; green, 47-8; sauce of bread and, 346; sauce of walnut and, 346; sauce of yoghurt and, 347; tomato sauce with, 344; vinegar, 348
*Garozi*, 127
Gerov, Najden, 92, 117 221, 257
*Gevrek*, 47, 231
*Gewürzküchlein*, 17
Gilthead bream, 130
Ginchev, Tsani, 30, 66, 74, 145
Giurgiu, Romania, 185
*Gjevrek*, 47
*Gkiousleméthes*, 262
Glazed apples with clotted cream and nuts, 288
Gllava Pass, Albania, 203
*Gobiidae*, 127
*Gobius exanthematicus*, 127
Goby, 127
Good King Henry, 49
Goose, roast with sauerkraut, 190
Gorenjska, Slovenia, 214
Gračanica, Serbia, 19
Graham bread, 233
Grains, 208-22
Grape biscuits, 275
Grape juice and walnut sausage, 323
Grape pudding, 298
Grapes, pickled, 321; sour, 43
Gratinated mixed vegetables, 107-8
Greece, 25
Green bean stew, 90
Green beans, lamb stew with, 164-5
*Green Newcomers, The*, 329
Green walnut preserve, 326
Grey mullet, 124, 127, 138
Griddles, 38
Grilled oysters, 144
Grilled pepper and tomato salad, 71
Grilled pepper salad, 70-1
Grilled quail on a rack, 206

Grilled trout with clotted cream, 133
Grills, 32
Guerilla kebab, 162
*Gulyas*, 17
*Güveç*, 104, 131, 181
*Gyozhe*, 28
*Gyulovitsa*, 14
*Gyuvech*, 104, 181, 182

Hadzhihristev, Dr Argir, 27
Hake, 128; fried in batter, 135
Halıcı, Nevin, 68-9, 78
Hall, D.J., 55
Halva, 48-9, 314-15; semolina, 315; walnut, 48; white, 49
Hamburg parsley, 52
*Hanoúm pagotó*, 306
Hare, hunter's style, 205
Haricot beans baked with white cabbage, 103
*Hašure*, 211-12
Hearths, 30, 33
Herbed sauce, 341
Hercegovinian pot with meat and vegetables, 174
*High Albania*, 93, 219, 240
Hilmo, Gerim, 32
'Hitur Peter', 290
*Hladna žetelačka supa*, 87
Hobhouse, John Cam, Lord Broughton, 11, 50, 124, 175, 218
Holbach, Maude M., 285
Honey bread, wholemeal, 248
Horseradish sauce, 147
*Hórta*, 49
*Hošaf*, 286
*Hurma*, 313
*Huso huso*, 124-5

Ice-cream, 285-303; salep, 303; white, 302; yoghurt, 301-2
Iced coffee, 336
Iced cucumber soup, 87
Illyrians, 5-7, 45
*Imam Bayildi*, aubergines, 96-7
*Instructions for all Kinds of Dishes*, 235
Islam, 11
Istanbul, Turkey, 277

Jam doughnuts, 256
Jam, quince, 330
*Japrak*, 22
Jelly, cornflour, 296; lemon, 300; raspberry, 300
*Jogurt tava*, 159
John Dory, 128

*Juha*, 24, 74
Juniper, wild piglet chops with, 204

*Kabuni-pilav*, 220
*Kachamak*, 28
*Kadaif*, 310-11
*Kadingöbeği*, 313
*Kajamak*, 18
*Kajmac*, 20, 50, 60
*Kapuciner*, 334
*Kaṣa, kaša, kasha* 17, 24, 27, 50, 214-15
*Kashkaval*, 1
*Kaskavál-sajt*, 18
*Katmer*, 263-4, 307
Katrandzhiev, Dr K., 12
*Katuk*, 12
*Kaymak*, 50, 57, 121
Kayseri, Turkey, 62
Kazanluk, Bulgaria, 329
Kebab, beef, baked in paper parcels, 162; bowl, 177; Shepherd's lamb, 175; sweet, 176
*Kek*, 277
Keta caviar, 60, 126
Khusru Parviz, King , 91
'King's Town sweets', 313
*Kisela chorba*, 19
*Kiselo mleko*, 18
*Klin*, 28
*Knödeln*, 17
Knuckle, pork, soup, 80
*Kolač*, 24
*Kolach*, 231
Kolašin, Yugoslavia, 21
*Komovica*, 19
Konstantinov, Aleko, 132
*Kos*, 10, 70
Kosovo, 11, 20
*Kotel*, 30, 33, 38
*Kourtmach*, 120
Kruševac, Serbia, 210
*Kuglof*, 242-4; with walnuts, 243-4
*Kuglov* with sunflower oil, 277-8
*Kyufteta*, 152-4

*Lactobacterium, acidophilus*, 120; *bulgaricum*, 120
'Lady's navel', 313
*Lakerda*, 61, 125
*Lakerdë*, 128
Lakišić, Alija, 173
Lamb, and yoghurt casserole, 159; chitterlings, 199; in vine-leaf rolls, 168-9; mixed grill, 150; offal roasted on a spit, 200; pan for cooking, 38; pluck, 196; pluck parcels, vegetarian, 107; Shepherd's kebab, 175; shish

kebab, 148-9; skinless sausages of, 151; sour soup, 75; stew with green beans, 164-5; stew with peas, 163; stew with potatoes, 165; stew with spinach, 164; stew with spring onions, 163; whole roast and stuffed, for St George's day, 147
Lambs' tongues, sour soup of, 76
Lang, George, 8, 22
Langer, 29
Langouste, 128, 140
*Lanher*, 29
Larisa, Greece, 56
Layered pastry with cheese, 268; with courgettes, 267; with minced meat, 169
Leaf pastry, 259-70; rolling out, 251
Leather carp, 125
Leaves, cabbage, 170; sauerkraut, 170-1; vine, 168-9
Leeks cooked in white wine, 90; stew with beef, rice and potatoes, 168
Leigh Fermor, Patrick, 57, 216
Lemon, egg and lemon finishing sauce, 349; jelly, 300; lemon-flavoured plain cake, 276-7; meze, 61; tea, 338;
Lemons, and cream, 293; preserved in sugar, 331
Leo V, Emperor, 57
*Lepus europaeus*, 205
Lettuce, cos, salad, 70
Leveret, 205
Light-as-air sweet fritters, 258
Lights, pork, 199
Lime-blossom tisane, 338
Limpets, 143
Linzer pastry, 281, 282
Liptauer, 117
*Lithograthus mormyrus*, 130
*Lithophaga lithophaga*, 143
Liver sausage, 197
Lobster, spiny, 128
Loksantra restaurant, Athens, 306
*Lomac*, 30
*Lonac*, 173-4
'Love Letters', 282
*Lyangyur*, 29
Lyaskovets, Bulgaria, 267

Macédoine, vegetable, to serve with roast beef, 102
Macedonia, 23-4, 238, 257, 263-4, 307
Macedonian baked beans, 40, 105
Macedonians, 5
Mackerel, 126, 128, 132; livers, 127
'Maiden's Breasts', 196-7
*Magkáli*, 32
Maize, 7, 28; bread, 239-40
*Makaronash*, 11

*Malebi*, 295
*Mămăligă*, 15, 216
Mangafish, 29
*Mangala*, 32
Maramureș, Romania, 17
Maraschino, 50
Market gardening, 8
Marmalade, plum, 332; pumpkin, 331-2
Marmora, Sea of, 127, 129
Marrow, vegetable, 7
Mastic, 50-1
*Mastika*, 14, 51
Matritsa, river, 124
Meat, Hercegovinian pot with vegetables and, 174; in cabbage-leaf rolls, 170; in sauerkraut-leaf rolls, 170-1; in vine-leaf rolls, 168-9; minced, layered pastry with, 169; minced, scrambled eggs with, 119; mixed vegetable casserole with, 181; peppers stuffed with, 182-3; potted, 186; see also under specific breeds
Meatball shish kebab, 149; soup (with vegetables), 81
Meatballs in egg-and-lemon sauce, 156; in onion sauce, 155; in tomato sauce, 154; see also *kyufteta*
*Mechka*, 117
Medlar, 296
*Melceü't-Tabbâhın*, 98
Melted cheese recipes, 114-6
*Merluccius merluccius*, 128
*Mesogobius batrachocephalus*, 127
Mesolonghi, 124
Metamorphoses, 38
Metchnikoff, Professor, 28
Meze, 59-73, 125-7
Milk, 120-3; fragrant, cake soaked in, 310; scalded bread with cheese and, 252; walnut, 352
Millet, 6, 24; *boza*, 45; porridge, 214
Minced meat, layered pastry with, 169; scrambled eggs with, 119
Minced steaks, venison, 202
Mirror carp, 125, 134
Mixed braised vegetables, 102-3
Mixed grill of lamb, 150
Mixed pickle, 322
Mixed summer salad, 72
Mixed vegetable casserole, 104; with meat, 181
*Mješinski sir*, 20
*Mlinci*, 225
*Močnik*, 24
*Mogul cephalus*, 130
Moldavia, 15
Monastery bean soup, 84-5
Montenegro, 11, 20
Morello cherries, 294; preserved in syrup, 327

Morello cherry compote, 287; sauce, 189, 351
Moussaka, 178-80
*Mugil cephalus*, 124, 127
Mullet, grey, see Grey mullet,
Mullet, red, see Red mullet,
*Mullus barbatus*, 129; *ponticus*, 129
*Mullus surmuletus*, 129
Mushrooms, pancakes stuffed with, 107; wild, 214-15
Mussels, 129, 143; fan, stewed, 141; in white wine, Dalmatian style, 142; stuffed, 142
Mycenaeans, 5
*Mytilus galloprovincialis*, 129

Nase, 129
'Nasreddin Hoca', 290
Nectarines, baked stuffed, 291-2
*Nephrops norvegicus*, 127
Nettle purée, 89
Nettle soup with walnuts or cheese, 86
New Year's Eve, 268
*Nigella sativa*, 232
Nikolas, St, 125, 136
*Njeguški sir*, 20
Novi Sad, Yugoslavia, 20
Numinagić, Ali efendi, 22
Nuts, glazed apples with clotted cream and, 288; salted, 61

Offal, 187-200; see also under individual cuts
Ohrid, lake, 125, 127, 130
Ohrid, Macedonia, 105, 212, 307
*Oidium lactis*, 120
Oil, red paprika, 347
Okra, 7
Old-fashioned soda biscuits the modern way, 272
Olive purée, black, 95
Olives, 61; black olive stew, 68
*Ömlesztett füstolt sajt*, 18
Omourtag, Khan, 57
Onion, aubergine stuffed with onion and garlic, 96-7; baked fish with, 139; tomato sauce with, 343
Onion sauce, meatballs in, 155
Onogur Turks, 223
Orange marmalade sauce, 351
Orange rinds preserved in syrup, 325
Orchids, 55-6
*Orchis latifolia*, 55; *maculata*, 55-6; *mascula*, 55; *militaris*, 55; *morio*, 55-6
*Oshaf(v)*, 46, 286
*Ovcho kiselo mleko*, 23
Ovens, bread, 3-4; lid, 33, 238
*Ovesena kasha*, 27
Ovid, 38

Oysters, grilled, 144

*Pain perdu*, 253
Palace bread, 253
*Palamud*, 125
*Palinurus vulgaris*, 128
Paluza, 296
Pancakes, 230-58; fast-day, 257; stuffed with mushrooms, 107; stuffed with vegetables, 106-8
*Panicum miliaceum*, 214
Paprika, 8; roast chicken with, 187
*Paprikash*, 131
Parsley, 7, 52; Albanian stew of lamb and, 160
Partridge, roast, in nests of straw potatoes, 206-7
*Pasatempo*, 45, 222
*Păsatul*, 15
Pasta, 11, 223-9; baked pudding, 226-7; broken baked, 225-6
Pasta shreds (*tarhana*), poached chicken with, 193
*Pastırma*, 58
Pastrami, 62
Pastries, 62, 281-84
Pastry amulets filled with cheese, 270
Pastry, layered, with cheese, 268; with courgettes, 267; with minced meat, 169
Pastry, leaf, see Leaf pastry,
*Pasturma*, 62
*Patatnik*, 28
Patties (*kyufteta*), 152-4
Peas, lamb stew with, 163; rice with, 218
Pejchev, Professor, 29
*Pekmez*, 52, 274, 298
Pelin, Elin, 84
*Penceta*, 131
Penev, Professor, 29
Pepper biscuits, 276
Pepper, grilled, salad, 70; and tomato, 71
Pepper, red see Red pepper,
Pepper, sweet, 8, 9
Peppers, stuffed with meat, 182-3; fried, stuffed with cheese, 110; fried, with tomato sauce, 110-11; scrambled eggs and tomato with, 118; stuffed with rice, 100
*Perca fluviatilis*, 129, 137
Perch, 129, 137
Pestle and mortars, 36
*Petmez*, 29; see also *Pekmez*
*Petroselinum sativum* var *foliosum*, 52; *tuberosum*, 52
Pheasant, roast, 207
Pickle, mixed, 322
Pickled cornelian cherries, 320
Pickled grapes, 321
Pickles, 62

Pig's head, 60
Pigs, Yorkshire, 80
Pike, 129, 132, 141
Pike-Perch, 129
Pilaff, 218-20; cracked wheat, 213
*Piryan*, 94
*Pita*, 231
*Pitka*, 236
Plaited bread, 246-7
*Plaki*, 125, 127, 129, 130, 131
*Plakiya*, 124
*Platanthera bifolia*, 55
*Platichthys flesus*, 127, 135; *luscus*, 127
*Pljeskavice*, 18
Plovdiv, Bulgaria, 115
Plum dumplings, 228-9
Plum marmalade or butter, 332
Plums, 19; baked sweet, 292
Poached chicken or turkey and wheat, 212
Poached chicken with pasta shreds, 193
Poached eggs with yoghurt, 118
Poached quinces filled with cream, 287-8
*Podesti*, 145
*Pogache*, 231
Polenta, 216-17; baked with cheese, 217
Poor Knights of Windsor, 253
Poor man's caviar, 64
*Popara*, 252
Poppy seed, 53
Pork, and rice casserole, 160-1; back fat, 62; cracklings, 60, 91; knuckle soup, 80; lights, 199; pot with white cabbage, 171; sauerkraut soup with, 76-7; sausages, 185; shish kebab of, 148-9; with sauerkraut, 172
Porridge, 208-22; buckwheat, 213; millet, 214; wheaten, with cheese, 214-15; see also Polenta.
Potato, 8; and walnut pudding, baked, 291; cakes, 112; cakes, spinach and, 112; casserole of rice and, 94; moussaka with, 180; chicken stew with, 192-3; lamb stew with, 165; stew with beef, rice and leeks, 168
Potatoes, straw, roast partridge in nests of, 206-7
Pots and pans, 30-42
Potted meat, 186
Poultry, 187-200
'Pour-and-bake' batter bread, 238
*Povesti*, 74
*Prakticheska Gotvarska Kniga*, 98
Prawn, Dublin Bay, 127
Prenj, Mount, Hercegovina, 201
*Prepenčenica*, 19
Preserves, 317-32
Priest's stew, 166
Prilep, Macedonia, 71

*Prošek*, 23
*Pršuta*, 21, 61
Prunes, beef stew with, 167
*Psetta maeotica*, 131
*Psetta maxima*, 131, 144
Pudding, baked pasta, 226-7; baked walnut and potato, 291
Puff pastry strudel, 266-7
Pumpkin, 7, 53; baked, 289; baked, purée, 290; butter, 331-2; marmalade, 331-2; seeds, 222; strudel, 266
Purandokht, Princess, 91

Quail, grilled on a rack, 206
Querns, 3
Quick tomato sauce, 345
Quince, creams with Cognac, 298; fritters, 258; jam, 330; poached, filled with cream, 287-8; salami, 293; stuffed with beef or veal, 184
*Qüvec*, 30

Radish, black, winter salad, 69-70
Rainbow trout, 131
*Raisiné simple*, 52
*Raki*, 53-4
*Rakiya*, 14
Raspberry jelly, 300; sorbet, 301
Ratatouille, 102
Razgrad, Bulgaria, 5, 335
*Ražnjići*, 18
Razor-shell, 143
Red deer, 202
Red mullet, 129, 140
Red paprika butter, 347; oil, 347
Red pepper baked with white cabbage, 103
Red pepper relish, 66
Rhodope mountains, Bulgaria, 27, 212
Rhodope, Bulgaria, 113
*Rhombus maeoticus*, 131; *maximus*, 131
Rice and potato casserole, 94
Rice, casserole of pork and, 160-1; courgettes with, 93; garden peas with, 218; peppers stuffed with, 100; pilaff, 218-20; pudding, 220-1; stew with beef, leeks and potatoes, 168; sweet saffron, 221; tomatoes with, 91-2 ; vine leaves stuffed with, 98-9
Risotto, 126, 127; scampi, 143
Roast duckling with morello cherry sauce, 189
Roast goose with sauerkraut, 190
Roast paprika chicken, 187
Roast partridge in nests of straw potatoes, 206-7
Roast pheasant, 207
Roast stuffed lamb for St George's day, 147
Roast sucking pig, 146

Roasted flour, 340
*Robinia pseudoacacia*, 330
Roe deer, 202
Rolling pins, 38
Rolls, cheese, 249; made with filo pastry, 265; made with *katmer* dough, 264
Romania, 15-18
*Romanian Furrow*, 55
*Rosa alba semiplena*, 328; *damascena oleifera* var *alba*, 328; *damascena* var *trigintipetala*, 328; *gallica officinalis*, 328; *gallica officinalis* var *conditorum*, 328
Rose petal preserve, 328
Rose-water sauce, 351
Rosenkranz, 17
Roses, 7
*Roupsko sirene*, 28
Roux, 340
Rusks with poached eggs, 253
Russe, Bulgaria, 113, 284

*Sach*, 38
Saffron rice, sweet, 221
*Sahan*, 39-40
*Saitperec*, 18
*Sakusliya rakiya*, 14
Salad, cos lettuce, 70; cucumber and yoghurt, 68-9; dried fish, 73; grilled pepper, 70-1; grilled pepper and tomato, 71; mixed summer, 72; sauerkraut, 72-3; winter black radish, 69-70; quince, 293
Salep, 55; drink, hot, 339; ice-cream, 303
*Salmo gairdneri*, 131; *salar*, 130; *trutta*, 131; *trutta fario*, 131
Salmon, 130; chum, 126
Salt cellars, 39-40
Salt cod, 126
Salted walnuts, 64
Samokov, Bulgaria, 123
Sarajevo, Bosnia, 32, 33, 189, 232
*Sarda sarda*, 125
Sardines, 132, 138
*Sarma*, 22
Sauce fricassée, 343
Sauce, cheese, 106-7; morello cherry, 189; walnut, 194
Sauces, 340-54
Sauerkraut, 62, 317-20; cold soup, 79; salad, 72-3; soup with pork, 76-7; pork with, 172; roast goose with, 190; roast pheasant with, 207; wild boar with, 203
Sauerkraut-leaf rolls with meat and rice, 170-1
Sausage, grape juice and walnut, 323
Sausages, 62; pork, 185; skinless, 151

*Sazdurma*, 63
Scalded bread with milk and cheese, 252
Scaly (King) carp, 125
Scampi, 127, 140; risotto, 143
Schnitzels, Universal, 157
*Scomber scomber*, 126
Scrambled eggs, with minced meat, 119; with peppers and tomato, 118
Sea bream, 130, 140
Seeds, 208-22
Sekels, 17
Semling, 130
Semolina, cake steeped in syrup, 309; caviar, 64; halva, 315
Sesame paste, 48, 55-6
Sevruga sturgeon, 125
Shapkarev, Kouzman, 212, 324
Sheat fish, 131
Shellfish, 124-44; meze, 63
Shepherd's casserole, 95; lamb kebab, 175
Sherbert, see also Spoonsweet
Shirvani, 220, 288
Shish kebab, 148-50
Shortbread biscuits, white, 272-3
Siebenburgen, 17
*Silurus glanis*, 131
*Simit*, 231
*Sirene*, 12, 28, 47
*Šiš ćevap*, 22
Skadar, lake, 125
Skinless sausages, grilled, 151
*Skorupaca*, 50, 60
*Skrob*, 24
*Skuta*, 115
*Slatko*, 18
Slav peoples, 6-7
*Slava*, 208
Slavejkov, Petko R., 25, 235
Slavonia, 22-3
*Sljivovica*, 19
Slovenia, 24-5, 69, 91, 201, 206, 214, 276
Slovenian melted cheese with bacon, 114-5
*Služba*, 208
Smoked meats, 61
*Smokvice*, 313
Smolyan centenarians, 27-9
Smolyan, Bulgaria, 94
Soda biscuits, 272
Sofia, Bulgaria, 261, 281, 290, 333
Soft fruit sauce, 350
Sole, 132, 135
*Solen vagina*, 143
*Solnitsa*, 40

Sorbet, raspberry, 301
Soul food, 316
Soungoulare wine, 14
Soup, fish, 30
Soup, recipes, 74-87
Sour cream sauce, 341
Sour grape, 43
Sour lamb soup, 75
Sour soup, 74; of lambs' tongues, 76
South Slavs, 21
*Soutzoúki*, 323
Sozopol, Bulgaria, 61
*Sparus auratus*, 130
Spearmint, 7
Spinach, and potato cakes, 112; cakes, 11; lamb stew with, 164; purée with fried eggs, 88-9
Spiny lobster, 128
Spit-roasted fillet of wild boar, 204
Sponge, fatless, 281-2; finger biscuits, 271
Spoonsweets, 324-30
Sprats, 132, 138
Spring onions, lamb stew with, 163
Squash, 53; cushaw, 54; winter turban, 289
St George's day, lamb for, 147
Stara Zagora, Bulgaria, 2-3
Starchev, K., 329
*Starets*, 186
Steaks, beef, 152
Sterlet, 125, 130, 138
Stew pot, 35, 41
Stew, Albanian lamb and parsley, 160; beef, with prunes, 167; beef, with rice, leeks and potatoes, 168; black olive, 68; chicken, 191; chicken with potatoes, 192-3; fish, 140; green bean, 90; lamb and green bean, 164-5; lamb and peas, 163; lamb, with potatoes, 165; lamb, with spinach, 164; lamb, with spring onions, 163; pork lights, 199; Priest's, 166
Stewed fan mussels, 141
Stews, enrichment sauce for, 349
*Stizostedion lucioperca*, 129
Stockfish, 126
Stoves, 32
Strained yoghurt, 123
Straw potatoes, roast partridge in nests of, 206-7
Straws, caraway, 283
*Streptococcus thermophilus*, 120
Strudel pastry, see Leaf pastry,
Strudel, puff pastry, 266-7; pumpkin, 266
*Strukeljci*, 24
Struma river, 124
Stuffed celeriac, like artichokes, 101
Stuffed chicken, 188
Stuffed mussels, 142

Stuffed peppers, 100
Stuffed vine leaves, 62, 98-9
Sturgeon, 124-5, 132, 138
Sucking pig, roast, 146
Sugar, vanilla, 352
Suleiman the Magnificent, 159
Sunflower oil, 8; kuglov with, 277-8
*Sus scrofa*, 203
*Sütlaç*, 220-1
Sweet kebab, 176
Sweet rice pilaff with currants and sultanas, 220
Sweet saffron rice, 221
Sweetbreads, 150
'Sweetheart' cake, Bosnian, 309
Sweetmeats, 304-16
Swordfish, 130, 132
Syrup turnovers, 308
Syrup-based biscuits, 274-5
Syruped biscuits, 313-14
Syruped sweets, 304-16

Tahan, 28, 48, 55-6
Tarama, 67, 127, 130
*Tarator*, 87, 346
*Tarhana*, 193, 223-9; with cheese, 225
*Tava*, 30, 40, 104, 181
*Tavche*, 30, 40
*Tavche so kompiri*, 94
*Tavë kosi*, 159
*Tavë me patate dhe oriz*, 94
Tea, lemon, 338
*Tel kadayıf*, 310-11
*Telemea*, 15, 57
*Teretur*, 63
*Test*, 34
Tetovo, Macedonia, 11, 105
Thessalonica, 49, 56
Thracian tomato casserole, 108
Thracians, 5-6, 317
*Through the Lands of the Serb*, 19, 21, 145
*Thunnus thynnus*, 128, 130, 131
*Tilia argentea*, 338; *cordata*, 338; *platyphyllos*, 338
Tirana, Albania, 135, 158, 255
Tisane, camomile, 339; lime-blossom, 338
*Tolmins*, 114
Tolstoy, Count Leo, 281
Tomato, and grilled pepper salad, 71; casserole, Thracian, 108; scrambled eggs and peppers with, 118; soup, 85;
Tomato sauce, fried peppers with, 110-11; meatballs in, 154; quick, 345; with fresh tomatoes and garlic, 344; with fresh tomatoes and onion, 343; with tomato purée, 345

Tomatoes, 8; with rice, 91-2
Tongue, lambs', sour soup of, 76
*Tónnolakértha*, 128
*Torouk*, 125
*Toutmanik*, 237
Transylvania, 17, 30, 57, 216
*Travels in Albania and Other Provinces of Turkey*, 11, 50, 124, 175, 218
Trifle creams, Albanian, 299
Trifonov, T., 329
*Trigonas*, 308
*Trigya*, 30
Tripe, 63; soup, 78-9
Trout, 131; grilled with clotted cream, 133
*Tsiganka*, 125
*Tuffâhiyye*, 288
*Ţuică*, 15, 55, 185
Tuna, 128, 130, 131, 140
Tundzha, river, 124
Turabi Effendi, 98
Turbot, 131, 135, 138, 140, 144
Turkey, 25-6
Turkey (the bird), 190; poached with wheat, 212; wheat with chicken and turkey, 61
Turkey wheat, 7
Turkish coffee, 333-5
*Turkish Cookbook*, 78
Turkish delight, quince, 293
Turnips, 'Alleluia', 91
Turnovers, cheese, 284
Turnovers, syrup, 308
Turnovo, Bulgaria, 84
*Tzatzíki*, 63
*Tzatzíki soupá*, 87

*Uha*, 16
*Under the Monastery Vine Arbour*, 84
*Under the Yoke*, 182
Universal schnitzels, 157
*Urs*, 117

Valac, Kosovo, 3
Vanilla sugar, 352
Vazov, Ivan, 182
Veal, 11, 146; escalopes, 157-8; escalopes, Viennese style, 158; quinces stuffed with, 184
Vegetables, 88-112; Bosnian pot, 173-4; casserole of mixed, 104; gratinated mixed, 107-8; Hercegovinian pot with meat and, 174; macédoine of, to serve with roast beef, 102; meatball soup with, 81; mixed braised, 102-3; mixed casserole of, with meat, 181; pancakes stuffed with, 106-8; soup, 83; see also under specific varieties

Venison, braised haunch of, 202; minced steaks, 202
Vinča, Serbia, 3
Vine, 6
Vine-leaf rolls, 98-9; with meat and rice, 168-9
Vinegar, garlic, 348
*Vitis vinifera* ssp *sylvestris*, 43; ssp *vinifera*, 43
Vlachs, 16
Vojvodina, 19-20, 201, 206, 282
*Vratnik*, 24
*Vrushnik*, 33

Wallachia, 15, 16, 328
Walnut, and aubergine caviar, 65; and garlic sauce, 346; and potato pudding, baked, 291; and yoghurt sauce, 346; biscuits, Albanian, 313-14; halva, 48; loaf, 278-9; milk, 352; sauce, 194
Walnuts, carp stuffed with, 136; crescent rolls filled with, 250; kuglof with, 243-4; nettle soup with cheese or, 86; preserve of green, 326; salted, 64; sausage of grape juice and, 323
Warty crab, 126, 140
Water buffalo, 57-8
Watermelon, and *mastika*, 61; Champagne compote in a, 286
Waxdick, 125
Weigand and Dorich, dictionary, 117
Wels, 131
Wheat, boiled, 208-10; cracked, pilaff of, 213; dessert, Bulgarian rose-scented, 211-12; durum, 7; poached chicken or turkey with, 212; porridge with cheese, 214-15; with chicken and turkey, 61
White cabbage, pork pot with, 171
White confectioner's custard, 354
White halva, 49
White ice-cream, 302
White pudding, 197
White sauce, 342
White shortbread biscuits, 272-3
Whitebait, fried, 133
Wholemeal bread, 233-4
Wholemeal honey bread, 248
Wild boar, spit-roasted fillet of, 204; with sauerkraut, 203
Wild piglet chops with juniper berries, 204
Winter black radish salad, 69-70
Wortley Montagu, Lady Mary, 26, 78

*Xiphias gladius*, 130

*Yahni*, 126, 129
*Yahniya*, 13
*Yaprák*, 175
Yasna Polyana restaurant, Sofia, 281
Yeasted fritters, 254-5

Yellow béchamel sauce, 342
Yoghurt, 10,12, 23-4, 27-9, 63, 120-3; Albanian casserole of lamb and, 159; and cucumber salad, 68-9; and garlic sauce, 347; custard, with *kyufteta*, 154; drink, 339; ice-cream, 301-2; poached eggs with, 118; sauce of walnut and, 346
Yugoslavia, 18-21

Zadar, Dalmatia, 50
*Zakouski*, 59-73
Zander, 129
*Zapruzhka*, 13
Zara, Croatia, 285
*Zelenite Prishultsi*, 329
*Zerde*, 221
*Zeus faber*, 128
*Zganci*, 24
*Zhito*, 208
*Zita*, 208
*Zupa*, 299

# WINNER OF THE LANGHE CERETTO PRIZE
# BEST EUROPEAN COOKERY BOOK 1997

Here is everything you ever wanted to know about the Balkan table: Croatia, Bulgaria, Romania, Macedonia, Slovenia, Serbia and Albania are all described with glorious recipes, detailed wordlists, and a mountain of extra information about the history of the people, their cookery, their pots and pans, and even the secrets of long life still treasured by the peasants of the Rhodope mountains in southern Bulgaria. Balkan cookery is a remarkable amalgam of the skills of the Ottoman Turks, the tastes and magnificence of the Austro-Hungarian empire, and the ancient history of the indigenous nations who settled this corner of the Earth: from the Illyrians of Homer's time to the Bulgars who thundered down from the icy steppes of Asia.

"THIS THOROUGH, DETAILED AND UNIQUE BOOK WORKS WONDERFULLY WELL ON SEVERAL LEVELS. THE RECIPES ARE ACCESSIBLE, WHOLESOME, APPEALING, AND NOT SOMETHING WE HAVE SEEN BEFORE; A WELCOME CHANGE FROM THE MEDITERRANEAN DIET."

**FRANCES BISSELL**

£14.99

**PROSPECT BOOKS**

ISBN 0 907325 96 3